The Future of International Courts

The end of World War II marked the beginning of a new golden era in international law. Treaties and international organisations proliferated at an unprecedented rate, and many courts and tribunals were established with a view to ensuring the smooth operation of this new universe of international relations. The network of courts and tribunals that exists today is an important feature of our global society. It serves as an alternative to other, sometimes more violent, forms of dispute settlement.

The process of international adjudication is constantly evolving, sometimes in unexpected ways. Through contributions from world-renowned experts and emerging voices, this book considers the future of international courts from a diverse range of perspectives. It examines some of the regional, institutional and procedural challenges that international courts face: the rising influence of powerful states, the turn to populism, the interplay between courts, the involvement of non-state actors and third parties in international proceedings, and more. The book offers a timely discussion of these challenges, with the future of several international courts hanging in the balance and the legitimacy of international adjudication being called constantly into question. It should also serve as a reminder of the importance of international courts for the functioning of a rules-based international order.

The Future of International Courts is essential reading for academics, practitioners and students who are interested in international law, including those who are interested in the role international courts play in international relations.

Avidan Kent is a Senior Lecturer at the University of East Anglia. His research interests include the fields of Sustainable Development Law, International Dispute Resolution, International Economic Law, and Public International Law. He holds a PhD from the University of Cambridge.

Nikos Skoutaris is a Senior Lecturer in EU Law at the University of East Anglia. He obtained his LLB from the University of Aberdeen, his LLM from Maastricht University and his PhD from the European University Institute. His research interests lie in the intersection between EU law, comparative constitutional law and conflict resolution theory. He has published extensively on Brexit and its effect on the UK territorial constitution.

Jamie Trinidad is a Fellow of Wolfson College, Cambridge and the Lauterpacht Centre for International Law, University of Cambridge. His research and publications address, among other things, issues of self-determination, territory (land and sea) and the practice of international courts and tribunals. He is a practising barrister and he has a PhD from Cambridge.

Routledge Research in International Law

Available:

Regional Developmentalism through Law
Establishing an African Economic Community
Jonathan Bashi Rudahindwa

China's One Belt One Road Initiative and Private International Law
Edited by Poomintr Sooksripaisarnkit and Sai Ramani Garimella

Transnational Terrorist Groups and International Criminal Law
Anna Marie Brennan

Confronting Cyberespionage under International Law
Oğuz Kaan Pehlivan

Russian Discourses on International Law
Sociological and Philosophical Phenomenon
Edited by P. Sean Morris

Backstage Practices in Transnational Law
Lianne Boer and Sofia Stolk

International 'Criminal' Responsibility
Antimonies
Ottavio Quirico

The Future of International Courts
Regional, Institutional and Procedural Challenges
Edited by Avidan Kent, Nikos Skoutaris and Jamie Trinidad

For a full list of titles in this series, visit https://www.routledge.com/Routledge-Research-in-International-Law/book-series/INTNLLAW

The Future of International Courts

Regional, Institutional and Procedural Challenges

Edited by Avidan Kent, Nikos Skoutaris and Jamie Trinidad

Routledge
Taylor & Francis Group
LONDON AND NEW YORK

First published 2019
by Routledge
2 Park Square, Milton Park, Abingdon, Oxon OX14 4RN

and by Routledge
605 Third Avenue, New York, NY 10017

First issued in paperback 2021

Routledge is an imprint of the Taylor & Francis Group, an informa business

Publisher's Note
The publisher has gone to great lengths to ensure the quality of this reprint but points out that some imperfections in the original copies may be apparent.

British Library Cataloguing-in-Publication Data
A catalogue record for this book is available from the British Library

Library of Congress Cataloging-in-Publication Data
Names: Kent, Avidan, editor. | Skoutaris, Nikos, editor. | Trinidad, Jamie, editor.
Title: The future of international courts : regional, institutional, and procedural challenges/edited by Avidan Kent, Nikos Skoutaris, and Jamie Trinidad.
Description: Abingdon, Oxon [UK] ; New York, NY : Routledge, 2019. | Series: Routledge research in international law | Includes index.
Identifiers: LCCN 2018052666 (print) | LCCN 2018053792 (ebook) | ISBN 9780429463280 (ebk) | ISBN 9781138615182 (hbk)
Subjects: LCSH: International courts. | International Court of Justice. | European Court of Human Rights. | Amicus curiae. | Justice, Administration of.
Classification: LCC KZ6250 (ebook) | LCC KZ6250 .F88 2019 (print) | DDC 341.5/5—dc23
LC record available at https://lccn.loc.gov/2018052666

Typeset in Galliard
by Apex CoVantage, LLC

ISBN 13: 978-1-03-224138-8 (pbk)
ISBN 13: 978-1-138-61518-2 (hbk)

DOI: 10.4324/9780429463280

Contents

Abbreviations

AB	Appellate Body
ACHPR	African Commission on Human and Peoples' Rights
ACFI	Agreements on Cooperation and Facilitation of Investments
ACtHPR	African Court on Human and Peoples' Rights
ACtJHR	African Court of Justice and Human Rights
ASEAN	Association of Southeast Asian Nations
BHRC	Bar Human Rights Committee of England and Wales
BIT	Bilateral Investment Treaties
BLEU	Belgium-Luxembourg Economic Union
BRI	Belt and Road Initiative
CCP	Chinese Communist Party
CETA	Comprehensive Economic and Trade Agreement
CIGI	Centre for International Governance Innovation
CJEU	Court of Justice of the European Union
CoE	Council of Europe
CPT	European Convention for the Prevention of Torture and Inhuman or Degrading Treatment or Punishment
CSOs	Civil Society Organisations
DSB	Dispute Settlement Body of the World Trade Organization
EACJ	East African Court of Justice
ECCC	Extraordinary Chambers in the Courts of Cambodia
ECHR	European Convention on Human Rights
ECtHR	European Court of Human Rights
ECJ	European Court of Justice
ECOWAS	Economic Community of West African States
EEZ	Exclusive Economic Zone
EHRAC	European Human Rights Advocacy Centre
FET	Fair and Equitable Treatment
FIPA	Foreign Investment Protection Act
FRA	Fundamental Rights Agency
FTAs	Free Trade Agreements
GATS	General Agreement on Trade and Services
GATT	General Agreement on Tariffs and Trade

IACtHR	Inter American Court of Human Rights
IADL	International Association of Democratic Lawyers
ICC	International Criminal Court
ICERD	International Convention on All Forms of Racial Discrimination
ICJ	International Court of Justice
ICSFT	International Convention for the Suppression and Financing of Terrorism
ICSID	International Centre for Settlement of Investment Disputes
ICSID Convention	Convention on the Settlement of Investment Disputes between States and Nationals of Other States
ICTY	International Criminal Tribunal for the former Yugoslavia
ICTR	International Criminal Tribunal for Rwanda
IDS	International Dispute Settlement
IHL	International Humanitarian Law
IIAs	International Investment Agreements
ILC	International Law Commission
IMTFE	International Military Tribunal for the Far East
ISA	Investor-State Arbitrations
ISDS	Investor-State Dispute Settlement
ITLOS	International Tribunal for the Law of the Sea
IWT	Indus Water Treaty
JCPS	Judicial Committee of the Privy Council
KSC	Kosovo Specialist Chambers
LCIA	London Court of International Arbitration
MEA	Ministry of External Affairs, Government of India
MES	Market Economy Status
MFN	Most Favoured Nation
MOFCOM	Ministry of Commerce of the People's Republic of China
NAFTA	North American Free Trade Agreement
NAFTA ITC	North American Free Trade Agreement International Trade Commission
OTP	Office of the Prosecutor (International Criminal Court)
PACE	Parliamentary Assembly of the Council of Europe
PCA	Permanent Court of Arbitration
PCIJ	Permanent Court of International Justice
PRC	People's Republic of China
ROC	Republic of China
RTA	Regional Trade Agreement
SADC	Southern African Development Community
SCOTUS	Supreme Court of the United States
SCSL	Special Court for Sierra Leone
SPC	Supreme People's Court of the People's Republic of China
STL	Special Tribunal for Lebanon
TEU	Treaty on European Union

TFEU	Treaty on the Functioning of the European Union
TPP	Trans-Pacific Partnership
TRIMS	Agreement on Trade-Related Investment Measures
TRIPS	Agreement on Trade-Related Aspects of Intellectual Property Rights
TTIP	Transatlantic Trade and Investment Partnership
UKHL	UK House of Lords
UKSC	UK Supreme Court
UNCITRAL	United Nations Commission on International Trade Law
UNCLOS	United Nations Convention on the Law of the Sea
UNCTAD	United Nations Conference on Trade and Development
UNESCO	United Nations Educational, Scientific and Cultural Organization
UNGA	United Nations General Assembly
UNSC	United Nations Security Council
WTO	World Trade Organization

Acknowledgments

We wish to thank Ms Amy Choi (LLB (UEA)) and Mr Sam Forsyth (MA (Cantab)) for their extremely valuable research assistance. We wish to acknowledge the financial support provided by the Society of Legal Scholars and the administrative support provided by the University of East Anglia's School of Law. We are grateful to Nicola Sharpe and Siobhán Poole from Routledge for their assistance throughout this project.

Contributors

Karen J. Alter is Professor of Political Science and Law at Northwestern University, a permanent visiting professor at the iCourts Center for Excellence, University of Copenhagen Faculty of Law, and the Co-director Research Group on Global Capitalism and Law at the Buffett Institute at Northwestern University. Alter's expertise concerns global and regional judicialization of international relations, with a particular focus on international adjudication.

Pushkar Anand is an assistant professor at Faculty of Law, University of Delhi. He teaches and researches in the field of Public International Law, International Investment Law, and the Law of the Sea. He has obtained his LLM from the South Asian University, New Delhi, India.

Bill Bowring is Professor of Law at Birkbeck College, University of London. As a practising barrister since 1974, he has represented applicants before the European Court of Human Rights in many cases since 1992, especially against Turkey and Russia. He has acted as a consultant and expert for the United Nations, Council of Europe, Organisation for Security and Cooperation in Europe (OSCE), European Union and the UK Government. He is the founder in 2003 and a member of the board of European Human Rights Advocacy Centre (EHRAC). He has more than 130 publications on topics of international law, human rights, minority rights, Russian law and philosophy. His latest book is *Law, Rights and Ideology in Russia: Landmarks in the Destiny of a Great Power* (Routledge 2013). He is President of the European Lawyers for Democracy and Human Rights (ELDH), with members in 21 European countries.

Armand de Mestral is Professor Emeritus and Jean Monnet Chair in Law of International Economic Integration at McGill University. He has served on World Trade Organization and North American Free Trade Agreement dispute settlement tribunals. He was made a Member of the Order of Canada in December 2007, and in 2017 was awarded the John E. Read Medal by the Canadian Council on International Law.

Zuzanna Godzimirska is a PhD fellow at iCourts, Centre of Excellence for International Courts at the University of Copenhagen. Her research explores issues of trust and legitimacy in the context of international courts.

Iryna Marchuk is an associate professor at the Faculty of Law at the University of Copenhagen.

Francesco Messineo is a legal officer at the Codification Division of the United Nations Office of Legal Affairs in New York, as well as an honorary research fellow at the University of Kent. He was previously an associate legal officer at the International Court of Justice and a lecturer in law at the University of Kent. He obtained his PhD at the University of Cambridge.

Joanna Nicholson is a postdoctoral fellow at Pluricourts, University of Oslo, specialising in international criminal law. She is the author of *Fighting and Victimhood in International Criminal Law* (Routledge 2018).

Jason Rudall is a researcher at the Faculty of Law of the University of Geneva and a lecturer on the LLM in international law at the Graduate Institute of International and Development Studies. He holds a PhD in international law from the Graduate Institute, Geneva.

Varsha Singh is a doctoral research candidate at the Centre for International Legal Studies, Jawaharlal Nehru University. She obtained her LLM from South Asian University, New Delhi, India.

Nanying Tao is a DCL candidate on international law at McGill University, and a recipient of CIGI (Centre for International Governance Innovation) graduate scholarship. She obtained her LLM from Xiamen University, LLB from Zhongnan University of Economics and Law and BA from Huazhong University of Science and Technology.

Sondre Torp Helmersen is an associate professor at the Inland Norway University of Applied Sciences.

Lukas Vanhonnaeker is a post-doctoral fellow at McGill University, Faculty of Law where he is conducting research in the field of international economic law with an emphasis on international investment law and arbitration, international trade law and international corporate law.

David Yuratich is a lecturer in law at Royal Holloway, University of London. His research interests revolve around the role of courts in democracies, particularly in the EU and UK.

1 What does the future hold for international courts?

Avidan Kent, Nikos Skoutaris and Jamie Trinidad

The twentieth century was the golden age of international law. Treaties and international organisations proliferated at an unprecedented rate, and many courts and tribunals were established to facilitate the smooth operation of this new structure of international relations. The network of international courts and tribunals (ICs) that exists today is an important feature of our global society. It serves as an alternative to other forms of dispute settlement, including gunboat diplomacy and even wars. Its emergence is widely regarded as a positive development; it is used by states and its authority is widely accepted. As former International Court of Justice (ICJ) president Gilbert Guillaume once wrote: 'Some decades ago the slogan was "Make love, not war". It could now be "Go to court, not to war".'[1]

A critical juncture?

In her book, *The New Terrain of International Law,* Karen Alter identifies three 'critical junctures' that have shaped the development of the ICs universe: the Hague Peace Conference; the end of World War II/the 'eruption' of the Cold War; and the end of the Cold War.[2] The post-Hague events led *inter alia* to the establishment of the Permanent Court of Arbitration and the later Permanent Court of International Justice. The political aftermath of World War II led to the establishment of tribunals such as the ICJ, European Court of Justice (ECJ), Inter-American Court of Human Rights (IACtHR), European Court of Human Rights (ECtHR) and the General Agreement on Tariffs and Trade's (GATT) dispute settlement system. The end of the Cold War led *inter alia* to the rise in prominence of the Bretton Woods Institutions (accompanied by the establishment of numerous trade and investment tribunals), and an increased international demand for accountability following atrocities in places such as Africa and the Balkans resulted in the establishment of international criminal tribunals.[3]

1 Gilbert Guillaume, 'The Future of International Judicial Institutions' (1995), 44 *Int'l & Comp. L.Q.* 848, 860.
2 Karen Alter, *The New Terrain of International Law: Courts, Politics, Rights* (Princeton University Press 2014).
3 See a comprehensive review of this historical process in Alter (n 2) chapter 4.

In her contribution to this volume, Alter claims that we are currently in the midst of yet another 'critical juncture'. While previous 'junctures' resulted in the proliferation of international courts and were motivated by states' willingness to entrust at least a portion of their sovereignty to ICs, the current 'juncture' is essentially different. Alter defines it as a systemic and broad 'shared loss of faith in the old order',[4] focused mostly on 'dismantling what exists'.[5] 'The dismantling nature of the current critical juncture', she explains, 'has put into question the entire international liberal order, which most international courts are part of.'[6]

We broadly share Alter's assessment of the disruptive potential of current developments for the future of ICs and it seems timely to reflect on some of the challenges that ICs currently face and are likely to face in the years ahead.

We have organised these challenges under three loose headings: regional, institutional and procedural. Our purpose in doing so was to span the perspective from the general to the specific, offering readers a range of bird's eye and worm's eye views on the future of ICs. We do not attach special significance to these headings – they are a mere organisational device and few, if any of the essays in this volume fall squarely under one heading or another.

Regional challenges

A key consideration in editing this volume was ensuring, as far as possible, that diverse voices from around the world were represented. While the possible shift away from an 'international liberal order' – which Alter examines by reference to developments in the United States, Poland, Hungary and post-Brexit-referendum UK – may be viewed with trepidation in some quarters, in others it could be viewed with indifference or even as a positive opportunity.

So-called 'new' and rising non-Western powers are increasingly involved in international adjudicatory processes and their actions are shaping the current 'critical juncture' in important ways. Nanying Tao describes in this context the transformation of China's attitude towards ICs; from a traditional position of hostility to that of an active litigant.[7] Tao defines China's current attitude towards ICs as a 'love-hate' relationship. On the one hand, China has embraced the use of economic tribunals to advance its economic agendas; it is now one of the most active users of the World Trade Organization (WTO) dispute settlement system and its approach towards the Investor-State Dispute Settlement (ISDS) has been favourable. On the other hand, Tao explains, when it comes to issues of sovereignty and territory, China is still haunted by the view that 'international adjudication essentially serves Western imperialistic interests'; it is a view that underpins its dismissive attitude towards the South China Sea Arbitration (as manifested in

4 Karen Alter, 'Critical junctures and the future of international courts', chapter 2 of this volume.
5 Ibid.
6 Ibid.
7 Nanying Tao, 'China's attitude towards international adjudication: Past, present and future', chapter 4 of this volume.

China's 'four noes' strategy: 'no acceptance, no participation, no recognition and no implementation').[8]

China is not the only rising giant that has shown ambivalence towards international adjudicative processes. Anand and Singh explain how India's insistence on a traditional, state-centric approach towards ICs has resulted in a rejection of certain progressive developments, notably regarding the participation of non-state actors, whether as amici curiae (in the WTO) or as litigants (ISDS).[9] India, the authors point out, is also generally hostile to developments which are perceived as increasing the reach of ICs into matters touching on sovereignty. It therefore insists, for instance, on the exhaustion of local remedies in its Model Bilateral Investment Treaties (BIT) ('even as the domestic judicial system in India already crumbles under the backlog of cases'[10]), and it rejects altogether any prospect of acceding to the Rome Statute of the International Criminal Court.

Brexit also denotes the effort of a state to distance itself from a highly integrated international legal order. Indeed, the prime minister Theresa May has declared that the ambition of the UK is to take back control of its laws by leaving the jurisdiction of the Court of Justice, among other things. Nikos Skoutaris, in his contribution to this volume,[11] shows that this may be a much more difficult exercise than proponents of Brexit might have anticipated. A close look at the UK's Withdrawal Agreement, the EU Withdrawal Act and even the UK's 'Chequers' proposal for a future relationship with the EU indicates that the influence of the Court of Justice of the European Union (CJEU) on the UK legal order is likely to remain significant after Brexit.

Will ICs survive this critical juncture? Alter notes that she 'do[es] not actually think that the international law project, or most of the existing substantive international law, is itself in question'.[12] 'International law', she believes, 'will endure,' due to its moral superiority, the fundamental values that it protects and the lack of an alternative.[13] Other contributors to this volume seem more reluctant to accept the moral superiority of international law as a given and some explicitly link the 'endurance' of international law with the willingness and ability of ICs to adapt their institutional practices.

Institutional challenges

Based on an empirical study of states' declarations, Zuzanna Godzimirska explains that historically, ICs such as the WTO's Appellate Body and the ICJ have 'enjoy[ed]

8 Tao (n 7).

9 Pushkar Anand and Varsha Singh, 'India and international dispute settlement: Some reflections on India's participation in international courts and tribunals', chapter 3 of this volume.

10 Anand & Singh (n 9).

11 Nikos Skoutaris, 'Taking back control? Brexit and the Court of Justice', chapter 6 of this volume.

12 Alter (n 4).

13 Alter (n 4).

substantial levels of support among their Members'.[14] She warns, however, that this state of affairs is rather fragile and even the actions of one state alone (referring to the United States' attempts to effectively dismember the Appellate Body) could potentially jeopardise this delicate state of affairs.

The critique of Investor-State Arbitrations (ISA, or ISDS) is even more stark. The perception of this dispute settlement mechanism as biased towards wealthy Western investors, conducted in a secretive manner obscured from public scrutiny, has resulted in certain Latin-American states denouncing the ISA and withdrawing from the Convention on the Settlement of Investment Disputes between States and Nationals of Other States (ICSID Convention). Many other states are revising their investment agreements.

Nevertheless, Armand de Mestral and Lukas Vanhonnaeker predict that the ISA will not disappear – 'the weight of over 3200 BITs and RTAs with investment chapters will be too great to allow this.'[15] In addition, the lack of a viable alternative supports this prognosis. Instead, these contributors argue, 'the most probable development of the international investment protection, including the ISA, is incremental change of both the substance and the procedure of the system.'[16] One example of such change is the adoption of rules on transparency, such as those adopted under the United Nations Conference on Trade and Development (UNCTAD) or in a variety of 'new generation' BITs. A more drastic change would be the arrival of the EU's proposed international investment tribunal including an appellate level. Such a measure would, it is hoped, increase transparency, consistency and coherence of jurisprudence.

International criminal tribunals have also been subjected to stinging criticism, much of it reflecting North/South tensions. '[T]he field of international criminal justice is experiencing a time of change,' writes Nicholson;[17] the International Criminal Tribunal for the former Yugoslavia (ICTY) and the International Criminal Tribunal for Rwanda (ICTR) are closing, a new generation of hybrid courts is emerging, and the International Criminal Court (ICC), perhaps the cornerstone of this system, is beginning to feel the weight of longstanding criticism reflected in the first withdrawals from the Rome Statute. The proliferation of hybrid courts is a countervailing trend, reflecting sentiment that forums like the ICTY and ICC are too remote from the communities most affected by their activities.

The ECtHR also faces a distinctive set of contemporary challenges, in part as a result of a resurgent populism in important Council of Europe (CoE) member states. In his chapter, Bill Bowring reflects on his decades of experience representing claimants against Turkey, Russia and the UK. On the one hand, Bowring's

14 Zuzanna Godzimirska, 'Delegitimation of global courts: Lessons from the past', chapter 8 of this volume.

15 Armand de Mestral and Lukas Vanhonnaeker, 'The future of investor-state dispute settlement', chapter 9 of this volume.

16 De Mestral and Vanhonnaeker (n 14).

17 Joanna Nicholson, 'Learning lessons through the prism of legitimacy: What future for international criminal courts and tribunals?', chapter 10 of this volume.

account documents the story of tenacious individuals who have persevered in the face of long delays and other institutional hurdles; on the other hand, it is a warning of what could happen if powerful states, in the grip of populist and authoritarian politics, disengage from the system. The twin aims of dispensing effective justice to individuals while retaining the 'buy in' of key states may not always be mutually compatible, which makes the challenge of ensuring that the ECtHR remains a relevant institution in the twenty-first century all the more formidable.

Amid all the turbulence, the reputation and authority of the ICJ has remained relatively solid. This is arguably due to the ICJ's traditionally narrow understanding of its own judicial remit. Philippe Sands has noted elsewhere in this respect: 'The Court had given a reasonably robust Opinion on the illegality of Israel's Wall, [FN omitted] but in other cases it had skirted around the difficult issues that really mattered, in the face of political divisions.'[18] Sands mentions the Court's Advisory Opinions regarding Kosovo and the legality of nuclear weapons as examples. One might also refer here to the Court's reluctance to deal with Russia's actions in Georgia and the Ukraine. In his contribution to this volume, Francesco Messineo rejects expectations such as those expressed by Sands (and others), according to which the Court should play the role of the 'ultimate authority speaking "eternal truth" on all questions of international law'.[19] Viewing the ICJ as the world's Supreme Court is misguided. Francesco Messineo reminds us that the Court's core function is to settle disputes and, as a result, to promote international peace and security.

Procedural challenges

The manner in which the process of litigation is itself changing will also play a role in shaping the future of ICs. Procedural rules often have a profound effect on the perceived legitimacy of ICs. The opacity of ISA proceedings, as mentioned above, is one example. The outrage within the WTO following the Appellate Body's decision to accept amicus curiae briefs and the lack of legal standing for NGOs in proceedings before the CJEU are others.

An interesting theme with respect to the process of litigation is the interaction between non-state actors and ICs. Non-state actors increasingly demand a larger role in international adjudicative processes and frequently attempt to intervene as amici curiae in court proceedings regardless of whether the relevant procedural framework permits such interventions. Civil society organisations will sometimes seek to link their participation to the legitimacy of the legal process and have had some success since the 1990s in persuading ICs that they should be permitted to intervene in proceedings. Today, amicus participation in ICs is almost as commonplace as it is in the domestic courts of the USA. ICs that have resisted

18 Philippe Sands, 'Climate Change and the Rule of Law: Adjudicating the Future in International Law' (2016) 28 *Journal of Environmental Law* 19, 20.

19 Francesco Messineo, 'The function of the International Court of Justice: Tending to the law while settling disputes?', chapter 7 of this volume.

this trend – most notably the ICJ – are the exception. Whether this development has had a positive impact on the legitimacy of ICs is, however, open to question. As Avidan Kent and Jamie Trinidad remind us, some states – especially in the developing world – view amicus participation as a vehicle for the promotion of narrow sectoral interests by rich Western NGOs.[20] The 'transaction costs' that result from a permissive approach towards amicus participation, not only for ICs but also for parties to proceedings, must be weighed against the benefits of third-party participation, but the benefits are not always easy to discern.

The role of international law scholars and scholarship within the work of ICs is another procedural area of interest. Occasionally, scholars are invited, or seek to participate in proceedings as amici curiae.[21] More frequently and significantly, international judges will draw on international legal scholarship, and the manner in which they do so can impact upon the legitimacy of ICs.[22] As Sondre Torp Helmersen explains, ICs rely almost exclusively on the work of white, male, Western authors. Referring to the ICJ, Torp Helmersen argues that while '[t]he heterogeneity of the Court's membership is mandated by the ICJ Statute Article 9', '[t]here is no similar regulation regarding teachings.'[23] Like others in this volume, Torp Helmersen argues that ICs will have to adapt and evolve in order to maintain their legitimacy. Judges, in his view, should be encouraged (perhaps even instructed) to be transparent in their use of scholarship and to draw on a diverse range of scholarly perspectives.

Other contributors to this volume point to interactions *between* ICs, as well as interactions between judges *within* ICs. David Yuratich discusses the importance of separate opinions in this context, and criticises the forced unanimity which guides the operation of tribunals such as the CJEU.[24] Drawing on the experience of the ICJ, Yuratich sees practical importance in the existence of separate opinions: '[S]eparate opinions are "speech acts" signalling the contestability of judgements and malleability of law.'[25] The delivery of separate opinions thus indicates that an IC has assessed different perspectives and has been meticulous in considering the arguments before it; losing parties are less likely to deem that they have been 'shut down' or that their arguments have been ignored. As such, Yuratich claims, by abandoning its 'univocal' tradition the CJEU may increase its own legitimacy.

20 Avidan Kent and Jamie Trinidad, 'Amicus Curiae Participation in International Proceedings: Forever Friends?', chapter 14 in this volume. See also the criticism in Patricia Birnie, Alan Boyle and Catherine Redgwell *International Law & the Environment* (OUP 2009) 254.

21 Avidan Kent and Jamie Trinidad, 'International law scholars as amici curiae: An emerging dialogue (of the deaf)? (2016) 29(4) *Leiden Journal of International Law* 2081.

22 Sondre Torp Helmersen, 'How the application of teachings can affect the legitimacy of the International Court of Justice', chapter 11 of this volume.

23 Ibid.

24 David Yuratich, 'Towards Separate Opinions at the Court of Justice of the European Union: Lessons in the deliberative democracy from the International Court of Justice and elsewhere' chapter 12 of this volume.

25 Ibid.

Jason Rudall discusses interactions *between* courts.[26] Like Yuratich, Rudall believes that judicial interaction is a positive thing. His main claim is that interactions and discourse between courts (a process conducted via what Rudall defines as 'legal vehicles') have led to the development of a 'human rights culture' serving the 'humanisation of international law' and has led to the extension of this 'culture' to tribunals such as the ICJ, WTO, ISA and more. According to Rudall, the spread of a human rights culture through institutional dialogue will ensure that human rights will 'continue to be a part of institutional responses' in the future.

Where next?

This volume is not the first attempt to examine the future of international courts. Earlier attempts (mostly from the late 1990s and early 2000s) have focused on issues such as the *proliferation* of international courts and the dangers of fragmentation.[27] These 'problems' reflected the political mood at the time ('go to court, not to war') and an increased reliance upon, and support for, ICs. Whether or not one accepts Alter's assessment that we are in the midst of a fourth 'critical juncture' for ICs, there can be little doubt that the focus of contemporary scholarship on ICs is no longer concerned with proliferation and fragmentation, but rather with issues such as 'legitimacy', 'backlash' and the sustainability of ICs. The contributions to this volume are no exception.

Some feel a need to reaffirm the raisons d'être of ICs, or to propose reforms that will enable ICs to survive this critical juncture. Others explain that emerging powers such as India or China are making only careful use of ICs, and are unlikely to fill any leadership vacuum. Even with respect to the ICJ, we would do well to keep our expectations in check.

The way forward will involve a process of evolution, in which some parts of the ecosystem disappear, the fittest survive and others adjust. ICs, their composition, procedures, and possibly also our expectations of them, will have to adapt in order to face future realities.

That being said, the existence of ICs is a condition *sine qua non* for the proper functioning of a rule-based international order. Despite contestations, conflicts and even the withdrawals of some states from certain legal orders, ICs will have a future for as long as there is an international order based on liberal values. For this reason, the issues raised in this volume shed light on a debate that is likely to continue in the years to come.

26 Jason Rudall, 'Not just a wit, but a cause of wit in others: The influence of human rights in international litigation', chapter 15 of this volume.

27 See for example *Symposium Issue: The Proliferation of International Tribunals: Piecing Together the Puzzle,* 31 N.Y.U. *J. Int'l L. & Pol.* (1998–1999), or vol 25(4) (Symposia) *Michigan Journal of International Law* (2004).

2 Critical junctures and the future of international courts in a post-liberal world order

*Karen J. Alter**

I have taken the opportunity of this book to reflect on the future of international courts (ICs) in the current political context. The book's title – *The Future of International Courts and Tribunals: Regional, Institutional and Procedural Challenges* – misses key social challenges that ICs increasingly face. What follows connects different social-constructivist theoretical understandings about international institutions, institutional change, legal politics, and legitimation, bringing them to bear on the question of the challenges ICs face in 2018. It is my nature to be optimistic, and thus I expect that when push comes to shove, people will prioritise order and human rights over chaos and rising violence. But, as I explain, we are surely in for a bumpy ride, and we cannot take for granted that the institutions under strain – including ICs – will endure this ride. At the end of the day, ICs depend on popular support for the rule of law. Whether this support will endure is currently at stake. Also, in the past (e.g. the 1950s, 1960s, 1970s and 1980s), ICs could avoid highly contentious issues by relying on gatekeepers, by stalling for time, or through procedural dodges. For reasons I shall explain, these tactics are harder to use in the current period. The worse the violations of international law are, the more likely ICs are going to be called upon to condemn state actors. Moreover, if popular support for the rule of law erodes, and if the compliance partners that ICs depend upon for their political influence are co-opted by authoritarian leaders, lying low will be an insufficient strategy.

The chapter first introduces the concept of a 'critical juncture', explaining that critical junctures can produce fundamental change, but they can also fail to produce fundamental change. The chapter then applies the critical juncture concept to think about the future of ICs. In the past, critical junctures provided moments where international courts proliferated in number, where the design of ICs shifted from the 'old' to the 'new style', and where litigation rates increased. In the past, however, ICs were seen as antidotes to the problem governments were facing. The fundamental question is, what will happen to ICs should they be seen as part of the problem?

* This chapter builds on arguments previously published in Karen J. Alter, 'The Evolution of International Law and Courts' in Orfeo Fioretos (ed.), *International Politics and Institutions in Time* (OUP 2017) 251–274; and Karen J. Alter, 'The Future of International Law' in Diana Ayton-Shenker (ed.), *The New Global Agenda: Priorities, Practices, and Pathways of the International Community* (Rowman & Littlefield 2018) 25–42.

I address this question by highlighting ideational and institutional changes across critical junctures that create lasting legacies affecting subsequent critical junctures.

I then draw on John Ruggie's argument that regimes fuse social purpose and power, reflecting on the likely future of ICs as part of the international liberal order. In *The New Terrain of International Law* I argued that ICs are designed to promote the objectives of economic and political liberalism written into the DNA of international law. 'ICs enforcing international economic rules will tend to promote market openness. ICs enforcing human rights rules will tend to promote a human rights agenda. International war crimes tribunals will tend to condemn state practices that harm noncombatants.'[1] By delegating legal interpretation to courts, the authors of the law gained a slow time-release mechanism that litigants could activate to push in the direction the law indicates.[2] The question then arises as to how the legal rules international judges are called upon to enforce affects the legitimacy and authority of ICs.

I then turn to what may be an even more fundamental challenge for ICs, namely a decreasing political commitment to the rule of law. I expect that ICs as institutions will endure, alongside international political support for a rules-based international system. The larger question, however, is whether a demand that governments respect the law will endure. The alternative path is that the rule of law can be transformed into a faux-brother, a rule-by-law system, where a genuine commitment to the rule of law (to governance restricted by law) gets replaced with a formalist commitment to law, where governments either totally control or are no longer accountable to legal checks and balances.

The chapter concludes by explaining why the international legal order is likely to weather this current critical juncture. ICs will not escape unscathed, and perhaps the current moment is a course correction for an international system that has encroached too far into the lives of governments and ordinary citizens. But I do not think we really can return to a world without international rules or multilateral governance, in which case both international law and ICs can be part of stabilising respect for international law and promoting legality in international relations.

Critical junctures: what happens in moments of great flux?

We are currently in the midst of what historical institutional scholars call a 'critical juncture'.[3] We can tell we are in a critical juncture because the upheaval in political

1 Karen J. Alter, *The New Terrain of International Law: Courts, Politics, Rights* (Princeton University Press 2014) 23.

2 Ibid xviii, 23.

3 Giovanni Capoccia catalogues the long history of the concept of critical juncture (and synonyms such as 'crisis', 'turning point', 'unsettled times'), see Giovanni Capoccia, 'Critical Junctures' in Orfeo Fioretos, Tulia G. Falletti and Adam Sheingate (eds.), *The Oxford Handbook of Historical Institutionalism* (OUP 2016) 89; Capoccio defines the study of critical junctures as 'the analysis of the politics of institutional change during a relatively brief phase which is characterized by the availability of different courses of action capable of affecting future institutional development in the longer term', see ibid. 92.

order is systemic: there is a broadly shared loss of faith in the old order and its institutions, and similar problems and complaints span countries and regions. Critical junctures create openings where previously taken-for-granted norms and policies are called into question and populations search for new answers for pressing problems. Clever political entrepreneurs can seize on the openings, and these entrepreneurs contribute to the uncertainty that abounds when we are living through a critical juncture.

Historical institutionalist scholarship has long focused on how critical junctures shape and change politics, simultaneously affecting multiple institutions in different parts of the world. Critical junctures can lead to fundamental changes that reorient politics, launching path-dependent political development down a new trajectory.[4] But not all critical junctures produce wide-scale change. For example, in the 1970s, the largest economic expansion in history ended with what economists thought impossible, a combination of rising inflation and rising unemployment (aka stagflation). Then the oil shock led to 400% increases in the price of oil, adding to inflation, increasing the cost of living and working in advanced industrial societies, and generating a global debt crisis as governments borrowed to keep energy flowing. Responding to these events, and exacerbating the political crisis, the US ended its promise of dollar-convertibility to gold, launching the uncertain era of floating exchange rates. At the same time, the mass protests against the Vietnam War and the demands launched by the civil rights movement engendered a conservative backlash that unfolded slowly in the 1980s. In short, in the 1970s economic uncertainty and strife abounded; there were mass protests in many parts of the world; presidents resigned; and governments fell. But the international order and the institutions of national political systems did not fundamentally change.

Where critical junctures do produce change, scholars observe that the direction of change is shaped by antecedent conditions, that is by local factors and conditions that combine with causal forces during a critical juncture to put different countries and regions on different trajectories.[5] Antecedent conditions can include shared beliefs and commitments that endure, localised factors that shape how global upheaval reverberates within a particular context, and prior experiences that inform how current events are interpreted. In this chapter, I argue that the liberal idea of a rule of law is an antecedent condition that is now being called into question, yet is perhaps more enduring than some fear. Meanwhile, where critical junctures do not produce rapid change, they can nonetheless unleash slower moving forces that redirect future politics. Indeed, in retrospect the conservative forces unleashed by the rocky 1970s have contributed to fundamental changes that were obscured by their slow-moving incremental nature.

4 Giovanni Capoccia and R. Daniel Kelemen, 'The Study of Critical Junctures in Historical Institutionalism' (2007) 59 *World Politics* 341.

5 Dan Slater and Erica Simmons, 'Informative Regress: Critical Antecedents in Comparative Politics' (2010) 43(7) Methodology Forum 886, 889; and Capoccia (n 3) 93.

I use the insights of historical institutionalism and the history of international courts to think about the prospects of international courts in the current moment. Before continuing, however, it is important to note that historical institutional trajectories may be path dependent – in that each choice is shaped by what came before – but path dependence is not the same thing as teleology or progressive development. My research has always included the idea that success can breed backlash, a response aimed at returning to an earlier condition. With respect to international courts, the earlier condition is one of formal sovereign equality, where national actors enjoy autonomy to decide when and how to apply international and supranational law. I argued that the more ICs succeed and the more they constrain, the more they encroach on national legal and political systems. This success breeds contestation that can slow, alter and even reverse the trajectory of international legal change.[6] Meanwhile, legal and political pushback can also be positive in that it can redirect international legal development to protect democratic choice.[7]

This section has argued that critical junctures create opportunities; they do not dictate what then happens. Yet during critical junctures, old understandings get called into question, and new untested ideas, or ideas that were once rejected, become possibilities. In the midst of a critical juncture, there will be experimentation during which different strategies are tried, refined, discarded or then institutionalised and emulated. This experimentation, refinement and emulation is what can launch future change down a new path-dependent trajectory. Meanwhile, periods of quiescence serve to consolidate past changes so that what were once maverick ideas – such as the idea that international law could subdue international relations, or that human rights can exist, independent of citizen rights – becomes normalised and even taken for granted, until a future critical juncture perhaps calls these normalised notions into question.

Critical junctures and international courts: how does the past guide the future?

International courts have, historically, been institutional beneficiaries of critical junctures. Why were past critical junctures so productive to the creation and use of ICs, and how is the current critical juncture different? One simple answer may be that when one starts from a baseline of zero, the only direction to go is up. All governance systems – international and domestic, economic and political – need mechanisms for dispute resolution. Before ICs, trans-border legal disputes were mediated or they were funnelled to courts or special bodies in colonial

6 Karen J. Alter, 'The European Legal System and Domestic Policy: Spillover or Backlash' (2000) 54 *International Organization* 489; Karen J. Alter, 'Who are the Masters of the Treaty?: European Governments and the European Court of Justice' (1998) 52 *International Organization* 125; Alter (n 1) Chapter 9.

7 Alter (n 1) Chapter 9.

countries, or turned over to special arbitrators or special supranational bodies created to deal with a class of legal disputes arising from particular historical events (e.g. mass claim courts, special slave courts).[8] The twentieth century replaced rule by empires with a network of multilateral institutions. International adjudicatory bodies may have been a natural (e.g. the most obvious) solution for the problem of managing transnational dispute settlement in what was a fundamentally different post-colonial global system.

But this basic answer is insufficient because it does not explain the timing or the trend towards creating more and more ICs, and towards creating 'new style' ICs, namely ICs with compulsory jurisdiction and access to non-state actors to initiate litigation. There are many modes of dispute resolution. ICs offer a highly legalised approach, where a standing body of judges from diverse countries apply pre-existing legal rules to adjudicate legal issues that arise. As a formal matter, international judges may not be bound by legal precedent, but because ICs issue public rulings, permanent courts must nonetheless attend to developing legal arguments and to the prospective effects of these arguments. In these and other important ways, permanent ICs differ from mediation, diplomacy and ad hoc arbitration where the parties appoint the mediators/adjudicators and where outcomes may only be known to the parties themselves.[9] Meanwhile, the jurisdiction of an IC does not have to be compulsory, nor do ICs need to include access for non-state actors. Both of these 'new-style' features widen the types of legal issues that may appear before ICs, making it harder for states to avoid inconvenient suits. The proliferation of new-style ICs is a particular historical phenomenon, arising from ideas and events as well as states' desire that ICs be able to do more than simply resolve disputes between states.[10]

Of course, there are many good reasons to create and invoke ICs. Scholars have long touted the many substantive and functional benefits that international law and international adjudication bring to the challenge of international cooperation and dispute resolution. In the liberal vision, international agreements allow countries to pursue collective goals, avoid conflicts, and achieve joint gains.

8 Jenny S. Martinez, 'Towards an International Judicial System' (2003) 56 *Stanford Law Review* 429; Ignacio de la Rasilla del Moral and Jorge E. Viñuales, *Experiments in International Adjudication: Historical Accounts* (Cambridge University Press 2018).

9 Cesare P. R. Romano, Karen J. Alter and Yuval Shany, 'Mapping International Courts and Tribunals, the Issues and Players' in Cesare P. R. Romano and others (eds.), *Oxford Handbook on International Adjudication* (OUP 2014) 9–12.

10 I explain the new-style term and trend, and offer an explanation of the trend arguing that as states enlarged the roles they wanted ICs to serve beyond inter-state dispute settlement, they adapted the design of ICs so that ICs could fulfil enforcement, constitutional and administrative review roles, Karen J. Alter, 'The Multiple Roles of International Courts and Tribunals: Enforcement, Dispute Settlement, Constitutional and Administrative Review' in Jeffrey L. Dunoff and Mark A. Pollack (eds.), *International Law and International Relations: Synthesizing Insights from Interdisciplinary Scholarship* (Cambridge University Press 2012). [Defining new-style ICs as courts with compulsory jurisdiction and access for non-state actors to initiate litigation]

Creating systems of rule enforcement clarifies ambiguities, makes international commitments more credible, fills in incomplete contracts, provides a justification to push back against rent-seeking domestic interests thereby helping governments prioritise longer-term objectives, and it allows domestic and international conflicts to be diverted into a law-based system where tempers can cool and international adjudicators can absorb the blame for disappointing local interests. There are also, of course, functional reasons to prefer compulsory jurisdiction and wider access to international adjudicatory bodies. These functional benefits could explain why creating ICs is attractive, and to the extent ICs deliver these benefits, the functional contributions of ICs could serve to legitimate ICs.[11]

The problem with relying on functional arguments, however, is that functional benefits should have always applied. Also, a problem is that functional arguments too sanguinely discount the downsides of legalising and judicialising international relations that critics that have long discussed.[12] In particular, it is not clear that legalisation is the best mode of international governance, or that international adjudication provides the best means of dispute resolution. Moreover, the fact that ICs increasingly have compulsory jurisdiction and access for non-state actors may itself contribute to the bringing of no-win legal suits, cases where IC rulings are surely going to be ignored and where rulings might even incite a political backlash.

In short, functional arguments will never be able to explain the timing or the nature of IC institutional development. One can also question whether the functional benefits can provide a sufficient basis for IC legitimacy, given that ICs and international law sometimes clash with nationally created laws, institutions and politicians who can also claim legitimacy.[13] What follows briefly recaps my argument of how past critical junctures have shaped the development of the

11 Andreas Follesdal adapts Joseph Raz's service conception of legitimacy to argue that ICs gain legitimacy by providing helpful services that stakeholders value. He qualifies, however, arguing that in order to be legitimate, IC outputs must also help compliance supporters realise objectively defensible objectives, see Andreas Follesdahl, 'The Legitimate Authority of International Courts and Its Limits: A Challenge to Raz's Service Conception?' in Patrick Capps and Henrik Palmer Olsen (eds.), *Legal Authority Beyond the State* (Cambridge University Press 2018).

12 Nationalist actors have long criticised the idea that international judges should assess the validity of state actions, arguing that international legal review violates national sovereignty, see Robert H. Bork, *Coercing Virtue: The Worldwide Rule of Judges* (American edn, AEI Press 2003). Third-World Approaches to International Law (TWAIL), a scholarly and activist movement that includes critical theory approaches to international law, has long sought to expose the colonial origins and exploitative aspects of the current international legal system, see Usha Natarajan and others, 'Introduction: TWAIL - On Praxis and the Intellectual' (2016) 37 Third World Quarterly 1946; Balakrishnan Rajagopal, *International Law from Below: Development, Social Movements, and Third World Resistance* (Cambridge University Press 2003).

13 Karen J. Alter, 'The Contested Authority and Legitimacy of International Law: The State Strikes Back' in Christopher Daase and others (eds.), *Beyond Anarchy: Rule and Authority in the International System* (forthcoming).

contemporary international judiciary. This historical institutional account sees institutional change (the creation of ICs, the change in IC design, and ICs' potential future dismemberment) in terms of path-dependent developments – changes inspired by the evolving institutional context as it interacts with recent history. During critical junctures, the functional benefits ICs offer still exist. What changes is the balance between supporters and critics, those who see the functional benefits in positive terms and those who let competing priorities trump arguments about potential functional benefits. I have written a longer history of these developments;[14] here I briefly summarise with the goal of moving to the present.

The Hague Peace to the end of the Cold War: laying the ideational and institutional groundwork for an international rule of law

The idea of international courts as a key part of a multilateral international political order emerged during the Hague Peace Era, a period that began before the outbreak of WWI and then responded to the emergency generated by the fact of the Great War. In this period diplomats convened in The Hague, where they negotiated and debated international law and international institutions, and dared to imagine that legalised inter-state dispute settlement might replace war as a tool of international politics. The Hague conferences generated a number of legal ideas that endured, and by some accounts marked the beginning of a new world order.[15] Not all of the institutions proposed or created during the Hague era succeeded, and indeed some were seen as failures, but the ideas and the actors promoting international adjudication as means to deal with inter-state conflicts continued their efforts, shaping legal and political developments within regions. I do not want to recap this history here.[16] Instead, I want to suggest how past critical junctures were fundamentally different from today.

In this post-Cold War moment, states consented to a number of deeply intrusive new-style international courts, as Tables 2.1 and 2.2 demonstrate. Table 2.1 overviews the international judicial institution-building that occurred following the different critical junctures. The periods of time are long because it can take many years for a draft court treaty to be ratified, for a funds to be allocated, a building to be found, judges appointed, and thus for an IC to be established. Table 2.1 also includes proposals that were rejected. The list of rejected bodies

14 Alter (n 1) Chapter 4.

15 Christian Reus-Smit, 'The Constitutional Structure of International Society and the Nature of Fundamental Institutions' (1997) 51 International Organization 555; Oona Anne Hathaway and Scott Shapiro, *The Internationalists and Their Plan to Outlaw War* (Simon & Shuster 2017).

16 Alter (n 1) Chapter 4; see also Jide Nzelibe, 'Strategic Globalization: International law as an extension of domestic political conflict' (2011) 105 *Northwestern University Law Review* 635.

Table 2.1 Periodisation of established v. proposed ICs

Critical Juncture	*International Courts (by year created)*	*Inoperative or abandoned ICs (by year proposed)*
Hague Peace Conference Juncture (1899–1935)	Permanent Court of Arbitration (1899) Central American Court of Justice (1908–1918) Permanent Court of Justice (1922–1946)	Central American Arbitration Tribunal (1902) International Prize Court (1907) Central American Tribunal (1923) Terrorism Court (1937) Inter-American Court of International Justice (1938)
Post-WWII Juncture (1945–1960)	1. International Court of Justice (1945) International Criminal Tribunal of Nurnberg (1945) *General Agreement on Tariffs and Trade 1948–1994 2. European Union's Court of Justice (1952) 3. European Court of Human Rights (1958) 4. Benelux Court (1974) 5. Inter-American Court of Human Rights (1979) 6. Andean Tribunal of Justice (1984)	Arab Court of Justice (1945) European Nuclear Energy Tribunal of the OECD (1957) *Arbitral College of the Benelux Economic Union (1958) *Court of Arbitration of the French Community (1959) *Arbitration Tribunal of the Central American Common Market (1960) European Tribunal on State Immunity (1972) *Judicial Board of the Organization of Arab Petroleum Exporting Countries (1980) Court of Justice of the Economic Community of Central African States (1983) International Islamic Court of Justice (1987) Court of Justice of the African Maghreb Union (1989)
Post-Cold War Juncture (1990–2010)	7. European Free Trade Area Court (1992) 8. Central American Court of Justice (1992) 9. International Criminal Tribunal for the Former Yugoslavia (1993) 10. Economic Court of the Commonwealth of Independent States (1993) 11. International Criminal Tribunal for Rwanda (1994) 12. World Trade Organization Appellate Body (formerly GATT) (1994)	Court of Justice of the African Economic Community (1991) Court of Conciliation and Arbitrage for the OECD (1994) ASEAN Appellate Body (2005) *Court of Union State between Russian Federation & Belarus (1999) Court of Justice of the African Union (2003) Multilateral Investment Court (2017)

(*Continued*)

Table 2.1 (Continued)

Critical Juncture	*International Courts (by year created)*	*Inoperative or abandoned ICs (by year proposed)*
	13. West African Economic and Monetary Union Court of Justice (1995) 14. International Tribunal for the Law of the Seas (1996) 15. Organization for the Harmonization of Corporate Law in Africa Common Court of Justice and Arbitration (1997) 16. Southern Common Market (1999) 17. Eastern and Southern Africa Common Market Court of Justice (1998) 18. Central African Economic and Monetary Community Court of Justice (2000) 19. East African Community Court of Justice (2001) 20. Caribbean Court of Justice (2001) 21. Economic Community of West African States Court of Justice (2001) 22. International Criminal Court (2002) 23. Arab Investment Court (2003) 24. Southern African Development Community (2005) (suspended in 2010)[1] 25. African Court on Human and Peoples' Rights (2006)	

* = proposals that were later created in a different form. # = 25 permanent ICs created by 2006. Reprinted from "The Evolution of International Law and Courts". In Orfeo Fioretos (ed.), *International Politics and Institutions in Time*, Oxford: Oxford University Press, 2017, p. 262.

1 The SADC summit agreed in 2012 to reconstitute a different SADC Tribunal, and in 2015 SADC leaders adopted a new draft protocol for the SADC Tribunal. The protocol has not been ratified by member states, and this decision remains a subject of adjudication in domestic courts.

is instructive because many of these ideas were eventually addressed, either by creating an IC (indicated by a *) or through evolutions in legal practice (e.g. creating arbitration bodies, limiting state immunity). In other words, the functional demand already existed, which is why proposals to create an IC were put forward,

Table 2.2 Trend towards ICs with new-style design features

	Optional Provisions	*Compulsory Jurisdiction*
State initiation rights only **(N = 4)**	International Court of Justice (binding rulings) International Tribunal for the Law of the—Sea (ITLOS) →	Economic Court of the Commonwealth of Independent States World Trade Organization *ITLOS seizing of vessels cases*
Supranational Commission or Prosecutor initiation rights (Total ICs with supranational actor initiation rights = 13 + ICJ advisory opinions)	*ICJ advisory opinions (opinions not binding)* African Court on Human and Peoples' Rights (ACtHPR) → Inter-American Court a of Human Rights (IACtHR) → International Criminal Court (ICC) →	International Criminal Tribunal for Former Yugoslavia International Criminal Tribunal for Rwanda Common Market of Eastern and Southern Africa Court of Justice *(requires Council assent for case to proceed)* *ACtHPR—26 of 54 member countries accept compulsory jurisdiction* *IACtHR—22 of 35 member countries accept charter and compulsory jurisdiction* ICC *jurisdiction compulsory for 120 signatory states and when Security Council refers case*
Supranational actor *and* private initiation rights D = Direct PR = via national courts (preliminary ruling references)		Andean Tribunal of Justice (D + PR) Central African Economic and Monetary Union (D + PR) East African Community Court of Justice (D + PR) Economic Community of West African States Court of Justice (D + PR) European Union Court of Justice (D + PR) European Free Trade Area Court (PR *advisory only)* West African Economic and Monetary Union Court of Justice (PR)
Private litigant initiation rights (Total ICs with private initiation rights = 16)		BENELUX Court (PR) Caribbean Court of Justice (D) Central American Court of Justice (D) Common Market of Eastern and Southern Africa (PR) European Court of Human Rights (D) Organization for the Harmonization of Business Law in Africa (D) ITLOS Seabed Chamber (D) Southern African Development Community (D + PR)* Southern Common Market (PR *advisory only)*

* Direct access is likely to be removed. PR access will likely remain.

Reprinted from *The New Terrain of International Law* Figure 3.2 p. 84.

but the political context either blocked or sidelined the proposal. At later times, when the context and the balance between opponents and supporters had shifted, many of the proposals were adjusted and adopted. Table 2.2 demonstrates the growth of new-style design features that limit the ability of governments to block inconvenient cases from proceeding. Elsewhere I document rising rates of litigation in general, and across these ICs.[17]

Earlier I argued that contextual factors of the moment combine with antecedent conditions to shape what occurs during critical junctures. Negotiating, creating and using the Hague-era ICs helped proponents hear and address logistical questions and concerns about how judges would be selected, and how international adjudication might work in practice. The Hague discussions were the antecedent condition shaping the post-WWII juncture, generating a number of proposals to create new international legal bodies, which were rejected yet came to fruition much later, in some cases carried forward by the very people who had been involved in Hague Peace Era conversations.[18]

The Cold War context limited the possibilities for creating global courts, and domestic divisions in the United States between internationalists and isolationists made the ratification of ambitious international agreements difficult.[19] As the next section will explain, however, the US government's commitment to principled multilateralism also generated an important permissive condition for the flourishing of international institutions and international law. Although the US did not join all human rights treaties, and it later withdrew its consent to compulsory international judicial review of its foreign policies, the US consistently preferred international agreements negotiated by collectivities of states.[20] These agreements established general principles that guided foreign policy and international political decision making at home and abroad, and later international legal decision making. Moreover, the US government's commitment to international law – notwithstanding occasional flagrant violations – and Congress's willingness to link respect for international law to various types of legal and political carrots and sticks made arguments based in international law politically useful.

17 Alter (n 1) 103–109.

18 Scholars have traced juris-diplomats from the inter-war years, to the post-WWII prosecution of war collaborators, to the founding of European integration projects, see Jean-Michel Guieu, 'The Debate About a European Institutional Order among International Legal Scholars in the 1920s and Its Legacy' (2012) 21 *Contemporary European History* 319; Mikael Rask Madsen and Antoine Vauchez, 'European Constitutionalism at the Cradle. Law and Lawyers in the Construction of a European Political Order (1920–1960)' in Alex Jettinghoff and Harm Schepel (eds.), *In Lawyers' Circles Lawyers and European Legal Integration* (Reed 2005). It is likely that a careful tracing of legal networks would reveal a direct lineage between the Hague Peace project and the creation of subsequent ICs.

19 Alter (n 1) 119–126.

20 John Ruggie, 'Multilateralism: The Anatomy of an Institution' in John Ruggie (ed.), *Multilateralism Matters* (Columbia University Press 1993) 585.

Finally, changes in national and international legal practices remained constraints on states in the post-Cold War era, and these changed practices are now antecedent conditions that shape the current moment. The post-Cold War period may well have been the apogee of IC creation (but not necessarily of the usage of ICs). New ICs were created, and a number of existing ICs were amended at this time to widen jurisdiction and access to the court. Overall, the number of operational permanent international courts grew from six in 1989, to 25 in 2010, and litigation rates in ICs also significantly increased.[21] The post-Cold War period was also different in that savvy transnational legal actors – cause lawyers, bar associations, non-governmental organisations – had learned how to use international litigation as part of their advocacy strategies. Post-Cold War ICs did not, therefore, experience the benign neglect of their predecessors. Whereas the early ICs could slowly build their case law, post-Cold War ICs faced higher litigation rates, including cases that were potentially politically explosive in that the issues divided whole polities.[22]

So far this review of international judicial development sounds a bit triumphal. I would be remiss if I did not also point out that the Washington Consensus, the collapse of a socialist political worry, and the expansion of international judicial authority (by state delegation and IC rulings) also unleashed a neo-liberalism that has directly contributed to eroded trust in international law and international institutions.

The end of the liberal consensus: how the current critical juncture is different

One way in which the current period differs from the 1930s, 1940s and 1950s is that many ICs now exist. Table 2.1 shows that during previous critical junctures, there were demands and proposals for creating ICs that were not yet met. Much of this demand, however, was met in the post-Cold War era, and at this point the proposals for creating ICs are few and relatively modest. Indeed, many of the proposals are designed to either create regional alternatives to global adjudicative bodies, or to consolidate existing adjudicatory systems into a slightly different configuration.[23] This difference alone means that we should not expect the trend towards creating ICs to continue.

Also different, however, is that many of these ICs have new-style design features (see Table 2.2), which make it harder for states to block litigation from proceeding, and thus compared to the past, ICs today face an increased likelihood that politically explosive cases may end up on their dockets.

21 Alter (n 1) Chapter 3.

22 Karen J. Alter, Laurence R. Helfer and Mikael Rask Madsen, *International Court Authority* (Oxford University Press 2018) 448–450.

23 Scholars have, however, offered some bold suggestions, such as creating a World Human Rights Court, a World Patent Court, a World Civil Court, or a permanent Investor Dispute Court.

Third, and perhaps more fundamentally, ICs today are associated with the old international order that is in decline and increasingly resisted. In *The New Terrain of International Law* I noted that:

> A focus on world history suggests that the spread of ICs in the post–Cold War period reflects the dominance of American and European hard and soft power. Even when the United States and Europe do not directly pressure regions around the world to create or enhance their international legal systems, belief in the benefits of liberal economics, democracy, and the rule of law drives US and European actors to support political parties and interest groups that pressure their governments to submit to judicial accountability. Moreover, the willingness of the United States and Europe to respond to well-developed legal arguments and judicial rulings makes emulating legalism an attractive strategy.[24]

We may have reached the end of European and American dominance. Asian markets now rival the US and European markets in size and influence; Western countries may be abandoning the values that conferred on these countries an international soft power advantage; and new technologies (drones and cyber war) may be changing the nature of military and coercive power and dominance.

A fourth difference is that resistance to ICs is more widespread, and it exists in places where ICs used to find many allies. This rising resistance may be an artefact of the growing success and confidence of ICs, which have moved from being primarily 'other binding' institutions to institutions that dare to confront powerful states.[25] Also, governments may have found ways to resist more effectively. To be sure, resistance to international courts is not at all new.[26] What may be different, however, is that attacks against the rule of law may be actually succeeding. I want to focus on the international level, but it is also important to note that judicial independence in a number of liberal democracies has been compromised or eviscerated. My previous work argued that state influence over ICs is less than what many expect, because recontracting requires collective action that is difficult

24 Alter (n 1) 159–160.

25 On the difference between self and other-binding international courts, see Alter (n 1) 35–41.

26 See, for example, Karen J. Alter, 'The European Court's Political Power' (1996) 19 *West European Politics* 458; Karen J. Alter, 'Who are the Masters of the Treaty?: European Governments and the European Court of Justice' (1998) 52 International Organization 125; Karen J. Alter, 'The European Legal System and Domestic Policy: Spillover or Backlash' (2000) 54 *International Organization* 489; Laurence R. Helfer, 'Overlegalizing Human Rights: International Relations Theory and the Commonwealth Caribbean Backlash Against Human Rights Regimes' (2002) 102 *Columbia Law Review* 1832; Alexandra Huneeus, 'Courts Resisting Courts: Lessons from the Inter-American Court's Struggle to Enforce Human Rights' (2011) 44 *Cornell International Law Journal*. Exit is another form of resistance that has long existed, see Laurence Helfer, 'Exiting Treaties' (2005) 91 *Virginia Law Review* 1579. See also Mikael Rask Madsen, Pola Cebulak and Micha Wiebush, 'Backlash against International Courts: Explaining the Forms and Patterns of Resistance to International Courts' (2018) 14 *International Journal of Law in Context.*

to organise.[27] While this remains true, states are turning to 'rule by law' tactics to undermine certain ICs. Unable to influence other governments to support radical change in international legal rules, the mandate or the rulings of an IC, Zimbabwe and the US have turned to a strategy blocking international judicial appointments with the goal of forcing others to acquiesce to their will. Zimbabwe maintained its strategy to the point that the Southern African Development Community (SADC) tribunal lost all of its staff, at which point other member states finally agreed to Zimbabwe's demand that the SADC Tribunal revert to a state-access-only international tribunal.[28] The US is currently drawing from Mugabe's playbook, blocking appointments to the World Trade Organization's (WTO) Appellate Body, although the ultimate goal of these tactics is not entirely clear.[29]

I need to pause for a moment, because I do not want to suggest that resistance to ICs is an inherently authoritarian act, or that resistance lacks legitimacy or merit. To the contrary, resistance to ICs may be a deeply democratic phenomenon, an effort to reclaim national control over issues of central importance.[30] That said, the governments that are willing to go to the greatest extremes to subvert both domestic and international courts often have authoritarian leanings. Seeing little value in either international institutions or the rule of law, frustrated that ICs are challenging their policies, and even more frustrated that other countries seem to not care about their strongly felt concerns, more authoritarian-minded leaders see little cost to castrating an international court.

Given these recent events, the question is whether the current critical juncture might launch ICs towards a new trajectory. This review of critical junctures and ICs has sought to demonstrate that today's critical juncture is fundamentally different from past junctures in a few ways. First, Table 2.1 suggests that unlike in past

27 Karen J. Alter, 'Delegation to International Courts and the Limits of Recontracting Power' in Darren Hawkins and others (eds.), *Delegation and Agency in International Organizations* (Cambridge University Press 2006); Karen J. Alter, 'Agent or Trustee: International Courts in their Political Context' (2008) 14 *European Journal of International Relations* 33. See also Alec Stone Sweet and Thomas Brunell, 'Trustee Courts and the Judicialization of International Regimes: The Politics of Majoritarian Activism in the ECHR, the EU and the WTO' (2013) 1 *Journal of Law and Courts.*

28 We discuss this strategy, and a different strategy used with some impact in the East African Community, see Karen J. Alter, James T. Gathii and Laurence R. Helfer, 'Backlash against International Courts in West, East and Southern Africa: Causes and Consequences' (2016) 27 *European Journal of International Law* 293. A draft treaty for the new SADC tribunal exists, but it has not been ratified so that the new tribunal does not yet exist.

29 Very soon, the Appellate Body will lack a quorum to rule, although litigation at the first stage of the process (the panel stage) can still proceed. Meanwhile, the larger US objective for this strategy – which began under the Obama administration – is not yet clear. See Greg Shaffer, 'Will the US Undermine the World Trade Organization?' (*HuffPost*, 23 May 2016) <https://www.huffingtonpost.com/gregory-shaffer/will-the-us-undermine-the_b_10108970.html> Last visited on September 19, 2018.

30 Eyal Benvenisti, 'Reclaiming Democracy: The Strategic Uses of Foreign and International Law by National Courts' (2008) 102 *American Journal of International Law* 241.

eras, the bank of proposals to create or expand existing ICs is much more limited. We may still see regional attempts to consolidate and/or improve the operation of existing ICs, but the big bang of IC creation may well be over. Second, in earlier periods ICs had little political salience. Today, however, ICs are associated with the establishment that is being repudiated, and ICs are increasingly 'self-binding' great powers.[31] Third, states may have finally figured out how to effectively sanction an IC.[32] Fourth, great powers are now part of the movement to resist ICs.[33]

That said, precisely because ICs represent a commitment to international law, those who still prefer international relations guided by international law may see ICs as a stabilising force for turbulent times. Perhaps enduring features of earlier periods include a popular belief in the benefits of the rule of law, a community of lawyers, scholars, activists and judges that have a know-how to work with and apply legal checks on governing power, and a global business preference for legal rules applied by independent legal bodies. These counter-trends supporting international law may keep the dockets of existing ICs populated with cases.

International courts and the international liberal order: a joint fate?

ICs developed and flourished as part of the international liberal order, and the legal rules that ICs most often adjudicate tend to be associated with the priorities and values of the international liberal order. What will happen to ICs if the international liberal order recedes? The next section will argue that there are many reasons to believe that states' commitments to a 'rules based international system' and to most existing international legal rules will survive. But it is nonetheless true that international law today is deeply wedded to the American-led international liberal order because many of the laws that ICs apply are designed to further liberal objectives.

Many years ago, John Ruggie argued that international regimes fuse power with a social purpose.[34] Power can wane or become separated from the social purpose,

31 Newspaper coverage of ICs has expanded, as has criticism of ICs and their judges. Indeed, supporters of Brexit were motivated in significant part by a desire to escape from the oversight and control of the ECJ (now called the Court of Justice of the European Union (CJEU)).

32 Shortly I will argue that the Trump administration is emulating Mugabe's strategy to cripple the WTO's dispute settlement system.

33 The Trump administration has soured on the WTO, and the president (erroneously) suggests that the US disproportionately loses cases adjudicated by the WTO, see Ana Swanson 'Once the WTO's Biggest Supporters, the US is its Biggest Skeptic' (*New York Times*, 10 December 2017). <https://www.nytimes.com/2017/12/10/business/wto-united-states-trade.html> Last visited on September 19, 2018. China and Russia, having lost important legal suits, have also articulated a revised interpretation of the extent of international legal obligations, see Kenneth Anderson, 'Text of the Russia-China Joint Declaration on Promotion and Principles of International Law' (*Lawfare*, 7 July 2016) <https://www.lawfareblog.com/text-russia-china-joint-declaration-promotion-and-principles-international-law> Last visited on September 19, 2018.

34 John Ruggie, 'International Regimes, Transactions and Change: Embedded Liberalism in the Postwar Economic Order' (1982) 36 *International Organization* 379, 198.

as occurred when the United Kingdom became unwilling to support the global economy during the interwar period, giving rise to the Great Depression and WWII. The international order then fell apart because there was no hegemon and no real commitment to the fledgling League of Nations. But, Ruggie argues, so long as the social purpose remains, momentum can keep the extant order in place.

Ruggie's argument suggests that the liberal international order can survive President Trump's inward turn so long as the social purpose it represents continues to be shared by others. The liberal international order could not, however, survive if the broader commitment to the liberal order's social purpose also changed. John Ruggie was writing in the 1980s, exposing the social underpinnings of the existing international order. The underpinnings were deeply shaped by the post-war consensus in Europe, and by American domestic and international values.[35] This means that the international liberal order can survive President Donald Trump, because it does not depend entirely on US support.

Yet, if one moves to a higher level, to consider what Christian Reus-Smit calls the 'fundamental institutions' and the 'constitutional structures', the full extent of the populist challenge is revealed. The constitutional structures are the ensembles of beliefs, principles and norms that define what constitutes a legitimate actor, entitled to all the rights and privileges of statehood; and they define basic parameters of rightful state action.[36] Reus-Smit argues that the constitutional structure of the modern era – what defines the moral purpose of the state – conceives of governance as a social contract designed to further the interests of citizens, and premised on constitutionalism, procedural justice and the rule of law. In other words, the constitutional structures are the same as one finds in liberal democracies.[37] Reus-Smit argues that the constitutional structures, including the social contract mode of governance, has also transferred to the international level, and with it came the understanding that 'The rules governing international society should be authored by those subject to them and equally binding on all.'[38] This idea of collective creation is inherent to multilateralism, and it is likely to endure. But as many international law critics note, international law has never truly been equally binding on all. The only way to make international law equally binding is either to let all international laws and institutions bind great powers (eliminating explicit and tacit veto rights for great powers), or to water down how international law binds weaker states.

In making historically contingent arguments regarding today's international liberal order, Ruggie and Reus-Smit remind us that a Chinese international order

35 Ibid; John Ruggie, 'Multilateralism: The Anatomy of an Institution' in John Ruggie (ed.) *Multilateralism Matters: The Theory and Practice of an Institutional Form* (Columbia University Press 1993) 3–47.

36 Christian Reus-Smit, *The Moral Purpose of the State: Culture, Social Identity and Institutional Rationality in International Relations* (Princeton University Press 1999) 30.

37 Christian Reus-Smit, 'The Constitutional Structure of International Society and the Nature of Fundamental Institutions' (1997) 51 *International Organization* 555, 576–583.

38 Ibid. 578.

might not value procedural justice, constitutionalism or individual rights. If international law becomes separated from the liberal social purpose that has defined the post-WWII period, then the nature of the international legal and political order will change. John Ruggie was clear: 'All hegemonies are not alike. The most that can be said about a hegemonic power is that it will seek to construct an international order in some form, presumably along lines that are compatible with its own international objectives and domestic structures. But, in the end, that really is not saying much.'[39]

It is in this light that we need to pay attention to what new political leaders are saying and doing. Populist leaders are challenging the constitutional structures of both domestic and international governance. Populist politicians tend to believe that they alone know what the people want; that they alone can protect the nationalist interest; and that their will is more important than human rights and systems of checks and balances. The populism we find in the United States, Latin America, Russia, the Middle East, and parts of Europe, tends to be deeply coupled with the charisma of particular political leaders. So long as populism depends on personalistic charisma, the movement may be ephemeral. China, however, has a longer-term commitment to a fundamentally different set of national and international values. Even if China's current president depends greatly on his own wily charisma, Ruggie is right that a Chinese hegemon is likely to promote a different sort of international order.

Yet the incentives to litigate in front of ICs remain, and in particular law-backed actors who continue to support the substantive issues at stake, and liberal values, may continue to want international legal validation of their claims. *The New Terrain of International Law* argued that ICs' real power is its speech-act of confronting power with law in the cases that are adjudicated. An IC's speech-act resonates only so far as it coalescences with values held by actors in society. I was careful in my claims:

> The altered politics argument suggests four necessary conditions for ICs to alter domestic and international politics: (1) litigants must be able to seize the court; (2) actors within states must care about legality; (3) entrepreneurs must invoke a court and help build a compliance constituency; (4) international rules must enjoy the political support of constituencies that have power. The first condition is met by new-style ICs but shaped by legal standing requirements and the substance of the law. Conditions two through four are determined by political factors, and variation in these factors will generate variation in the influence of ICs across institution, issue area, and case.[40]

In other words, if domestic and/or international politics affects litigant ability or willingness to seize an international court, if populism leads politicians or

39 Ruggie (n 36) 585–586.
40 Alter (n 1) 62.

voters to no longer care about legality, and/or if the size or power of an IC's compliance constituency substantially shrinks (if only because national judiciaries are 'reformed' into subservience), then the ability of ICs to alter domestic and international politics will diminish.

How might changes in the contemporary period affect conditions? Legal scholarship tends to treat ICs and specific legal rules in isolation from the larger institution of which they are a part, suggesting that so long as international judges do their job well, the institution will enjoy legitimacy. But the resonance of an international legal victory may decline if the larger institution issuing the legal ruling lacks legitimacy and/or political support, or if the substantive issue at stake in the case lacks domestic support. Meanwhile, governments are unlikely to heed pressure to comply with international laws that are deeply unpopular at home. These factors are related: violations may abound, but litigants are more likely to raise an international legal case if they believe that an international judicial ruling can help their cause.[41] If national populations and Western countries care about international legal violations then an international legal victory becomes increasingly attractive. By contrast, if domestic actors no longer support the legal rule in question, and if the US and Europe also do not care, then the attractiveness and effectiveness of an international litigation strategy may decline. Litigants may therefore choose not to raise a legal suit, appealing to political rather than legal strategies to promote their objectives.

While many actors may eschew litigation in favour of other political strategies, litigation has always been a tool of the weak. When nothing else is working (e.g. governments seem impervious to the individual's or group's demands), and when the voice of local actors has been suppressed at home, international litigation may be the only way to have legal and regional claims recognised. This last dynamic means that the more powerless supporters of the rule of law are – either domestically or internationally – the more likely they may be to turn to international legal and quasi-legal fora to receive symbolic validation of their claims.

This last incentive creates a real dilemma for international judges. The future for ICs lies between these competing dynamics – a growing desperation to hold governments accountable can collide with a growing indifference as to whether governments violate international law. This argument raises two inextricably linked yet distinct questions, both of which are mostly empirical in nature: 1) Is the political commitment to substantive international law actually waning, so that the international value of an international legal ruling is declining? 2) Is the domestic commitment to legality waning so that the domestic value of an international legal ruling is also declining? I address these in turn.

41 These strategies may be aimed at increasing compliance, but as James Gathii points out, local activists may have agendas that are not really focused on forcing compliance with international law, see James Thuo Gathii, 'Variation in the use of subregional integration courts between business and human rights actors: the case of the East African Court of Justice. (Symposium: The Variable Authority of International Courts)' (2016) 79 *Law and Contemporary Problems* 37.

The future of international law in a changing international order

Historical institutionalism teaches us that institutions are sticky – particular policies and institutions may recede in importance but institutions are seldom dismantled. International courts are sleeper institutions that wait to be activated by litigants. When litigants want international law enforced, and should compliance consti-tuencies emerge that also want international law enforced, ICs can awake and become newly relevant. This is what I mean when I say that ICs might enter "Sleeping Beauty" mode. The lovely institutions that are ICs might repose, remaining largely out of sight, until the Prince (litigants and compliance constituencies) arrives to awaken them.

Meanwhile, although some political leaders may want international law to be less domestically intrusive and personally constraining, the larger project of codifying international agreements in the form of binding and enforceable international law is likely to endure, along with most of the existing substantive international law.[42] There are a few reasons why I am cautiously sanguine that international law will survive, mostly unchanged. First, the current debate in the US is basically a cyclical debate. While President Trump likes to suggest that everything he does is a fundamental change from what came before, in reality anti-globalist and non-interventionist voices have always been part of the American policy debates. One might even say that the Republican Party is basically reverting to its pre- and post-WWII protectionist and isolationist origins.[43] In these cyclical politics, domestic opponents of internationalism win important victories, but they have generally failed to turn back the tide of global internationalism.[44] If American support for multilateralism endures, and if anything support is growing in opposition to President Trump's actions,[45] then this cyclical moment will

42 Karen J. Alter, 'The Future of International Law' in Diana Ayton-Shenker (ed.), *The New Global Agenda: Priorities, Practices, and Pathways of the International Community* (Rowman & Littlefield 2018)

43 Douglas A. Irwin, 'From Smoot-Hawley to Reciprocal Trade Agreements: Changing the Course of U.S. Trade Policy in the 1930s' in Michael D. Bordo, Claudia Goldin and Eugene N. White (eds.) *The Defining Moment: The Great Depression and the American Economy in the Twentieth Century* (University of Chicago Press 1998) 325–352; Nelson Richards, 'The Bricker Amendment and Congress's Failure to Check the Inflation of the Executive's Foreign Affairs Powers, 1951–1954' 94 *California Law Review* 175

44 For example, in the 1950s US-based opponents of the International Trade Organization managed to block the adoption of a fully drafted global trade agreement that the United States had championed. This victory slowed down, but it did not stop the construction of a global trading system via GATT, which later became the WTO, see John H. Barton and others, *The Evolution of the Trade Regime* (Princeton University Press 2006). Concerned that international human rights agreements might render America's Jim Crow laws illegal, vocal critics within the United States slowed and blocked the domestic ratification of human rights agreements that the United States had championed, see Elizabeth Borgwardt, *A New Deal for the World: America's Vision for Human Rights* (Belknap Press of Harvard University Press 2005). And conservative Americans convinced President Ronald Reagan not to sign or ratify the UN Law of the Seas Treaty that President Nixon had fought so hard to achieve.

45 See Dina Smeltz and others, 'What Americans Think about America First' (The Chicago Council on Global Affairs) <https://digital.thechicagocouncil.org/what-americans-think-about-

pass.[46] That said, this optimism depends on whether populist parties can remain in power long enough to hollow and reform domestic judiciaries and governance institutions, crippling ICs' compliance partners in enduring ways.

Second, while specific political leaders may dislike certain international laws, there really is no alternative to international law as a tool for coordinating state policies. International law scholar Louis Henkin famously made a point that no one contests: 'Almost all nations observe almost all principles of international law almost all of the time.'[47] For most international legal issues – diplomatic immunity, navigation of the seas, rules prohibiting against foreign invasion, rules governing air traffic and the postal service, and even open markets (within limits) etc. – countries tend to be mostly happy with international law as it exists. As such, these rules are unlikely to change, and countries that repeatedly flaunt international rules might find themselves on the losing side of softer and harder forms of retaliation (e.g. non-cooperation, withholding courtesies and benefits, diverting purchases etc.).[48] Part of this calculation is a realisation which President Trump does not yet grasp: while the current rules may be imperfect, particular governments are unlikely to be able to negotiate an agreement that is more to their liking. In this respect, asking the public if they like rule X or would prefer rule Y is really beside the point. International agreements are negotiated bargains, not a statement of what the population or the president of any one country would most like at a particular moment of time. Meanwhile, given the more plausible political choice between no international rules or a rules-based international system (e.g. a world where clear and articulated international rules operate), most people and governments would prefer the latter, if only because rules-based systems are more predictable.

Third, the current international system is densely institutionalised in ways that are likely irreversible. Eliminating institutions is always difficult, if only because some set of actors will want them to remain. Yet most international laws and norms are embedded in multiple institutions, so that eliminating one institution will be insufficient. For example, most trade regimes replicate the rules of the WTO. Even if the WTO disappeared, the core legal principles of 'national treatment' would endure because it is replicated in so many treaties. The same is true for torture, mass atrocities and other international legal rules.

The America First agenda prefers bilateralism, as this is the best way for the US to force its wishes on others. Yet eliminating the whole idea of multilateralism – wherein groups of states come together to reach principled

america-first?_ga=2.104059401.801395235.1521145581-1585603661.1516033141> Last visited on September 19, 2018.

46 A larger danger may lie in Europe. During the post-WWII period, mainstream European political parties were united in their internationalist position, and these parties worked very hard to keep radical left- and right-wing parties from assuming power. But should populist parties seize government, European support may experience a change which is not so clearly cyclical in nature.

47 Louis Henkin, *How Nations Behave* (Columbia University Press 1979) 47.

48 Oona Hathaway, and Scott J. Shapiro,'Outcasting: Enforcement in Domestic and International Law' 121(2) (2001) *Yale Law Journal* 252–469.

collective agreements – is also unlikely, if only because existing regimes include exceptions that apply to multilateral endeavours, so that countries that want different regimes will be tempted to legislate through new forms of multilateralism. All of this means that key elements of the current international institutional and legal order are likely to endure.

The current order can, however, be changed. It is easier to layer new agreements and institutions on top of existing agreements than it is to dismantle existing institutions. This tendency to add rather than subtract contributes to the rise of international regime complexity, to the creation of arrays of partially overlapping and non-hierarchical institutions that empower a range of actors to strategise within and around regime complexes.[49] So while the current system may change to reflect the social purpose of emerging powers, its development is likely to be shaped by the existing set of international regimes that endure, and by the new regimes that get layered on top.

The final question to address, however, is whether international courts can survive if the constitutional structures of the international order change, and thus if liberal democracy and the rule of law are no longer valued.

The future of a political commitment to legality

Along with others, I have long argued that the authority of international law hinges on a political commitment to legality as an indicator of whether or not a policy or action is legitimate.[50] Indeed it is the social value that liberal democratic societies place on legality – the quality of being in accordance with the law – that leads governments to justify their policy in international law terms, even when their actions are widely perceived to violate international law in fairly obvious and transparent ways. This argument about legality as a source of legitimacy is insufficient, however, in that legality is not itself the same thing as legitimacy.

On the one hand, the conflation of legality and legitimacy is understandable. Legality arguments draw on Weberian rational-legal modes of legitimation that are promoted and sustained by scholars, and by law-compliant and law-violating states.[51] To observe that states and international actors use rational-legal legitimisation strategies, however, is not to show that these strategies are convincing

49 Karen J. Alter and Kal Raustiala, 'The Rise of International Regime Complexity', 14 (2018) *Annual Review of Law and Social Science* 329–349.

50 This view is so widely argued that it is hard to make a list of who has made this claim, but here are a few recent examples: Jutta Brunnée and Stephen J. Toope, *Legitimacy and Legality in International Law an Interactional Account* (Cambridge University Press 2010); Ian Hurd, *How to Do Things With International Law* (Princeton University Press 2017); Christian Reus-Smit, 'The Politics of International Law' in Christian Reus-Smit (ed.), *The Politics of International Law* (Cambridge University Press 2004); Jutta Brunnée and Stephen J. Toope, 'Interactional Legal Theory, the International Rule of Law and Global Constitutionalism' in Anthony F. Lang and Antje Wiener (eds.), *Handbook on Global Constitutionalism* (Edward Elgar 2017).

51 Fernando G. Nuñez-Mietz, 'Legalization and the Legitimation of the Use of Force: Revisiting Kosovo' (2018) 72 International Organization 725; Ian Hurd, 'The Strategic Use of

or successful. Personally, I have been more persuaded by Lon Fuller's social-philosophical justification of the criteria of legality, which according to Fuller confer a morality on the law that generates a sense of obligation. Crisply stated, Fuller's definition of legality is as follows:

> Legal norms must be general, prohibiting, requiring, or permitting certain conduct. They must also be promulgated, and therefore accessible to the public, enabling actors to know what the law requires. Law should not be retroactive, but prospective, enabling citizens to take the law into account in their decision making. Actors must also be able to understand what is permitted, prohibited, or required by law – the law must be clear. Law should avoid contradiction, not requiring or permitting and prohibiting at the same time. Law must be realistic and not demand the impossible. Its demands on citizens must remain relatively constant. Finally, there should be congruence between legal norms and the actions of officials operating under the law.[52]

In linking these legal criteria to claims of legal morality and a felt sense of obligation, Fuller suggests that legality in fact confers legitimacy.[53] To be sure, Fuller's criteria are, on balance, normatively desirable and perhaps even necessary for legal morality. But because they are rather formalist and subject to manipulation, they are not sufficient conditions for legitimacy.[54]

We are increasingly aware that often unstated and taken for granted normative commitments underpin respect for rules and institutions, which is why any system of rules and institutions can be subverted.[55] In constitutional democracies, Fuller's principles are augmented by norms and practices that have a particular notion of how legality works. The norms and practices add features, such as the practice of having democratic legislatures (and thus legitimated actors) producing the laws. Also, liberal democracies follow procedures that allow input into the law-making process, including free and fair elections and notice-and-comment processes which feed back into legal drafting and administrative policymaking. Constitutional democracies also have independent judiciaries and constitutional checks that ensure that no one, not even governments or political leaders, are above the law. These larger sets of 'rule of law' institutions and norms have a long lineage, which is not to say that they are unproblematic or uncontroversial.[56]

Liberal Internationalism: Libya and the UN Sanctions, 1993–2003' (2005) 59 *International Organization* 495.

52 Brunnée and Toope (n 50) 310, citing Coleen Murphy, 'Lon Fuller and the Moral Value of the Rule of Law' (2005) 24 Law and Philosophy 239, 240–241.

53 Lon L. Fuller, *The Morality of Law* (Yale University Press 1964). In the international realm the work of Brunnée and Toope has extended this notion, see Brunnée and Toope (n 51).

54 David Luban, 'The Rule of Law and Human Dignity: Re-examining Fuller's Canon' (2010) 2 *Hague Journal on the Rule of Law* 29.

55 Steven Levitsky and Daniel Ziblatt, *How Democracies Die* (First edn, Crown 2018).

56 Brian Z. Tamanaha, *On the Rule of Law: History, Politics, Theory* (Cambridge University Press 2004).

Authoritarian leaders construct a faux-twin that combines a formalist mimicry of rule of law structures found in liberal democracies, and suppression of the normative foundations promoted by liberal democracies. Scholars of law in authoritarian contexts have dubbed this faux-twin 'ruling by law'.[57] In rule-by-law systems, the making, interpretation and enforcement of the law becomes a tool to control and/or punish political opponents. Formally, the two systems look similar – constitutions and even constitutional courts exist, legislative bodies make laws, the laws are facially neutral in form, and prosecutors and judges enforce the laws. Legal institutions may even have the formal trappings associated with judicial independence, and they may adhere to Fuller's formal rules of legality. But in its faux rule-by-law twin, group privileges are codified into law; laws may be designed to entrap both well-intended and criminal elements;[58] the judiciary is stacked with loyalists; violations by friends are overlooked while through legal enforcement, political outsiders are rendered lesser people, and even enemies. In rule-by-law systems, genuine legal checks are dismantled so that 'illegality' can be politically constructed and deployed as a weapon to disenfranchise, dehumanise and punish political opponents. In such a context, legality cannot confer legitimacy.

We are learning that the normative underpinnings of the rule of law and the legal institutions constructed to uphold a democratic 'rule of law' system may be more easily subverted than we previously imagined, allowing for the proliferation of rule-by-law tactics. These days, a chief preoccupation of law and politics scholars is to understand when institutions involved in law enforcement – including courts – are and are not controlled, weaponised or legitimate.[59] The rise of populism focuses greater attention on this debate, because it helps to reveal the strategy that populist leaders use to convert democratic institutions into a rule-by-law regime, what Kim Scheppele calls a 'worst practices' strategy to create

57 Tom Ginsburg and Tamir Moustafa, *Rule by Law: The Politics of Courts in Authoritarian Regimes* (Cambridge University Press 2008); Jothie Rajah, *Authoritarian Rule of Law: Legislation, Discourse and Legitimacy in Singapore* (Cambridge University Press 2012).

58 This statement would seem to violate Fuller's legality requirement that it 'must be able to understand what is permitted, prohibited, or required by law – the law must be clear. Law should avoid contradiction, not requiring or permitting and prohibiting at the same time. Law must be realistic and not demand the impossible' see Jutta Brunnée and Stephen Toope, (n 50) 310. No one is disputing these points. A law that required people not to eat or breathe would be impossible to follow, and thus prohibited. Similarly, a human rights provision without any exceptions – for example a requirement that all humans have complete and full access to all medical interventions – is simply not possible for many parts of the world, and thus it would be unreasonable. The critical distinction is whether governments weaponised laws, applying them as a tool to control political opponents. Thus, if a tax code is extremely complex so that most taxpayers make small errors, or if the US government requires 15 years of biographical information to obtain a visa, then the law is perhaps designed to provide governments with a ready tool to selectively punish political opponents.

59 See for example Tom R. Tyler and Jonathan Jackson, 'Popular Legitimacy and the Exercise of Legal Authority: Motivating Compliance, Cooperation, and Engagement' (2014) 20 *Psychology, Public Policy, and Law* 78.

'democratorship'.[60] Meanwhile, there are many longstanding legal systems that mimic in form Western versions of the rule of law, mimicking the institutions found in liberal democracies, and even the formal rules of judicial independence. In practice, however, the absolute control wielded by governments over lawmaking, legal interpretation and the judicial branch ensures that these governments can rule-by-law. The persistence of rule-by-law twins in many parts of the world may even explain the regional and national variation in support for and respect of international law. Moreover, the belief in many parts of the developing world that the United States and Europe have always employed rule-by-law tactics vis-à-vis them imparts a cynicism about international law, even if the very same individuals aspire to the rule of law systems of the West.

I stick by my claim that the populist playbook used to subvert judicial independence at the national level is much harder to deploy internationally. International law is much harder to change compared to domestic law, because changing extant law requires the assent of multiple and sometimes all participating governments. International courts are also much harder to control or stack. Presidents Mugabe and Trump may, through force of will, block every attempt at an international judicial appointment.[61] But the appointment process for international judges remains decentralised in that each country gets to choose who it nominates to the international judicial bench. It takes an iron will, willingness to compromise the survival and/or legitimacy of the larger institution, and very long political tenures, to stack an IC. And eventually the reign of individual authoritarian leaders will end. Inertia therefore makes it more likely that ICs will survive, so long as ICs and their judges avoid drawing the sort of political attention that might incite an even greater backlash, such as the referendum on membership in the European Union (aka Brexit).

But the minefield that current international judges face today, especially compared to past eras, is formidable. During past critical junctures, it was fairly easy for international adjudicators to avoid entering into major international and domestic political disputes. Access rules limited the types of cases ICs were called upon to adjudicate whether because no ICs had legal jurisdiction to enforce contested legal rules, because ICs lacked compulsory jurisdiction (so that motivated states could block the case from proceeding) or because international commissions could and did screen out the most controversial suits.[62] Certainly during the Hague Peace era,

60 The worst practices include instituting seemingly neutral judicial reforms that conveniently oust independent judges, allowing governments to then stack the judiciary with loyalists. The playbook also involves muzzling the media and human rights groups. Kim Scheppele, 'Worst Practices and the Transnational Legal Order (or How to Build a Constitutional "Democratorship" in Plain Sight)' (2017) Unpublished manuscript.

61 With respect to the WTO's appellate body, this strategy actually began under President Obama. The difference is that President Trump will not even allow the vetting of candidates to begin, and he is challenging attempts to let sitting judges continue to adjudicate the cases that have begun.

62 Former European Human Rights Commissioner Henry Schermers wrote that 'In the early years virtually all individual applications were registered whilst as of 1973 the Secretariat of the Commission played a more active role in dissuading applicants with hopeless cases from

and for most of the post-WWII era, the most contested international legal rules lacked any enforcement mechanism which is to say that international criminal law could not be enforced, and most human rights and trade law violations were never adjudicated. When polemical cases did arise, ICs avoided controversial rulings by being highly formalist, using procedure to avoid controversial rulings or sticking to the plain language of the law.[63] If the law and the case were such that a controversial ruling could not be avoided, international judges could buy time, dragging out the litigation in the hopes that the political climate might improve.

We see some of these strategies still in operation. The African Court on Human and Peoples' Rights (ACtHPR) relies on the African Commission on Human and Peoples' Rights (ACHPR) to screen cases; despite the formal 'automaticity' of the WTO's dispute settlement system the China-European dispute over China's market economy status remains greatly delayed; and the Andean Tribunal of Justice has drawn on legal formalism to avoid political controversies. But today's new-style ICs are more likely to be presented with cases involving major violations of international law, and these cases are harder (although not impossible) to delay or circumvent. Litigants can also draw on a greatly expanded body of international law, including international criminal law and a large body of international legal rulings that have developed and applied international law over the years. The more that states violate international law, the more difficult it might become for ICs to avoid politically explosive rulings, meanwhile one can ask whether ICs can remain legitimate if they fail to call out clear violations of international law.

Conclusion: whither the (international) rule of law?

The global liberal order represents a surprising realisation of a vision first articulated during the Hague Peace talks, but immediately dismissed as utopian. According to Christian Reus-Smit, this vision succeeded because it built on the traditions that animated the American and French Revolutions, replacing absolutist right with the 'self-evident' truth that 'all men are created equal, that they are endowed by their Creator with certain unalienable Rights, that among these are Life, Liberty

continuing their case, which meant that in 1973 out of 1632 provisional files only 442 cases were registered. But even of all provisional files (9323 in 1993) the percentage of admissible cases in 1993 was considerably higher than in 1961 (2.3%, compared to 0.5%)', see Henry G. Schermers, 'Acceptance of International Supervision of Human Rights' (1999) 12 *Leiden Journal of International Law* 821, 825. The screening performed by the Commission was eliminated in 1998, but already before then the Commission had begun to allow more cases to proceed to the Court.

63 Stuart Scheingold's historic treatment of the European Court of Justice during the era of the Coal and Steel Community provides a guidebook of how international judges could avoid political controversies, see Scheingold (n 9); Alter and Helfer, analysing the jurisprudence of the Andean Tribunal of Justice provide a more recent analysis of how international judges can rely on legal formalism to escape political controversy, see Karen J. Alter and Laurence R. Helfer, *Transplanting International Courts: The Law and Politics of the Andean Tribunal of Justice* (Oxford University Press 2017).

and the pursuit of Happiness. – That to secure these rights, Governments are instituted among Men, deriving their just powers from the consent of the governed.'[64]

The primary political question of the day is whether populations are willing to trade democracy, individual rights and the rule of law for nationalist glory or economic opportunity. In the past, populations have proven willing to do so. Should the constituent people collectively cede liberal democratic values, then it would be foolish to expect international law or domestic legal systems to survive in their current form. In this respect, what Timothy Snyder refers to as 'the road to unfreedom'[65] is paved by the willingness of populations to look the other way when governments and powerful actors violate the law, and trample the rights of groups and individuals. The path down this road will be led by individuals who profit when they are unleashed from legal checks and balances; these are the actors who actively work to undermine institutions that check them, including independent judges, free elections and the media. The road to unfreedom may also, however, be paved by the failure of the elite to acknowledge or remedy the inequality that existing domestic and international order facilitate.[66]

The political zeitgeist is currently different compared to the end of the Cold War and the end of WWII. But the current international system is also different in that international relations has become multilateralised and highly legalised, with a dense array of international regimes and laws and a number of legal institutions that can be called upon to adjudicate violations of these laws. Compared to previous international orders, the key language and primary medium of contemporary international relations is international law and collective international law-making. Moreover, political events like trade wars and the proliferation of nuclear weapons might mean that we are reminded again that the alternatives to a system of global governance governed by international law are far less attractive.

ICs sit at the crossroads of these changes. The current moment is dangerous for ICs, because violations of international law are rising and the compliance supporters of ICs and the international liberal order are under siege. ICs can survive as institutions that enter a sort of Sleeping Beauty mode, waiting until publics remember what a world without individual rights and the rule of law actually looks like. Yet, if the key compliance partners of ICs are domestically dismantled, if litigants bring to ICs cases that put them on direct collision courses with great powers, and if international judges decide that legal hari-kari is the most honourable way, the current critical juncture could become a major turning point in world history. All of this is to say that the future lies in the hands of citizens, litigants and judges.

64 The United States Declaration of Independence (US 1776), discussed in Reus-Smit (n 36), 127–154.

65 Timothy Snyder, *The Road to Unfreedom: Russia, Europe, America* (Crown Publishing Group 2018).

66 Jeff D. Colgan and Robert O. Keohane, 'The Liberal Order is Rigged: Fix it Now or Watch it Wither' (2017) 96 *Foreign Affairs* 36.

Part I
Regional Challenges

3 India and international dispute settlement

Some reflections on India's participation in international courts and tribunals

*Pushkar Anand and Varsha Singh**

Introduction

The settlement of international disputes through peaceful means is the only way one can assure the 'supremacy of law in the community of nations'.[1] However, international law is not entirely divorced from power and politics, which affect international legal frameworks including the effectiveness of international dispute settlement (IDS).[2] As the dominance of the traditional great powers under international law is in a state of flux, the centre of global power arguably shifts to Asia where India is an important player.[3]

While the economic development of India and its status as an emerging world power may be of relatively recent origin, its involvement in the international legal order dates back to the pre-independence days. India was the only non-self-governing British dominion which participated in the 1919 Paris Peace Conference and became one of the founding members of the League of Nations,[4] and later of the United Nations (UN) in 1945. As such, India has

* The authors are grateful to Avidan Kent, Nikos Skoutaris, Jamie Trinidad and Vyoma Jha for their valuable comments in the development of this chapter. Views and errors, if any, are solely the authors' responsibility.

1 RP Anand, 'Enhancing the Acceptability of Compulsory Procedures of International Dispute Settlement' in JA Frowein and R Wolfrum (eds.), *Max Planck Yearbook of United Nations Law Volume 5 2001* (Kluwer Law International 2001) 1–20, 1.

2 See Congyan Cai, 'New Great Powers and International Law in 21st Century' (2013) 24(3) European Journal of International Law 755–795, examining how the rise of 'new great powers' such as China, Brazil and India would impact the international law; see generally, on international law and politics, Shirley V Scott, *International Law in World Politics: An Introduction* (Viva Books 2012).

3 See Amrita Narlikar, 'India's role in global governance: A Modi-fication' (2017) 93(1) International Affairs 93–111; Dan Steinbock, 'The global economic balance of power is shifting', World Economic Forum (20 September 2017) <www.weforum.org/agenda/2017/09/the-global-economic-balance-of-power-is-shifting> accessed 12 June 2018.

4 See for detailed analysis of the 'anomalous position' of India under international law due to the membership of the League of Nations, RP Anand, 'The Formation of International Organizations and India: A Historical Study' (2010) 23 *Leiden Journal of International Law* 5–21.

played an important role in the shaping of the international legal frameworks, institutions, and IDS following the Second World War.[5] Post-independence, the constitution of India made it a directive principle to 'foster respect for international law and treaty obligations' and to 'encourage settlement of international disputes by arbitration'.[6] India was one of the founding members of the General Agreement on Tariffs and Trade (GATT) in 1947 and later of the World Trade Organization (WTO) in 1995. Similarly, India actively participated in the Third Law of the Sea Conference and became a party to the United Nations Convention on the Law of the Sea (UNCLOS) in 1982. India is also a party to all major multilateral human rights instruments, with the notable exception of the Rome Statute, where India participated in the deliberations but did not become a party. Similarly, India was actively involved in the negotiating process that resulted in the Convention on the Settlement of Investment Disputes between States and Nationals of Other States (ICSID Convention) but did not become a party thereto.[7] Bilaterally, India has signed numerous agreements, including more than 80 bilateral investment treaties (BITs) and investment chapters in free trade agreements (FTAs) with investor-state dispute settlement (ISDS) provisions.[8]

India has participated actively at various international courts and tribunals; for instance, it has been involved in six cases before the ICJ, although mostly as a respondent. India has also actively resorted to the WTO's dispute settlement body (DSB) to secure its trade interests, as well as settled its maritime boundary disputes with Bangladesh through UNCLOS arbitration in 2014.[9] However, the land boundary dispute with Bangladesh was settled through the 1974 Land Boundary Agreement which was ratified by India in 2015.[10] The water sharing disputes with Pakistan under the Indus Water Treaty (IWT) were settled

5 See Narlikar (n 3).

6 Constitution of India 1950, art 51(c) and (d); however, it has been argued that the clause relating to settlement of international disputes by arbitration was included in the constitution without 'adequate understanding of system of international dispute settlement'. See, RP Anand, *Studies in International Law and History – An Asian Perspective* (Lancer Books 2004) 11.

7 See ICSID, *History of the ICSID Convention – Documents Concerning the Origin and Formulation of the Convention on Settlement of Investment Disputes between States and Nationals of Other States, Volume II-1* (ICSID, 1968).

8 See UNCTAD, India <http://investmentpolicyhub.unctad.org/IIA/CountryBits/96#iiaInnerMenu> accessed 24 June 2018. However, India has terminated many BITs and the current number of BITs in force is 61.

9 *Bay of Bengal Maritime Boundary Arbitration between Bangladesh and India* (*Bangladesh v India*) ('*Bay of Bengal Arbitration*') PCA Case No 2010–16 <https://pca-cpa.org/en/cases/18/> accessed 24 June 2018.

10 Agreement between the government of the Republic of India and the Government of the People's Republic of Bangladesh concerning the demarcation of the land boundary between India and Bangladesh and related matters (16 May 1974).

once through a World Bank-appointed neutral expert,[11] and in another instance through the Permanent Court of Arbitration.[12]

Although with much unease, India has also been involved in more than 20 ISDS cases under various BITs since 2011, with two awards rendered against it.[13]

India's attitude towards the IDS fora like the ICJ, WTO and UNCLOS has been that of deference. Some resistance to IDS, however, does exist. For example, the ISDS has been an issue of concern for India. In the context of the general backlash that ISDS has been facing, India fits perfectly as an example of the 'non-unidirectional nature of IDS'.[14] Of late, India has adopted a resistant stance regarding the BITs after a spate of arbitral awards rendered against it in ISDS cases.[15] Another case in point is the rejectionist stance of India towards the International Criminal Court (ICC).[16]

Against this backdrop, this chapter attempts to reflect on India's participation at various international courts and tribunals.[17] This chapter will review India's practice and approach towards different international courts and tribunals, albeit briefly. It will then reflect on issues such as India's preference for diplomatic negotiations over adjudication, compromise of sovereignty, invocation of the principle of exhaustion of local remedies, and the accommodation of non-state entities or individuals in IDS.

India at the International Court of Justice

The 1940 Declaration of India accepting the compulsory jurisdiction of the Permanent Court of International Justice (PCIJ) was applicable to the ICJ until 1956, when a new declaration with more reservations was made.[18] India has expanded over the years the scope of its reservation, thus limiting the compulsory

11 *Baglihar Hydroelectric Plant, Expert Determination on points of difference referred by Government of Pakistan under the provisions of Indus Water Treaty* ('*Baglihar Dispute*') (12 February 2007) <http://siteresources.worldbank.org/SOUTHASIAEXT/Resources/223546-1171996340255/BagliharSummary.pdf> accessed 20 June 2018.

12 *Indus Waters Kishenganga Arbitration (Pakistan v India)* ('*Kishenganga Arbitration*') PCA Case No 2011–01 <https://www.pcacases.com/web/view/20> accessed 20 June 2018.

13 UNCTAD, India <http://investmentpolicyhub.unctad.org/ISDS/CountryCases/96?partyRole=2> accessed 21 June 2018.

14 See Cesare PR Romano, 'The Shift from the Consensual to the Compulsory Paradigm in International Adjudication: Elements for a Theory of Consent' (2007) 39 *New York University Journal of International Law* and Politics 791, 837.

15 See *White Industries v India*, UNCITRAL, Final Award (30 November 2011); *Devas v India,* PCA Case No 2013–09. In both these case awards have been rendered against India.

16 See Usha Ramanathan, 'India and the ICC' (2005) 3 Journal of International Criminal Justice 627.

17 See also, VG Hegde, 'India and International Settlement of Disputes' (2016) 56 *Indian Journal of International Law* 1–40

18 See, Bimal N Patel, *The State Practice of India and the Development of International Law: Selected Areas* (Brill Nijhoff 2015) 260–285, 284.

jurisdiction of the ICJ greatly. For instance, the 1940 Declaration limited the Court's jurisdiction to only five grounds,[19] which have later increased to 11 under the 1974 Declaration.[20]

India's first experience at the ICJ in the *Right of Passage over Indian Territory* case is of relevance here.[21] India raised several preliminary objections to the jurisdiction of the ICJ in this case. Notably, India argued that Portugal had acted contrary to the principles of equality, reciprocity and mutuality when filing an application within only three days of submitting its declaration accepting the compulsory jurisdiction of the ICJ.[22] This objection was not sustained by the ICJ which held that there was no additional requirement in Article 36 of the ICJ statute that information transmitted by the secretary-general must reach the parties to the statute, or that some period must elapse subsequent to the deposit of the declaration before it can become effective.[23]

This outcome presumably prompted India to modify its reservation in 1959 along the lines of the United Kingdom, according to which the disputes with the states, which accepted compulsory jurisdiction only for a particular dispute, or which accepted the compulsory jurisdiction less than 12 months prior to the filing of a dispute before the ICJ, were ousted from the jurisdiction of the ICJ.[24] This reservation has been retained by India in its 1974 Declaration which is presently in force.[25]

India has also removed from the scope of the ICJ's jurisdiction all the disputes which arose before 15 September 1974 (the date when the latest declaration was filed), thus removing a large proportion of disputes from the ICJ's jurisdiction.[26] India has also removed disputes involving hostilities, armed conflict, self-defence,

19 The five reservations contained in the 1940 Declaration were – 1) Disputes in regard to which the Parties to the dispute have agreed or shall agree to have recourse to some other method of peaceful settlement; 2) Disputes with the government of any other Member of the League which is a Member of the British Commonwealth of Nations, all of which disputes shall be settled in such manner as the Parties have agreed or shall agree; 3) Disputes with regard to questions which by international law fall exclusively within the jurisdiction of India; 4) Disputes arising out of event occurring at a time when the Government of India were involved in hostilities; 5) India also reserved a right to suspend the judicial proceedings under certain conditions in case of disputes under consideration by the UN Security Council. See, Patel, *The State Practice of India and the Development of International Law* (n 18) 284–285.

20 See declaration recognising as compulsory the jurisdiction of the International Court of Justice, in conformity with Article 36, paragraph 2, of the Statute of the International Court of Justice, New Delhi ('The 1974 Declaration') (15 September 1974) <https://treaties.un.org/doc/Publication/UNTS/Volume%20950/volume-950-I-13546-English.pdf> accessed 20 June 2018.

21 See *Case concerning Right of Passage over Indian Territory* (Merits) [1960] ICJ Rep 6; *Case concerning Right of Passage over Indian Territory (Portugal v India)* (Preliminary Objections) ('*Right to Passage* (Preliminary Objections)') [1957] ICJ Rep 125.

22 *Right to Passage* (Preliminary Objections) (n 21) 145–147.

23 Ibid.

24 India's Declaration of 14 September 1959, cl 5, see Patel (n 18) 284.

25 The 1974 Declaration (n 20) cl 5.

26 Ibid. cl 11.

belligerency or military occupation from the Court's compulsory jurisdiction.[27] Further, all the disputes concerning land and maritime boundaries, various maritime zones and airspace have also been put out of the ICJ's reach.[28]

Interestingly, in its 1956 Declaration, India introduced a 'self-judging' reservation in respect of disputes which fell within its domestic jurisdiction. This reservation mirrored the Connally reservation of the US.[29] The reservation was, however, withdrawn in subsequent declarations, probably due to the controversial nature of 'self-judging' reservations which drastically impacted the effectiveness of the ICJ, as well as due to similar withdrawals made by other states.[30]

The *Right of Passage* case is also illustrative of India's emphasis on diplomatic negotiations as a preferred method for settlement of disputes. India had objected that Portugal did not undertake or exhaust diplomatic negotiations to an extent which would render the subject matter of the dispute as 'determined'. India contended that it was a 'rule of customary international law that the filing of a unilateral application must be preceded by a full trial of diplomatic negotiations' and Portugal failed to comply with this rule. India further argued that the states accepting compulsory jurisdiction of the ICJ should bring a dispute before the Court only when a settlement by negotiation was not possible.[31] The ICJ however, did not accept this objection.

The emphasis of India on the exhaustion of diplomatic means is a recurrent theme in its position on IDS. This emphasis could be seen in the more recent *Marshall Islands* case where the Marshall Islands filed a number of applications to the ICJ, one of which was against India,[32] alleging that India did not comply with customary international law obligations relating to 'cessation of arms race' and 'nuclear disarmament'.[33] India once again raised the objection that 'in order for a dispute to arise, there has to be an attempt to raise an issue the failure to resolve which gives rise to a dispute' and there was no such attempt on the part of the Marshall Islands before seizing the Court. While the Court asserted that there was no requirement of prior exhaustion of negotiation, it nevertheless held that it lacked the jurisdiction under Article 36(2) of the ICJ Statute for want of a legal dispute.[34]

27 Ibid. cl 4.
28 Ibid. cl 10.
29 Carsten Stahn, 'Connally Reservation' in *Max Planck Encyclopedia of Public International Law* (Oxford 2006).
30 See RP Anand, 'India and the World Court', in *Studies in International Adjudication* (Vikas Publications, New Delhi, 1969).
31 *Right to Passage* (Preliminary Objections) (n 21) 148–149.
32 See *Obligations Concerning Negotiations Relating to Cessation of the Nuclear Arms Race and to Nuclear Disarmament* (*Marshall Islands v. India)* (Jurisdiction and Admissibility) ('*Marshall Islands* (Jurisdiction and Admissibility)') [2016] ICJ Rep 255. The other states against whom Marshall Islands filed applications were the US, the UK, China, DPRK, France, Israel, Russia, Pakistan.
33 Ibid.
34 Ibid.

The *Trial of Pakistani Prisoners of War* case also serves to reflect on India's preference for bilateral negotiations. India did not consent to the jurisdiction of the ICJ in this case. India's argument was based on a reservation appended to Article XI of the Genocide Convention, according to which consent of all the parties to the dispute was essential to submit disputes to the ICJ.[35] India and Pakistan consequently signed an agreement with a view to facilitate negotiations to resolve the dispute, and the case was discontinued.

India has also invoked the 'commonwealth exception' against Pakistan in the *Aerial Incidents Case*[36] to successfully challenge the jurisdiction of the ICJ. More recently, unlike most of the cases before the ICJ where India has been the respondent, in the *Jadhav* case[37] India approached the ICJ against Pakistan, for the alleged violation of the obligations under the Vienna Convention on Consular Relations[38] in relation to an Indian national – Kulbhushan Jadhav – who was sentenced to death in Pakistan on charges of espionage, sabotage, and terrorism. India filed an application for provisional measures to withhold Pakistan from executing Mr Jadhav. The ICJ has made an order indicating Pakistan to take all measures at its disposal to prevent the execution of Mr Jadhav, until the Court renders its final judgment on the merits.[39]

India's approach towards the ICJ generally can be said to be one of deference. This is borne out by the fact that while five other states did not choose to appear before the ICJ in the application by Marshall Islands, India appeared before the ICJ and made submissions, which undeniably reflects the respect that India has for the ICJ. However, India has consistently supported bilateral negotiations as a preferred choice, as reflected by arguments made in cases such as the *Right of Passage*, *Marshall Islands*, and the approach it took in *Trial of Pakistani Prisoners*. However, in the context of the *Right to Passage*, it is pertinent to note that within one year of the ICJ rendering the final judgment in the case, India had to use force to throw out the Portuguese in 1961, after waiting for 14 years since independence. This attracted criticism that India had violated the UN Charter by resorting to the use of force and had failed to exhaust peaceful methods of dispute resolution.[40] However, for India, it was the 'question of getting rid of the last vestige of colonialism . . .'.[41]

35 *Trial of Pakistani Prisoners of War*, Order of 15 December [1973] ICJ Rep 347.

36 *Case Concerning the Aerial Incident of 10 August 1999 (Pakistan v. India)* (Jurisdiction of the Court) ('*Aerial Incidents Case*') [2000] ICJ Rep 12.

37 *Jadhav Case* (*India v. Pakistan*) (Request for the Indication of Provisional Measures: Order) ICJ (18 May 2017) <http://www.icj-cij.org/files/case-related/168/168-20170518-ORD-01-00-EN.pdf> accessed 22 June 2018.

38 Vienna Convention on Consular Relations (signed 24 April 1963, entered into force 19 March 1967).

39 See *Jadhav Case* (n 37).

40 See Quincy Right, 'The Goa Incident', (1962) 56 *American Journal of International Law* 617, 626–627. For a different view, see Anand (n 6) 5–8.

41 See Anand (n 6) 5–8, quoting India's ambassador C.S. Jha.

In terms of the factors that affect India's decision to approach the ICJ, 'national interest' can be said to take precedence. While in the *Jadhav* case an Indian national faces the death sentence over espionage charges in Pakistan, the *ICAO Council* case arose as a result of suspension of overflights of Indian territory by Pakistani aircrafts, owing to a hijacking incident where the hijacked flight was directed to Pakistan.[42] Given the often strained political relationship between India and Pakistan it is unsurprising that the 'commonwealth reservation', adopted by India through its 1974 Declaration, is aimed at excluding disputes with Pakistan from the jurisdiction of the ICJ. This aspect of India's reservation to the ICJ jurisdiction was dealt with at length in the dissenting opinion of Judge Al-Khasawneh in the *Aerial Incidents* case.[43]

Notably, apart from the contentious cases, India has also actively participated in various advisory opinions of the ICJ by making written submissions.[44] These, however, will not be addressed in this chapter due to space and scope limitations.

India at the WTO dispute settlement body

India has consistently used the WTO dispute settlement body to secure its trade interests. To date, India has been involved in 24 disputes as a complainant, 25 disputes as a respondent, and 130 disputes as a third party.[45] Nedumpara classifies India as a 'repeat player' in terms of recourse to the WTO dispute settlement mechanism.[46] The majority of the cases filed by and against India concern measures adopted by the EU and the US, highlighting the high stakes involved with these trading partners. An important point that Das and Nedumpara illustrate in respect of India's approach, is that 'India has not hesitated to file disputes even against countries with which it shares friendly political ties' in order to secure its trade interests.[47] The *Brazil – Jute Bags* dispute is an illustration in point, where India requested consultation with Brazil regarding the latter's decision to continue imposing anti-dumping duties on jute bags made in India. This was done at a time when both India and Brazil were working closely at the WTO as well as within the BRIC framework.[48] Similarly, in *EC – Tariff Preferences* India challenged tariff concessions that were given by the EU to ACP countries as well as Pakistan, all of which are developing countries. This move might have jeopardised the interests of these countries with which India is collaborating in the Doha

42 See *Appeal Relating to the Jurisdiction of the ICAO Council (India v. Pakistan)* (Judgment) [1972] ICJ Rep 46.

43 See *Aerial Incidents Case* (n 36) 48 (Dissenting Opinion of Judge Khasawneh).

44 See Patel (n 18) 280.

45 See WTO, Cases involving India <https://www.wto.org/english/thewto_e/countries_e/india_e.htm> accessed 22 June 2018.

46 James J Nedumpara, 'Naming, Shaming and Filing': Harnessing Indian Capacity for WTO Dispute Settlement', (2013) V (1) *Trade, Law, and Development* 68, 96.

47 Abhijit Das and James J Nedumpara, *WTO Dispute Settlement at Twenty – Insiders' Reflections on India's Participation* (Springer 2016) 10.

48 Ibid.

round of trade negotiations.[49] Other examples include *EC – Sugar Subsidies*, where India chose not to intervene as a third party in favour of Mauritius despite having strong political, historical and cultural ties with this country.[50] Even internal political pressures have not dissuaded India from litigating a dispute at the WTO dispute settlement body.[51]

Despite the above, it should be noted that India prefers to settle WTO disputes rather than litigate.[52] For instance, India requested consultations with Poland on the issue of preferential tariffs being granted to the EU for automobiles, which was settled by a mutually agreed solution, without recourse to the establishment of a panel.[53] Similarly, a dispute with the EU regarding the imposition of definitive anti-dumping measures on imports of certain flat-rolled products of iron or non-alloy steel from India was settled by way of an agreement, as the EU agreed to terminate the disputed measure.[54] Following the *Turkey – Textiles* report, as Turkey was unable to implement the rulings and recommendations of the DSB, India concluded a mutually acceptable solution with this country by way of an agreement.[55]

India indeed requested authorisation to retaliate only in the case of *US – Byrd Amendment*.[56] This request, however, as explained by Das and Nedumpara, should be seen as an exception and in the larger context of the 'overwhelming sentiment of the several WTO members against the failure of the US to comply with the recommendations of the DSB'.[57]

As a respondent, India's preference for settlement by agreement was reflected by its ability to arrive at a mutually agreed solution in *India – Quantitative Restrictions* with Australia, Canada, New Zealand, Switzerland and the European Union. The exception was the United States, where India followed the decision of the DSB.

Further, India has complied with all the decisions of the DSB, even when such compliance led India to make substantive changes to its domestic laws and policies. Cases such as *India – Patents (US)* and *India – Quantitative Restrictions* are a testimony to this fact. After India lost the latter case, it did away with quantitative restrictions on imports in respect of all items, thus marking a major change to its existing trade policy. Similarly, as a result of the decision of the Appellate Body in *India – Patents (US)*, India amended its patent legislation in 1999 and

49 Ibid.
50 Ibid. 11.
51 Ibid. 11.
52 Abhijit Das and James J Nedumpara, *WTO Dispute Settlement at Twenty – Insiders' Reflections on India's Participation* (Springer 2016) 8.
53 See WTO, *Poland – Import Regime for Automobiles* (11 September 1996) WT/DS19/1.
54 See WTO, *European Communities – Anti-Dumping Duties on Certain Flat Rolled Iron or Non-Alloy Steel Products from India* (27 October 2004) WT/DS313/2.
55 See WTO, *Turkey – Restrictions on Imports of Textile and Clothing Products* (19 July 2001) WT/DS34/14.
56 See WTO, *United States – Continued Dumping and Subsidy Offset Act of 2000* (11 November 2004) WT/DS217/40.
57 Das and Nedumpara (n 52) 12.

provided for the system of mailbox applications for pharmaceutical and agricultural chemical products with retrospective effect from 1995, the date on which India was supposed to have instituted a mailbox facility under the Agreement on Trade-Related Aspects of Intellectual Property Rights (TRIPS).[58]

India has also resisted certain proposed reforms in the Dispute Settlement Understanding (DSU), emphasising the state-centric nature of this framework. In the *US – Shrimp*,[59] the Appellate Body held that the DSU accorded a panel ample and extensive authority under art 13 to accept non-requested information from non-governmental sources in a dispute, which was objected to by India.[60] As a result of the experience in *US – Shrimp*, in the context of amicus curiae briefs, India later asserted that 'allowing non-members to participate and submit amicus curiae briefs would undermine' the intergovernmental character of the WTO dispute settlement,[61] and raised a cautionary note regarding the possibility of non-governmental entities advancing their sectoral interests.[62] India also asserted that allowing non-governmental entities to influence the process and outcome of disputes would severely erode the member governments' authority and ability to participate effectively in the dispute settlement process.[63] India also suggested that if non-governmental entities are allowed, such entities in the developing and the least developed countries would not be able to effectively participate for lack of resources.[64]

On the other hand, several procedural proposals have been made by India. For example, India proposed to fix the timeline for notification of mutually agreed solutions within 60 days and in sufficient detail,[65] and to adjust the terms of Appellate Body members as non-renewable for a period of six years, so as to ensure that they do not have to depend upon WTO membership in order to secure a second term.[66] India has also advocated greater rights for third parties at the appellate stage. It has asserted the right of third states having substantial interest and which have so notified the DSB, to make written submissions and to be heard by the appellate body, which shall be reflected in the report of the appellate body.[67] India has also proposed to give a complaining party which is a developing

58 See Shamnad Basheer, 'India's Tryst with TRIPS: The Patents (Amendment) Act 2005' (2005) 1 *Indian Journal of Law and Technology* 15, 27.
59 See, WTO, *United States – Import Prohibition of Certain Shrimp and Shrimp Products* WT/DS58/AB/R.
60 Ibid.
61 See, WTO, *Negotiations on the Dispute Settlement Understanding, Proposals on DSU by Cuba, Honduras, India, Malaysia, Pakistan, Sri Lanka, Tanzania and Zimbabwe*, TN/DS/W/18 (7 October 2002), <http://commerce.gov.in/international_nextDetail_WTO.aspx?LinkID=31&id=43> accessed 20 June 2018.
62 Ibid.
63 Ibid.
64 Ibid.
65 Ibid.
66 Ibid.
67 Ibid.

country 'the right to seek authorization for suspension of concessions or other obligations with respect to any or all sectors under any covered agreements'.[68]

India and dispute settlement under UNCLOS and IWT

Disputes under UNCLOS

India is a party to UNCLOS 1982 and made a declaration at the time of ratification reserving 'the right to make at the appropriate time the declarations provided for in articles 287 and 298, concerning the settlement of disputes'.[69] This means, effectively, that India did not indicate any preferred forum for dispute resolution from those set out in Article 287(1) of UNCLOS. The cases of the *Bay of Bengal Arbitration*[70] and the *Enrica Lexie Incident*[71] were both heard by the arbitral tribunal constituted in accordance with Annex VII, which acts as a default forum if any party to UNCLOS does not make a declaration as to the choice of forum,[72] or where the two parties in the dispute have made a declaration choosing different fora.[73] The dispute in the *Bay of Bengal Arbitration*[74] concerned the location of the land boundary terminus, delimitation of the territorial sea, exclusive economic zone (EEZ) and continental shelf within and beyond 200 nautical miles, in the Bay of Bengal area. The award rendered by the arbitral tribunal was in favour of Bangladesh, for as a result of the delimitation done by the tribunal it was entitled to 19,467 sq. km out of 25, 602 sq. km area in the Bay of Bengal.[75] It is important to note that, apart from India, Bangladesh had initiated arbitration against Myanmar at the International Tribunal for the Law of the Sea (ITLOS) in order to settle its maritime boundaries.[76] Prior to the initiation of the arbitration, India, Bangladesh, and Myanmar had unsuccessfully been negotiating the delimitation of maritime boundaries in the Bay of Bengal area since the 1970s.[77] India did not object in this case to the jurisdiction of the arbitral tribu-

68 Ibid.

69 Declaration of India made upon ratification (29 June 1995) <http://www.un.org/depts/los/convention_agreements/convention_declarations.htm#India%20Declaration%20made%20upon%20ratification> accessed 20 June 2018.

70 See *Bay of Bengal Arbitration* (n 9).

71 See *The Enrica Lexie Incident (Italy v India)* PCA Case No 2015–28.

72 See United Nations Convention on the Law of the Sea, art 287.

73 Ibid.

74 See *Bay of Bengal Arbitration* (n 9).

75 Haroon Habib, 'Bangladesh wins Maritime Dispute with India' *The Hindu* (9 July 2014) <http://www.thehindu.com/news/national/bangladesh-wins-maritime-dispute-with-india/article6191797.ece> accessed 23 July 2018.

76 *Delimitation of the Maritime Boundary in the Bay of Bengal (Bangladesh/Myanmar)* (14 March 2012) 12 ITLOS Rep 4.

77 Naomi Burke, 'Annex VII Arbitral Tribunal Delimits Maritime Boundary Between Bangladesh and India in the Bay of Bengal' (2014) 18(20) ASIL Insights <https://www.asil.org/insights/volume/18/issue/20/annex-vii-arbitral-tribunal-delimits-maritime-boundary-between#_edn3> accessed 20 June 2018.

nal. When the tribunal decided eventually against India, the official spokesperson of the Ministry of External Affairs (MEA) of the Indian government stated that India 'respects the verdict of the Tribunal' and 'that the settlement of the maritime boundary will further enhance mutual understanding and goodwill between India and Bangladesh by bringing to closure a long-pending issue'.[78] In a reply given in the Lok Sabha, the MEA stated that this award will 'enable both countries to fully exploit the resources in that part of the Bay of Bengal', and the 'peaceful settlement of this issue on the basis of international law symbolizes friendship, mutual understanding, and goodwill between the two countries'.[79]

The dispute of *Enrica Lexie,* on the other hand, did not lead to similar cordiality. Such an attitude could be attributed to the facts of the case, which involved the killing of two Indian fishermen at the hands of two Italian marines on board the *Enrica Lexie,* an Italian oil tanker, approximately 20.5 nautical miles off the Indian coast. From the very beginning, Italy challenged the jurisdiction of the Indian authorities and asserted sovereign immunity for the marines.[80] Italy requested the establishment of an Annex VII arbitral tribunal for the resolution of the dispute.[81] Italy asserted that by detaining the marines and exercising criminal jurisdiction against them in a manner that was allegedly inconsistent with UNCLOS, India had violated its obligations under international law to respect the sovereign immunity of the marines as officials exercising state functions.[82] In the hearing before the ITLOS for provisional measures requested by Italy, India raised an objection that the Annex VII arbitral tribunal can exercise jurisdiction only if local remedies have been exhausted. The tribunal rejected India's objection, stating that 'since the very nature of the dispute concerns the exercise of jurisdiction over the *Enrica Lexie* incident, the issue of exhaustion of local remedies should not be addressed in the provisional measures phase'.[83]

The case of *Enrica Lexie* differs greatly from the *Maritime Boundary Delimitation* dispute. This case involves the exercising of criminal jurisdiction – a highly sensitive topic, regarded as inseparable from, and a paramount attribute of, the sovereignty of a state. This case, therefore, evoked stronger reactions in the

78 Ministry of External Affairs, Government of India, official spokesperson's response to a question on the award of the Tribunal on the Maritime Boundary Arbitration between India and Bangladesh, (8 July 2014) <http://www.mea.gov.in/Speeches-Statements.htm?dtl/23575/Official+Spokespersons+response+to+a+question+on+the+award+of+the+Tribunal+on+the+Maritime+Boundary+Arbitration+between+India+and+Bangladesh> accessed 23 June 2018.

79 Government of India, Ministry of External Affairs, Lok Sabha, Unstarred Question No. 2920 (30 July 2014), <http://164.100.47.194/Loksabha/Questions/QResult15.aspx?qref=5718&lsno=16> accessed 20 July 2018.

80 The Supreme Court of India in the case *Republic of Italy and Ors. v Union of India and Ors* (Writ Petition (Civil) No135 of 2012), directed the Union of India to establish a special court to try the case inter alia in accordance with the provisions of UNCLOS which are not inconsistent with the India laws.

81 *The Enrica Lexie Incident* (n 70).

82 Ibid.

83 Ibid. [64–67].

Indian national space.[84] Nonetheless, the attitude of India has been respectful towards the awards and provisional measures rendered by the Annex VII arbitral tribunal and ITLOS in both the cases.

Disputes under the Indus Waters Treaty

Before India and Pakistan agreed on the IWT, Pakistan decided to take the matter to the ICJ owing to disagreements over water sharing. India, however, objected and in an official communication 'proposed a model based on international commission established between US and Canada, and argued that any reference to third party would mean confession of our continued dependence on others'.[85]

The IWT provides for the establishment of a Permanent Indus Commission, consisting of commissioners appointed by both India and Pakistan. As for the settlement of disputes, the treaty provides for the appointment of a neutral expert or a court of arbitration.[86] So far, only two disputes have been initiated under the treaty, both by Pakistan.

The first case, *Baglihar Hydropower Project*, was decided by the neutral expert appointed by the World Bank.[87] It is important to note that India's acceptance of submitting the 'difference' to the neutral expert was a 'major policy shift',[88] as the Indian position on such issues generally had been tilting against third-party intervention. For instance, the primary reason due to which India abstained from voting in the United Nations General Assembly on 21 May 1997 during the adoption of the Convention on the Law of Non-Navigational Uses of International Watercourses related to the aspect of 'fact-finding' from outside experts in art 33 (4) of the said Convention.[89]

The second case which was referred to the Court of Arbitration under the IWT was the *Kishenganga* arbitration, arising out of the construction of a hydroelectric power plant by India, which, Pakistan claimed, was not in accordance with the criteria provided in the IWT.[90] While India did not object to the jurisdiction of the Court of Arbitration in the *Baglihar Hydropower Project* dispute, it did so in respect of the *Kishenganga* arbitration. India asserted its position that the 'Commission should resolve these questions by agreement and that it was unnecessary to address the issue outside the Commission – in particular because

84 See VS Mani, 'It's our Boat, our Courts', *The Hindu* (23 March 2013).

85 See Hegde (n 17), quoting Niranjan D Gulhati, *Indus Water Treaty: An Exercise in International Mediation* (Allied Publishers, Bombay, 1973).

86 Treaty Between the Government of India and the Government of Pakistan concerning the most Complete and Satisfactory Utilisation of the Waters of the Indus System of Rivers (signed 19 September 1960).

87 See *Baglihar Dispute* (n 11); For a general overview of the Indus Water Treaty and Baglihar Dispute see, VG Hegde, 'Neutral Expert and Indus Water Treaty', 9 *Himalayan & Central Asian Studies* (2005) 47–59.

88 Hegde (n 17).

89 Ibid.

90 *Kishenganga Arbitration* (n 12).

the authoritative precedent of the *Baglihar* expert determination was available to assist the Commission in understanding the substance of the Second Dispute'.[91] Kumar commented on this dispute, stating that given the politically loaded circumstances within which any Indo-Pakistani issue is placed, settlement of issues relating to water sharing in a cooperative and peaceful manner serves as a 'useful reminder of the potential of pacific dispute settlement in resolving complex disputes in tense settings'.[92]

India and the ISDS

India has had a rather discordant view of ISDS. Despite the existence of an extensive BIT programme, ISDS did not garner much attention in India until 2011, when an adverse arbitral award was rendered in *White Industries v. India*.[93] The Indian government found itself, over the next seven years, as a respondent in more than 20 ISDS claims under various BITs.[94] The most concerning issue for India in the context of ISDS has been the alleged lack of sovereign regulatory space. Besides, India has not been very comfortable with the whole idea of a foreign investor having the right to challenge a sovereign state. This is best reflected by the reservation that India expressed during the negotiations of the ICSID Convention. Indian delegate Mr Adarkar asserted that 'The Convention involved an important departure in international law' as it 'aimed at setting up a forum where States and individuals were placed on a par'.[95] Further, it was asserted that 'No investor should be able to challenge any measure taken by a State in the lawful pursuance of its national policy unless such measure involved discrimination against a class of investors, or was in conflict with the terms of a contract between the State and an investor.'[96] However, the Indian delegate was not opposed to the possibility where India, as a host state, chose to place herself on a par with foreign investors through investment contracts for a particular purpose. The problem, however, with the ICSID according to India, was that 'It placed the foreign investor and the State on a par regardless of any law, national or international, or the terms of any contract or other arrangements between the State and the foreign investor.'[97] This reflects India's inclination to the traditional notion of the primacy of states and their consent, under international law. India never became a party to the ICSID convention. However, because of changes in economic policy

91 Ibid. [277].
92 See Shashank Kumar, 'The Indus Waters Kishenganga Arbitration (Pakistan v. India),' (2013) 17(3) ASIL Insights (13 May 2013) <https://www.asil.org/insights/volume/17/issue/13/indus-waters-kishenganga-arbitration-pakistan-v-india> accessed 20 June 2018.
93 *White Industries v India* (n 15).
94 See above (n 13).
95 ICSID, *History of the ICSID Convention – Documents Concerning the Origin and Formulation of the Convention on Settlement of Investment Disputes between States and Nationals of Other States, Volume II-1* (ICSID, 1968) 468–469.
96 Ibid.
97 Ibid.

and the perceived benefits of BITs, India has signed a large number of BITs containing an ISDS clause.

In a statement at the United Nations Conference on Trade and Development (UNCTAD) World Investment Forum in 2014, however, India flagged several issues such as encroachment into the policy space available to governments, and the susceptibility of provisions such as most favoured nation (MFN) and fair and equitable treatment (FET) to wide interpretations which may have far-reaching and unintended consequences for the host states, to name a few.[98] India alleged that ISDS has contributed to inconsistent jurisprudence, simultaneously alleging lack of independence of arbitrators. India decried the absence of an institutional basis resulting in arbitral awards that lack any precedential value, as well as the absence of an appeals facility in the ISDS system.[99] Consequently, India reviewed its BIT programme and came up with a new Model BIT in 2016,[100] which now represents the official position of India in respect of the ISDS system.[101]

It is pertinent to note that despite the problems that India has had with ISDS, it has retained this dispute settlement mechanism in its Model BIT. However, the access to ISDS under the new model is heavily qualified with the scope restricted only to disputes that arise out of the breach of certain specific obligations. Another notable feature is the absence of an 'umbrella clause', thus keeping the breach of investment contracts out of the purview of ISDS, which again is welcome owing to the divergent views of the arbitral tribunals on the issue.[102] However, India has once again turned the clock back and resorted to exhaustion of local remedies as a precondition to ISDS. The Model BIT requires the foreign investors to exhaust local remedies for a period of five years, which is problematic as the domestic judicial system in India already crumbles under a heavy backlog of cases.[103] This limitation is compounded by additional conditions in the form of strict time frames that have to be complied with in order to submit the claim to arbitration under the ISDS. There are other provisions which are problematic. These include

98 UNCTAD, Statement by India at the World Investment Forum 2014 (16 October 2014) 1–2 <http://unctad-worldinvestmentforum.org/wp-content/uploads/2014/10/Mayaram.pdf> accessed 20 June 2018.

99 Ibid.

100 2016 Indian Model Bilateral Investment Treaty ('2016 Model Indian BIT') <http://mof.gov.in/reports/ModelTextIndia_BIT.pdf> accessed 20 June 2018. For a comprehensive analysis of the provision of the 2016 Indian Model BIT, see Prabhash Ranjan and Pushkar Anand, 'The 2016 Model Indian Bilateral Investment Treaty: A Critical Deconstruction' (2017) 38(1) *Northwestern Journal of International Law and Business* 1–55.

101 For a detailed analysis of the ISDS provision of the 2016 Indian Model BIT see, Prabhash Ranjan and Pushkar Anand, 'Investor State Dispute Settlement in the 2016 Indian Model Bilateral Investment Treaty: Does it Go Too Far?' in Julien Chaisse and Luke Nottage (eds.), *International Investment Treaties and Arbitration Across Asia* (Brill Nijhoff 2018) 579–611.

102 Ibid.

103 Ibid. Ironically the tribunal in White Industries v. India, the first ISDS case that India lost, has held that the undue delay in the judicial process amounts to a violation of FET. See, *White Industries v. India* (n 15).

the bar on arbitral tribunals from 'reviewing the merits of a decision made by a domestic judicial authority',[104] and the requirement of a high deferential standard of review reducing the scope of arbitral review of the host state's regulatory measures.[105] Taken together, these qualifications make it difficult for foreign investors to effectively use the system, taking India closer to being an abolitionist, even if it has formally retained the ISDS mechanism.[106]

India has also laid down comprehensive rules related to the appointment of arbitrators in its Model BIT, along with detailed provisions relating to the prevention of arbitrators' conflict of interests and challenges to their appointment, as well as providing a wide scope to the parties to challenge appointments. This points to the scepticism of India with respect to the impartiality and independence of ISDS arbitrators.[107] The ISDS provision in India's Model BIT also focuses on transparency, placing an obligation on the host state to make public the notice of arbitration, pleadings, submissions by non-disputing parties, awards and orders.[108] Lastly, while India decried the absence of an institutionalised system of ISDS in 2014 at the UNCTAD World Investment Forum, and despite the fact that India's Model BIT contains a provision that contemplates the establishment of an appeals facility, it rejected the idea of a multilateral investment court proposed by the EU and Canada in January 2017.[109]

India and the International Criminal Court

There are several factors which dissuaded India from joining the ICC.[110] In a reply to a question asked in the Rajya Sabha, the government said that it did not sign the Rome Statute as it brought several crimes under the purview of the ICC, which are subject to national jurisdiction, and makes the primacy of national

104 2016 Model Indian BIT (n 100) art 13.5(1).
105 2016 Model Indian BIT (n 100) art 23.1.
106 See Ranjan and Anand (n 101).
107 Ibid. One of the grounds for justifiable doubts under art 19.10(h) of the 2016 Indian Model BIT – 'where the arbitrator has publicly advocated a fixed position regarding on an issue in the case that is being arbitrated', institutionalises the arguments of India regarding 'issue conflict' in the case of *CC Devas Mauritius Ltd and Ors. v. Republic of India* PCA Case No 2013–09, where India successfully challenged the appointment of Prof Francisco Orrego Vicuna. For more details see, Ranjan and Anand (n 101).
108 2016 Model Indian BIT (n 100) art 22.1.
109 See Prabhash Ranjan, 'Summary rejection of a multilateral investment agreement at the WTO is not the best strategy. It would be better to make sure the agreement addresses India's concerns,' *The Wire* (13 February 2017) <https://thewire.in/external-affairs/india-investment-agreement-wto> accessed 21 June 2018.
110 See statement by Mr Dilip Lahiri, Additional Secretary (UN), Ministry of External Affairs, Head of the Indian Delegation at the United Nations Diplomatic Conference of Plenipotentiaries on the Establishment of International Criminal Court, Rome, Italy (16 June 1998) <https://www.legal-tools.org/en/doc/ebc5e9/>. See, Haris Jamil, 'Critical evaluation of India's position on the Rome Statute' (2017) 57 *Indian Journal of International Law* 411–442.

jurisdiction subject to the satisfaction of the ICC.[111] Also, the fact that the Rome Statute did not allow for any opt-out or reservation was perceived as 'representing a violation of consent of State' and accordingly a threat to sovereignty.[112] An important factor for India's disapproval of the ICC has been the fear of being targeted in respect of various internal armed conflicts ongoing in Kashmir, the north-east, and the Maoist insurgency in central India.[113] Dilip Lahiri, head of the Indian delegation at the Rome Conference, while writing in a personal capacity in 2010, conceded that the possibility of being politically targeted was the primary reason for the strong Indian opposition to the ICC. While accepting that the sympathisers and front organisations of the insurgents could lobby to have investigations launched by the ICC prosecutors against Indian leaders and commanders, he emphasised that the fear of 'high ranking Indian civil and military officials being on the run to evade ICC arrest warrants if they travel abroad is farfetched'.[114] India has also cited the special and discriminatory powers to the United Nations Security Council (UNSC) to refer cases or block consideration of cases by the ICC, as reasons for staying away from this institution.[115] However, the opposition of India in respect of the role of the UNSC and the consequent politicisation is at variance with its practice as argued by Pillai, pointing to India's vote as a UNSC member in favour of referring the situation in Libya to the ICC, and to India's support for the UNSC resolution providing immunity to peacekeeping troops in Bosnia from the jurisdiction of the ICC.[116]

Conclusion and some reflections for the future

There is a general acceptance and respect for a rule-based international legal order on the part of India, reflected broadly by its participation at various courts and tribunals, and also its compliance with their decisions, awards and orders. However, with the exception of the WTO where India has actively pursued disputes as complainant, India has mostly been involved as a respondent before various international courts and tribunals, which shows the approach of dispute avoidance, marked by a preference for settlement through diplomatic negotiations.

111 See Government of India, Ministry of External Affairs, Rajya Sabha, Unstarred Question No-1740 <http://164.100.47.5/qsearch/QResult.aspx> accessed 23 June 2018.
112 See Usha Ramanathan, 'India and the ICC' (2005) 3 *Journal of International Criminal Justice* 627.
113 See Priya Pillai, 'India Wants UN Security Council Seat but Runs Shy of International Criminal Court Facing Desertion' *Outlook* (23 February 2017) <https://www.outlookindia.com/website/story/india-wants-un-security-council-seat-but-runs-shy-of-international-criminal-cour/298037> accessed 9 August 2018.
114 See Dilip Lahiri, 'Should India continue to Stay out of ICC?' *Observer Research Foundation* (24 November 2010) <https://www.orfonline.org/research/should-india-continue-to-stay-out-of-icc/> accessed on 9 August 2018, suggesting that India should engage more actively and constructively with the ICC.
115 See Ramanathan (n 112).
116 See Pillai (n 113).

Further, India prefers a state-centric model of IDS. For instance, although India has retained 'a highly qualified' ISDS in its new Model BIT, it is now reportedly preferring to enter into investment treaties with state-state dispute settlement.[117] The rejection of a proposed multilateral investment court confirms the aversion that India has for the ISDS. This also goes on to highlight the selectivity of India in pursuing the causes of reform. For instance, the zeal with which India is advocating multilateralism[118] and engaging at the WTO is absent in the case of ISDS where India seems to be fighting a 'sovereignist battle'[119] against foreign investors' right of action against host states. Indian officials have even gone to the extent of stating that if arbitral awards are rendered against India in a tax-related ISDS case, India would not enforce it.[120] Similar selectivity is visible in the case of the ICC, which has been totally rejected by India citing primacy accorded to the international court over the national jurisdiction, and political interference by the UNSC. It is of note that India shuns the ICC, even as it claims a permanent seat in and advocates reform at the UNSC. If India wishes to emerge as a leader advocating reforms in the UNSC, it would be unwise to isolate itself from the ICC which is functionally linked to the UNSC. More so, when India is already a party to several human rights instruments imposing legal obligations on India. Otherwise, it runs the risk of being dubbed as an opportunist at a time when India's clout on the world stage both politically and economically is increasing.[121] Further, India puts huge diplomatic effort into placing its representatives on all the major multilateral courts and tribunals such as the ICJ, WTO and ITLOS. In sum, the approach of India seems dictated by self-interest and zeal for protection of its sovereignty, which is generally the approach taken by any other

117 See 'Brazil and India initial bilateral investment treaty (BIT); text yet to be published' *Investment Treaty News* (12 December 2016), <https://www.iisd.org/itn/2016/12/12/brazil-and-india-initial-bilateral-investment-treaty-bit-text-yet-to-be-published/> accessed 9 August 2018.

118 Amiti Sen, 'India invites over 40 WTO members for mini-ministerial meet', The Hindu Business Line, (5 February 2018) <https://www.thehindubusinessline.com/economy/macro-economy/india-invites-over-40-wto-members-for-mini-ministerial-meet/article22661302.ece> accessed 20 June 2018.

119 See Relja Radović, 'Defending the Undefendable: Asia's Sovereignist Battles against Easy Access to Investment Treaty Arbitration' in Junji Nakagawa (ed.), *Asian Perspectives on International Investment Law* (forthcoming).

120 See 'India may not accept arbitration orders annulling Cairn, Vodafone tax demands', *The Economic Times* (22 May 2018) <https://economictimes.indiatimes.com/news/economy/policy/india-may-not-accept-arbitration-orders-annulling-cairn-vodafone-tax-demands/articleshow/64271201.cms> accessed 9 August 2018.

121 See Sreemoy Talukdar, 'Justice Dalveer Bhandari's re-election to ICJ reflects India's clout, leadership of nations marginalized at UN' *Firstpost* (21 November 2017), <https://www.firstpost.com/india/justice-dalveer-bhandaris-re-election-to-icj-reflects-indias-growing-clout-leadership-of-nations-marginalised-at-un-4220945.html> accessed 9 August 2018; see 'NITI Aayog vice chairman: India, 6th largest economy, has long way to go as per capita income still low' *The India Express* (12 July 2018) <https://indianexpress.com/article/india/niti-aayog-vice-chairman-india-6th-largest-economy-has-long-way-to-go-as-per-capita-income-still-low-rajiv-kumar-5257117/> accessed 9 August 2018.

state. However, since India has transformed itself into an indispensable power in the international community, it cannot afford a selective approach towards IDS. In these turbulent times of ever-increasing unilateralism, India needs to actively engage with all the IDS fora with equal zeal and push for reforms or the creation of new IDS mechanisms where they are needed, with the objective of establishing a rule-based, peaceful, just and equitable multilateral international legal order.

4 China's attitude towards international adjudication

Past, present and future

Nanying Tao

Introduction

There is bifurcation in China's attitude towards international adjudication. In recent decades, China has been expanding its engagement with international adjudication on economic issues. It has joined the Convention on the Settlement of Investment Disputes between States and Nationals of Other States (ICSID Convention) and has included investor-state arbitration (ISA) in most of its international investment agreements (IIAs). Since 2001 it has actively participated in the World Trade Organization (WTO) Dispute Settlement Mechanism (DSM): it was a respondent in 40 disputes (the third highest number of all 164 members), a complainant in 17 cases (top ten initiator of cases before the WTO), and a third party in 145 cases.[1]

However, China is wary of international adjudication concerning maritime boundaries, territory, human rights and criminal law. It has not accepted the compulsory jurisdiction of the International Court of Justice (ICJ). Recently when the Republic of the Philippines instituted arbitral proceedings against it concerning maritime rights in the South China Sea, China flatly refused to appear in the proceedings, describing the South China Sea Arbitration ('the Arbitration') as 'essentially a political farce attempting to undermine China's interest over the South China Sea'.[2]

Why is China by turns enthusiastic and hostile towards international adjudication? How did this bifurcation come into being? Will it continue to exist in the future? This chapter attempts to answer these questions by exploring the evolution of China's attitude to international courts and tribunals. Part I traces China's interaction with international courts and tribunals in the Qing dynasty, the Republican era and the Mao era, with the purpose of investigating the sources of China's hostility towards international adjudication. Through the study of

1 'Disputes by Member' (*World Trade Organization*) <https://www.wto.org/english/tratop_e/dispu_e/dispu_by_country_e.htm> accessed 20 June 2018.

2 'Remarks by Chinese Foreign Minister Wang Yi on the Award of the So-Called Arbitral Tribunal in the South China Sea Arbitration' (*The South China Sea Issue*, 12 July 2016) <http://www.fmprc.gov.cn/nanhai/eng/wjbxw_1/t1380003.htm> accessed 14 May 2017.

China's attitude towards WTO adjudication, ISA and the South China Sea Arbitration, Part II examines how contemporary China's attitude to international courts and tribunals shifted from a pure 'hate' to a 'love-hate' position. Part III predicts that China in the future will show more ambition in exploring a Chinese approach to international adjudication: previously it was 'asked' to accept international adjudication and to abide by many West-centric norms; now it attempts to reinterpret, or even to remake the rules of international adjudication. China's recent moves in the WTO DSM and the Belt and Road Initiative (BRI) demonstrate this direction. The Conclusion briefly discusses the implications of the rise of a Chinese approach towards international adjudication that could have important implications in the future.

Past: Hostility towards international adjudication

The Qing dynasty

China's encounter with international adjudication dates back to the late nineteenth century when the Qing government was invited to join the Permanent Court of Arbitration (PCA). China at first was suspicious of the idea that any state aggrieved in a legal dispute could have that dispute adjudicated by a court or tribunal. The Qing officials generally questioned the nature of international adjudication: 'It could be an alternative, peaceful way to settle disputes, but we are afraid that it would probably become a Western conspiracy to hide their use of force in the wars,'[3] 'When facing issues involving Eastern affairs, the European states always conspire together against China. If we were in a dispute, they would take peaceful dispute settlement as a plot to stall us . . .' (author's translations).[4]

Qing China's suspicion of international adjudication might stem from the Sino-Western clashes that originated in the First Opium War (1839–1842) and the 'international treaties' it signed with the Western powers.[5] The treaties that Qing China concluded were inherently unequal, though they often proclaimed to promote peace, freedom and equity. For instance, the Treaty of Nanking not only requested China to pay an indemnity, but also ceded Hong Kong to Great Britain to compensate 'its loss in the war'.[6] The perceived injustice soon

3 *Grand Council's Reply to Zongli Yamen: On the accession of The Convention for the Pacific Settlement of International Disputes* (1899), Taibei, Archives of Modern Chinese History (No. 01–28–001–02–006).

4 *Zongli Yamen: Explanation: the accession of The Convention for the Pacific Settlement of International Disputes* (1899), Taibei, Archives of Modern Chinese History (No. 01–28–001–02–007).

5 The First Opium War happened between Great Britain and the Qing dynasty over the legalisation of the British opium trade with China. Since then, Qing China had suffered defeat in a series of military conflicts with the West and signed treaties with the victorious states.

6 *Treaty of Perpetual Peace and Friendship between China and Great Britain (Treaty of Nanking)* (Windsor Castle, United Kingdom: 28 December 1842).

generated resentment among the Chinese,[7] and the hatred was extended to the entire international legal regime. When international law was systemically introduced to China in 1863,[8] it was regarded by the Chinese as a tool that Westerners used for dealing with, or even bullying China.[9]

Because of the bias against international law, Qing China never settled disputes through PCA arbitration.[10] A request to refer to the PCA was once made to the Qing government by Portugal when it disputed the interpretation of the right of 'perpetual occupation and governance of Macau' under the Sino-Portuguese Treaty of Peking.[11] However, China rebuffed the Portuguese proposal, arguing that 'the Westerners have a long-term racial discrimination against East Asian ethnics . . . if the Macau dispute was submitted to the PCA for arbitration, the Western powers that controlled the PCA would be partial towards the Portuguese' (author's translation).[12]

The Republican era

The Qing dynasty was replaced by the Republic of China (ROC) in 1912. The new government abandoned the thousand-year long imperial rule and sought to transform China into a modern nation state by adapting elements of Western civilisation.[13] The Chinese attitude to the international legal regime during this period became moderate. China also became more skilful at using international rules to further its own practical interests. For example, campaigns for the end of 'unequal treaties' were often orchestrated through a combination of the knowledge of international law and broad appeals to the international community aimed at winning sympathy and foreign support.[14]

Accordingly, international adjudication began to be viewed as an instrument that could help China shake off the yoke of foreign domination and secure a

7 John K Fairbank and Kwang-Ching Liu (eds.), *The Cambridge History of China, Vol. 11: Late Ch'ing, 1800–1911, Part 2* (Cambridge University Press 1980) 194.

8 W.A.P. Martin translated Henry Wheaton's *Elements of International Law* to Chinese and published it in 1863, marked as the formal and systematic introduction of international law into China, ibid. 96; Bardo Fassbender and others, *The Oxford Handbook of the History of International Law* (Oxford University Press 2013) 460.

9 Jia Zhen et al. (eds.), *A Complete Account of the Management of Barbarian Affairs under the Tongzhi Regime*, Vol 27 (Zhonghua Press 1979) 25–26.

10 'Cases' (*Permanent Court of Arbitration*) <https://pca-cpa.org/en/cases/> accessed 20 June 2018.

11 *Sino-Portuguese Treaty of Peking*, the Kingdom of Portugal and China, 1 December 1887.

12 The First Historical Archives of China, Macau Foundation and The Historical Material Study Institute of Jinan University, *Collection of Macau Archives During Ming & Qing Dynasty*, Vol 4 (People Press 1999) 301–302.

13 Keping Yu, '"Westernization" vs."Sinicization": An Ineffaceable Paradox Within China's Modernization Process' in Tian Yu Cao, Xueping Zhong and Liao Kebin (eds.), *Culture and Social Transformations in Reform Era China* (Brill 2010) 151.

14 Julia C Strauss, *Strong Institutions in Weak Polities: State Building in Republican China, 1927–1940* (Oxford University Press 1998) 155–156.

respected place in the international community. In a case presented before the Permanent Court of International Justice (PCIJ) concerning China's denunciation of the Sino-Belgian Treaty of 1865, the majority of the Chinese Republican government agreed with China's appearance before the court, saying, 'Without attendance, other states would have no way of knowing the truth of the denounciation' (author's translation).[15] Some officials even strongly advocated it: '. . . but we cannot surrender to the unequal provisions; we should respond to Belgium's claim and expose our grievance to the world, even at the cost of losing the lawsuit and withdrawing from the League' (author's translation).[16]

However, the susceptibility of international adjudication to political influence, as the ROC had discovered in the Tokyo Trial,[17] ultimately shattered Chinese expectations. A prominent example is the exoneration of Emperor Hirohito of Japan. The Chinese government planned to prosecute Emperor Hirohito for his role in declaring the war and as the supreme commander of the army.[18] However, the United States saved Hirohito from trial as a war criminal, because it believed the occupation of Japan would be greatly facilitated if the emperor, who was regarded as the God of Japan, could remain on the throne.[19] The US intervention provoked criticism in China and increased scepticism of international adjudication. At the 5th Annual International Association of Democratic Lawyers (IADL) Congress, Shen Chun-jun considered that the International Military Tribunal for the Far East (IMTFE) had failed to punish war atrocities.[20]

The Mao era[21]

China's hostility towards international adjudication intensified during the Mao era, especially after the escalation of the Cold War. The US and its allies grouped the People's Republic of China (PRC) into the eastern socialist bloc and refused to recognise it as the legitimate representative of China in the international

15 *Minute of Treaty Research Committee*, Taibei, Diplomatic Archives of Republican China (No.05000–143) 330 to 355).

16 Ibid. at 393–419, quoted from Chi-hua Tang, 'A Study of Treaty Revision Negotiations between China and Belgium, 1926–1929' (2009) 31 *Journal of National Chengchi University* 115, 128.

17 After WWII, the ROC as a member of the victorious Allies was invited to join the International Military Tribunal for the Far East (IMTFE) and adjudicate the Japanese war criminals.

18 Zhiyong Song,"Tokyo Trials and China' 41 (2001) *The Journal of Studies of China's Resistance War against Japan* 144, 155.

19 John K Fairbank and Albert Feuerwerker, *The Cambridge History of China: Volume 13, Republican China 1912–1949* (Cambridge University Press 1986) 540.

20 Shen Chun-jun, 'On the Indictment and Punishment of War Criminals, PC, no.6,' in Jerome Cohen and Hungdah Chiu, *People's China and International Law,* Vol 2 (Princeton University Press 1974) 1584.

21 Historians often divide the history of the PRC into the 'Mao era' and the 'post-Mao era'. The Mao era lasted from the founding of the PRC in 1949 to Deng Xiaoping's consolidation of power and policy reversal in 1978. John King Fairbank and Merle Goldman, *China: A New History, Second Enlarged Edition* (Harvard University Press 2006).

community. Likewise, the Chinese Communists rejected the existing international legal regime, describing it as Western bourgeois international law that 'defend[ed] the aggressive or colonial policy of the strong capitalist countries'.[22] They further insisted that, in the course of interpreting and executing international law, there always existed struggles in terms of 'ideological standpoint, understanding of the question, etc.' between the socialist viewpoint and the bourgeois viewpoint.[23]

The PRC's attitude towards the ICJ embodies its ideological struggles with the so-called bourgeois international law. In theory, the Chinese denounced the ICJ interpretation of international law for 'merely reflect[ing] the bourgeois and imperialist nature of international law'.[24] In practice, the PRC did not have any direct interaction with the ICJ. It never brought cases to the ICJ, appeared before the Court as a respondent, or participated in proceedings as a third party;[25] it did not accept clauses providing for judicial settlement by the ICJ in treaties to which the PRC was a party.[26] During the 1962 Sino-Indian border conflicts,[27] India proposed that the dispute could be referred to the ICJ.[28] But China rejected the proposal: '. . . the Chinese Government could not agree to refer the Sino-Indian boundary question to international arbitration and that the International Court of Justice at The Hague is an organ of the United Nations, among whose judges there is an element of the Chiang-Kai-shek clique[29]. . . .'[30]

Present: the PRC's love-hate relationship with international adjudication in the post-Mao era

In the post-Mao era the PRC experienced significant policy changes. Internationally, due to the restoration of its permanent seat in the United Nations and

22 Ho Wu-shuang and Ma chun, 'A Criticism of the Reactionary Viewpoint of Ch'en T'i-ch'ang on the Science of International Law' in Cohen and Chiu (n 20)Vol 1, 34.
23 Lin Hsin, 'On the System of International Law after the Second World War' in ibid., Vol 1 55 to 60.
24 Meng Kong, 'A Criticism of the Theories of Bourgeois International Law Concerning the Subjects of International Law and Recognition of State' (1960) 2 *International Studies* 44, 49.
25 'List of Contentious Cases by date of introduction' (*International Court of Justice*) <http://www.icj-cij.org/docket/index.php?p1=3&p2=3> accessed 20 June 2018.
26 Julian Ku, 'China and the Future of International Adjudication' (2012) 27 *Maryland Journal of International Law* 154, 160.
27 China and India disputed their Himalayan border in 1962. See details in Neville Maxwell, *India's China War* (Natraj Publishers 1997).
28 'Letter from the Prime Minister of India to the Prime Minister of China, 1 January 1963' in Government of India Ministry of External Affairs, *Notes, Memoranda and Letters Exchanged and Agreements Signed Between the Governments of India and China, 1962–1963*, Vol 8 (Government of India Press 1963) .
29 The Chiang-Kai-shek clique refers to the Communist government's rival – the Republican government led by Chiang-Kai-shek. From 1949 to 1971, the Republican government, which ruled Taiwan and its surrounding waters, represented China at the ICJ.
30 'Text of Chinese Foreign Ministry Note to India' (9 October 1963), NCNA-English. Peking (12 October 1963) in Cohen and Chiu (n 20) 1441–1442.

the end of the Cold War, China resumed diplomatic relations with most states and began to actively take part in many international institutions.[31] Domestically, the Chinese Communist Party (CCP) decided to open China to the West and develop a 'socialist market economy with Chinese characteristics'.[32] As ideological elements were gradually played down, the Chinese started to rethink international law. In 1981, Tieya Wang, one of the leading Chinese international legal scholars of his day, defined international law as 'the sum of principles, rules, regulations and systems which are binding and which mainly regulate inter-state relations'.[33] Wang overturned the prevailing socialist viewpoint, stating that the basis of international law is attributed to the willingness of various states with different ideologies and cultures to cooperate for the common good.[34] The process of 'de-ideologicalisation' promoted the development of international law in China, paving the way for China to integrate into the international legal regime, and influencing the government's attitude towards international courts and tribunals.

WTO adjudication and changes of China's attitude

When the PRC joined the WTO in 2001, it complied with the terms of the treaty package and accepted the DSM as a formal mechanism for settling disputes arising out of the WTO legal system. The PRC's acceptance of the DSM is considered as a dramatic shift in policy.[35] Prior to 2001, the government stuck to the principle of non-intervention and had limited interest in international adjudication. However, its membership in the WTO and the treaty obligation compelled China to interact with the DSM.

The PRC's first WTO case was *US-Steel Safeguards*,[36] in which it acted as a co-complainant. The Chinese representative of that time, Guohua Yang, recalled his team's first-ever appearance at the WTO consultation. At the start of the consultation, the Chinese were very serious, 'glanc[ing] at the seats of the United States, the respondent, with a sense of hostility – the U.S. restricted the import of steel products including those from China, and hence it was a "rival" to China in the case'.[37] When Yang sat down, he found '. . . documents and materials were full on the tables of the people from all the other eight members.'[38] In contrast,

31 Hungdah Chiu, 'Chinese Attitudes toward International Law in the Post-Mao Era' (1988) 1988 Maryland Series in Contemporary Asian Studies 1.
32 Fairbank and Goldman (n 21) 407–410.
33 Tieya Wang, *International Law* (Law Press 1981) 2.
34 Ibid. 9.
35 Marcia Don Harpaz, 'China and International Tribunals: Onward from the WTO' in Lisa Toohey, Colin B Picker and Jonathan Greenacre (eds.), *China in the International Economic Order: New Directions and Changing Paradigms* (Cambridge University Press 2015) 43.
36 *United States – Definitive Safeguard Measures on Imports of Certain Steel Products* (DS252).
37 Guohua Yang, 'China in the WTO Dispute Settlement: A Memoir' (2015) 49 *Journal of World Trade* 1, 1.
38 Ibid. 2.

'. . . only a few pieces of papers . . . were in front of [his] Chinese colleagues.'[39] Yang described his following days as 'suffering'.[40] While other complainants kept asking the US delegation facts and legal issues about the safeguards against steel imports, the Chinese were extraordinarily silent, as they 'did not even know to bring a copy of the Report of the United States International Trade Commission' (USITC).[41] Yang eventually admitted that China 'could not contribute much to this case', because '[w]e could not even understand what they were talking about!'[42]

This embarrassing experience reminded China of the importance of WTO adjudication. Previously, the Chinese viewed the WTO as a hallowed mechanism that could bring benefits to China's economy, but they neglected other aspects of the system, such as the high level of preparation necessary for settling trade disputes.[43] The other lesson China learned from this case was the spirit of 'the rule of law' embedded in international adjudication. In his memoir, Yang expressed his surprise at the outcome of the *US-Steel Safeguards* case: a thousand pages of Panel and Appellate Body Reports, in which every legal issue of the case was addressed in detail, finally determined that the US safeguard measures were inconsistent with the WTO obligations; but the US accepted and enforced the ruling with good grace.[44] This fact, described by Yang as 'unprecedented', rectified China's misunderstanding of international adjudication and further increased its trust in WTO adjudication:

> WTO is a big family with many members. There are rules of rights and obligations to make the family work, but disputes are inevitable. What can we do with the disputes which could not be resolved through negotiations? 'Judicial remedy' seemed to be the only rational and efficient way.[45]

After this case, China embarked on what some scholars call a 'learning and socialisation' process.[46] During this process China brought very few cases to the WTO; rather, it preferred to resolve disputes through non-adversarial, diplomatic exchanges such as bilateral negotiations.[47] In handling the cases against China,

39 Ibid.
40 Ibid.
41 Ibid.
42 Ibid.
43 Wenhua Ji and Cui Huang, 'China's Path to the Center Stage of WTO Dispute Settlement: Challenges and Responses' (2010) 5 *Global Trade and Customs Journal* 365, 369.
44 Yang (n 37) 6–7.
45 Ibid. 6.
46 See e.g. in Xiaojun Li, 'Understanding China's Behavioral Change in the WTO Dispute Settlement System' (2012) 52 Asian Survey 1111, 1113; Marcia Don Harpaz, 'Sense and Sensibilities of China and WTO Dispute Settlement' (2010) 44 *Journal of World Trade* 1155; Stuart Harris, *China's Foreign Policy* (John Wiley & Sons 2014) 130.
47 Harris (n 46) 130; Li (n 46) 1130.

the Chinese were said to be 'anxious' and 'scared'.[48] Chenggang Li, the assistant minister of the Ministry of Commerce of the People's Republic of China (MOFCOM), reminisced about the government's reaction to *China — Value-Added Tax on Integrated Circuits*:[49] 'We treated the multilateral trade mechanism with awe, preparing every proposal under supervision of ministers' (author's translation).[50] Meanwhile, China observed the operation of WTO adjudication through participating in the proceedings as a third party. By 2006, it had been a third party in 54 cases, which surpassed the level of participation of many developing countries that joined the WTO much earlier than China.[51]

The year 2006 was a watershed year for China, as it signalled the expiration of the *de facto* five-year grace period at the WTO[52] and WTO members began to frequently challenge China.[53] Faced with a flood of disputes, China revamped its former image as a passive observer. The turning point occurred in the *China – Auto Parts* dispute.[54] Instead of settling the dispute out of court as it did previously, the Chinese government determined to go for adjudication: '. . . China would defend its position and interests before the panel and remained confident that China's relevant measures were consistent with its accession commitments and the relevant WTO rules . . .'[55] In the following three years, China went through the entire adjudicatory process, ranging from the establishment of a panel to appealing to the Appellate Body (AB). Despite losing the case, the MOFCOM was willing to implement the decision, explaining that China was successful in the sense that the proceedings, especially the first-ever appeal to the AB, had offered it valuable experience in managing WTO adjudication.[56]

After the *Auto Parts* case, China filed its first WTO case as an independent complainant in September 2007,[57] and by 2018 it had lodged 17 complaints.[58]

48 Guohua Yang and Xiaoli Shi, *Womenzai WTO Daguansi (We Are Litigating in WTO)* (Zhishi Chanquan Press 2015) 1.
49 *China – Value-added tax on Integrated Circuits* (DS309).
50 Yang and Shi (n 48) 4.
51 'Disputes by Member' (n 1).
52 There was no explicit clause that forbids WTO members to sue China immediately after its accession. To respect the commitments subject to the transitional period made upon China's accession, however, most potential complainants chose to wait until the end of that period – this is the so-called *de facto* grace period. Wei Zhuang, 'An Empirical Study of China's Participation in the WTO Dispute Settlement Mechanism: 2001–2010' (2011) 4 *Law and Development Review* 218, 219–220.
53 From 2006 to 2010, China was a respondent in almost a quarter of all WTO disputes, see in ibid. 221. Marcia Don Harpaz has similarly observed that, of the 19 cases brought against China between 2004 and 2012, 18 were filed in or after 2006. Toohey, Picker and Greenacre (n 35) 50.
54 *China – Measures Affecting Imports of Automobile Parts* (DS342).
55 WTO, Minutes of Meeting held on 26 October 2006, Dispute Settlement Body, WT/DSB/M/221 (4 December 2006), para. 53, quoted from Harpaz (n 46).
56 Li (n 46) 1134.
57 *United States – Preliminary Anti-Dumping and Countervailing Duty Determinations on Coated Free Sheet Paper from China* (DS368).
58 'Disputes by Member' (n 1).

Contrary to its performance in *US-Steel Safeguards*, through these cases China has grown into a seasoned complainant. When Yang recorded his attendance at the *U.S.-Poultry* consultation in 2009, he said:

> . . . we asked a series of questions on the measure . . . I had all the related documents in front of me, i.e., the paragraph from the act, the legislative history, the background of the congresswoman who introduced the bill, the study on its WTO consistency, and above all, the question list we sent to the U.S. one week before this consultation, with the follow-up questions marked in my copy . . .[59]

Moreover, the experience in the WTO cultivated China's sense of the 'rule of law'. This is evident in a MOFCOM official's reflection on China's policy towards the DSM:

> We came to the WTO having a lot of reservations about using the dispute settlement system. We made a lot of commitments in the negotiations leading up to the signing of the [accession] agreement and do not want to be seen as breaking our promises. That's why we only adjudicated when we felt 100% sure that we were going to prevail, such as in the U.S. Steel case. As we became more familiar with the system by learning and observing actual disputes, however, we found that our reservation was totally unnecessary. Countries as large as the U.S. win and lose WTO cases all the time and it's all part of the game. China needs to be playing the same game.[60]

Spillover effect: China's increasing embrace of ISA

The shift of attitude towards WTO adjudication has a positive spillover effect on China's embrace of international adjudication in other areas, especially the resolution of investor-state disputes. This can be observed in the evolution of the investor-state dispute settlement (ISDS)[61] clauses in the Chinese IIAs.

At the very beginning of its contracting activities, China did not include an ISDS clause in the IIAs. The situation started to change after the mid-1980s, marked by the China-BLEU (Belgium-Luxembourg Economic Union) Bilateral Investment Treaty (BIT) (1984) that unprecedentedly granted investors the right to settle disputes through ISA, albeit for limited purposes.[62] In 1993 China rati-

59 Yang (n 37) 2–3.
60 Li (n 46) 1132.
61 Here the ISDS generally refers to any settlement for investor-state disputes, including international arbitration, amicable settlement, administrative settlement and judicial settlement.
62 Article 10 (3) of the China-BLEU BIT provides that 'A dispute which arises from an amount of compensation for expropriation, nationalization or other similar measures and has not been settled within six months from the date of notification may, as the investor prefers be referred for settlement either to: (1) a judicial body of the Contracting Party accepting the investment, or, (2) an international arbitration without resort to any other means.'

fied the ICSID Convention, making it possible to submit investment disputes to the International Centre for Settlement of Investment Disputes (ICSID) for arbitration. However, at the time of accession, China declared a reservation, limiting the jurisdiction of ICSID to disputes over 'compensation resulting from expropriation and nationalization'.[63] Alongside this, in the IIAs China imposed the 'fork in the road' requirement on the investor's choice of ISA,[64] indicating that the investor irrevocably elects a procedural remedy when (s)he commences the legal proceedings in either the courts of the host state or international tribunals.

But since 2001, China has gradually removed the jurisdictional hurdle, as the admissibility requirements of arbitration changed from the compensation-relevance to what Manjiao Chi and Xi Wang call 'investment-relevance'.[65] A typical example is the China-Netherlands BIT (2001) that allows 'disputes which might arise between . . . concerning an investment' to be submitted to the ICSID or *ad hoc* arbitration.[66] Later, a new type of admissibility requirement – the 'legal nature' requirement – was introduced.[67] For instance, Art. 8(1) of China-BLEU BIT (2005) states: 'When a legal dispute arises between an investor of one Contracting Party and the other Contracting Party, either party to the dispute shall notify the other party to the dispute in writing.'[68] The 'legal nature' clause is believed to further loosen the limitation on ISA, for it gives any legal disputes access to arbitration, including those arising from treatments the investors receive from the host state.[69]

After 2008, China began to borrow from the North American Free Trade Agreement (NAFTA) model to articulate its ISDS clauses. Part C of the China-Canada BIT (2012), which covers aspects such as consent to arbitration, submission of a claim to arbitration, appointment of arbitrators, consolidation and enforcement of an award, resembles the structure of Chapter 11 Section B of NAFTA. Some wording in Part C also echoes that in the NAFTA. For instance, Article 20 provides that an investor may submit a claim arising from breaches of certain provisions of the treaty to arbitration and that (s)he is entitled to request for loss or damage by reason of, or arising out of that breach as well, which is in line with the scope of consent to arbitration set up under Article 1116 of NAFTA. The 'NAFTA-isation' pattern frequently appears in recent Chinese IIAs, including the ASEAN-China Investment Agreement (2009), China-Japan-Korea, Republic of Trilateral Investment Agreement (2012), and China-Australia Free Trade Agreement (2015).

63 Christoph H Schreuer, *The ICSID Convention: A Commentary* (Cambridge University Press 2009) 342.
64 See e.g. Article 9(3) of China-Chile BIT (1994).
65 Manjiao Chi and Xi Wang, 'The Evolution of ISA Clauses in Chinese IIAs and Its Practical Implications' (2015) 16 *Journal of World Investment & Trade* 869, 884.
66 Art.10 (1) of China-Netherlands BIT (2001).
67 Chi and Wang (n 65) 885.
68 Art. 8(1) of China-BLEU BIT (2005).
69 Chi and Wang (n 65) 886.

Another index reflecting China's acceptance of ISA is its changing attitude towards appearing before investment tribunals. Although China has provided ICSID arbitration in an increasing number of IIAs since the 1990s, for over ten years there had been no ICSID case involving China, in sharp contrast to the enormous share China has in international investment. This is due to China's long-term endeavour to settle investor-state disputes within domestic fora. Amicable settlement in particular is advocated by the Chinese government, which fears the loss of reputation and investment if disputes with foreign investors are not handled properly and submitted to international tribunals.[70] To limit the adverse effects of disputes, the government is prepared to make heavy concessions and pays compensation following negotiations with foreign investors.[71] Similarly, Chinese investors follow tenets of Confucianism which emphasises the importance of settling disputes amicably.[72] They are said to regard disputes as a kind of shame and try to avoid them; if disputes are inevitable, informal persuasion and negotiation are used for creating harmony between parties.[73]

However, since 2006, China has shifted its approach and started to appear before investment arbitral tribunals. In 2007, 14 years after China's accession to the ICSID Convention, a Chinese investor initiated the first arbitration request in the ICSID.[74] At the time of writing (June 2018), seven investment arbitration cases involving China or Chinese investors had been filed: one in 2010,[75] one in 2011,[76] one in 2012,[77] two in 2014,[78] and two in 2017.[79] It is not possible to claim that there is clear evidence proving a causal link between China's recently frequent participation in ISA and its behavioural change in WTO adjudication; however, it is very likely that China's experience with the WTO provided a momentum to change its conservative attitude towards ISA. First, China's enhanced legal capacity building and experience with litigation, attributed to its involvement as a third party in WTO cases, laid the intellectual and institutional foundations for China to cope with international adjudication more

70 Stephan W Schill, 'Tearing down the Great Wall: The New Generation Investment Treaties of The People's Republic of China' (2007) 15 *Cardozo J. Int'l & Comp. L.* 73, 89–94.

71 Guiguo Wang, 'Chinese Mechanisms for Resolving Investor-State Dispute' (2011) 1 *Jindal J. Int. Affairs* 204, 209.

72 See e.g. Anne Judith Farina, 'Talking Disputes into Harmony China Approaches International Commercial Arbitration' (1989) 4 *Am UJ Int'l l & Pol'y* 137, 139–141.

73 Kenneth J Keith, 'Asian Attitudes to International Law' [1967] *Aust. YBIL* 1, 27.

74 *Señor Tza Yap Shum v. The Republic of Peru*, ICSID Case No. ARB/07/6.

75 *Beijing Shougang Mining Investment Company Ltd and others v. Mongolia*, PCA Case No. 2010–20.

76 *Ekran Berhad v. People's Republic of China*, ICSID Case No. ARB/11/15.

77 *Ping An Life Insurance Company, Limited and Ping An Insurance (Group) Company, Limited v. The Government of Belgium*, ICSID Case No. ARB/12/29.

78 *Ansung Housing Co., Ltd. v. People's Republic of China*, ICSID Case No. ARB/14/25; *Beijing Urban Construction Group Co. Ltd. v. Republic of Yemen*, ICSID Case No. ARB/14/30.

79 *Hela Schwarz GmbH v. People's Republic of China*, ICSID Case No. ARB/17/19; *Sanum Investments Limited v. Lao People's Democratic Republic (II)*, ICSID Case No. ADHOC/17/1.

broadly. Second, understanding and even accepting the culture of the 'rule of law' strengthens China's confidence in using adjudication to settle its investment disputes.

Lingering hostility: China's '4 Noes' policy towards the South China Sea Arbitration

It is true that, since its accession to the WTO, China's stance on international adjudication has been evolving towards greater acceptance and engagement. Yet this does not mean China has embraced international adjudication as a whole. In 2013, the Republic of the Philippines instituted arbitral proceedings against the PRC concerning the role of historic rights and the source of maritime entitlements in the South China Sea. Instead of attending the proceedings and responding to the claims, China declared that it would not participate in the Arbitration, as the Hague-based tribunal that heard the case lacked jurisdiction.[80] The tension increased to a higher level when the arbitral tribunal issued its final award in favour of the Philippines in 2016. Regarding the Arbitration as illegal, China released the 'No Acceptance, No Participation, No Recognition, and No Implementation' (the '4 Noes') policy soon after the announcement of the award.[81]

China's 4 Noes policy can be traced to the country's historical position as a victim of the international legal regime. From the perspective of China, the Arbitration essentially addresses a dispute involving its sovereignty and territorial rights that were seriously impaired historically by foreign powers.[82] As the position paper published on 13 July 2016 stated: during the 1930s and the 1940s 'France and Japan invaded and illegally occupied by force some islands and reefs of China's Nansha Qundao (Spratly Islands)';[83] since the 1950s, this area has been coveted by the neighbouring states – for instance, 'The Philippines has been raising illegal territorial claims over these places since the 1950s.'[84] Connecting past foreign wrongdoings with the present case, the Arbitration was seen as the embodiment of foreign invasion, which easily provoked the Chinese sense of humiliation and resentment.

80 'Position Paper of the Government of the People's Republic of China on the Matter of Jurisdiction in the South China Sea Arbitration Initiated by the Republic of the Philippines' (*The South China Sea Issue*, 7 December 2014) <http://www.fmprc.gov.cn/nanhai/eng/snhwtlcwj_1/t1368895.htm> accessed 21 June 2018.

81 'China Adheres to the Position of Settling Through Negotiation the Relevant Disputes Between China and the Philippines in the South China Sea' (*Ministry of Foreign Affairs of the People's Republic of China*, 13 July 2016) <http://www.fmprc.gov.cn/mfa_eng/zxxx_662805/t1380615.shtml> accessed 13 May 2017.

82 But the tribunal held that the Philippines' submission 'is not a dispute concerning sovereignty or maritime boundary delimitation'. See in Award on Jurisdiction and Admissibility, *The South China Sea Arbitration (The Republic of Philippines v. The People's Republic of China)*, PCA Case N° 2013–19, 140.

83 'China Adheres to the Position of Settling Through Negotiation the Relevant Disputes Between China and the Philippines in the South China Sea' (n 81) para 23.

84 Ibid. 58–61.

The view that the Arbitration is a foreign plot against China is clearly discernible in the critique of the arbitral tribunal. At the subsequent press conference, Zhengming Liu, the vice minister of the Ministry of Foreign Affairs of the People's Republic of China (MOFA), asserted that the award should be null because: (1) the Japanese appointed four arbitrators and exerted influences on the proceedings; (2) most arbitrators are from Europe and know little about Asian culture, Asian history and the South China Sea; (3) the arbitrators were paid by the Philippines and other states.[85] To be sure, an arbitral award can be challenged on certain grounds, but generally the challenges confine themselves merely to the facts supported by rules and real evidence. Obviously, some of the allegations made by China are based on its prior experience of prejudice in international adjudication. The doubt of the impartiality of the European arbitrators is essentially consistent with the traditional images of international adjudicators in the eyes of Chinese authorities: the Qing government rejected the use of PCA arbitration in the Macau disputes because 'the Westerners have a long-term racial discrimination against Chinese ethnics'[86]; the PRC objected to a resort to the ICJ for the Sino-Indian disputes because 'there is an element of the Chiang-Kai-shek clique' among the ICJ judges.[87]

Some might regard China's hostility towards the Arbitration as a reflection of political expediency: it rejected the Arbitration because its claim in the case is arguably weak and the participation in the proceedings would damage its interests; had its claim been strong in law, China would probably attend the proceedings. This claim is difficult to dismiss. After all, a state always makes its foreign policy based on national self-interest – China is no exception, and political calculation sometimes takes precedence over the international rule of law. Yet if China rejects the Arbitration merely because it sees it as compromising, rather than advancing, its interests, why does it still refuse international adjudication for settling other sovereign or territorial disputes in which its legal argument might be strong?[88] As a matter of fact, when acceding to conventions of a political nature, the PRC always makes reservations to adjudication clauses therein.[89] Thus there appears to be some historical continuity in China's dislike of international adjudication concerning territorial or sovereignty issues: from the Qing dynasty to the PRC, China has never required or agreed to submit its sovereignty-related disputes to international courts or tribunals, regardless of the subject of the dispute or the strength of China's legal arguments.

85 'Vice Foreign Minister Liu Zhenmin at the Press Conference on the White Paper Titled China Adheres to the Position of Settling Through Negotiation the Relevant Disputes Between China and the Philippines in the South China Sea' (*The South China Sea Issue*, 13 July 2016) <http://www.fmprc.gov.cn/nanhai/eng/wjbxw_1/t1381980.htm> accessed 14 May 2017.

86 See n 12.

87 See n 30.

88 A prominent example is the handover of Hong Kong and Macau as a result of negotiations between China and the United Kingdom and Portugal respectively.

89 Muthucumaraswamy Sornarajah and Jiangyu Wang (eds.), *China, India and the International Economic Order* (Cambridge University Press 2010) 318, 323.

Future: paradigm shift and challenges

China's historical humiliation at the hands of the West can now be consigned to the past: the contemporary international community is arguably more civilised than in the nineteenth century, and China is rising as a great power with a gradual acceptance of the 'rule of law'. But Chinese discourse regarding the Arbitration suggests the ongoing relevance of the humiliating history. Why does China's historical perception of international adjudication, referred to as 'the tool serving Western interests', still loom large in its foreign policy? Admittedly, many concrete circumstances that shape China's attitude have changed in the past century, yet these changes do not alter the nature of China's role in the international adjudicatory regime throughout the history: since the nineteenth century international adjudication has constantly remained Western-led and China is often seen as the 'other'.

Status quo: Western-led international adjudication

Implicit in the Chinese rebuff to the Arbitration is the conviction that the West leads international adjudication and intends to undermine China's interests. This belief might overestimate Western power, yet there exists some truth in that international adjudication is basically Western-led. International adjudication from the past until today has been built on the architecture of the Western discourse – its applicable rules are imported from Western systems, its institutions are shaped by Western powers, and its underlying rationales are Western values.[90] The West is regarded as the 'self' of international adjudication:[91] Western views, such as the interpretation of international treaties, represent 'universal' international norms that should be applied to describe, evaluate and authorise commentaries on disputes. Non-Western states including China, as countries with substantially different domestic political and economic contexts, are regarded as the 'others', 'rule takers' or 'passive responders' who are supposed to follow, accept and comply with 'universal' international norms. Hence too often we find that, within the current literature, China's attitude towards international adjudication equates to 'China's integration into the global system',[92] 'whether China accepts international dispute settlement or not'[93] or 'China's socialisation into the international legal regime'.[94]

90 Yasuaki Onuma, *A Transcivilizational Perspective on International Law* (Brill Academic Publishers 2010) 47–48.

91 Edward W. Said, *Orientalism* (New York: Vintage Books 1979). Said's 'self' and 'other' categories are applied by Teemu Ruskola and Lisa Toohey in their description of contemporary international legal studies on China. Teemu Ruskola, 'Legal Orientalism' (2002) 101 Michigan Law Review 179, 182–183; Lisa Toohey 'Regarding China: Images of China in the International Economic Order' in Toohey, Picker and Greenacre (n 35) 29–32.

92 E.g. Marcia Don Harpaz in Toohey, Picker and Greenacre (n 35) 43.

93 E.g. Harriet Moynihan, 'China's Evolving Approach to International Dispute Settlement' (*Chatham House*, 29 March 2017) <https://www.chathamhouse.org/publication/chinas-evolving-approach-international-dispute-settlement> accessed 1 June 2018.

94 E.g. Harpaz (n 46).

Such a scenario has been realistically, and also painfully, recognised by China. Early in the 1990s, Deng Xiaoping gave China a '24-Character' principle to guide its foreign policy: 'Observe calmly; secure our position; cope with affairs calmly; hide our capacities and bide our time; be good at maintaining a low profile; and never claim leadership.'[95] By saying so, Deng suggested China take a compromised position and accommodate the West in its support of the country's domestic reform and economic development, regardless of the differences in political systems and values. Deng's principle has been continuously implemented and has become a central tenet of Chinese foreign policy for decades, resulting in China's increasing integration into the international adjudicatory regime from the 2000s through the 2010s. Acknowledging that international adjudication is 'a product of Western civilisation',[96] China sees itself as a novice entering the 'game' that has been designed by others and thus trying its best to suit terms set by the West.[97] This can be clearly manifested in China's prescription-oriented study of WTO adjudication, where Western legal practice is used as a standard for China to imitate, and legal advice is often given to help China improve its performance in WTO cases so as to meet Western standards.[98]

Indeed, China has benefited a lot from the security and economic dividends brought by such an integration: it has been the world's largest recipient of foreign direct investment, the world's largest manufacturing economy and exporter of goods, and the world's second largest economy. But accepting the fact that it is more profitable to act in line with the West is arguably out of pragmatism rather than a free choice. Hence, China's acceptance of international adjudication is changeable and selective, depending on national interests: on the one hand, it welcomes the economic benefits brought by commercial and trade related international adjudication; but on the other hand, it rejects other forms of international adjudication related to sovereignty which developed without its participation, considering them contrary to its interests.

However, this situation may be unsustainable in the future, as China's ability (and perhaps willingness) to reframe the Western-led regime increases. From a historical perspective, nostalgia for China's great past, including the glorious Middle Kingdom and the splendid Chinese civilisation, together with the humiliation brought by foreign wrongdoings, generates a 'burning hope' that someday China can once again become great and reassert its rightful place in the world.[99] Economically, as China's economy rapidly develops and becomes a major contributor to global governance, the existing rules, institutions, and procedures of

95 Honghua Men, '"Keeping Low Profile and Striving to Make Achievements" Strategy and China's Diplomacy in 1990s' (2016) 56 Jilin University Journal Social Sciences Edition 81.

96 Zhipeng He and Lu Sun, *Chinese Theory of International Law* (Law Press 2017) 53–54.

97 Xiaohong Su, 'International Adjudication in the Changing World', doctoral thesis, 130.

98 E.g. Julia Ya Qin, 'Pushing the Limits of Global Governance: Trading Rights, Censorship, and WTO Jurisprudence – A Commentary on the China-Publications Case' (2011) 10 Chinese Journal of International Law 62.

99 Immanuel Chung-yueh Hsü, *China's Entrance into the Family of Nations: The Diplomatic Phase, 1858–1880* (Harvard University Press 1960) 210.

international adjudication, which are originally designed by and for the West, will hardly accommodate China's increasing needs and interests. This has already been revealed in some Chinese scholarly writings.[100] Politically, China's identity as a major economic power implies that it has increasing leverage in international politics. It can use its economic power, such as its considerable influence on trade and investment flows, to achieve its political objectives.[101] Legally, China's 'learning and socialisation' strategy has proven to be successful in enhancing its legal capacity. After years of participation, China gradually developed its own international legal professionals. Some Chinese lawyers can now handle international cases independently – the most prominent figure may be the first Chinese counsel appearing before the WTO panel, Jun Peng.[102]

Paradigm shift: exploring the Chinese approach

There is some evidence that China is unwilling to continue its role as an 'other' of international adjudication. The most significant sign comes from the revision of Deng's '24-Character' principle. Soon after taking his position as general secretary of the CCP, Xi Jinping proclaimed that 'the greatest dream for the Chinese now is to realize the great rejuvenation of the Chinese nation.'[103] This call was later applied to foreign policy in an address Xi made at the Central Conference on Work Relating to Foreign Affairs. There, he urged China to 'develop a distinctive diplomatic approach matching its role as a major country . . . conduct diplomacy with a salient Chinese character, Chinese feature and a Chinese vision' (author's translation).[104] Xi's account, which was later summarised as seeking 'a major power diplomacy with Chinese characteristics, or what we call "Chinese approach"' (author's translation),[105] illustrates that China no longer wants to just follow,

100 E.g. Chongli Xu, 'The "Outsider" Mentality and the Poor Chinese International Legal Research' (2006) 24 Tribune of Political Science and Law 33; Congyan Cai, 'New Great Powers and International Law in the 21st Century' (2013) 24 European Journal of International Law 755; Zhiyun Liu, 'Redefinition of China's National Interests and Its Transformation on International Law under the New Situation' (2014) 4 *Journal of International Relations and International Law* 96.

101 Harris (n 46) 139.

102 'Jun Peng: The First Chinese WTO Counsel' (*Sina Finance*, 27 October 2015) <http://finance.sina.com.cn/leadership/mroll/20151027/151523594935.shtml> accessed 1 June 2018.

103 Xi Jinping described his declaration as 'Chinese dream' in his visit to the National Museum of China in 2012. Since then, 'Chinese dream' has been regarded as the embodiment of the political ideology of the leadership under Xi. 'Chinese Dream' (*China Daily*, 26 March 2014) <http://www.chinadaily.com.cn/china/Chinese-dream.html> accessed 14 May 2017.

104 'Xi Jinping Attended the Central Conference on Work Relating to Foreign Affairs and Made an Important Speech' (*Xinhuanet*, 29 November 2014) <http://www.xinhuanet.com/politics/2014-11/29/c_1113457723.htm> accessed 10 June 2018.

105 'Wang Yi: Implement the Principle of "Major Power Diplomacy with Chinese Characteristics" and Serve for the Chinese Dream' (*Ministry of Foreign Affairs of the PRC*,

accept and reinforce Western theories and practice of international adjudication. Rather, as what the CCP announced at the Fourth Plenary Session of the 18th Central Committee, China should:

> vigorously participate in the formulation of international norms, promote the handling of foreign-related economic and social affairs according to the law, and strengthen our country's discourse power and influence in international legal affairs, use legal methods to safeguard our country's sovereignty, security, and development interests.[106]

China's recent behaviour in WTO adjudication may be the most obvious manifestation of its pursuit for the Chinese approach. Having familiarised itself with WTO rules and procedures, China has shifted to what Saadia Pekkanen describes as 'aggressive legalism', actively using 'the legal rules in the treaties and agreements overseen by the WTO to stake out positions, to advance and rebut claims, and to embroil all concerned in an intricate legal game . . .'[107] In two claims it recently brought to the DSM,[108] China seems to challenge the WTO legal regime: unlike other complaints made by China that address disputes on specific products, these two cases are essentially about the definition of market economy status (MES) provided in Section 15 of China's Protocol of Accession and the interpretation of Section 15(d).[109] This bold move by China represents a landmark in its approach. For a long time, China has put considerable diplomatic effort into being recognised as a market economy by individual trading partners, though with limited success after the US and the EU formally opposed China's MES. Aside from continuing its diplomatic lobbying tactics, China now uses the dispute settlement process to fill gaps in the WTO agreements and sets forth new norms that may justify its MES. Its courage in countering the *status quo* in a visibly confrontational, legitimate manner appears to astonish the US. The US trade representative Robert Lighthizer warned the Senate Finance Committee that the MES fight '. . . is without question the most serious litigation matter we have

---

11 December 2014) <http://www.mfa.gov.cn/chn//gxh/tyb/gdxw/t1218445.htm> accessed 10 June 2018.

106 'Decision of the CPC Central Committee on Major Issues Pertaining to Comprehensively Promoting the Rule of Law' *People's Daily* (Beijing, 29 November 2014) 1.

107 Saadia M Pekkanen, 'Aggressive Legalism: The Rules of the WTO and Japan's Emerging Trade Strategy' (2001) 24 *The World Economy* 707, 732.

108 *United States — Measures Related to Price Comparison Methodologies* (DS515); *European Union — Measures Related to Price Comparison Methodologies* (DS516).

109 Section 15 provides that if China can clearly show the market economy conditions in its domestic industry, then the Chinese producers have a right for any anti-dumping determination to be based on Chinese prices. The issue is, however, what the criteria of the so-called market economy are and who has the right to set the criteria. Another issue is the legal interpretation of Section 15 (d), namely, does the language of (d) indicate that MES shall be granted to China automatically 15 years after the date of China's accession?

at the WTO right now . . . a bad decision with respect to non-market economy status with China . . . would be cataclysmic for the WTO.'[110]

The increasing self-awareness of an independent Chinese approach is also revealed in the concrete steps that China has taken to explore and construct its own international courts. On 28 June 2018, the Supreme People's Court of the PRC (SPC) announced that China would establish two international commercial courts in July – one in Shenzhen, for disputes arising from the Maritime Silk Road; and one in Xi'an, for disputes from the overland 'Belt' – for resolving commercial and investment disputes arising out of projects forming part of the BRI.[111] Although the courts were initially designated as a place to hear disputes between commercial parties, their establishment appears to be a strong signal of China's desire to play a more expansive role in international adjudication – whilst China is emerging as the world's economic and political power, until today it has only actively engaged in WTO adjudication. Thus, many expectations have been placed on the creation of the courts. First, it is supposed to serve the BRI and become an international dispute resolution hub like those in London, Singapore and Hong Kong.[112] Second, given the worldwide trend of establishing courts to hear investor-state disputes (e.g. the investment court under the Comprehensive Economic and Trade Agreement (CETA)), the courts are regarded as an initial step to explore whether China can do so as well.[113] Third, as some European observers have pointed out, the courts reflect China's hope to become a great judicial power in international adjudication.[114]

Challenges

It is too soon to tell for certain whether the Chinese approach will develop rapidly and propose a new mechanism of international adjudication that can supplement and coexist with the dominant Western one. The road ahead will not be easy.

The risks of a backlash against China from the existing regime may increase. Samuel Huntington, in *The Clash of Civilizations*, predicted that China and the West, as two different cultural groups, would compete for relative military and economic strength, struggle over the control of international institutions, and competitively promote their particular political, cultural and religious values.[115]

110 'Lighthizer: U.S. loss in China NME dispute would be "cataclysmic" for WTO' (*World Trade Online*, 23 June 2017) <https://insidetrade.com/inside-us-trade/lighthizer-us-loss-china-nme-dispute-would-be-cataclysmic-wto> accessed 1 July 2017.

111 'China to launch two international commercial courts' (*Xinhuanet*, 2 July 2018) <http://www.xinhuanet.com/english/2018-06/28/c_137287616.htm> accessed 2 July 2018.

112 Susan Finder, 'Update on China's International Commercial Court' (*Supreme People's Court Monitor*, 11 March 2018) <https://supremepeoplescourtmonitor.com/2018/03/11/update-on-chinas-international-commercial-court/> accessed 22 June 2018.

113 Ibid.

114 'New Courts for the Belt and Road Initiative' (*OBOREurope*, 2 June 2018) <http://www.oboreurope.com/en/bri-courts/> accessed 13 June 2018.

115 Samuel P Huntington, *The Clash of Civilizations and the Remaking of World Order* (Simon & Schuster 1996) 28–29.

Huntington's prediction parallels the longstanding 'China threat' theory which believes that China, with its long-term objectives that are not compatible with the international (mostly Western) system, values and beliefs, would constitute a major threat to world peace and development.[116] Indeed, China's culture, historical development and socialist polity have created a view of law that may be distinguished from the mainstream international legal regime. For example, China has shown reluctance to being heavily involved in international adjudication relating to human rights, arguing that its conception of rights prioritise collective (e.g. state sovereignty) rather than individual rights.[117] This reflects an apparent incompatibility between China and the existing international legal regime in which human rights occupy an important place.

The significant distinctions between China and the existing regime in legal values and concepts could make the Chinese approach less likely to be accepted and supported by other states. Perhaps China can employ its political, economic and even military power to have the approach endorsed: for example, states that are economically dependent upon China, such as those in Africa, the Middle East and Central Asia, have voiced their support for China's '4 Noes' policy towards the South China Sea Arbitration.[118] However, it is uncertain at this stage whether the Chinese approach will also represent the voices and interests of other states (especially developing states), or whether it will attract more buy-in and form a strong power base that can influence the existing international legal regime.

It is also too early to say whether China can transform from a rule-taker to a rule-maker and whether it will be competent in its new role. The West may treat China's rise as a major rule-maker in the international legal regime as an irreversible trend. Yet it is possible that the Chinese approach to international adjudication could go off the rails with potentially disastrous consequences; for a century, China's focus has been on how to act within the existing rules, and it remains to be seen how it will behave as its ability to change the rules increases.

At present, numerous issues loom over China. The cases on China's MES are still pending, and it is difficult to predict what the panels will decide. If the judges rule against China, the outcome will have major repercussions. Another challenge is how to build the international commercial courts. The normal trajectory for establishing an international tribunal or court is top-down: state(s) at the outset define(s) a fixed, clear, unified legal framework with pre-established rules and principles that can operate in the court/tribunal for collective management of resources and issues. However, as many observers have noted, it appears to be impossible for China to provide the courts with such a framework, for too many changes would need to be made to the existing Chinese legal system to

116 See e.g. Shaun Breslin, 'China's Emerging Global Role: Dissatisfied Responsible Great Power' (2010) 30 Politics 52.

117 Raymond John Vincent, *Human Rights and International Relations* (Cambridge University Press 1986) 41–42.

118 'African countries back China's approach to South China Sea dispute' (*Xinhuanet*, 9 July 2016) <http://news.xinhuanet.com/english/2016-07/09/c_135500830.htm> accessed 10 July 2017.

accommodate international courts.[119] The Judges Law may be amended, because it currently prohibits foreign judges[120] – but without an international panel, how can an international court be called 'international'? Another factor is the language issue, since the Chinese Civil Procedure Law provides that only Chinese can be used in proceedings.[121] Whether foreign lawyers can handle cases and appear before the court is also a problem, because the Civil Procedure Law requests foreigners and foreign enterprises to appoint Chinese lawyers to represent them in proceedings.[122]

Conclusion

One prevailing presumption in the existing scholarship on international adjudication is that the proliferation of international courts and tribunals requires standards of adjudication in developing non-Western states to be brought into line with those of the developed Western world. As the study of China suggests, however, we can no longer assume that influence flows only one way from the West to the non-Western world. More attention needs to be focused on the ways in which change is already moving in the other direction and will do so increasingly in the years ahead.

Do the emerging non-Western approaches, in particular the Chinese approach, necessarily generate fundamentally different, or even challenging paradigms and lead to a clash with the established Western-led international adjudicatory regime? People who ask this question tend to conceive the Western and non-Western approaches in a mutually exclusive and conflicting manner, assuming that non-Western states like China would abandon the Western paradigm and develop their own perspectives, rules and institutions for international adjudication. Admittedly, differences between the Western and the non-Western approaches exist, but they are not impossible to reconcile. Both sides are not fixed in stone; in fact, they are evolving like organisms. The Chinese are traditionally said to be less legalistic and more prone to settle disputes out of court, but their performance in the WTO suggests that China's recourse to adjudication can be like that of the West. Similarly, even within the West where there is a strong legal tradition, some states are also reluctant to resort to international courts and tribunals.

We should avoid viewing future international adjudication as a battlefield of competing values, perspectives and approaches. International adjudication is developed not only for the realisation of certain values, but also for the promotion of peaceful coexistence and the cooperation of different values and belief systems.[123] The dominance of one approach in the long term will hamper this mission

119 See e.g. Finder (n 112).
120 Article 9 (1) of Judges Law of the People's Republic of China.
121 Article 240 of Civil Procedure Law.
122 Article 241 of Civil Procedure Law.
123 Andreas Paulus, 'International Adjudication' in Samantha Besson and John Tasioulas (eds.), *The Philosophy of International Law* (Oxford University Press 2010) 217.

and undermine the legitimacy of international adjudication: non-Western states may reject the jurisdiction of an international court or tribunal that heavily relies on the Western approach because they consider it contrary to their interests, and vice versa. In this sense, a plurality of approaches to international adjudication may be beneficial. The real issue for future international adjudication is how to accommodate global interests on the one hand, and diverse approaches on the other.

5 The crisis of the European Court of Human Rights in the face of authoritarian and populist regimes

*Bill Bowring**

Introduction

This chapter asks whether the future of the European Court of Human Rights (ECtHR) has recently been compromised by the Court's apparent deference to three states which have at different times perpetrated gross violations of human rights in the context of internal armed conflict: Turkey, Russia and the United Kingdom. More than one commentator has raised the question whether the decisions of the ECtHR were 'politically motivated'. I therefore analyse recent developments in respect of each of these countries in turn, concluding with some observations on the current state of affairs. I do not pretend to be able to predict the future of the ECtHR, but it is surely less certain than it appeared to be some years ago.

My own experience taking cases to Strasbourg against Turkey and Russia

Ten years ago, in 2008, I participated in a conference in Ankara organised by the leading Turkish human rights scholar and activist, Kerem Altiparmak. The following year he published an edited collection which contains my only article in Turkish.[1] In my presentation at the conference and in the article I reflected on ten

* An outline of this chapter was delivered as a paper at the conference in Istanbul on 7–9 September 2018, of the Istanbul Bar Association, *International Conference on Law, State of Emergency and Judicial System in Turkey-2*, where useful feedback and suggestions were given. See <www.eldh.eu/events/event/dark-side-of-the-moon-2-the-normalization-of-the-state-of-emergency-and-the-situation-of-judiciary-in-turkey-307/> accessed 21 September 2018. I am the president of the European Lawyers for Democracy and Human Rights (ELDH), in 21 European countries: the two main progressive lawyers' organisations in Turkey are members, Progressive Lawyers Association (Çağdaş Hukukçular Derneği) CHD, and Platform of Lawyers for Freedom (Özgürlükçü Hukukçular Platformu), ÖHP.

1 Bill Bowring, 'Avrupa İnsan Hakları Mahkemesi İçtihadında Parçalanma, lex specialis ve Gerilimler' (Gökçen Alpkaya ile birlikte) 50. Yılında Avrupa İnsan Hakları Mahkemesi: Başarı mı Hayal Kırıklığı mı?, (Yay. Haz. Kerem Altıparmak), (2009) Ankara Barosu Yayınları, Ankara, s. 206–221. This appeared in English as Bill Bowring, 'Fragmentation, *Lex Specialis* and the

years of taking cases on behalf of Kurdish applicants against Turkey from 1992, and eight years taking cases on behalf of Chechen applicants against Russia.

Turkish cases

My most important cases against Turkey (I was advocate in about 30 cases) were *Özgür Gündem v Turkey*,[2] *Aktaş v Turkey*,[3] and *İpek v Turkey*.[4] These were important cases, but it will be noted that the first case took seven years from lodging the application, the second nine years, and the third ten years. Of course, the gross violations of human rights in each case predated the application. This is for certain a violation, by the ECtHR, of the right in Article 6 of the ECHR to a hearing 'within a reasonable time'.

In Ankara I asked the question – why on earth the applicants wanted to take a case to the ECtHR, when the case would take so many years.

The applicant in İpek, Abdurrezak İpek, who was born in 1942, suffered the 'disappearance' of his two sons, Servet and İkram İpek, in the course of an operation conducted by security forces in his village on 18 May 1994. His village was also burned to the ground. He was then 52. From 18 to 20 November 2002, when he was 60, he gave evidence to the ECtHR sitting in the Turkish Supreme Court in Ankara. I represented him. The Court held that:

> . . . taking into account that no information has come to light concerning the whereabouts of the applicant's sons for almost nine and a half years, the Court is satisfied that Servet and İkram İpek must be presumed dead following their unacknowledged detention by the security forces. Consequently, the responsibility of the respondent State for their death is engaged. Noting that the authorities have not provided any explanation as to what occurred following the İpek brothers' apprehension, and that they do not rely on any ground of justification in respect of any use of lethal force by their agents, it follows that liability for their death is attributable to the respondent Government. Accordingly, there has been a violation of Article 2 on that account.[5]

That is, Turkey murdered his sons. The ECtHR awarded him €51,400 in compensation.

Tensions in the Jurisprudence of the European Court of Human Rights' (2009) 14 *Journal of Conflict and Security Law* 485.

2 *Özgür Gündem v Turkey* App no 22492/93 (ECtHR, 16 March 2000); Turkish Kurdish newspaper, violations of Article 10, freedom of expression – also positive duty under Article 10 to protect freedom of expression.

3 *Aktaş v Turkey* App no 24351/94 (ECtHR, 24 April 2003); death of young man in police custody – oral fact-finding hearing in Turkey – findings of torture and death by asphyxiation – violations of Articles 2 and 3.

4 *İpek v Turkey* App 25760/94 (ECtHR, 17 February 2004; abduction by Turkish army of two of the applicant's sons – oral fact-finding hearing in Turkey – violations of article 2 and 3.

5 Ibid. [168].

I need not emphasise that Mr İpek did not go to the ECtHR and wait ten years, 12 from the events concerned, in order to receive some money. His prime motivation in taking his case was not even the search for justice. The perpetrators of the murder of his sons have never been brought to trial. He, like my other Kurdish and Chechen clients, demanded vindication of the truth as to what had happened to them and to their children.[6] In his own case the Turkish government went to extraordinary lengths for several years to try to persuade the Court that nothing had happened to Mr İpek or his sons, and that there was no case for Turkey to answer.

I had personal experience of the consistent practice of the Turkish state in accusing advocates of the very crimes for which their clients are accused. For example, in the oral hearing in Strasbourg in *Özgür Gündem v Turkey*, the Turkish government representative turned to me in front of the judges and shouted, 'Professor Bowring is a terrorist! He is a member of the PKK!', because I was representing a newspaper accused of inciting terrorism. The ECtHR held that the newspaper had not incited terrorism: in fact, it had used the words 'Kurd' and 'Kurdish', which Turkey considered to be 'separatism', and therefore terrorism.

Russian cases

I started taking cases against Russia in 2000; Russia ratified the ECHR in 1998. In 2003 I obtained a grant of €1 million from the EC's Human Rights and Democracy Initiative, and founded the European Human Rights Advocacy Centre (EHRAC),[7] in partnership with the Bar Human Rights Committee of England and Wales (BHRC)[8] and the leading Russian civil society organisation 'Memorial', and its Human Rights Centre.[9]

My activity started a few years earlier. In September 1999 the then prime minister of Russia started the Second Chechen War – the Russian Federation had lost the First Chechen War, 1994–1997, and Chechnya was de facto independent for two years. This was an act of revenge. On 24 September 1999, at a press conference in Astana, while the capital of Chechnya, Grozny, was being bombed by Federal Russian bombers, Mr Putin said, using the language of street gangsters: 'We will pursue the terrorists everywhere. If they are in the airport – at the airport. So, you'll excuse me, if we catch them in the toilet, we'll piss on them in the toilet, after all. We will do everything, and that's the end of it.'[10]

6 See for example Dermot Groome, 'The Right to Truth in the Fight against Impunity' (2011) 29 *Berkeley Journal of International Law* 175; Federico Fabbrini, 'The European Court of Human Rights, Extraordinary Renditions and the Right to the Truth: Ensuring Accountability for Gross Human Rights Violations Committed in the Fight Against Terrorism' (2014) 14 *Human Rights Law Review* 85, 85–106.

7 <http://ehrac.org.uk/> accessed 21 September 2018.

8 <www.barhumanrights.org.uk/> and <www.barhumanrights.org.uk/country/russia/> both accessed 21 September 2018.

9 <www.memo.ru/ru-ru/pravozashita/> in Russian, accessed 21 September 2018.

10 See more, 'Putin's Chechen Remark Causes Stir' (*BBC News*, 13 November 2002) <http://news.bbc.co.uk/1/hi/world/europe/2460305.stm> accessed 21 September 2018, and

At the beginning of 2000 with Memorial I helped to start the first six Chechen cases against Russia, representing the mothers of children who were killed in the Russian bombardment of a refugee column, and victims of massacres in Grozny and another town, *Isayeva and others v Russia*.[11] Russia denied that any such things had happened. On 24 February 2005 the ECtHR delivered a set of detailed judgments, establishing what the applicants wanted – the incontrovertible truth of what had happened to them and their families.

Since then I and my EHRAC colleagues have represented Chechen victims of a range of gross violations of their rights at the hands of the Russian Federation.[12] For example, April 2017 marked an important milestone for survivors and victims' families in their 13-year battle for justice, as the ECtHR ruled that failings in the Russian authorities' response to the Beslan school siege contributed to the 334 fatalities and hundreds of casualties in 2004. In a robust judgment, the Court found that the authorities had failed to take preventative measures despite prior intelligence about such an attack, and that there were serious shortcomings in the planning and control of the security operation.[13]

In my presentation in Ankara I spoke with guarded optimism about taking cases to the ECtHR, and why victims of violations should be encouraged to take their cases and to wait for years for a result. Ten years later, was my optimism justified?

Turkey since the attempted coup

The attempted coup took place on 15 July 2016. On 6 June 2017 a chamber of the ECtHR ruled that the application in *Gökhan Köksal v Turkey*[14] was inadmissible.[15] The case concerned a teacher's dismissal by emergency Decree No. 672,[16] along with 50,875 other public servants who were regarded as having membership of or an affiliation, link or connection with terrorist organisations or structures, formations or groups determined by the National Security Council to engage in activities against the national security of the Turkish state.

The applicant complained of a breach of his right of access to a court, his right to be presumed innocent and his right to be informed of the accusation against

also for analysis Gregory Simons, 'The Use of Rhetoric and the Mass Media in Russia's War on Terror' (2006) arbetsrapporter Working Papers No. 98, <https://uu.diva-portal.org/smash/get/diva2:131143/FULLTEXT01.pdf> accessed 21 September 2018.

11 *Isayeva and others v Russia* App nos. 57947–9/00 (ECtHR, 24 February 2005).

12 See for a brief summary Bill Bowring, 'Ten years of successful litigation at the European Court of Human Rights' (*Counsel*, December 2013) <www.counselmagazine.co.uk/articles/ten-years-of-successful-litigation-the-european-court-of-human-rights> accessed 21 September 2018.

13 <http://ehrac.org.uk/about-our-work/where-we-work/russia/#northcaucasus> accessed 21 September 2018.

14 *Köksal v Turkey* App no 70478/16 (ECtHR, 6 June 2017) (only available in French and Turkish).

15 For analysis, see Emre Turkut, 'The Köksal Case Before the Strasbourg Court: A Pattern of Violations or a Mere Aberration?' (*Strasbourg Observers*, 2 August 2017) <https://strasbourgobservers.com/2017/08/02/the-koksal-case-before-the-strasbourg-court-a-pattern-of-violations-or-a-mere-aberration/#more-3868> accessed 21 September 2018.

16 Text in English at <https://rm.coe.int/16806a2e17> accessed 21 September 2018.

him (Article 6 paragraphs 1, 2 and 3 (a) of the European Convention of Human Rights (ECHR). He also complained that he had been dismissed on the basis of acts which did not constitute a criminal offence at the time they were committed (Article 7 – no punishment without law), and that his rights and freedoms under Articles 8 (right to respect for private and family life), 10 (freedom of expression), 11 (freedom of assembly and association), 13 (right to an effective remedy) and 14 (prohibition of discrimination) had been violated.

The Court dismissed the application for failure to exhaust domestic remedies, finding that a new remedy was available to the applicant, provided by Decree No. 685,[17] which was adopted on 2 January 2017. Decree No. 685 provided for the creation of a commission, namely the 'State of Emergency Inquiry Commission', tasked with assessing the measures adopted directly by the emergency decrees issued in the context of the state of emergency, including the dismissals of civil servants. After several months, the rules of procedure of the Commission were finally published on 12 July and the Commission finally began receiving applications on 17 July.

Kerem Altiparmak has provided a highly convincing explanation as to why the Commission cannot be an effective remedy.[18] Emre Turkut too concluded that '. . . the Strasbourg Court has adopted a narrow approach in order to reduce the overwhelming number of pending cases before it and has thus turned a blind eye to the shattered lives of the purged public servants in Turkey.'[19] He pointed out that this is against the background of the fact the ECtHR is granting a wider margin of appreciation to states by providing more subsidiarity, particularly with regard to Article 35, over the past half-decade following the Brighton Declaration.[20] Oleg Soldatov and Gülden Deniz Tokmak went further:[21]

> . . . some of the decisions of the European Court of Human Rights could be regarded as politically motivated: the way the judges are appointed to the Court[22] and the dynamics of relationships between the Court and the Council of Europe Member States[23] are vaguely hinting at this. At the same time,

17 Text in English via the Venice Commission at <www.venice.coe.int/webforms/documents/default.aspx?pdffile=CDL-REF(2017)014-e> accessed 21 September 2018.

18 Kerem Altiparmak, 'Is the State of Emergency Inquiry Commission, Established by Emergency Decree 685, an Effective Remedy?' 23 February 2017) <https://papers.ssrn.com/sol3/papers.cfm?abstract_id=2943518> accessed 21 September 2018.

19 Turkut (n 16).

20 See on this Mikael Madsen, 'Rebalancing European Human Rights: Has the Brighton Declaration Engendered a New Deal on Human Rights in Europe?' (2018) 9 *Journal of International Dispute Settlement* 199.

21 Oleg Soldatov and Gülden Deniz Tokmak, 'Köksal v. Turkey: Excessive Formalism or Strict Adherence to Admissibility Criteria?' (*Resource Centre on Media Freedom in Europe*, 11 January 2018) <www.rcmediafreedom.eu/Tools/Legal-Resources/Koeksal-v.-Turkey-Excessive-Formalism-or-Strict-Adherence-to-Admissibility-Criteria> accessed 21 September 2018.

22 Erik Voeten, 'The Politics of International Judicial Appointments: Evidence from the European Court of Human Rights' (2007) 61 *International Organization* 669.

23 Roger Masterman, *Supreme, Submissive or Symbiotic? United Kingdom Courts and the European Court of Human Rights* (The Constitution Unit 2015).

> if one hypothesizes that this inadmissibility decision in the Köksal category of cases was part of the efforts of the Council of Europe community to 'pacify' Turkey and to leave room for future negotiations on other issues, this tactic has most likely failed: Turkey withdrew its extra-budgetary funding of the Council of Europe.[24]

On 9 March 2018 the Rules Committee of the Parliamentary Assembly of the Council of Europe (PACE) proposed that Turkish should be removed from PACE's list of working languages. According to the committee, 'the draconian reduction' of the Assembly's budget for 2018 and 2019 – which is a consequence, among other things, of the Turkish decision to return to its original status as an ordinary contributor to the Council of Europe budget – 'calls for drastic measures'.[25]

At the Istanbul Bar Association conference this year, Kerem Altiparmak argued that the ECtHR should find that the actions of the Turkish government since 2016 amount to an 'administrative practice'.[26] The former Commission of Human Rights had stated, in the Greek case,[27] that, where

> there is a practice of non-observance of certain Convention provisions, the remedies prescribed will of necessity be side-stepped or rendered inadequate. Thus, if there were an administrative practice of torture or ill-treatment, judicial remedies prescribed would tend to be rendered ineffective by the difficulty of securing probative evidence, and administrative enquiries would either be not instituted, or, if they were, would be likely to be half-hearted and incomplete.

Kevin Boyle and Hurst Hannum, counsel in *Donnelly v United Kingdom*,[28] took the view[29] that:

> It is difficult to consider separately the two primary holdings, concerning the competence of the individual to raise the substantive issue of the

24 'Turkey Withdraws as Main Contributor in European Council, Cites Monitoring Process' *Daily Sabah* (Ankara, 9 November 2017) <www.dailysabah.com/politics/2017/11/10/turkey-withdraws-as-main-contributor-in-european-council-cites-monitoring-process> accessed 21 September 2018.

25 'Budgetary Crisis at the Council Of Europe: Rules Committee Outlines Impact on the Work of the Assembly' (*Parliamentary Assembly*, 9 March 2018) <http://assembly.coe.int/nw/xml/News/News-View-EN.asp?newsid=6984&lang=2&cat=28> accessed 21 September 2018.

26 See Kevin Boyle and Hurst Hannum, 'Individual Applications under the European Convention on Human Rights and the Concept of Administrative Practice: The Donnelly Case' (1974) 68 *American Journal of International Law* 440, 440–453.

27 *The Greek Case* App nos. 3321–3/67, 3344/67 Series 12(A) (Report of the Commission, 1969) 12 Yearbook 194.

28 *Donnelly and others v. the United Kingdom* App nos. 5577–5583/72 (ECtHR, 15 December 1975).

29 Boyle and Hannum (n 27) 452.

> existence of an administrative practice contrary to the Convention and the effect of such an alleged practice on the exhaustion of domestic remedies rule, for each is strongly supportive of the other. In addition, it is clear from a reading of the Commission's decision that both are based on the similar premise of the inherent equality of procedures under Articles 24 and 25 (apart from the specific distinctions set out in Article 25 itself and Article 27(1) and (2)).

But even if the ECtHR held that Turkey was responsible for an 'administrative practice', so that Turkish applicants were no longer required to exhaust domestic remedies, there would be no guarantee that the ECtHR would find in their favour on the merits.

Russia

As I already mentioned, Turkey has withdrawn its extra-budgetary funding from the Council of Europe (CoE). Russia is now paying no money at all to the CoE. This poses a very serious problem: Turkey, Russia and the UK are three of the six states which contribute an exceptionally large amount to the CoE's budget. On 16 March 2018 *The Guardian* reported that the CoE is facing 'an unprecedented budgetary crisis', following Russia's decision to suspend payments in 2017 over its representation in the council's Strasbourg assembly and Turkey's decision to slash its contributions. The CoE faces a shortfall of at least €42.65m (£37.6m), 10% of its annual budget, meaning it could be forced to cut jobs.[30]

Following Russia's illegal annexation of Crimea in 2014,[31] PACE imposed sanctions on the Russian delegation. On 28 January 2015 it decided to ratify the credentials of the Russian delegation, citing the need to 'foster dialogue', but at the same time decided to suspend its voting rights and its right to be represented in the Assembly's leading bodies 'as a clear expression of condemnation of continuing grave violations of international law in respect of Ukraine' by Russia. In addition, PACE also suspended – for the duration of the Assembly's 2015 session – the right of its Russian members to be appointed as a rapporteur, to observe elections or to represent the Assembly in other CoE or external bodies.[32] These sanctions have been continued.

30 Jennifer Rankin, 'Human Rights Body Faces Cash Crisis After Clash with Russia' *The Guardian* (Brussels, 16 March 2018) <www.theguardian.com/law/2018/mar/16/human-rights-body-faces-cash-crisis-after-clash-with-russia> accessed 21 September 2018.

31 See Bill Bowring, 'Who Are the "Crimean People" or "People of Crimea"? The Fate of the Crimean Tatars, Russia's Legal Justification for Annexation, and Pandora's Box' in Sergey Sayapin and Evhen Tsybulenko (eds.) *The Use of Force against Ukraine and International Law: Jus Ad Bellum, Jus In Bello, Jus Post Bellum* (T M C Asser Press 2018) 21–40.

32 'Citing Ukraine, PACE Renews Sanctions Against Russian Delegation' (*Parliamentary Assembly*, 28 January 2015) <http://assembly.coe.int/nw/xml/News/News-View-EN.asp?newsid=5410&lang=2&cat=8> accessed 21 September 2018.

However, on 22 January 2018 the secretary general of the CoE, Thorbjorn Jagland, said that sanctions against the Russian Federation should be removed in order to restore its participation in PACE by 2019.[33]

The June 2018 CoE visit to Russia

From 19–21 June 2018, Mr Jagland went to Russia on a working visit. The fact of his visit, to meet President Putin, Minister of Foreign Affairs Lavrov, and Human Rights Ombudsman Moskalkova, was reported very briefly on the CoE website.[34] However, in what follows I have deliberately set out at greater length than usual what was said by various protagonists. This is highly relevant to my overall argument in this chapter.

The Russian Ministry of Foreign Affairs provided its own commentary on 19 June 2018.[35] It recalled that Russia had joined the CoE on 28 February 1996, becoming the 39th member state, and had ratified 65 conventions and protocols out of the 224 CoE legal documents, including the ECHR,[36] the European Convention for the Prevention of Torture (CPT), the European Social Charter and the European Cultural Convention. In 2017–2018 alone, Russia had ratified six important Council of Europe documents, including the Convention on an Integrated Safety, Security and Service Approach at Football Matches and Other Sports Events, the Convention on Laundering, Search, Seizure and Confiscation of the Proceeds from Crime and on the Financing of Terrorism, and the Convention on the Counterfeiting of Medical Products and Similar Crimes Involving Threats to Public Health (Medicrime Convention).

The Russian MFA added:

> Russia is currently actively involved in all the entities of the Council of Europe, except for its Parliamentary Assembly (PACE). Unfortunately, CE's parliamentary dimension was taken hostage by a rather small, albeit well-organised, group of people representing anti-Russia forces.

33 'PACE Should Remove Sanctions Against Russia by 2019, Jagland Says' (*Research Concorde Capital*, 23 January 2018) <https://concorde.ua/rs/daily/item_72621/> accessed 21 September 2018.

34 'Secretary General Jagland to meet Russian President Putin and Foreign Minister Lavrov in Moscow' (*Council of Europe*, 19 June 2019) <www.coe.int/en/web/portal/-/secretary-general-jagland-to-meet-russian-president-putin-and-foreign-minister-lavrov-in-moscow> accessed 21 September 2018.

35 'Comment by the Information and Press Department on the Upcoming Visit of Secretary General of the Council of Europe Thorbjorn Jagland' (*The Ministry of Foreign Affairs of the Russian Federation*, 19 June 2018) <www.mid.ru/en/foreign_policy/news/-/asset_publisher/cKNonkJE02Bw/content/id/3263025> accessed 21 September 2018.

36 See Bill Bowring, 'Politics and Pragmatism: The Constitutional Court of the Russian Federation and Its 20 Years of Engagement with the European Convention on Human Rights' (2018) 1 *East European Yearbook on Human Rights* 5, 5–31.

> Seeking to express its concern over the deepening crisis within PACE, the Russian Federation decided not to pay its contributions to the Council of Europe for 2017 until the delegation of the Federal Assembly of the Russian Federation is fully and unconditionally restored in its rights within the Parliamentary Assembly. At the same time, the Russian Federation remains proactive within the Council of Europe, and continues to honour its commitments under conventions it has acceded to.[37]

The Russian media reported that Mr Jagland had congratulated Russia on successfully hosting the football world championship.[38] Mr Jagland's comments were published verbatim on the Kremlin's website.[39] As to Russia's problems with the CoE, Mr Jagland said:

> There is always a lot of focus on the European Court, and for all of the member countries there are judgments that they dislike, but, all in all, I would say that the justice of the court has been very important for all of the member states.
>
> We have here a small brochure, which shows how the court has influenced, in a positive way, many ways of life in the Russian Federation. This is, actually, the meaning of the court: to help its member states come closer together by adopting laws that are in conformity with the Convention. So again, thank you for all these twenty years and thank you for your strong commitment to the Council of Europe.

Mr Lavrov said, in his meeting with Mr Jagland:

> Today, we cannot fail to mention that the organisation is going through a system-wide crisis related to the situation within the Parliamentary Assembly of the Council of Europe. We greatly appreciate your efforts to find a way out of this crisis, Mr Secretary General. The solution must be based on the principles that govern the work of the Council of Europe and were devised by its founding fathers. One of these principles is equality among all member countries.[40]

37 See n 36.

38 'Ягланд на встрече с Путиным назвал успешным проведение ЧМ-2018' (*TVC*, 20 June 2018) <www.tvc.ru/news/show/id/140043> accessed 21 September 2018.

39 'Встреча с Генеральным секретарём Совета Европы Турбьёрном Ягландом' (*Kremlin*, 20 June 2018) <http://kremlin.ru/events/president/news/57818> accessed 21 September 2018.

40 'Foreign Minister Sergey Lavrov's Opening Remarks at the Talks with Secretary General of the Council of Europe Thorbjørn Jagland, Moscow, June 20, 2018' (*Embassy of the Russian Federation in Ireland,* 20 June 2018) <https://ireland.mid.ru/web/ireland_/home/-/asset_publisher/jMdQKPys2LHL/content/foreign-minister-sergey-lavrov-s-opening-remarks-at-the-talks-with-secretary-general-of-the-council-of-europe-thorbj-rn-jagland-moscow-june-20-2018?inheritRedirect=false> accessed 21 September 2018.

Mr Jagland did not raise the question of Ukrainian political prisoners with Mr Putin, although it was reported that he had raised it with Mr Lavrov and Ms Moskalkova.[41]

Finally, on 24 June 2018, Mr Jagland finally submitted a petition to Russia in his capacity as secretary general of the CoE, pursuant to the ECHR, calling on President Putin to pardon the Ukrainian filmmaker Oleh Sentsov, illegally, according to experts, convicted in Russia.[42] And on 19 September 2018 the EU's Justice Commissioner Věra Jourová called on Russian Justice Minister Alexander Konovalov to release Mr Sentsov from the Russian prison where he has been in custody for more than four years.[43] Mr Sentsov was arrested in 2014 and sentenced to 20 years in jail on terrorism charges. He is a vocal critic of Russia's annexation of Crimea. He has been on hunger strike since May 2018, calling for the release of 64 Ukrainians he says are also political prisoners.

Mr Sentsov complained to the European Court of Human Rights following his arrest in 2014, and on 8 July 2014 his application was given priority. On 21 June 2018 Natasha Dobreva, Sentsov's lawyer at the ECHR and a representative of the international human rights group Agora reported that the ECtHR is asking the Russian authorities to provide all available information about the state of health of Mr Sentsov, on the 38th day of a hunger strike. She said: 'The Court sent a request to the Government of Russia on information on compliance with the requirements of articles 2 (the right to life), 3 (prohibition of torture) and 4 (prohibition of forced labour) of the Convention for the Protection of Human Rights and Fundamental Freedoms in connection with [Sentsov's] hunger [strike].'[44]

According to Ms Dobreva, the ECHR also asked for the provision of information about Mr Sentsov's current condition, as well as his medical documentation prior to 27 June.

A politically motivated denial of justice?

Despite these recent interventions, it remains the case that Mr Sentsov's application was lodged with the Court, and given priority status, more than four years ago. A recent comment asks whether the ECtHR is guilty of a politically motivated denial of justice.[45] The article cites Pavel Chikov, who leads Agora and is

41 'CoE Secretary General Jagland to Submit Petition to Putin for Pardoning Sentsov' (*Unian*, 24 June 2018) <www.unian.info/politics/10163789-coe-secretary-general-jagland-to-submit-petition-to-putin-for-pardoning-sentsov.html> accessed 21 September 2018.

42 Ibid.

43 'EU Calls on Russia to Release Ukrainian Filmmaker Oleh Sentsov – Media' (*UNIAN*, 19 September 2018) <www.unian.info/politics/10266075-eu-calls-on-russia-to-release-ukrainian-filmmaker-oleh-sentsov-media.html> accessed 21 September 2018.

44 'European Court of Human Rights Asks Russia to Provide Information about Sentsov's Health' (*UAWIRE*, 21 June 2018) <www.uawire.org/european-court-of-human-rights-asks-russia-to-provide-information-about-sentsov-s-health> accessed 21 September 2018.

45 Halya Coynash, 'The European Court of Human Rights' Politically-Motivated Denial of Justice for Oleg Sentsov' (*KHPG*, 31 August 2018) <http://khpg.org/en/index.php?id=1535462098> accessed 21 September 2018.

another lawyer in the ECtHR case, as saying that he believes that the Court is taking so long to consider Mr Sentsov's case because it does not want to address the issue of Russia's annexation of Crimea. He added that there is no point in expecting a judgment in less than a year and that the ECtHR is somewhere 'in the middle' of the process. In fact, even a year seems optimistic as there is no sign of movement at all.

Asked on *Hromadske Radio* why the ECtHR is taking its time with the case, Mr Chikov suggested that the issue cannot be resolved without addressing the issue of Crimea's legal status. The Sentsov case is very complex, he says, and unquestionably political: 'It concerns the legal status of Crimea which arouses very serious discussion within the Council of Europe and European Court of Human Rights. The European Court is evidently unwilling to raise the issue and give its assessment.'[46] This is despite universal condemnation of Russia's annexation of Crimea, and findings by authoritative bodies that it was illegal. Halya Coynash added that it was impossible not to agree with Mr Chikov that the ECtHR's delaying tactics do not cast them in a good light. While it is not at all guaranteed that Mr Sentsov would be released merely on the basis of an ECtHR judgment, the lack of such a judgment helps Russia to continue lying both about the charges against him, and about the fact that he has only Ukrainian citizenship.[47]

Foreign agents

The case of Mr Sentsov is not the only controversial case in which the ECtHR has more than taken its time. In July 2012, the Russian parliament enacted legislative amendments concerning civil society organisations (CSOs), which are collectively known as the 'Foreign Agents Act'.

Russian organisations receiving any funding at all from any foreign donors, or from other Russian organisations receiving foreign funding, and which engage in 'political activity' very widely defined, are required to register as 'foreign agents'. Any organisation carrying that label is subject to stricter accounting requirements than other CSOs, and must report to the Ministry of Justice more frequently on how it spends its funds. Publications by 'foreign agents' must be labelled as such; failure to comply with this provision leads to the risk of substantial fines. The term 'foreign agent' implies spying and illicit activity as a result of the term's usage during the Soviet era. CSOs are faced with a difficult choice: either receive foreign funding and accept the repercussions of the label; or rely exclusively on Russian sources, including presidential or governmental grants, which may result in a loss of independence and self-censorship. In June 2018, according the Ministry of Justice, there were currently 76 NGOs on the 'foreign agents' register. A total of 158 groups have been designated as 'foreign agents' to date, including

46 Ibid.

47 See Halya Coynash 'Russia Pushes Lies and Defamation While Hiding Sentsov Who Is Reportedly Very Weak' (*KHPG*, 29 June 2018) <http://khpg.org/index.php?id=1530232129> accessed 21 September 2018.

30 which have shut down rather than bear the label, and more than 40 which have stopped accepting foreign funding.[48]

On 6 February 2013 the EHRAC lodged a 'collective complaint' to the ECtHR on behalf of several of the affected CSOs, and altogether there are now 49 applications to the ECtHR.[49]

However, these cases were not communicated to Russia until 22 March 2017,[50] four years after lodging the application, despite the fact that the Act had been condemned by the CoE's own Commissioner for Human Rights in 2013[51] and 2015,[52] the CoE's Venice Commission in 2014,[53] the Human Rights Resource Centre in 2015, and Amnesty International in 2016. On 5 July 2017 the Commissioner lodged a Third Party Intervention in the case,[54] as did Amnesty International and the International Commission of Jurists on 3 October 2017.[55] On 12 March 2018 EHRAC lodged its Reply to the Russian Government Observations. Again, the case is highly unlikely to be decided for at least a year.

It is not possible to find out what has been going on behind closed doors at the CoE in Strasbourg. But it is clear from the public materials reviewed above that the COE, led by Mr Jagland, is doing everything it can to prevent Russia from 'crashing out' of the ECHR system as a result of sanctions imposed because of the annexation of Crimea. I noted above that Mr Jagland is on record as insisting that sanctions must be lifted by 2019; and his efforts are greatly appreciated by Russia.

The United Kingdom

As I indicated at the start, the United Kingdom has joined Turkey and Russia as a state which, in the context of the internal armed conflict in Northern Ireland from

48 See European Human Rights Advocacy Centre (EHRAC), 'The 'Foreign Agents Act' is Stifling Independent Civil Society' (*EHRAC*, 12 March 2018) <http://ehrac.org.uk/news/foreign-agents-act-stifling-independent-civil-society/> accessed 21 September 2018.

49 Application no. 9988/13 ECODEFENCE and others against Russia and 48 other applications.

50 *Ecodefence and ors Against Russia and 48 other applications* App no 9988/13 (ECtHR, 22 March 2017).

51 <https://rm.coe.int/opinion-of-the-commissioner-for-human-rights-on-the-legislation-of-the/16806da5b2> accessed 21 September 2018.

52 'Council of Europe Commissioner for Human Rights Reiterates his Call to Bring Russian NGO Legislation in Line with European Standards' (*Council of Europe*, 9 July 2015) <www.coe.int/en/web/commissioner/-/council-of-europe-commissioner-for-human-rights-reiterates-his-call-to-bring-russian-ngo-legislation-in-line-with-european-standards?desktop=true> accessed21 September 2018; his Opinion is at <https://rm.coe.int/16806da772> accessed 21 September 2018.

53 <www.venice.coe.int/webforms/documents/default.aspx?pdffile=cdl-ad(2014)025-e> accessed 21 September 2018.

54 <https://rm.coe.int/third-party-intervention-by-the-council-of-europe-commissioner-for-hum/1680731087> accessed 21 September 2018.

55 <www.icj.org/russia-icj-and-amnesty-international-intervene-on-foreign-agents-law/> accessed 21 September 2018.

1969 to 1997, is being shown surprising – and in the view of many, dangerous – deference by the ECtHR.

During the Troubles in Northern Ireland, the UK government arrested hundreds of men suspected of terrorism as part of 'Operation Demetrius' in the summer of 1971. Some 342 people were interned (imprisoned without trial) as part of the operation. Fourteen men were chosen for 'special treatment' and were taken to a secret interrogation centre. The men were forced to wear hoods and were thrown to the ground from low-flying helicopters while hooded. These 14 men became known as the 'Hooded Men'. On top of brutal beatings and death threats, the men were then subjected to what would become known as the 'five techniques', use of which had been authorised at a high level: hooding; stress positions; white noise; sleep deprivation; deprivation of food and water. None of the 14 men was ever convicted of any criminal offence.[56]

The case was investigated by Amnesty International. What they found was shocking. The men were severely beaten, and when they collapsed, the beatings would start again. Some were still black and blue with bruises. Some felt they were on the brink of insanity – one alleged he tried to kill himself by banging his head against some metal piping in his cell. Their findings were clear: this was a case of brutality and torture by the British state.

The Irish government made history by taking the UK government to the ECtHR – the first 'interstate case'. The UK denied torture, but the (former) European Commission on Human Rights disagreed, ruling in 1976 that the UK had tortured the men, a violation of Article 3 of the ECHR. The UK government appealed to the ECtHR, which in 1978 (seven years after the complaints were filed) found that the techniques amounted to 'inhuman and degrading treatment' – but not torture.

New information came to light in 2014 in a television documentary, *The Torture Files*, by the Irish broadcaster RTÉ. Files had been discovered in the UK state archives suggesting that the UK had misled the ECtHR in 1978. The documents show that the UK knew that the torture techniques had long-term health impacts on the victims, and had been authorised at the very highest levels of UK government. In 2014, following Judicial Review proceedings initiated by the Hooded Men, the Irish Government requested the ECtHR to revise its 1978 judgment, and to find, on the basis of the new information, that use of the techniques was indeed torture.

On 20 March 2018, the Chamber of the ECtHR, by six votes to one, decided to dismiss the application.[57] There was a very strong dissenting opinion by the Irish judge, Síofra O'Leary. She concluded:[58]

56 'The Hooded Men: Torture, Lies and a Quest for Justice' (*Amnesty International UK*, 24 April 2018) <www.amnesty.org.uk/hooded-men-torture-uk-ireland> accessed 21 September 2018.

57 *Ireland v. the United Kingdom* (request for revision of the judgment of 18 January 1978) App no 5310/71 (ECtHR, 20 March 2018).

58 Ibid. [77].

> In my view, it was the Court and the Convention system and not the respondent State which was primarily under scrutiny in the context of this revision request. I regret that my colleagues in Chamber were not able or willing to see this. Revision must remain exceptional and requests should, where appropriate, be defeated by the very legitimate and fundamental principle of legal certainty. However, in the present case it is difficult to avoid the impression that it is the Court which has sought to shelter itself behind that principle. By doing so it risked damaging the authority of the case-law which that principle seeks to safeguard and overlooking its own responsibilities pursuant to Article 19 of the Convention. I can only conclude with regret – in a similar vein to my predecessor in the original case – that there is much in the general approach of the original and revision judgments that must discourage Member States from invoking Article 33 of the Convention and, regrettably, much to encourage future respondent States with reference to which that article may be invoked.

In his analysis published on *Strasbourg Observers*, Dr Alan Greene of Durham University described what had happened as a 'missed opportunity'.[59] The ECtHR had in his view '. . . missed an opportunity to correct an historic wrong; one that has had a pernicious effect across the globe.' He added that '. . . the public interest in this case is particularly salient in light of the fact that the original judgment was utilised by, amongst others, the United States to legitimise and defend what it termed "enhanced interrogation techniques" during the war on terror.'

On 12 June 2018 it was reported that not only the Hooded Men themselves but the Irish government had requested a referral to the Grand Chamber of the ECtHR – in effect an appeal.[60] This request is likely to be granted. At the same time, also with the support of Amnesty International, the Hooded Men have a case pending at the Belfast court of appeal, seeking permission to bring a case against former members of the military and the Royal Ulster Constabulary, whom the 14 men claim were responsible for beating and torturing them in 1971 during a mass security clampdown known as internment. Grainne Teggart, Amnesty International's Northern Ireland campaigns manager, said: 'The torture of these men was authorised at the highest levels of government. In line with the UK's international human rights obligations, those responsible for sanctioning and carrying out torture, at all levels, must be held accountable and, where possible, prosecuted.'[61]

59 Alan Greene 'Ireland v the UK and the Hooded Men: A Missed Opportunity?' (*Strasbourg Observer*, 25 April 2018) <https://strasbourgobservers.com/2018/04/25/ireland-v-the-uk-and-the-hooded-men-a-missed-opportunity/> accessed 21 September 2018.

60 'Irish Government to Appeal Hooded Men decision' (*BBC News*, 12 June 2018) <www.bbc.co.uk/news/uk-northern-ireland-44455415> accessed 21 September 2018.

61 Henry McDonald, ' "Hooded men" seek Northern Ireland Torture Investigation' *The Guardian* (Northern Ireland, 18 April 2018) <www.theguardian.com/uk-news/2018/apr/18/hooded-men-seek-northern-ireland-torture-investigation> accessed 21 September 2018.

This is against the background of the group of historic cases from Northern Ireland concerning the inadequacy of the investigation of the use of lethal force by state agents (the so-called 'McKerr Group', which comprises six cases: *McKerr*, *Jordan*, *McShane*, *Shanaghan*, *Kelly and Finucane*).[62] Patrick Finucane, commonly known as Pat Finucane, was an Irish human rights lawyer, a practising solicitor, who was allegedly killed by loyalist paramilitaries acting in collusion with the British government intelligence service MI5. In all these cases the UK was found by the ECtHR to have violated the right to a prompt and effective investigation following a suspected killing by state agents. Every year CoE's Committee of Ministers, which supervises the execution of judgments of the ECtHR, records that the UK has so far failed to comply with its obligations.

On 26 June 2018 the United Kingdom Supreme Court was told that the UK government had 'subverted the rule of law and obstructed justice' by refusing to hold an inquiry into the 1989 murder of Mr Finucane. Their barrister said that the decision to conduct a paper review meant government officials 'have been insulated from further scrutiny'. He added: 'The army, police and security service officers responsible for facilitating the murder of a solicitor whose only "crime" was to represent his clients effectively have all been guaranteed impunity.'[63] He said the question for the Supreme Court was whether the refusal to hold a public inquiry 'could ever be regarded as compatible with either the rule of law or article 2 of the ECHR [which guarantees the right to life]'. The murder was '. . . exactly the kind of case where the court needs to interfere in a hard-edged way to discharge its constitutional obligations and to protect the rule of law, not to mention Mrs Finucane's human rights,' he said. 'Where the executive has subverted the rule of law and obstructed justice, they should not expect the guarantors of law and justice to look the other way.'[64]

What is the ECtHR for, anyway?

In his recent book *The Conservative Human Rights Revolution: European Identity, Transnational Politics, and the Origins of the European Convention*,[65] Marco

62 *Hugh Jordan v the United Kingdom* App no 24746/94 (ECtHR, 4 May 2001); *Kelly and Ors v the United Kingdom* App no 30054/96 (ECtHR, 4 August 2001); *McKerr v the United Kingdom* App no 28883/95 (ECtHR, 4 August 2001); *Shanaghan v the United Kingdom* App no 37715/97 (ECtHR, 4 August 2001); *McShane v the United Kingdom* App no 43290/98 (ECtHR, 28 August 2002); *Finucane v the United Kingdom* App no 29178/95 (ECtHR, 1 October 2003).

See <https://publications.parliament.uk/pa/jt201415/jtselect/jtrights/130/13005.htm> and <www.patfinucanecentre.org/european-convention-human-rights/pfc-submission-committee-ministers-re-mckerr-ors-v-uk> both accessed 21 September 2018.

63 McDonald (n 62).

64 Owen Bowcott, 'Government Subverted Law by Refusing Finucane Inquiry, Court Told' *The Guardian* (London, 26 June 2018) <www.theguardian.com/uk-news/2018/jun/26/finucane-inquiry-refusal-subverted-rule-of-law-court-told>; see also Vincent Kearney, 'Pat Finucane: Supreme Court Urged to Quash Inquiry Decision' (*BBC News*, 26 June 2018) <www.bbc.co.uk/news/uk-northern-ireland-44620236> both accessed 21 September 2018.

65 Marco Duranti *The Conservative Human Rights Revolution: European Identity, Transnational Politics, and the Origins of the European Convention* (OUP 2017).

Duranti shows on the basis of thorough research that the CoE and ECHR were indeed the brainchild of Winston Churchill, in whose mind acceding to a binding human rights treaty and accepting the jurisdiction of an international court were necessary in the context of the Cold War, as a bulwark against communism in the shape of the USSR and its allies – and the spectre of socialism in the UK, especially following Labour's landslide victory in 1945.

This was also despite the long Conservative tradition in England, since 1789, of horror at the implications of the Declaration of Rights of Man and of the Citizen.[66] The Declaration was regarded by Edmund Burke, Jeremy Bentham, and William Pitt the Younger as at best nonsense and at worst intellectual terrorism.[67] From the left, Karl Marx declared that '. . . so-called rights of man, the ***droits de l'homme*** as distinct from the ***droits du citoyen***, are nothing but the rights of a member of civil society – i.e., the rights of egoistic man, of man separated from other men and from the community.'[68]

It is not hard to see that the ECHR is almost word for word the Declaration; and the First Protocol to the ECHR, promulgated simultaneously with the ECHR, contains a right to private property; a right of parents to decide the (religious) education of their children;[69] and a right to regular elections which has been the basis for excluding a former communist, my client Tatjana Zdanoka, from standing as a candidate for the Latvian Parliament.[70] The Labour Party and the trade union movement were, unsurprisingly, for the most part strongly opposed both to the CoE and the ECHR. In the cases of the Irish Republicans against the UK, the Chechens against Russia, and the Kurds against Turkey, the ECHR became the means by which peoples in struggle for self-determination could reawaken the revolutionary content of the Declaration, even though the ECtHR was very reluctant to see other than individual rights.[71]

Conclusion

Will the ECHR system survive? There is a significant risk that Turkey, Russia and the UK could each leave the CoE and the ECHR system. Russia and the UK have both refused to comply with judgments against them, in relation to prisoners' voting rights and in Russia's case a refusal to pay a very large sum to the former shareholders of YUKOS. The Court's decisions on admissibility mean that it is

66 See Bill Bowring, 'England's Terror of the French Revolution: the Historical Roots of Resistance to the Rights of Man and the Case Against the Human Rights Act' in Frederick Cowell (ed.), *Critically Examining the Case Against the 1998 Human Rights Act* (Routledge 2017).

67 Jeremy Waldron, *Nonsense Upon Stilts: Bentham, Burke and Marx on the Rights of Man* (Routledge 2014).

68 Karl Marx, 'On the Jewish Question' in *Deutsch-Französische Jahrbücher* (1844), see <www.marxists.org/archive/marx/works/1844/jewish-question/> accessed 21 September 2018.

69 Bill Bowring, 'Geopolitics and the Right to Education, and Why "No Person" Is in Fact a Child' (2014) 26 *Child and Family Law Quarterly* 196.

70 *Ždanoka v Latvia* App no 58278/00 (ECtHR, 16 March 2006).

71 For a more lengthy presentation of these ideas, see Bill Bowring, 'Human Rights and Public Education' (2012) 42 *Cambridge Journal of Education* 53.

less likely that Turkey will refuse to comply with the judgment in a particular case. The present prime minister of the UK in 2016 made it clear that in her view the UK should denounce the ECHR and leave the CoE.[72] It could be argued that if these states refuse to comply with their international legally binding obligations, then the CoE should bite the bullet and expel them, the 'nuclear option'. Moreover, the argument could continue, if the CoE fails to take robust action then the integrity of the whole system will be at stake. However, all three states gain significant advantages from CoE membership, and Russia in particular continually declares that it wants to stay in, as shown above. Mrs May will not be prime minister indefinitely. And Turkey remains a democracy, albeit with an authoritarian government. So perhaps it is more likely that with a sufficient degree of goodwill from a sufficient number of key actors, the Court and these three member states will muddle through, at least for the present. Long-term survival is beyond the ability of this writer to predict.

72 Anushka Asthana and Rowena Mason "UK must leave European convention on human rights, says Theresa May" 25 April 2016 at <https://www.theguardian.com/politics/2016/apr/25/uk-must-leave-european-convention-on-human-rights-theresa-may-eu-referendum> accessed 21 September 2018.

6 Taking back control? Brexit and the Court of Justice

Nikos Skoutaris

Introduction

On 23 June 2016, 52 per cent of voters that participated in the Brexit referendum voted to leave the EU. The message of the Leave Campaign to 'take back control' struck a chord with the majority of the electorate. Notwithstanding the separate reasons that led each and every one of those voters to vote in favour of the withdrawal of the UK from the EU, it is interesting to note that the UK government has interpreted this vote as an urge to shield the UK legal order from the influence of EU law. The prime minister, Theresa May, in her first speech in a party conference as leader of the Conservative party noted: 'Our laws [should be] made not in Brussels but in Westminster. Our judges [should be] sitting not in Luxembourg but in courts across the land. The authority of EU law in this country [should be] ended forever.'[1]

The stance of the UK government towards EU law and its main interpreter, the Court of Justice is hardly surprising, if one takes into account the following. First, even from the very beginning of the UK's EU membership, the EU law principles of primacy and direct effect upon which the EU constitutional order is founded were sitting uncomfortably with parliamentary sovereignty which consists of the paramount principle of the UK legal order. Brexit offers an unprecedented opportunity to the UK legal order to 'divorce' from those 'foreign' legal principles that have created tectonic changes to it. Second, the result of the referendum shed light on the fact that the UK electorate was not in support of the current level of EU integration. Of course, 'integration is fundamentally a political process' but 'law has a vital role to play in the process.'[2] In that sense, the detachment of the UK legal order from that of the EU and its institutions is almost a logical consequence of that vote.

1 <https://www.telegraph.co.uk/news/2016/10/05/theresa-mays-conference-speech-in-full/> accessed 1 October 2018.
2 Mauro Cappelletti, Monica Seccombe & Joseph H.H. Weiler, '1.1 Integration through law' in Mauro Cappelletti, Monica Seccombe & Joseph H.H. Weiler (eds.) *Integration Through Law: Europe and the American Federal Experience* (de Gruyter, 1985), 1.

Having said that, the EU and the UK legal orders have been in a symbiotic relationship for more than four decades. To give but one example, there are thousands of directly applicable EU regulations, binding in their entirety, that have 'parachuted' within the UK legal order without any national transposing measure. So, an abrupt 'clean' end to that relationship would be almost impossible without the domestic legal order suffering from a seismic ripple effect. Moreover, given that the EU is a 'community of law', 'designing an ambitious economic partnership which respects the freedoms and principles of the EU, and the wishes of the British people' as the prime minister declared in her Florence speech[3] means that the Court of Justice of the European Union (CJEU) will inevitably be influencing the UK legal order for the foreseeable future.

The present chapter focuses on the aforementioned themes by analysing the relationship between the Court of Justice and the UK legal order after Brexit takes place. It revisits the challenge that the EU principles of primacy and direct effect raised for the UK constitutional order. It explains the role that the Agreement on the UK's Withdrawal from the EU (hereafter WA) envisages for the CJEU.[4] Finally, it describes the role of the Court of Justice in the UK legal order after Brexit takes place by reference to the EU Withdrawal Act 2018 and the Agreement on the Future Relationship (hereafter FRA).

The analysis of the strained relationship between the UK and the EU and its apex court provided in this chapter can be seen in the broader context of the challenges that international organisations and international courts face at the moment from various states. The United States has not contributed to the United Nations Educational, Scientific and Cultural Organisation (UNESCO) budget since 2011 and plans to quit in 2018, while it has been delaying the process of appointments in the World Trade Organization (WTO) Appellate Body. Burundi left the International Criminal Court and it remains unclear whether South Africa will also exit the Rome Statute system. In that sense, the UK's withdrawal from the EU institutional framework is a symptom of a more widespread global phenomenon. At the same time, as a result both of the symbiotic relationship of the UK and EU legal orders and of the role that is envisaged for the CJEU in the future relationship between the UK and the EU, the CJEU will remain an important actor in the UK order.

The past: the UK and the judge-made EU law principles

'The question of the legal status of norms of European Union law within the legal order of the Member States' has been omnipresent since the very first years

3 <https://www.gov.uk/government/speeches/pms-florence-speech-a-new-era-of-cooperation-and-partnership-between-the-uk-and-the-eu> accessed 1 October 2018.

4 Draft Agreement on the withdrawal of the United Kingdom of Great Britain and Northern Ireland from the European Union and the European Atomic Energy Community, as agreed at negotiators' level on 14 November 2018. <https://ec.europa.eu/commission/sites/beta-political/files/draft_withdrawal_agreement_0.pdf> accessed 1 December 2018.

of the life of the EU.'[5] Even at that early period, the Court of Justice understood the then European Economic Community as 'a new legal order of international law for the benefit of which the states have limited their sovereign rights, albeit within limited fields and the subjects of which comprise not only member states but also their nationals.'[6] As an answer to that question, the Court established the principles of direct effect and primacy (or supremacy) in its early case law.[7]

Direct effect allows individuals to rely on an EU law provision before a national court. It is the capacity of any EU law provision whose wording is *clear*, *precise* and *unconditional* to be applied in domestic court proceedings.[8] At the same time, the Court in *Costa* held that whenever there is a conflict between a norm of EU law and one of national law, EU law '. . . could not . . . be overridden by domestic legal provisions . . . without being deprived of its character as [Union] law and without the legal basis of the [EU] itself being called into question.'[9] This is why 'Primacy denotes the capacity of [an EU law provision] to overrule inconsistent norms of national law in domestic court proceedings.'[10] In *Simmenthal*, the CJEU went a step further by ruling that national courts have the power to disapply/set aside a national law provision and apply an EU law one in case they are in conflict. This may happen even in cases where the national legal framework does not provide the courts with such power of judicial review.[11]

Primacy and direct effect were 'certainly well established in the jurisprudence of the European Court of Justice long before the United Kingdom joined the [then] Community'.[12] It was foreseeable that those norms would sit somewhat uncomfortably with a legal order which is founded on the principle of parliamentary sovereignty.

According to the Diceyan orthodoxy, the principle of parliamentary sovereignty means 'that Parliament . . . has, under the English Constitution, the right to make or unmake any law whatsoever; and, further, that no person or body recognised by the law of England as having a right to override or set aside the legislation of Parliament'.[13] This means, first, that the UK Parliament possesses supreme lawmaking power that allows itself to pass legislation concerning anything.[14] Second, no Parliament can bind its successors. Third, and more impor-

5 Bruno de Witte, 'Direct Effect, Primacy and the Nature of the Legal Order' in Paul Craig and Gráinne de Búrca (eds.), *The Evolution of EU Law* (2nd ed, OUP 2011) 323, 323.

6 Case 26/62 *NV Algemene Transport en Expeditie Onderneming Van Gend en Loos v Nederlandse administratie der belastingen*, [1963] ECR 1.

7 The two terms are used interchangeably in the English language literature. But the Court of Justice never refers to the term 'supremacy'.

8 *Van Gend en Loos* (n 6).

9 Case 6/64 *Costa v ENEL* [1964] ECR 585.

10 De Witte (n 5).

11 Case 106/77, *Amministrazione delle Finanze v Simmenthal SpA* [1978] ECR 629.

12 *R v Secretary of State for Transport ex p Factortame* (No 2) [1991] 1 AC 603, para 379.

13 Albert Venn Dicey, *An Introduction to the Study of the Law of the Constitution* (6th edn, Macmillan and Co, 1885) 40.

14 For example, the Parliament can legislate on issues relating to itself (See Septennial Act 1716, Parliaments of 1910–1918, 1935–1945); with 'extra-territorial' effect (see War Crimes Act

tant for the purposes of the present chapter, a valid Act of Parliament cannot be set aside/disapplied by a court.

Bearing that in mind, the seismic impact of the *Factortame* decision is unsurprising.[15] In that case, the then highest court of the land, the House of Lords disapplied – for the first time since the Glorious Revolution – an Act of the UK Parliament so as to give priority to a directly effective principle of EU law. The effect of EU law, however, has not been limited to introducing a limited form of judicial review in a constitutional system that is founded on parliamentary sovereignty. In *Thoburn,* Sir John Laws introduced the idea that the UK legal order recognises a hierarchy of statutes by accepting the distinction between 'ordinary statutes' and 'constitutional statutes'.[16] The latter are immune from implied repeal. According to Lords Neuberger and Mance, '[T]he United Kingdom has no written constitution, but we have a number of constitutional instruments. They include [. . .] the European Communities Act 1972.'[17] This finding has been reaffirmed in *Miller.*[18]

So the influence of EU law in the transformation of the UK legal order cannot be overestimated. Lord Denning has described EU law as an '. . . incoming tide. It flows into the estuaries and up the rivers.'[19] It is therefore unsurprising that the UK government decided to limit, if not eliminate, the influence of EU law from the domestic legal order after Brexit takes place. In fact, Prime Minister Theresa May declared in her Lancaster House speech that after Brexit all laws governing the UK will be made in the UK and 'will be interpreted by judges not in Luxembourg but in courts across this country'.[20] But can the UK legal order become watertight from the tide of EU law and CJEU case law even after Brexit takes place? A brief examination of the currently negotiated Withdrawal Agreement (WA) and the recently approved EU (Withdrawal) Act 1998 might suggest otherwise.

The present I: the CJEU and the Withdrawal Agreement

To start with, 'the Court of Justice of the European Union shall have jurisdiction as provided for in the Treaties' for the duration of the transition period.[21] But

1991); retrospectively (see Indemnity Act 1920 and War Charges Validity Act 1925; Enemy Property Act 1953); in (alleged) breach of International Law and the UK's international obligations (*Mortensen v Peters* (1906) 8 F(J) 93, 100; *Cheney v Conn* [1968] 1 All ER 779,782); even immorally (*Madzimbamuto v Lardner-Burke* [1969] 1 AC 645,723).

15 *Factortame* (n 12).

16 *Thoburn v Sunderland City Council* [2003] QB 151.

17 *(HS2 Action Alliance Ltd) v Secretary of State for Transport* [2014] UKSC 3, [207].

18 *R (on the application of Miller and another) v Secretary of State for Exiting the European Union* [2017] UKSC 5. [67].

19 *HP Bulmer Ltd v J Bollinger SA* [1974] Ch 401, 418.

20 Lancaster House Speech, The government's negotiating objectives for exiting the EU: PM speech, <https://www.gov.uk/government/speeches/the-governments-negotiating-objectives-for-exiting-the-eu-pm-speech> accessed 1 October 2018.

21 Art 131 WA.

even after the end of the transition, the CJEU and its case law will continue to play a significant role especially in the area of citizens's rights.

Despite the polarised rhetoric concerning free movement of persons during the Brexit referendum, the UK and the EU managed to agree fairly quickly on the issue of post-Brexit citizens' rights. Accordingly, all EU citizens residing at the UK and all UK citizens in the EU 27 at the end of the transition period (31 December 2020) will retain their rights of residence and work and most notably the right to equal treatment as currently derived from EU law. In the December Joint Report, the UK and the EU pointed out that the WA should 'enable the effective exercise of rights derived from Union law and based on past life choices.'[22] Part 2 of the WA (Articles 9 to 39) enshrines those rights through direct references to the relevant primary and secondary EU legislation including the citizens' rights Directive,[23] Regulation 492/2011[24] and Regulation 883/2004.[25]

To protect those rights both for UK citizens living in the EU and EU citizens living in the UK and to give them legal certainty, the two parties accepted that appropriate mechanisms should be established[26] and that the CJEU is the 'ultimate arbiter of the interpretation of EU law.'[27] So, the WA provides for a 'voluntary preliminary reference procedure'. According to Article 158 WA, the UK courts will be able to send preliminary references related to the part of the WA that regulates citizens' rights. This avenue of judicial assistance will be available for any litigation that has started up to eight years after the end of the transition period. The only difference between this voluntary procedure and the one described in Article 267 TFEU is that the UK courts of last instance will not be obliged to refer. In other words, the obligation of the courts of last instance to refer to the CJEU in accordance with Article 267(3) TFEU and the *CILFIT* case law[28] on 'acte clair' will not be part of the legal framework established by the WA. Despite this, the Court of Justice will be able to influence the British legal life for a number of years after Brexit at least with regard to the very sensitive issue of citizens' rights.

22 Joint report from the negotiators of the European Union and the United Kingdom government on progress during phase 1 of negotiations under Article 50 TEU on the United Kingdom's orderly withdrawal from the European Union <https://ec.europa.eu/commission/sites/beta-political/files/joint_report.pdf> accessed 1 October 2018 (hereafter Joint Report), para 6.

23 Directive 2004/38/EC of the European Parliament and of the Council of 29 April 2004 on the right of citizens of the Union and their family members to move and reside freely within the territory of the Member States [2004] OJ L 158/77.

24 Regulation (EU) 492/2011 of the European Parliament and of the Council of 5 April 2011 on freedom of movement for workers within the Union [2011] OJ L141/1.

25 Regulation (EC) No 883/2004 of the European Parliament and of the Council of 29 April 2004 on the coordination of social security systems [2004] OJ L 166/1.

26 Joint Report, para 37.

27 Ibid., para 38.

28 Case 283/81 *Srl CILFIT and Lanificio di Gavardo SpA v Ministry of Health* ECLI:EU:C:1982:335.

However, citizens' rights is not the only area of the WA where a dispute settlement mechanism should be established. According to the European Council's guidelines, the WA 'should include appropriate dispute settlement and enforcement mechanisms regarding the application and interpretation of the [whole] withdrawal agreement'.[29] According to Article 167 WA, the EU and the UK should 'make every attempt through cooperation and consultations' to reach a settlement of any dispute concerning the WA. Judicial mechanisms should be considered as a last resort when it comes to the settlement of any dispute. This is why at first instance, the two parties 'shall endeavour to resolve any dispute regarding the interpretation and application of the provisions of this Agreement by entering into consultations in the Joint Committee in good faith, with the aim of reaching a mutually agreed solution.'[30] Such Joint Committee will be comprised of representatives of both the UK and the EU.[31]

According to Article 170 WA, '[W]here no agreed solution can be reached, either party to the WA may request the establishment of an arbitration panel.'[32] The arbitration panel will be comprised of five persons.[33] The EU and the UK will each nominate two persons from a list of ten they will have submitted by the end of the transition period.[34] The chairperson will be selected by consensus by the four members of the panel.[35] The existence of such arbitration panel was not part of the initial draft WA. As such, it 'can be considered a negotiating success for the UK which had been pressing for an arbitration mechanism (instead of the ECJ as the ultimate arbiter).'[36]

More interestingly, for the purposes of the chapter,

> Where a dispute submitted to arbitration in accordance with this Title raises a question of interpretation of a concept of Union law, a question of interpretation of a provision of Union law referred to in this Agreement or a question of whether the United Kingdom has complied with its obligations under Article 89(2), the arbitration panel shall not decide on any such question. In such case, it shall request the Court of Justice of the European Union to give a ruling on the question. The Court of Justice of the European Union shall have jurisdiction to give such a ruling which shall be binding on the arbitration panel.[37]

29 European Council Guidelines of 29 April 2017, point 17.
30 Art 169(1) WA.
31 Art 164(1) WA.
32 Tobias Lock 'On Thin Ice: The Role of the Court of Justice under the Withdrawal Agreement', Verfassungsblog <https://verfassungsblog.de/on-thin-ice-the-role-of-the-court-of-justice-under-the-withdrawal-agreement/> accessed 1 December 2018.
33 Art 171(3) WA.
34 Art 171(1) and (5) WA.
35 Ibid.
36 Lock (n 32).
37 Art 174(1) WA.

This means that notwithstanding the existence of an arbitration panel, the CJEU will still have an important role in the monitoring of the correct implementation of the WA.

Be that as it may, the biggest obstacle that the two parties faced in reaching an agreement on the WA related to the border between Ireland and the UK. Theresa May's government had been trying to find the balance between two seemingly irreconcilable goals. The UK aimed to leave the single market and the customs union, without returning to a hard border on the island of Ireland.[38]

The text of the Joint Report, reached between the UK and the EU in December 2017 included a formula to 'square the circle'. It stated that the aim of the future trade negotiations would be to address the challenge of the Irish border through the overall EU-UK relationship. If the future trade agreement finds it impossible to provide for a frictionless invisible border, then, 'specific [technological] solutions' will apply to Northern Ireland. If the UK and the EU cannot agree on those 'specific solutions', then either the UK as a whole, or Northern Ireland, will remain aligned to the single market and the customs union after Brexit takes place.[39]

That third 'backstop option' was legally codified in a protocol contained in the Draft WA. It said that – should no specific solution be found – a common regulatory area comprising the European Union and Northern Ireland will be established and Northern Ireland will remain in the EU customs territory. May vehemently rejected the plan and said that 'No UK prime minister could agree to it'[40] because it 'threatens [the UK] constitutional integrity'.[41] This is why the final draft of the WA included a significant compromise. According to it, the UK as a whole will be in a 'bare bones' customs union with the EU while Northern Ireland will remain aligned to those rules of the single market that are necessary to maintain the free movement of goods across the Irish border.[42]

More interestingly for the purposes of the present chapter, the 'Court of Justice of the European Union shall have jurisdiction as provided for in the Treaties' with regard to the application of the EU *acquis* in Northern Ireland.[43] In particular, the Court of Justice will have jurisdiction over the interpretation of EU customs legislation;[44] the rules of the single market in goods as far as they apply

38 <http://www.independent.co.uk/news/uk/politics/article-50-letter-read-full-brexit-theresa-may-takes-uk-out-of-eu-statement-a7655566.html> accessed 1 October 2018.

39 Joint Report, para 49.

40 <https://www.irishtimes.com/news/world/theresa-may-rejects-draft-brexit-withdrawal-agreement-1.3409215> accessed 1 October 2018.

41 Nikos Skoutaris, 'Why the EU's Brexit "backstop option" for Northern Ireland doesn't threaten the UK's constitutional integrity' <https://theconversation.com/why-the-eus-brexit-backstop-option for-northern-ireland-doesnt-threaten-the-uks-constitutional-integrity-92869> accessed 1 October 2018.

42 Protocol on Ireland/Northern Ireland, WA.

43 Art 14(4), Protocol on Ireland/Northern Ireland, WA.

44 Art 8, Protocol on Ireland/Northern Ireland, WA.

under the backstop;[45] VAT and excise rules;[46] agriculture and environment;[47] the single electricity market;[48] and state aid.[49] Thus, it is obvious that the CJEU will continue playing a significant role with regard to a part of the UK at least.

The present II: the European Union (Withdrawal) Act 2018

On 26 June 2018, the European Union (Withdrawal) Act 2018 received royal assent. The constitutional significance of that piece of legislation cannot be overstated. Section 1 repeals the European Communities Act 1972 which is considered one of the 'constitutional statutes' of the United Kingdom.[50] Crucially, however, its purpose is to preserve and carry over into UK law the full body of EU law even after Brexit takes place as provided in sections 2, 3 and 4 of the Act.

The reason why a legislative act that was initially called 'the Great Repeal Act' 'copies and pastes' huge swathes of EU law in the legal order of a future third country is the following. Given the symbiotic relationship of the two legal orders for more than 40 years, there are thousands of directly applicable and directly effective pieces of EU law that would cease to apply to the UK after Brexit takes place. This would mean that legal vacuums would be created in a number of areas such as environmental law, consumer protection, workers' rights etc. In order to avoid such a situation, it was of utmost importance that the UK administration and Westminster would find a way to bridge those gaps without clogging up the parliamentary timetable for years to come.

Interestingly, the arrangement is very similar to the 'continuance clauses' of former colonies on independence from the UK as Douglas-Scott has noted.[51] For instance, section 4(1) of the Constitution of Jamaica reads:

> All laws which are in force in Jamaica immediately before the appointed day shall (subject to amendment or repeal by the authority having power to amend or repeal any such law) continue in force on and after that day, and all laws which have been made before that day but have not previously been brought into operation may (subject as aforesaid) be brought into force, in accordance with any provision in that behalf, on or after that day, but all such laws shall, subject to the provisions of this section, be construed, in relation to any period beginning on or after the appointed day, with such adaptations

45 Ibid.
46 Art 9, Protocol on Ireland/Northern Ireland, WA.
47 Art 10, Protocol on Ireland/Northern Ireland, WA.
48 Art 11, Protocol on Ireland/Northern Ireland, WA.
49 Art 12, Protocol on Ireland/Northern Ireland, WA.
50 *Thoburn* (n 16).
51 Sionnaidh Douglas-Scott 'The 'Great Repeal Bill': Constitutional Chaos and Constitutional Crisis?', UK Constitutional Law Blog <https://ukconstitutionallaw.org/2016/10/10/sionaidh-douglas-scott-the-great-repeal-bill-constitutional-chaos-and-constitutional-crisis/> accessed 1 October 2018.

> and modifications as may be necessary to bring them into conformity with the provisions of this Order.[52]

Be that as it may, section 5 of the EU (Withdrawal) Act addresses the role of the judge-made EU law principle of primacy post-Brexit. The general rule is that the principle of primacy does not apply to any UK law that is passed after the exit day.[53] However, if Parliament intends that primacy should apply with regard to a certain post-Brexit legislative modification, then the UK courts should act accordingly.[54] More importantly for the purposes of the present chapter, section 5(2) 'introduces a new legal hierarchy into the UK's constitutional system'.[55] According to this section, the principle of primacy will apply to retained EU law, that is to say, EU law that has been passed before Brexit including rights created by the case law of the Court[56] as it relates to other pre-Brexit legislation. So, the retained EU law will have priority over any law enacted before Brexit pointing to the fact that the most important principle that was laid out by the Court will have a lasting effect in the UK legal order for years to come.

Consistent with the aim of the government to remove the influence of the CJEU on the UK legal order,[57] section 6(1)(a) provides that after Brexit, the UK courts are 'not bound by any principles or decisions made . . . by the European Court'. They are also prohibited from sending a preliminary reference question to the Court of Justice[58] with the exception of cases on citizens' rights that are raised within the first eight years after the end of the transition period. However, even after Brexit takes place, any UK court may take into account the case law of the Court of Justice.[59] In any case, UK courts regularly engage with the jurisdiction of foreign courts which they treat as persuasive but not a binding authority. In fact, the UK government has admitted that it is possible that 'Account is to be taken of CJEU decisions [. . .] where there is a shared interest in reducing or eliminating divergence in how specific aspects of an agreement with the EU are implemented.'[60]

Concerning retained EU law, section 6(3) of the Act requires the UK courts to interpret the retained EU law 'in accordance with any retained case law and any retained general principles of EU law'. The term 'retained EU case law' refers to 'any principles laid down by, and any decisions of, the European Court,

52 Jamaican Constitution, s 4(1).
53 EU (Withdrawal) Act, s 5(1).
54 EU (Withdrawal) Act, s 5(3).
55 Jack Simson Caird, Vaughne Miller and Arabella Lang, 'European Union (Withdrawal) Bill' House of Commons Briefing Paper No 8079.
56 EU (Withdrawal) Act, s 4(1).
57 See Theresa May's speech in the 2016 Conservative Party conference (n 1).
58 EU (Withdrawal) Act, s 6(1)(b).
59 EU (Withdrawal) Act, s 6(2).
60 Department for Exiting the EU, 'Enforcement and Dispute Resolution – A Future Partnership Paper' <https://www.gov.uk/government/publications/enforcement-and-dispute-resolution-a-future-partnership-paper> accessed 1 October 2018.

as they have effect in EU law' before Brexit unless there is an explicit exception either in section 5 or in Schedule 1.[61] As previously discussed, section 5 excludes the principle of primacy of EU law. Schedule 1 on the other hand, provides that 'There is no right in domestic law [after Brexit takes place] to damages' for non-contractual state liability in accordance with *Francovich*.[62]

Notwithstanding those exceptions, it seems certain that the case law of the Court of Justice will influence the legal status of a significant part of UK legislation (namely, retained EU law) and as such the UK legal order. This body of legislation, in fact, will have primacy over any other piece of pre-Brexit national legislation.

However, not all the UK courts will be obliged to provide for legal continuity by following the retained EU law. The UK Supreme Court and the Scottish High Court of Judiciary are asked to treat this retained EU case law in the same way that they would treat their own.[63]

So far, we have seen how the WA – which at the time of writing is still being negotiated – and the recently approved EU (Withdrawal) Act will allow the Court of Justice and its well-established case law to influence the UK legal order even after Brexit takes place. A question remains, however, as to what the influence of the Court will be in the future relationship between the UK and the EU. How might the Agreement on the Future Relationship (hereafter FRA) – that will only be negotiated once the UK becomes a non-member of the EU – envisage the role of the CJEU?

The future: the future agreement

According to Article 50(2) TEU (Treaty on European Union), the EU 'shall negotiate and conclude an agreement with [the UK], setting out the arrangements for its withdrawal taking account of the framework for its future relationship with the Union.' Indeed, a political declaration that sets out the framework of the future UK-EU relationships was published at the same time as the WA.[64] The negotiations for the agreement, however, will only start after Brexit takes place on 29 March 2019 and will be conducted in accordance with Article 218 TFEU (Treaty on the Functioning of the European Union). The latter is of significant importance. It means that the FRA may be subject to an opinion of the CJEU according to Article 218(11) TFEU.

61 EU (Withdrawal) Act, s 6(7).
62 Joined Cases C-6/90 and C-9/90, *Francovich and Bonifaci v Italy* ECLI:EU:C:1991:428.
63 EU (Withdrawal) Act, s 6(5).
64 Political Declaration Setting out the Framework for the Future Relationship between the European Union and the United Kingdom (hereafter Political Declaration) <https://assets.publishing.service.gov.uk/government/uploads/system/uploads/attachment_data/file/758557/22_November_Draft_Political_Declaration_setting_out_the_framework_for_the_future_relationship_between_the_EU_and_the_UK__agreed_at_negotiators__level_and_agreed_in_principle_at_political_level__subject_to_endorsement_by_Leaders.pdf> accessed 1 December 2018.

The Court has a long history of judicially reviewing international agreements of the EU with often unexpected results. A recent example is *Opinion 1/13* where the Court struck down the agreement on the accession of the EU to the European Convention on Human Rights (ECHR) because it violated the principle of autonomy of the Union legal order, among other things.[65] It did so, despite the fact that it took part both in the negotiations and in the drafting of that agreement. So, given its history in judicially reviewing international agreements, it is important to understand the limits that its case law sets in designing the dispute settlement mechanisms of the FRA.

The EU has made clear from the beginning that any dispute settlement scheme would need to respect the principle of autonomy of the Union legal order including the role of the Court of Justice[66] and the UK has tacitly accepted that.[67] According to the settled case law of the CJEU, this principle sets certain constraints in the event that international agreements concluded by the EU provide for dispute settlement through judicial or quasi-judicial bodies other than the Court of Justice itself. Such dispute settlement bodies 'must not have the effect of binding the EU and its institutions, in the exercise of their internal powers, to a particular interpretation of the rules of EU law'.[68] So any judicial or quasi-judicial body established by the Agreement on the post-Brexit relationship of the EU with the UK to settle disputes may not interpret provisions 'which are identical to provisions of [Union] law'.[69] Finally, it is possible for the agreement on the future relationship to 'confer new powers on the Court, provided that in so doing it does not change the nature of [its] function' as conceived in the EU treaties.[70]

Recently, the UK put forward a blueprint for the future relationship: the Chequers agreement.[71] The new plan proposes to establish a free trade area for goods between the UK and the EU where 'a common rulebook for goods including agri-food' will exist.[72] The UK will commit, by international agreement, 'to ongoing harmonisation with EU rules on goods'.[73] This echoes the mechanism of the European Economic Area whose members have to adopt the new or reformed regulations that the EU institutions produce. At the same time, the government contends that parliament can guard the UK legal order from future

65 Opinion 2/13 *Re Accession of the EU to the ECHR* ECLI:EU:C:2014:2454.
66 See points 1 and 17 of the European Council Guidelines of 29 April 2017; point 39 of the Negotiating Directives.
67 Political Declaration, para 83.
68 Opinion 2/13 (n 65) para 184 citing Opinions 1/91, EU:C:1991:490, paras 30 to 35; and 1/00, EU:C:2002:231, para 13.
69 Opinion 1/92 *Re EEA*, ECLI:EU:C:1992:189, para 36.
70 Ibid., para 32.
71 White Paper on 'The Future Relationship between the United Kingdom and the European Union' <https://www.gov.uk/government/publications/the-future-relationship-between-the-united-kingdom-and-the-european-union> accessed 1 October 2018.
72 Ibid.
73 Ibid.

EU legislation in an arrangement that somehow resembles the EU's relationship with Switzerland.

Be that as it may, in the White Paper on the future relationship, the UK states that disputes under this arrangement should be raised in the Joint Committee comprised of representatives both of the UK and the EU. In the event that the Committee fails to resolve the dispute by negotiation, an independent arbitration panel should be formed.[74] In the area of goods where the UK has decided to adhere to the common rulebook, a referral to the CJEU for interpretation of the relevant rules will also be available to the Joint Committee and the arbitration panel.[75] In other words, the UK wants to opt for a system of dispute resolution through arbitration with an in-built possibility of referring to the Court of Justice, similar to the WA. The EU has accepted that in principle.[76] This again shows that the influence of the CJEU to the UK legal order will remain significant for years to come.

To be sure, the negotiations on the future relationship have barely started while the EU has remained lukewarm if not totally unconvinced with regard to the Chequers proposal.[77] Having said that, it is worth noting two distinct but interrelated issues that relate to the dispute resolution system that the Political Declaration favours. There is nothing particularly innovative about the establishment of a Joint Committee as the primary venue of dispute settlement. Apart from the WA itself that provides for such a body, a number of free trade agreements also establish a Joint Committee responsible for the overall functioning of the agreement. Such Committee has the primary role for resolving disputes through negotiations. The recent EU-Singapore Free Trade Agreement, for instance, establishes a Trade Committee.[78]

The Trade Committee shall:

(a) ensure that this Agreement operates properly;
(b) supervise and facilitate the implementation and application of this Agreement, and further its general aims;
(c) supervise the work of all specialised committees, working groups and other bodies established under this Agreement;
(d) consider ways to further enhance trade relations between the Parties;
(e) without prejudice to Chapter Fourteen (Dispute Settlement) and Chapter Fifteen (Mediation Mechanism), seek to solve problems which might arise in areas covered by this Agreement, or resolve disputes that may arise regarding the interpretation or application of this Agreement; and
(f) consider any other matter of interest relating to an area covered by this Agreement.[79]

74 Ibid. 93.
75 Ibid.
76 Political Declaration, para 134.
77 <https://www.independent.co.uk/news/uk/politics/brexit-michel-barnier-theresa-may-chequers-proposal-no-deal-eu-a8519636.html> accessed 1 October 2018.
78 Free Trade Agreement between the European Union and the Republic of Singapore, Article 16.1.
79 Ibid.

Second, given the insistence of the Court of Justice on the principle of autonomy, an arbitration system could only be established if there was a mandatory preliminary reference procedure from the arbitration to the CJEU whenever the dispute turned on interpretation of a reference to EU law or a concept identical to EU law. Such mandatory preliminary reference procedures exist already in a few international agreements concluded between the EU and non-members of the EU. For example, Articles 267 of the EU-Georgia Association Agreement,[80] 322 of the EU-Ukraine Association Agreement,[81] and 403 of the EU-Moldova Association Agreement[82] provide that 'Where a dispute raises a question of interpretation of a provision of Union law [. . .], the arbitration panel shall not decide the question, but request the Court of Justice of the European Union to give a ruling on the question [. . .] The ruling of the Court of Justice of the European Union shall be binding on the arbitration panel.'

The difference with the aforementioned models, however, will be the scope of such arbitration system. Given the ambition of the future relationship, it is expected that the EU-UK arbitration system will have largely unprecedented competence in international law practice as it could reach far beyond trade disputes and extend across many areas of law. And if within this dispute settlement mechanism there is space for a mandatory preliminary reference procedure, the influence of the Court of Justice will continue in the post-Brexit era.

Conclusion

Brexit is arguably the most significant constitutional moment for the UK in decades. The gradual detachment of the UK legal order from the EU, with which the UK has shared more than 40 years of symbiotic relationship, raises a number of questions, one of which relates to the role of the main arbiter and interpreter of EU law, the Court of Justice.

The UK government has declared that in 'taking back control of its laws' it needs to distance itself from the jurisprudence of the Court of Justice and should put an end to the primacy of its case law. It is true that the role of the Court of Justice and EU law in general will be more limited after Brexit takes place than it is at present. However, it is almost impossible to envisage the UK legal order becoming completely 'watertight' from the 'tide' of EU law.

The WA that regulates the terms of withdrawal of the UK provides for a significant role for the CJEU with regard to citizens' rights and with regard to dispute

80 Council Decision of 16 June 2014 on the signing, on behalf of the European Union, and provisional application of the Association Agreement between the European Union and the European Atomic Energy Community and their Member States, of the one part, and Georgia, of the other part (2014) OJ L261/1.

81 Association Agreement between the European Union and its Member States, of the one part, and Ukraine, (2014) OJ L161/3.

82 Association Agreement between the European Union and the European Atomic Energy Community and their Member States, of the one part, and the Republic of Moldova, of the other part (2014) OJ L260/4.

settlement more generally. If there is a compromise on the 'Irish border question' along the lines described by the Commission, the CJEU will also remain a court for part of the UK. In addition, the terms of the EU (Withdrawal) Act acknowledge that UK courts will be influenced by the case law of the Luxembourg court. Finally, the principle of autonomy suggests that an ambitious FRA should acknowledge and take into account the role of the CJEU.

In other words, the rumours of the death of the CJEU are greatly exaggerated . . .

Part II

Institutional Challenges

7 The functions of the International Court of Justice

Tending to the law while settling disputes?

*Francesco Messineo**

Introduction: The tension between eternal truth and settling disputes

One of the most striking elements of the scholarly writings about the settlement of international disputes published in the early twentieth century is the radical nature of some of the solutions proposed. At that time, a permanent international judicial institution was seen as essential for the completeness of the international legal system. Writers such as Hans Wehberg and, later on, Hersch Lauterpacht, advocated its establishment;[1] and diplomats as well as politicians seemed pervaded by a willingness to build new international institutions which has only rarely resurfaced since.

Initially, such aspirations found tangible outlets. Article 14 of the Covenant of the League of Nations (1924) provided that:

> [T]he Council shall formulate and submit to the Members of the League for adoption plans for the establishment of a Permanent Court of International Justice. The Court shall be competent to hear and determine any dispute of an international character which the parties thereto submit to it. The Court may also give an advisory opinion upon any dispute or question referred to it by the Council or by the Assembly.

When the Council of the League of Nations set out to create the Court, it appointed an Advisory Committee of Jurists 'for the purpose of preparing plans

* The views expressed herein are those of the author and do not necessarily reflect the views of the United Nations. With many thanks to Tamar Sarjveladze.

1 See Hans Wehberg, *The Work of The Hague*, vol 2 (Clarendon Press 1918); the book is the English translation of *Das Werk vom Haag*, vol 2 (Duncker & Humblot 1912); Hersch Lauterpacht, *The Function of Law in the International Community* (Clarendon Press 1933).

for the establishment' thereof.[2] At the first meeting of the Committee, Mr Léon Bourgeois of France, speaking as a Member of the Council, employed language that left no doubts as to the solemnity of the task at hand – no less than building the 'empire of justice':

> You are about, Gentlemen, to give life to the judicial power of humanity. Philosophers and historians have told us of the laws of the growth and decadence of empires. We look to you, Gentlemen, for laws which will assure the perpetuity of the only empire which can show no decadence, the empire of justice, which is the expression of eternal truth.[3]

Nowadays, international courts and tribunals do not purport to express 'eternal truth' or to speak as the 'judicial power of humanity' (nor, fortunately, are such matters exclusively entrusted to 'Gentlemen').[4] Nonetheless, it would be difficult to overstate the importance of the Permanent Court of International Justice and its successor, the International Court of Justice ('the Court' hereinafter), as key actors in the international legal system.[5] Statements of the International Court of Justice concerning the scope and content of rules of international law are generally deemed authoritative, if not conclusive, in view of its unique role as the principal judicial organ of the United Nations. Indeed, the Court is the only permanent court of general jurisdiction potentially open to all states (including non-member states of the United Nations).[6]

This centrality of the Court is especially vivid in the perception of international law academics. As a recent editorial in a prominent European journal seeking

2 Permanent Court of International Justice, Advisory Committee of Jurists, *Procès-verbaux of the Proceedings of the Committee, June 16th – July 24th 1920, with annexes* (Van Langenhuysen Brothers 1920) III.

3 Ibid. 11.

4 However, for a contemporary natural law perspective on the functions of the International Court of Justice, see the collection of individual opinions by Judge Antônio A. Cançado Trindade, *The Construction of a Humanized International Law*, vol. 1–3 (Brill/Nijhoff 2015 and 2017).

5 The close relationship (often perceived as a *de facto* continuity) between the Permanent Court of International Justice in the League of Nations system and the International Court of Justice in the United Nations system is hinted at by Article 92 of the United Nations Charter, which recalls that the Statute of the Court 'is based upon the Statute of the Permanent Court of International Justice', and is buttressed by explicit continuity provisions concerning the extent of the Court's jurisdiction (see Article 36(5) and Article 37 of the Statute of the Court). This chapter focuses on the International Court of Justice.

6 See articles 34 and 35, Statute of the International Court of Justice; United Nations Security Council resolution 9 (1946); United Nations General Assembly resolution 246 (III) of 8 October 1948; see also *Application of the Convention on the Prevention and Punishment of the Crime of Genocide (Bosnia and Herzegovina* v. *Yugoslavia (Serbia and Montenegro))* (Provisional Measures) [1993] ICJ Rep 3, 12–14 ('[T]he Court therefore considers that proceedings may validly be instituted by a State against a State which is a party to [. . .] a special provision in a treaty in force, but is not party to the Statute, and independently of the conditions laid down by the Security Council in its resolution 9 of 1946').

further contributions on the Court's jurisprudence put it, 'The pronouncements of law made by the Court generally become instant classics in our discipline and trustworthy references as to the state of the law.'[7] The function, structure, procedure and jurisprudence of the Court have benefited from unremitting attention in legal literature. One need only consult the imposing annual bibliographies issued by the Court itself to assess the breadth of academic writing thereupon: more than 1,000 bibliographical references concerning the Court were received by its Registry during the year 2003 alone.[8] The total number of articles, books and other writings concerning the Court that have been recorded in all such annual bibliographies over time now runs 'into five figures'.[9]

A number of these commentators expect the Court to seize all available opportunities to authoritatively 'say what the law is' in the abstract, almost for the benefit of the legal system as a whole rather than the parties before it. However, this is not the Court's primary function – not even in the context of the exercise of its advisory jurisdiction. Indeed, the jurists entrusted by the Council of the League of Nations to prepare plans for the Permanent Court of International Justice in 1920 had a rather more pragmatic approach than the proposals of Wehberg and the solemn words of Mr Bourgeois might have suggested. The president of the Advisory Committee of Jurists, Baron Descamps of Belgium, saw the primary function of the nascent Court as solving disputes: 'The first duty of the judge is to render a sentence,' he opined.[10] Similarly, Arturo Ricci-Busatti, the Italian legal adviser, highlighted that it was 'the aim and nature of the *function* of the Court that must be considered. The Court was intended to settle disputes between States by an authority other than that of the States themselves.'[11] Similarly, in 1945, the Committee of Jurists entrusted with preparing the draft Statute of the International Court of Justice explicitly indicated in what became Article 38 of the Court's Statute that its primary role was deciding 'in accordance with international law such disputes as are submitted to it'.[12]

The aim of this chapter is to discuss the role and functions of the International Court of Justice in light of this recurrent tension between the perceived role of the Court as the ultimate authority speaking 'eternal truth' on all questions of

7 Santiago Villalpando, 'On the International Court of Justice and the Determination of Rules of Law' (2013) 26 LJIL 243, 245.

8 *ICJ Bibliography No 57* (concerning 2003, International Court of Justice 2012), <http://www.icj-cij.org/files/publications/bibliography-en.pdf>. This is the last year for which an annual bibliography was published at the time of writing.

9 Ibid. 117.

10 Advisory Committee of Jurists (n 3) 48; see also ibid. 45–48 (for his argument that international arbitration and judicial proceedings before the nascent court were similar in their primary purpose, i.e. solving disputes).

11 Ibid. 107.

12 The addition was pursuant to a proposal by Chile: United Nations Conference on International Organization, 'Summary Report of Nineteenth Meeting of Committee IV/1', Doc. 799, IV/1/63, 5 June 1945, *Documents of the United Nations Conference on International Organization*, vol. 13, 279, 285.

international law and its actual mandate – settling disputes between states and advising on legal questions upon the request of the General Assembly, the Security Council, or any other organ of the United Nations system so authorised by the General Assembly. This chapter will describe such a role by reference to the Charter of the United Nations, the Statute of the Court, and the Court's own pronouncements on its own purpose.[13]

The settlement of international disputes as the core function of the Court

Resolving disputes is the core function of the Court. This is plainly stated in Article 38 of the Statute of the Court, which is devoted to the sources of applicable law. Before enumerating such sources, the Article incidentally asserts that the 'function' of the Court 'is to decide in accordance with international law such disputes as are submitted to it'.[14] The Court itself sees its own mandate in these terms. As it remarked on two separate occasions in 1998 and 1999, while dealing with complex situations concerning consular rights in the context of domestic criminal proceedings involving foreign nationals, 'The function of [the] Court is to resolve international legal disputes between States, *inter alia* when they arise out of the interpretation or application of international conventions.'[15]

13 In view of the mentioned multifariousness of academic writing on the Court, it is not possible to do justice here, even cursorily, to the many authoritative publications thereupon. See, among many other seminal works in the last decade: Paula Wojcikiewicz Almeida, Jean-Marc Sorel, *Latin America and the International Court of Justice: Contributions to International Law* (Routledge 2017); Philippe Couvreur, *The International Court of Justice and the Effectiveness of International Law* (Brill 2017); Pierre Michel Eisemann, Photini Pazartzis, *La jurisprudence de la Cour internationale de Justice* (Pedone 2008); Xue Hanqin, *Jurisdiction of the International Court of Justice* (Brill Nijhoff 2017); Giorgio Gaja, Jenny Grote Stoutenburg (eds.), *Enhancing the Rule of Law through the International Court of Justice* (Brill Nijhoff 2014); Gleider I. Hernández, *The International Court of Justice and the Judicial Function* (OUP 2014); Robert Kolb, *La Cour internationale de Justice* (Pedone 2014; English edn Hart 2013); Max Planck Institute for Comparative Public Law and International Law, *World Court Digest* <http://www.mpil.de/en/pub/publications/archive/wcd.cfm> accessed 1 June 2018; Malcom N. Shaw, *Rosenne's Law and Practice of the International Court: 1920–2015* (5th edn, Brill Nijhoff 2016); Juan José Quintana, *Litigation at the International Court of Justice: Practice and Procedure* (Brill Nijhoff 2015); Christian J. Tams, James Sloan (eds.), *The Development of International Law by the International Court of Justice* (OUP 2013); Hugh Thirlway, *The International Court of Justice* (OUP 2016); Hugh Thirlway, *The Law and Procedure of the International Court of Justice: Fifty Years of Jurisprudence* (OUP 2013); Andreas Zimmermann, Karin Oellers-Frahm, Christian Tomuschat, and Christian J. Tams (eds.) *The Statute of the International Court of Justice: A Commentary* (2nd edn, OUP 2012).

14 Tellingly, the equivalent provision in the Statute of the Permanent Court of International Justice did not mention the functions of that Court, perhaps because this had been enshrined in Article 14 of the Covenant of the League of Nations.

15 And, it continued, 'not to act as a court of criminal appeal': *Vienna Convention on Consular Relations (Paraguay* v. *United States of America)* (Provisional Measures) [1998] ICJ Rep

In this regard, it is worth recalling the definition of 'dispute', the key aspects of which have been summarised by the Court in the *Obligations concerning Negotiations relating to Cessation of the Nuclear Arms Race and to Nuclear Disarmament* cases in 2016:

> According to the established case law of the Court, a dispute is 'a disagreement on a point of law or fact, a conflict of legal views or of interests' between parties (*Mavrommatis Palestine Concessions, Judgment No. 2, 1924, P.C.I.J., Series A, No. 2*, p. 11). In order for a dispute to exist, '[I]t must be shown that the claim of one party is positively opposed by the other' (*South West Africa (Ethiopia v. South Africa; Liberia v. South Africa), Preliminary Objections, Judgment, I.C.J. Reports 1962*, p. 328). The two sides must ' "hold clearly opposite views concerning the question of the performance or non-performance of certain" international obligations' (*Alleged Violations of Sovereign Rights and Maritime Spaces in the Caribbean Sea (Nicaragua v. Colombia), Preliminary Objections, Judgment, I.C.J. Reports 2016 (I)*, p. 26, para. 50, citing *Interpretation of Peace Treaties with Bulgaria, Hungary and Romania, First Phase, Advisory Opinion, I.C.J. Reports 1950*, p. 74).[16]

The function of settling international disputes is not exclusive to the Court. The Charter of the United Nations designates the Court as 'the principal judicial organ of the United Nations' (Article 92) – the 'principal', not the 'only' judicial organ. As the other contributions in this book attest, judicial institutions are now aplenty in the system of international law. Article 95 of the Charter explicitly alludes to 'other tribunals' as possible methods for states to solve 'their differences'. Furthermore, the designation of the Court as a 'judicial organ' must be considered alongside Article 33 of the Charter, which mentions 'judicial settlement' as one of many available methods of dispute settlement. Thus, the role of the Court must be understood in the broader context of the settlement of international disputes under the United Nations Charter. A non-exhaustive list of the many other strategies available to states is contained in Article 33 (1) of the Charter, which mentions 'negotiation, enquiry, mediation, conciliation, arbitration, judicial settlement, resort to regional agencies or arrangements' as well as 'other peaceful means of [the parties'] own choice'. This vast array of options counterbalances the prohibition of the use of force as a method of dispute

248, 257, para. 38; reiterated *verbatim* at *LaGrand (Germany* v. *United States of America)* (Provisional Measures) [1999] ICJ Rep 9, 15, para. 25.

16 *Obligations concerning Negotiations relating to Cessation of the Nuclear Arms Race and to Nuclear Disarmament (Marshall Islands* v. *United Kingdom)* (Preliminary Objections) [2016] ICJ Rep 833, 849, para. 38. See also *Obligations concerning Negotiations relating to Cessation of the Nuclear Arms Race and to Nuclear Disarmament (Marshall Islands* v. *Pakistan)* (Jurisdiction and Admissibility) [2016] ICJ Rep 552, 566, para. 34; *Obligations concerning Negotiations relating to Cessation of the Nuclear Arms Race and to Nuclear Disarmament (Marshall Islands* v. *India)* (Jurisdiction and Admissibility) [2016] ICJ Rep 255, 269, para. 34.

settlement, as per Articles 2 (4) and 39 to 51 of the Charter. In a nutshell, the Charter prescribes that states are free to employ any method they wish to settle their differences, except war.

Because the Court is just one method of dispute settlement among many, the existence of proceedings before the Court does not preclude the concomitant use of a number of different methods in relation to the same dispute. As the Court remarked in *Passage through the Great Belt (Finland/Denmark)*, 'Pending a decision of the Court on the merits, any negotiation between the Parties with a view to achieving a direct and friendly settlement is to be welcomed.'[17] In this regard, the Permanent Court of International Justice had also had the occasion to remark that 'The judicial settlement of international disputes, with a view to which the Court has been established, is simply an alternative to the direct and friendly settlement of such disputes between the parties; [. . .] consequently it is for the Court to facilitate, so far as is compatible with its Statute, such direct and friendly settlement.'[18]

Indeed, strategies of dispute settlement are not necessarily alternative, but they are often complementary to each other. Proceedings before the Court may be best suited for some but not all aspects of a given situation, or the Court may only have jurisdiction to intervene on one aspect of a much more complex situation. For example, the case concerning *Questions relating to the Seizure and Detention of Certain Documents and Data (Timor-Leste* v. *Australia)* arose in 2013 in the context of a pending arbitration under the 2002 Timor Sea Treaty between Timor-Leste and Australia, and was eventually discontinued after two orders by the Court indicating provisional measures had positively contributed to the resolution of one crucial but circumscribed aspect of a broader dispute.[19] Many years earlier, in 1986, at the end of the *Nicaragua* v. *United States of America* judgment on the merits, the Court, while recalling that Article 33 of the Charter reflected 'the principle of customary international law that prescribes the peaceful settlement of international disputes', underlined that, even after the judgment on the merits the Court had just rendered, the 'difficult situation in the region' would still now require 'delicate and difficult negotiations'.[20] Even in those cases where it found that it lacked jurisdiction, the Court has sometimes reminded states of 'their obligation to settle their disputes by peaceful means'.[21]

Article 33 of the Charter makes clear that the pacific settlement of international disputes revolves around the key principle of consent: the methods to be employed

17 *Passage through the Great Belt (Finland/Denmark)* (Provisional Measures) [1991] ICJ Rep 12, 20, para. 35.

18 *Free Zones of Upper Savoy and the District of Gex*, PCIJ Series A No. 22, 13.

19 See *Questions relating to the Seizure and Detention of Certain Documents and Data (Timor-Leste* v. *Australia)* (Provisional Measures) [2014] ICJ Rep 147, (Modification of Provisional Measures) [2015] ICJ Rep 556, and (Discontinuance) [2015] ICJ Rep 572.

20 *Military and Paramilitary Activities in and against Nicaragua (Nicaragua* v. *United States of America)* (Merits) [1986] ICJ Rep 14, 145.

21 *Aerial Incident of 10 August 1999 (Pakistan* v. *India)* (Jurisdiction of the Court) [2000] ICJ Rep 12, 53.

are those 'of their [that is, the parties'] own choice'. Article 36 of the Court's Statute gives effect to the principle of consent in relation to the Court's exercise of jurisdiction. As Judge *ad hoc* Elihu Lauterpacht clearly explained in his separate opinion in the *Bosnia and Herzegovina* v. *Yugoslavia (Serbia and Montenegro)* decision on provisional measures of 1993, such consent may take many forms:

> The Court can only act in a case if the parties, both applicant and respondent, have conferred jurisdiction upon it by some voluntary act of consent. This can be given in various forms: a treaty undertaking to that effect; a contracting-in to the compulsory jurisdiction of the Court under the so-called 'optional clause' (Article 36 (2) of its Statute); or an acceptance of jurisdiction by a respondent through its conduct following upon a unilateral commencement of proceedings by an applicant – a method known as *forum prorogatum*. Whatever form the consent may take, the range of matters that the Court can then deal with is limited to the matters covered by that consent.[22]

The principle of consent, he added, often severely restricted the ambit of what the Court could pronounce itself upon.[23] While it might be tempting to criticise the Court for only focusing on genocide in the context of complex situations involving a great number of grave breaches of international humanitarian law, as was the case in both cases concerning the application of the Genocide Convention in the former Yugoslavia,[24] such a narrow focus was the result of the extent of the Court's jurisdiction, rather than the Court's choosing:

> The possibility must be recognized and accepted that there are a number – alas, a very great number – of substantive rights protected by international law which, for want of a suitable jurisdictional link to the Court, cannot be made the subject of consideration and decision by it. This is not the fault of the Court. It is simply a reflection of the present unsatisfactory state of the international legal system – a reflection, many consider, of a lack of appropriate political will on the part of States, not a reflection of any shortcoming in the Court. If jurisdiction exists, the Court will exercise it. That, after all, is what the Court is for.[25]

A corollary to the principle of consent is enshrined in Article 59 of the Court's Statute, which provides that the decisions of the Court have 'no binding force

22 *Application of the Convention on the Prevention and Punishment of the Crime of Genocide (Bosnia and Herzegovina* v. *Yugoslavia (Serbia and Montenegro))* (Provisional Measures) [1993] ICJ Rep 325, 412 (Sep Op Judge *ad hoc* Lauterpacht).

23 Ibid. 412–413.

24 Ibid.; and *Application of the Convention on the Prevention and Punishment of the Crime of Genocide (Croatia* v. *Serbia)* (Merits) [2015] ICJ Rep 3.

25 Ibid. 412–413.

except between the parties and in respect of [the] particular case' that was decided. As the Court remarked in the *Frontier Dispute* between Burkina Faso and Mali:

> A judicial decision . . . merely substitutes for the solution stemming directly from [the] shared intention [of the parties], the solution arrived at by a court under the mandate which they have given it. In both instances, the solution only has legal and binding effect as between the States which have accepted it, either directly or as a consequence of having accepted the court's jurisdiction to decide the case.[26]

There is thus no *stare decisis* before the International Court of Justice. In practice, however, the Court will 'follow the reasoning and conclusions of earlier cases' – at times religiously so – unless it finds 'cause' to do otherwise.[27] This means that it is certainly possible to analyse the Court's established jurisprudence in particular areas of the law. Prudence, however, is required in that regard. The fact that settling disputes is the core function of the Court and that its decisions in principle only bind the parties should caution against making hasty inferences about the state of international law from judgments of the Court, especially if they are isolated. A contextual analysis is always required to determine whether a finding of law which appears implied in the Court's reasoning on a particular case is in fact a finding reached by the Court or simply the practical result of the parties' litigation strategies. It is important not to jump to the conclusion that established jurisprudence exists on a particular matter.

One of many possible examples in this respect was discussed by Judge Yusuf in his separate opinion on the *Burkina Faso / Niger* case of 2013, which concerned a territorial boundary delimitation.[28] In his view, it was erroneous to assume the equivalence of *uti possidetis juris* with the principle on the respect of boundaries at the time of independence that is now enshrined in Article 4 (b) of the Constitutive Act of the African Union.[29] Such an equivalence, having been embraced by the parties in their pleadings in *Burkina Faso / Niger*, may also appear to have been implied in the judgment of the Court, which, as to this point, mostly followed the precedent of the *Burkina Faso / Mali* case of 1986.[30] The implication of such an equivalence was an over-reliance on French colonial law,

26 *Frontier Dispute (Burkina Faso/Mali)* [1986] ICJ Rep 554, 577–578, para. 46.

27 *Land and Maritime Boundary between Cameroon and Nigeria* (Preliminary Objections) [1998] ICJ Rep 275, 292, para. 28 ('It is true that, in accordance with Article 59, the Court's judgments bind only the parties to and in respect of a particular case. There can be no question of holding Nigeria to decisions reached by the Court in previous cases. The real question is whether, in this case, there is cause not to follow the reasoning and conclusions of earlier cases.').

28 *Frontier Dispute (Burkina Faso/Niger)*, [2013] ICJ Rep 44, 134–148 (Sep Op Judge Yusuf).

29 Ibid. 146, para. 39.

30 Ibid. 147–148, paras. 44–46. See also *Frontier Dispute (Burkina Faso/Mali)*, [1986] ICJ Rep 554, 565–566, para. 22.

or '*droit d'outre-mer*', which may in fact be unwarranted.[31] Thus, a commentator reading only the two *Frontier Dispute* judgments involving Burkina Faso of 1986 and of 2013 may reach the hasty inference that the state of international law on the matter is that the principle on the respect of boundaries at the time of independence in the African context is the same as the *uti possidetis juris* principle. Whether this is indeed the case is beside the point here. The issue is that such inference would arise from the way in which the cases were pleaded before the Court in the 1980s and in the 2010s (including in part by the same lawyers), rather than because of a full consideration by the Court of this complex issue. However, these two decisions should not be read as having settled the matter. On their own, the parties to a case before the Court should not inadvertently be treated as the legislators of international legal principles.

Tending to the law as an ancillary function

Many commentators would argue that reducing the Court's function to dispute settlement discounts the profound impact of the Court's jurisprudence on the system of international law. The aim of the present chapter is certainly not to deny such impact. The established jurisprudence of the Court has made a fundamental contribution to international law.

Such contribution is explicitly recognised in the system of sources of international law. Article 38 of the Court's Statute indicates that, 'subject to the provisions of Article 59', judicial decisions, including decisions of the Court itself, are among the sources that the Court shall apply 'as subsidiary means for the determination of rules of law', that is, to assist in identifying rules of law arising from treaties, custom, or general principles of law. In relation to custom, in particular, the International Law Commission clarified that asserting that judicial decisions are subsidiary means 'is not intended to suggest that such decisions are not important'.[32] The Commission went on to clarify, however, that one should not automatically rely thereupon – once again, prudence is key:

> Decisions of courts and tribunals on questions of international law, in particular those decisions in which the existence of rules of customary international law is considered and such rules are identified and applied, may offer valuable guidance for determining the existence or otherwise of rules of customary international law. The value of such decisions varies greatly, however, depending both on the quality of the reasoning of each decision (including primarily the extent to which it results from a thorough examination of evidence of an alleged general practice accepted as law) and on the reception of the decision, in particular by States and in subsequent case law.[33]

31 *Frontier Dispute (Burkina Faso/Niger)*, [2013] ICJ Rep 44, 147–148, para. 45 (Sep Op Judge Yusuf).

32 Commentary to draft conclusion 13 on the identification of customary international law, para. (2), UN Doc. A/73/10, 149.

33 Ibid. para. (3) of the commentary to draft conclusion 13.

In other words, according to the Commission, before drawing any conclusions as to the existence of a rule of customary international law from a judicial decision, be it domestic or international, it is necessary to conduct an analysis of that decision, *inter alia* to consider whether the court in question actually conducted any examination of evidence of the existence of the customary international law rule being considered. This applies *mutatis mutandis* to the determination of rules of law arising from other sources such as treaties or general principles of law. The example provided above concerning *uti possidetis juris* is a case in point. Decisions of the Court should not be read as if each statement of the law they contain is a provision binding on all states, but as possible guidance in navigating through the many available sources of international law.

It is nonetheless undeniable that, over the years, the established jurisprudence of the Court has contributed to our understanding of many areas of international law.[34] In addition to its classic pronouncements on foundational matters such as the sources of international law, the formation and evidence of customary international law,[35] *erga omnes* obligations,[36] and many aspects of the law of treaties (especially interpretation),[37] the Court has also significantly contributed to the law of the sea (especially maritime delimitation),[38] the law of territorial boundaries,[39] the jurisdictional immunities of states,[40] state responsibility,[41] the law of international organisations,[42] the use of force in international law,[43] the law of armed conflict (especially self-defence),[44] and, more recently, international environmental law[45] and international human rights law.[46] Of course, the Court

34 The examples provided in the text and notes below (n 34 to n 46) are purely illustrative in nature.

35 See e.g. *Jurisdictional Immunities of the State (Germany* v. *Italy: Greece intervening)* [2012] ICJ Rep 99, 121–142.

36 See e.g. *Barcelona Traction, Light and Power Company, Limited (Belgium* v. *Spain)* (Second Phase) [1970] ICJ Rep 3, 32, para. 33; *Legal Consequences of the Construction of a Wall in the Occupied Palestinian Territory* (Advisory Opinion) [2004] ICJ Rep 136, 199, para. 155.

37 See e.g. *Dispute regarding Navigational and Related Rights (Costa Rica* v. *Nicaragua)* [2009] ICJ Rep 213, 232–253.

38 See e.g. *Maritime Dispute (Peru* v. *Chile)* [2014] ICJ Rep 3.

39 See e.g. *Frontier Dispute (Burkina Faso/Niger)* [2013] ICJ Rep 44.

40 See e.g. *Jurisdictional Immunities of the State (Germany* v. *Italy: Greece intervening)* [2012] ICJ Rep 99.

41 See e.g. *Application of the Convention on the Prevention and Punishment of the Crime of Genocide (Bosnia and Herzegovina* v. *Serbia and Montenegro)* [2007] ICJ Rep 43.

42 See e.g. *Difference Relating to Immunity from Legal Process of a Special Rapporteur of the Commission on Human Rights* (Advisory Opinion) [1999] ICJ Rep 62.

43 See e.g. *Armed Activities on the Territory of the Congo (Democratic Republic of the Congo* v. *Uganda)*, [2005] ICJ Rep 168.

44 See ibid.

45 See e.g. *Certain Activities Carried Out by Nicaragua in the Border Area (Costa Rica* v. *Nicaragua)* and *Construction of a Road in Costa Rica along the San Juan River (Nicaragua* v. *Costa Rica)*, [2015] ICJ Rep 665.

46 See e.g. *Ahmadou Sadio Diallo (Republic of Guinea* v. *Democratic Republic of the Congo)* (Merits) [2010] ICJ Rep 639; (Compensation) [2012] ICJ Rep 324.

has also developed a rich jurisprudence on its own jurisdictional and procedural law, which is often relevant to the settlement of international disputes more generally.[47] It is only to be expected that such contribution will continue in future, as the Court continues to be employed by states to settle their disputes.

It is crucial, however, that the Court itself views the elucidation of rules of international law as ancillary to its main function of solving disputes. When discussing its function in relation to the finding of rules of law, the Court generally underlines that its role is to find all the law needed to solve the dispute at hand, and nothing but the law that is in fact needed to solve that dispute. As the Court put it in the *Fisheries Jurisdiction* cases, the law that the Court must consider on its own initiative under the principle of *jura novit curia* is the law 'relevant to the settlement of the dispute'.[48] In practice, the Court will often take pains to avoid making judicial pronouncements on a given issue of law unless such a pronouncement is necessary to its line of reasoning. For example, in the *Croatia* v. *Serbia* case concerning the application of the Genocide Convention, the Court avoided ruling on the 'serious questions of law' arising from a subsidiary claim of Croatia based on the principle of succession of states to international responsibility by addressing the merits of the case in a certain order, so that it effectively became unnecessary to examine the law on succession to state responsibility.[49] While the question of succession to international responsibility is one on which a pronouncement by the Court would have been most welcome by academics and practitioners alike (customary international law still being unsettled thereupon), judicial caution was carefully embedded in the line of reasoning itself.

It is of course true that, under Article 96 of the Charter, the Court may give advisory opinions 'on any legal question' when requested to do so by the General Assembly or the Security Council, as well as advisory opinions on legal questions arising within the scope of the activities of other entities in the United Nations system authorised by the General Assembly to seek such advisory opinions. In this context, the Court may find itself confronted with legal questions that are more abstract in nature than those arising during the exercise of its contentious jurisdiction. However, even when exercising its advisory jurisdiction, the Court has generally limited itself to answering the question at hand. For example, in the *Legality of the Threat or Use of Nuclear Weapons* Advisory Opinion, the Court

47 See e.g. the *Marshall Islands* cases, above n 17.

48 *Fisheries Jurisdiction (United Kingdom* v. *Iceland)* [1974] ICJ Rep 3, 9, para. 17; *Fisheries Jurisdiction (Federal Republic of Germany* v. *Iceland)* [1974] ICJ Rep 175, 181, para. 18 ('The Court [. . .], as an international judicial organ, is deemed to take judicial notice of international law, and is therefore required in a case falling under Article 53 of the Statute, as in any other case, to consider on its own initiative all rules of international law which may be relevant to the settlement of the dispute. It being the duty of the Court itself to ascertain and apply the relevant law in the given circumstances of the case, the burden of establishing or proving rules of international law cannot be imposed upon any of the parties, for the law lies within the judicial knowledge of the Court.').

49 See *Application of the Convention on the Prevention and Punishment of the Crime of Genocide (Croatia* v. *Serbia)* (Merits) [2015] ICJ Rep 3, 55–56, paras. 112–114, and 129, para. 442.

explicitly avoided pronouncing itself in the abstract about the *jus cogens* nature of rules of international humanitarian law (and famously came close to a *non liquet* as to the main question addressed thereto).[50] Indeed, the Court clearly described the practical nature of its advisory function in the 1989 Advisory Opinion on the *Applicability of Article VI, Section 22, of the Convention on the Privileges and Immunities of the United Nations*:

> The jurisdiction of the Court under Article 96 of the Charter and Article 65 of the Statute, to give advisory opinions on legal questions, enables United Nations entities to seek guidance from the Court in order to conduct their activities in accordance with law. These opinions are advisory, not binding. As the opinions are intended for the guidance of the United Nations, the consent of States is not a condition precedent to the competence of the Court to give them.[51]

The fact that clarifying international law is an ancillary function of the Court's jurisprudence, and not its main role, puts into question the meaningfulness of the recurring debates on the fragmentation of international law in light of the proliferation of international courts and tribunals.[52] These debates often highlight the inconsistencies between statements concerning the law in decisions by different courts and tribunals. A common example is the difference of opinion between the International Criminal Tribunal for the former Yugoslavia and the International Court of Justice on issues of attribution of conduct for internationally wrongful acts committed in the context of armed conflict.[53] It may be tempting to encourage the International Court of Justice to settle such inconsistencies as a 'first among peers', at least insofar as general international law is concerned, as the Court seems to have usefully done in the *Bosnian Genocide* case.[54] However, despite the aspirations concerning universal and permanent compulsory jurisdiction at the turn of the twentieth century,[55] the Court was not designed primarily as a mechanism for achieving uniformity in international law, but as a dispute settlement mechanism. Although it is certainly beneficial when the Court finds itself in a position to create such uniformity, expecting the Court to play such a role as a matter of course is a tested recipe for disappointment.

50 *Legality of the Threat or Use of Nuclear Weapons* (Advisory Opinion) [1996] ICJ Rep 226, 258; and see para. 2(E) of the operative clause, ibid., 266.
51 *Applicability of Article VI, Section 22, of the Convention on the Privileges and Immunities of the United Nations* (Advisory Opinion) [1989] ICJ Rep 177, 188.
52 International Law Commission, 'Report of the study group on the fragmentation of international law, finalized by Martti Koskenniemi', UN Doc. A/CN.4/L.682, A/CN.4/L.682/Corr.1 and A/CN.4/L.682/Add.1.
53 E.g. at ibid., paras. 49–52.
54 *Application of the Convention on the Prevention and Punishment of the Crime of Genocide (Bosnia and Herzegovina* v. *Serbia and Montenegro)* (Judgment) 2007 ICJ Rep 43, 209.
55 See above n 2.

This may be contrasted with the role of supreme courts, especially in civil law countries, whose explicit function is to correct and clarify matters of law arising from lower courts. In Italian legal circles, for instance, the *Corte di Cassazione* is described as having the function of *nomofilachia*, or 'tending to the law'.[56] Such a function entails the authoritative selection of the 'correct' interpretation of legal provisions among the multifarious statements that a legal system without *stare decisis* inevitably engenders. International law similarly has no *stare decisis*, and thus would benefit from authoritative final statements on the state of the law. However, as Judge Mbaye famously put it in the *Guinea Bissau* v. *Senegal* case, the International Court of Justice is not 'the *Cour de cassation* for all States'.[57] It may indeed be called to clarify international law, but always in relation to the dispute at hand or the question before it. When considering the possible contribution of the Court to the evolution of international law, it is imperative to manage one's expectations as to the role that the Court is properly called to play.

Conclusion: is there a 'right' type of dispute for the Court?

The practical orientation of the Court's work is one of its strengths, not a weakness. It would perhaps be desirable for more states to unreservedly accept the Court's jurisdiction under the optional declaration of Article 36(2) of its Statute, thus recognising 'as compulsory ipso facto and without special agreement, in relation to any other state accepting the same obligation, the jurisdiction of the Court'. If states so willed, a universal system of compulsory jurisdiction could thus arise, and the nature of the Court might swing more heavily towards the *Cour de cassation* role. However, in the absence of such political will (and perhaps irrespective thereof), the Court is best suited to solve those disputes in which the parties are fully committed to the process. From the perspective of dispute settlement more generally, the unwitting participation of one of the parties to proceedings before the Court is less likely to solve the underlying dispute.

Over the years, the Court has accumulated a wealth of experience in solving precisely those types of disputes, such as maritime and territorial boundary delimitations, where the interest of both parties in reaching an authoritative determination of the underlying dispute is strong. For a state having a theoretical maritime claim to a large Exclusive Economic Zone that conflicts with a similar claim by another state, it might be difficult to attract investment or otherwise exploit resources; the benefits of an authoritative judicial determination are evident even if the ultimately determined Exclusive Economic Zone happens to be

56 See Italian Law (decreto legislativo) n 40 of 2 February 2006, explicitly mentioning the 'funzione nomofilattica' of procedures before the Court of Cassation. For a general assessment thereof, see Michele Taruffo, 'Precedente e giurisprudenza' [2007] Rivista trimestrale di diritto e procedura civile 709.

57 *Arbitral Award of 31 July 1989 (Guinea Bissau* v. *Senegal)*, [1991] ICJ Rep 53, 80 (Decl. Judge Mbaye).

smaller. In other words, the legal certainty of one's maritime entitlements has a value of its own. In this type of case, the Court usually benefits from a full commitment of both parties to the process and its outcome (even if partly unfavourable). *Actio finium regundorum*, the Roman law suit of delimitation of boundaries between neighbours, comes to mind: the practical solution of conflicting claims, rather than the grandiloquent statement of 'eternal truth', is the core function the Court has performed best in practice.

Does such an account of the Court's role – dispute settlement at its core, statement of the law as ancillary thereto – diminish its possible function as 'the judicial power of humanity', as its first proponents hoped in the 1920s? This depends on the perspective one favours. The Court's central role in the system of peaceful settlement of international disputes is, above all, a contribution to international peace and security. When states employ the Court to settle their differences, they are not engaging in armed conflict, which might well have been an option to settle boundary disputes in the pre-Charter era. The system envisaged by the Charter to 'save succeeding generations from the scourge of war' is thus reaffirmed through the Court's work.

8 Delegitimation of global courts

Lessons from the past

Zuzanna Godzimirska

International courts need to be perceived as legitimate by their constituents in order to function effectively, to ensure compliance with their decisions, and ultimately to survive.[1] Recent strikes at the World Trade Organization's (WTO) Appellate Body (AB) by the United States and the stalling of the selection of new AB members, remind us why perceived legitimacy is important, and demonstrate that low perceptions of legitimacy may have paralysing effects on a court. Often, however, the delegitimation of an international court is less dramatic and far more subtle, with the rejection of a court's claims to authority being expressed through language. A court's constituents may signal, in more or less categorical terms, that they do not approve of the way in which a court exercises its authority, by criticising it for instance for expansive treaty interpretation, impartiality or inefficiency. Communicative means like these may also be used to *legitimate* international courts. Constituents may praise a court when they believe a case has been settled in a fair manner, or that the court has interpreted a treaty text in accordance with the majority's view on the matter.[2]

This chapter sheds new light on the extent to which states have accepted two global courts' claims to authority over the past 20 years. Drawing on a dataset comprising government statements issued in two political bodies, the United Nations General Assembly (UNGA) and the WTO's Dispute Settlement Body (DSB), and 36 interviews with government and court officials at the UN and WTO,[3] this chapter provides an analysis of the (de)legitimation of the International Court of Justice (ICJ) and the WTO AB, in the period 1996–2016.

1 Daniel Bodansky, 'The Legitimacy of International Governance: A Coming Challenge for International Environmental Law?' (1999) 93 *American Journal of International Law* 596, 603; Mark Kersten, *Justice in Conflict: The Effects of the International Criminal Court's Interventions on Ending Wars and Building Peace* (Oxford University Press 2016) 168.

2 Cosette Creamer and Zuzanna Godzimirska, '(De)Legitimation at the WTO Dispute Settlement Mechanism' (2016) 49 *Vanderbilt Journal of Transnational Law* 275.

3 Twenty-eight interviews were conducted during 13–17 January 2014 in Geneva, Switzerland. Three interviewees were officials within the WTO Secretariat; 25 interviews were conducted with current or former delegates representing their respective members within DSB meetings. Eight interviews were conducted during 25–30 October 2017 in New York, United States. All of these interviewees were current legal advisors involved in the process of drafting statements

The chapter proceeds as follows. The first section lays the conceptual foundations and outlines the actors engaged in, and the means of, international court legitimation. The section that follows presents the data and methods employed to map the extent to which states have accepted the AB's and the ICJ's claims to authority over the past 20 years. This is followed by an empirical analysis, which sheds light on states that have engaged in debates on the two courts and evaluated their exercise of authority. Finally, it explores the specific issues that have caused concern among UN and WTO members over the past 20 years. Building on these findings, the final section reflects on what we can learn from past views expressed by governments in assessing the future of these two global, inter-state courts.

Legitimation of international courts

The term legitimacy connotes both a normative and descriptive dimension. In normative terms, legitimacy is about the rightfulness of institutions.[4] Whether an institution is considered legitimate from a normative perspective depends on arguments put forth by moral, political and legal theory.[5] The descriptive dimension of legitimacy, in turn, relates to the acceptance of an institution's claims to authority.[6] In this sense, legitimacy may be empirically assessed or measured, by tracing various constituents' attitudes or beliefs.[7] It is this latter form of legitimacy that is the subject of this chapter.

In his seminal work on the legitimacy of international governance, Bodansky defines perceived legitimacy as the 'justification of authority'.[8] This definition suggests that legitimacy is not merely a static quality possessed by an institution. Legitimacy in this sense needs to be continually claimed, and these claims need to be *perceived* as justified for legitimacy to be obtained and maintained. For this reason it is more fruitful to talk of legitimation, rather than legitimacy, as this better captures the relational and temporal character of legitimacy – as an interactive process between an institution and its constituents that changes over time. This is

---

on the Report of the International Court of Justice in meetings of the UNGA. Members interviewed in Geneva and New York varied across relevant characteristics, including size, wealth, use of ICJ or WTO dispute settlement systems, and vocal participation within meetings of the DSB in the context of adoption of AB reports and UNGA meetings on the Report of the ICJ. The identities of all interviewees have been redacted and replaced with random numbers, to ensure interviewee confidentiality.

4 Achim Hurrelmann, Steffen Schneider and Jens Steffek, 'Introduction: Legitimacy in an Age of Global Politics' in Achim Hurrelmann, Steffen Schneider and Jens Steffek (eds.), *Legitimacy in an Age of Global Politics* (Palgrave Macmillan 2007) 3.

5 Daniel Bodansky, 'Legitimacy in International Law and International Relations' in Jeffrey Dunoff and Mark A Pollack (eds.), *Interdisciplinary Perspectives on International Law and International Relations. The State of the Art.* (Cambridge University Press 2013).

6 Max Weber, *Economy and Society, an Outline of Interpretive Sociology* (Bedminster Press 1968).

7 Henning Schmidtke and Frank Nullmeier, 'Political Valuation Analysis and the Legitimacy of International Organizations' (2011) 7 *German Policy Studies* 117; Bodansky (n 5).

8 Bodansky (n 1) 602.

also more in line with more recent research, which sees legitimation as a process of the making of claims by an institution and the subsequent rejection or attribution of these claims by its various constituents.[9] Within this understanding of legitimation, institutions like international courts are thus *legitimated* when their claims to authority are accepted by their various constituents, and conversely, *delegitimated* when instead they are rejected.

While some contend that the process of legitimation occurs primarily *within* the institution,[10] it is widely acknowledged that the process of legitimation also, and maybe primarily, concerns the acceptance of practices by *outside* constituents. As such, it is an interactive process between those in possession of a certain type of authority and their subjects.[11] For an international court, and in particular one that settles inter-state disputes, its primary concern is the acceptance of its claims to authority by the body of states that have conferred jurisdiction upon it, whose compliance with its decisions matter the most and whose withdrawal from the court may altogether determine the survival of the court. That said, delegitimation may take place by the entire membership of a court, by subsets of it, or just one state.

One can distinguish between communicative and institutional means of legitimation. Institutional legitimation encompasses 'substantive forms of behavioural adaptation and institutional change'.[12] The stalling of the initiation of the AB selection process by the US is one example of such institutional delegitimation. Communicative means of legitimation, on the other hand, comprise discursive practices about an institution, its identity and (exercise of) authority. The African Union and its member states' discursive attack on the International Criminal Court in recent years as a biased and racist court, is one of the more severe examples of delegitimation through communicative means.[13]

The focus of this chapter is on these latter means. More specifically, I examine the communicative means that member states of two international courts – the ICJ and the WTO AB – have employed to evaluate the acceptability of these institutions over the past 20 years.

Data and methods

Government statements

To shed light on the discursive (de)legitimation of international courts by states, I analyse government statements made in UNGA debates on the annual report of

9 Jennifer Gronau and Henning Schmidtke, 'The Quest for Legitimacy in World Politics – International Institutions' Legitimation Strategies' (2016) 42 *Review of International Studies* 535.

10 Rodney Barker, *Legitimating Identities. The Self-Presentations of Rulers and Subjects.* (Cambridge University Press 2004).

11 Gronau and Schmidtke (n 9) 539.

12 Gronau and Schmidtke (n 9) 541–542.

13 Creamer and Godzimirska (n 2).

the ICJ,[14] and DSB debates on AB reports[15] (i.e. judgments). The judicial organs of the WTO and UN formally enjoy full judicial independence from the political bodies. Yet both report to the political organs on their activities allowing states the opportunity to comment on and evaluate their exercise of authority.[16] In contrast to the UNGA, which meets once a year to discuss the annual report of the ICJ, the number of DSB meetings on reports of the AB relate to the number of reports issued in a given year.[17] Both the annual report of the ICJ and AB reports are circulated in advance of the meeting, allowing UN and WTO members to read the report and prepare statements. Statements in both fora are considered to be verbatim – and not summaries – of member statements.[18] While not all members attend the meetings or issue statements on the ICJ and the WTO AB, formally, both UNGA and DSB meetings are open to accredited representatives of all UN[19] and WTO members.[20]

The relevance and importance of these meetings to the functioning of these two courts – and indirectly for their legitimation – has been stressed within interviews and DSB and UNGA meetings by states and Court officials alike.[21] For example, in his speech to the UNGA on one of the annual reports of the ICJ, the Court's then President Judge Shi Jiuyong emphasised that 'The Court (. . .) views the close exchanges between these two principal organs of the [UN] as a guarantee of the successful accomplishment of their respective tasks and of the aims of the Organization.'[22] In a similar vein, government representatives underlined within interviews that the UNGA debate on the Report of the ICJ was 'the only way' to signal (dis)satisfaction with the ICJ, and that they were moreover useful as a way of 'taking the temperature of the UN Member States' and their attitudes towards the ICJ.[23] Similar views have been expressed within interviews with WTO officials and government representatives, with one WTO official, saying that 'Through the Secretariat the members of (. . .) the AB are

14 Meeting records of the UNGA on the Report of the ICJ were obtained through the United Nations Bibliographic Information System (UNBISNET): http://unbisnet.un.org:8080/ipac20/ipac.jsp?profile=speech&menu=search&submenu=power#focus

15 Meeting records of the DSB on AB reports were obtained through WTO Documents Online: https://docs.wto.org/dol2fe/Pages/FE_Search/FE_S_S001.aspx

16 UN Charter Article 93(1).

17 At times, the DSB will debate and adopt multiple AB reports in the same meeting. Following the debate, the DSB must adopt the report unless there is a consensus against it, cf. DSU Article 17.14.

18 Rules of Procedure of the UNGA, Rule 58. Interview 2.3, Geneva, Switzerland (14 January 2014).

19 Rules of Procedure of the UNGA, Rule 25.

20 Mary E Footer, *An Institutional and Normative Analysis of the World Trade Organization*, vol 46 (Martinus Nijhoff Publishers 2006) 48.

21 Interview 10.1, UN, New York, USA (30 October 2017).

22 Statement by ICJ Judge Shi Jiuyong, UNGA meeting held on 27 October 2005, A/60/PV.39, 1–6.

23 Interview 10.3, UN, New York, USA (30 October 2017).

able to listen and pay attention. Views on reports are a way to send to them a concrete message.'[24]

States may use various other avenues to signal (dis)satisfaction with the ICJ and the WTO AB, but for three reasons debates on their reports form the best basis for an analysis of states' acceptance of these courts' claims to authority. First, focusing on debates that occur on a regular basis in the same forum provides an opportunity to track changes over years while holding the contexts constant.[25] Second, debates on these agenda items provide the most systematic way of identifying the extent and content of criticism on these two courts and their exercise of authority. Although states may issue statements under other agenda items in the UNGA or DSB, or in meetings of the UN Sixth Committee or WTO General Council, references to the ICJ and AB are unsystematic and far apart. Moreover, while states sometimes do make references to or mention the courts under other agenda items, they rarely provide evaluative comments on their exercise of authority outside the report context. Classifying statements that explicitly evaluate these courts' practices allows one to identify *which* claims to authority, or in other terms, which practices that have been rejected or accepted by these courts' main constituents. Third, representatives of the ICJ and the AB Secretariat sit in on these particular meetings[26] and what is said by members during the report debates may form a basis for these courts' legitimation practices and, as such, further fuel the process of legitimation.

Individual text classification

From meeting records in the years 1996–2016 a total of 2070 and 3410 individual paragraphs of 854 and 377 government statements on the AB and ICJ respectively were manually extracted. Each unit was coded for relevant meta-data such as the issuing state's income level, regional location, regime type, domestic legal tradition and level of independence in its judiciary, in order to examine variation in engagement on the two courts and (de)legitimation across these various state characteristics. Using paragraphs of the government statements as the unit of analysis, instead of the entire statements, allows for a more fine-grained analysis of which practices members accept or reject, or believe to merit improvement. Relying in large part on political valuation analysis,[27] a detailed coding scheme[28] was developed to manually classify all units into one of three categories: those

24 Interview 3.1, Geneva, Switzerland (15 January 2014).

25 Martin Binder and Monika Heupel, 'The Legitimacy of the UN Security Council: Evidence from Recent General Assembly Debates' (2014) 59 *International Studies Quarterly* 1.

26 Interview 2.3 and 4.4, Geneva, Switzerland (14 and 16 January 2014), Interview 9.2, UN, New York, USA (27 October 2017) and participant observation in UNGA meeting, 26 October 2017.

27 Schmidtke and Nullmeier (n 7).

28 Detailed coding rules are on file with the author.

that 1) are supportive of the court or its exercise of authority ('Supportive'),[29] 2) those that are critical towards the court or its exercise of authority ('Critical'),[30] or 3) those that are neutral about it ('Neutral').[31]

The next section provides a descriptive analysis of the classification of evaluative views on the ICJ and the WTO AB to discern the level to which these courts' authority has been accepted by their primary constituents over the past 20 years and to identify which issues have caused concern among their respective memberships.

Empirical analysis

Between 1996 and 2016, the DSB discussed and adopted 129 reports issued by the AB.[32] WTO members have engaged consistently in debates prior to the adoption of these reports, issuing a total of 854 statements, with an average of 6.6 statements per report. In the context of the ICJ, the picture is slightly more complex. While the ICJ began operating in 1946, it only began submitting annual reports to the UNGA in 1969. Yet it took states another three decades to begin engaging in debates on the Court in this forum.[33] Between 1996 and 2016, UN members made 353 statements, with an average of 17.6 statements per report/a year.

Which UN and WTO members speak and (de)legitimate the ICJ and WTO AB?

While a number of UN and WTO members engage in debates, many do not formulate views on the courts. Overall, though, more UN members are prone to voicing a view on the report of the ICJ than WTO members are on the AB, with 41.5%[34] of the UN and merely 32.9% of the WTO membership having made at least one statement on their respective court. Accounting for those UN

29 These units fell into one of four sub-categories and 1) expressed explicit support for the court or the way it exercises its authority, 2) expressed both support and criticism, but overall expressed more support, 3) contained words of positive valence when describing the court or its exercise of authority, or 4) expressed commitment to, confidence in or support for the court.

30 These units fell into one of four sub-categories and 1) expressed explicit criticism of the court or the way it exercises its authority, 2) expressed both support and criticism, but overall expressed more criticism, 3) contained words of negative valence when describing the court or its exercise of authority, or 4) expressed potential for improvements of the court or its exercise of authority.

31 This category encompassed units that concerned the courts' budget, the political bodies of the UN or WTO, or members' non-compliance with decisions. If such units additionally contained an evaluative view on the court at hand, they are classified as 'Critical' or 'Supportive'.

32 This consists of 108 regular reports and 21 Article 21.5 reports (compliance proceedings).

33 Statement by Denmark, UNGA meeting held on 15 October 1993, A/48/PV.31, 4–5 (para. 1).

34 This does not account for those statements that are made on behalf of multiple states. Iran, for example, regularly makes a statement on behalf of the Non-Alignment Movement, speaking on behalf of 120 UN members. Joint statements like these are uncommon in the context of AB report adoption.

members that have accepted the ICJ's jurisdiction as compulsory adds another dimension.[35] While one might expect the 72 UN members that have accepted the Court's jurisdiction under Article 36(2) of the Statute to be more vocal about the Court, the fact is that only 43 of them have ever issued a statement on the Court. Conversely, of the 121 UN members that have *not* accepted the ICJ's jurisdiction as compulsory, 37 have issued at least one statement on the Court.[36]

Among those states that *do* engage in UNGA and DSB debates on courts' reports, the distribution of statements varies depending on states' experience with the system as well as direct involvement in a dispute at the time of issuing a statement.[37] First, given it is customary for the parties to a dispute to make a statement prior to the adoption of an AB report, it is unsurprising that the majority of AB statements (44%) are made by parties to the dispute with the remaining statements distributed between third parties (36%) and non-parties (20%). What is surprising, in comparative terms, is the hesitancy many UN members experience in voicing a view on the ICJ when they are involved in disputes before it; as such, only a quarter of all statements are made by states that at the time of issuing a statement were involved in a dispute before the Court.[38]

Figure 8.1 compares the distribution of statements on the ICJ and AB across six state characteristics: the issuing state's dispute experience before the courts,[39] the issuing state's income level,[40] regime type,[41] geographical location, domestic legal tradition[42] and level of judicial independence.[43] Disaggregating statements

35 While all UN members are ipso facto parties to the ICJ (UN Charter Article 93), they need to accept its jurisdiction, see ICJ Statute Article 36.

36 This does not account for all those UN members that have accepted the ICJ's jurisdiction through optional clauses or in treaties.

37 Numbers provided are based on the author's database.

38 Among the few exceptions that exist, were statements by Russia in the UNGA meetings in October 2009 and 2010 arguing why the ICJ should declare that it did not have jurisdiction in the dispute brought before it by Georgia. The ICJ issued its judgment on the preliminary objections in April 2011. Statement by Russia, UNGA meeting 30 October 2009, A/64/PV.32, 6–7, and 28 October 2010, A/65/PV.38, 22–23.

39 In the WTO, the high usage category comprises the US and the EU; the medium category includes the next ten most active users; the low category includes all members that have participated as a party within at least one empanelled dispute. In the ICJ, the high usage category comprises states that have been involved in five or more disputes; the medium category comprises those states that have been involved in two to four disputes, and the low category includes those that have been involved in one dispute before the ICJ. Non-users within both UN and WTO members comprise members that have never been involved in a dispute as a party.

40 States are divided into low, lower middle, upper middle, and high income categories. Measures of GDP per capita were obtained from the World Bank.

41 The data was classified based on panel data from Monty G Marshall, Ted Robert Gurr and Keith Jaggers, 'Polity IV Project: Political Regime Characteristics and Transitions, 1800–2012' <http://www.systemicpeace.org/polity/polity4.htm>. The NA category encompasses statements issued in 2016, for which no data was available.

42 For domestic legal tradition, classification relies on data provided by Sara McLaughlin Mitchell and Emilia Justyna Powell, *Domestic Law Goes Global. Legal Traditions and International Courts* (Cambridge University Press 2011).

43 For judicial independence, data was obtained from David Cingranelli, David L Richards and Chad K Clay, 'The CIRI Human Rights Dataset' <http://www.humanrightsdata.com>.

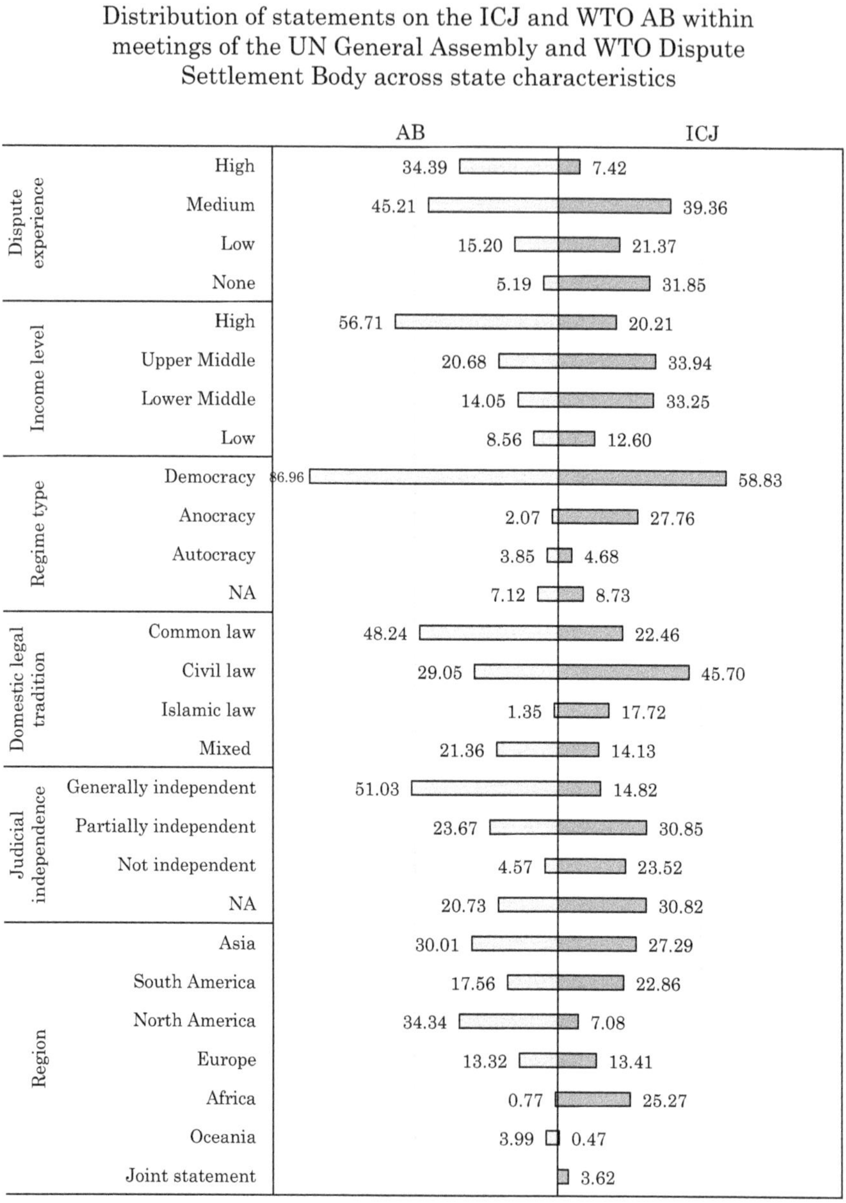

Figure 8.1 The graph shows the distribution of entire statements on each court across six state characteristics.

into paragraphs, and classifying them into the three categories described above ('Supportive', 'Neutral' and 'Critical'), Figure 8.2, in turn, provides us with a picture of how various subsets of states engage in de- or legitimation of the two courts – or evaluate them. Due to space constraints, the following analysis focuses on variation in engagement and evaluations by states' dispute experience, income level, regional distribution and domestic legal tradition.

Accounting for overall experience with the two courts, first, Figure 8.1 shows that medium and low users of the ICJ and AB engage in comparable ways on both courts. For the remaining statements, there are, however, great divergences; while the high users account for 34.39% of statements on AB reports, high users of the ICJ account for only 7.42% of all statements. Conversely, UN members that have never been involved in disputes make up almost one third of all statements, whereas non-users of the AB almost never issue statements. Interestingly, in terms of support expressed, the trends on ICJ and WTO AB go in opposite directions (Figure 8.2). With the exception of non-users, increased experience before the WTO Dispute Settlement Mechanism (DSM)[44] seems to go hand in hand with increased expressed satisfaction. The high users of the ICJ, on the other hand, express lower proportions of positive evaluations compared to the remaining UN members. While levels of expressed support are equal among these lower users of the ICJ, low and non-users express slightly more criticism of the ICJ in relative terms with almost 5% of all units being classified as critical. The opposite is true for those with no experience before the WTO DSM.

Second, turning to distribution of statements and views according to a state's wealth, Figure 8.1, moreover shows that vocality on AB reports increases along with income levels. Given that the majority of statements are made by disputing parties, which for the most part are high income level countries, this is not very surprising. What is surprising, in comparative terms, is the distribution of statements on the ICJ, where the dominant part of statements – 67.19% – are issued by middle income level countries (33.25% by lower and 33.94% by upper middle countries respectively). Contrary to the WTO, where the high income level countries account for more than half of all statements, in the ICJ these states are among the least vocal (21.41%). The distribution of evaluative views (Figure 8.2) on the two courts also varies across income level, with the high income level countries generally expressing the largest proportion of support on the two courts as compared to the lower income level states. Although variation is subtle, in the ICJ, expressed satisfaction with the Court generally decreases alongside decreasing levels of income. In the AB a similar trend comes to show, although upper and lower middle income members express similar proportions of (dis)satisfaction. Among WTO members, however, the low income level

The measure indicates the extent to which the judiciary is independent of control from other sources, such as another branch of the government or the military. Data was available for the period 1996–2011, excluding small states and the EU. All statements issued by these states, and all statements issued after 2011 were classified as NA.

44 Comprising panels and the AB.

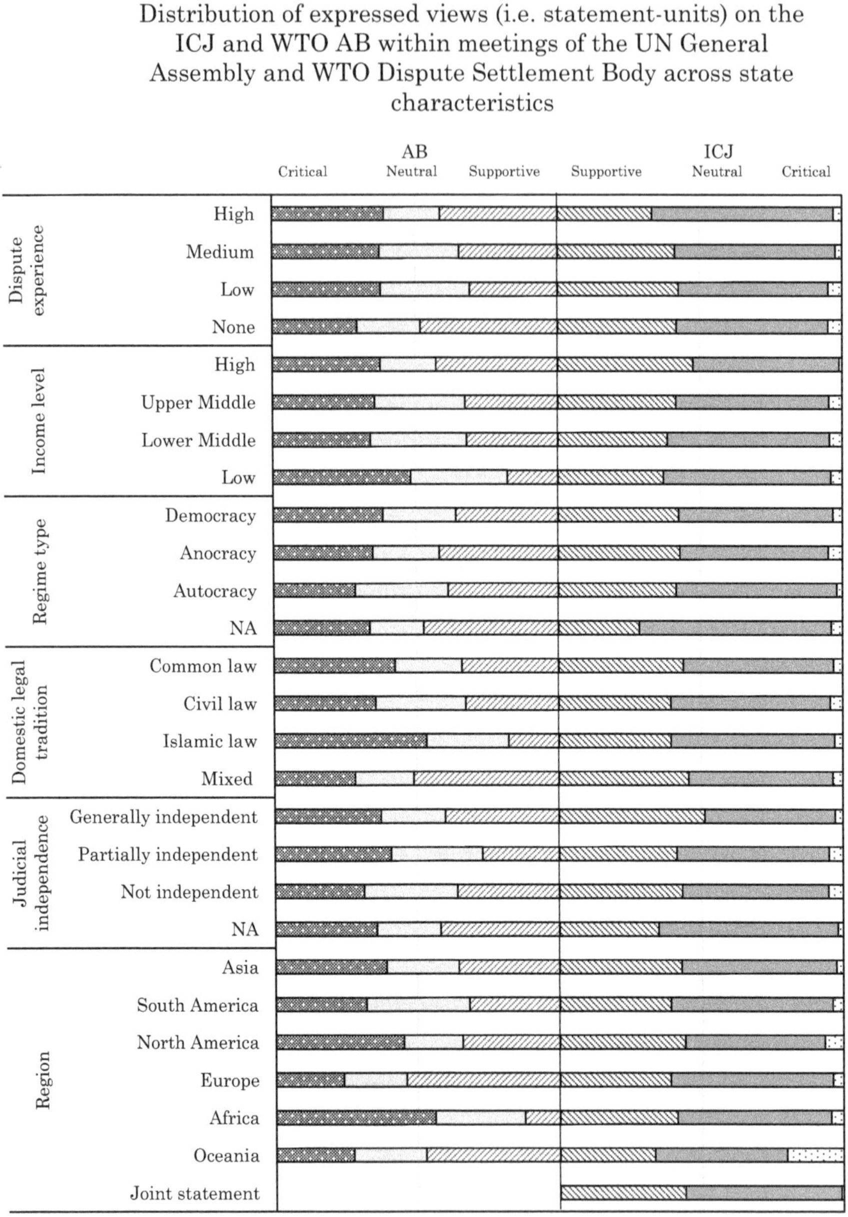

Figure 8.2 The graph shows the distribution of expressed views, i.e. statement-units, on ICJ and AB reports within the three categories, Critical, Neutral and Supportive, across the six state characteristics.

countries stand out in terms of criticism of the AB, with almost half of their views expressed being classified as 'Critical'. While they rarely make statements, when they do, it is to send a message of concern to the AB.

Third, with two exceptions, there is a quite similar distribution of statements on the two courts across regions.[45] The two exceptions concern statements made by African and North American states. While North American members – consisting of the high and medium AB users, US, Canada and Mexico – account for about a third of all statements on AB reports, they only make up 7% of statements on the ICJ. Quite the opposite is true for statements by African states; they account for more than a quarter of all ICJ statements, but make up a mere 0.77% of statements on AB reports. In terms of their satisfaction with the courts, Figure 8.2 demonstrates that, with the exception of Oceania, there is not great variation in terms of (de)legitimation of the ICJ across regions. Oceania stands out in the proportion of criticism expressed,[46] but given that this region only stands for 3.99% of ICJ statements, it is not very telling of its overall satisfaction with the Court. As for the distribution of expressed views on the AB across regions, European WTO members – who speak with one voice through the representative of the EU – express, in relative terms, the most satisfaction with the AB with more than half of all units (53.79%) classified as 'Supportive' and merely a quarter as 'Critical'. Oceanian members of the WTO express similar proportions of (dis) satisfaction as European ones, while African members figure on the other side of the spectrum. More than half of all views expressed by this group criticise the AB, and only 12.5% express positive evaluations of it. Although these statements comprise less than 1% of all statements on AB reports, it is worth noting that criticism has been voiced by a wide selection of African states over the years, including Cameroon, Côte d'Ivoire, Egypt, Mauritius, Morocco and Senegal.

Turning to the legal characteristics of states that engage in debates on the ICJ and AB, Figure 1 shows that vocality on both courts also greatly varies according to the states' domestic legal tradition. Whether this is in any way related to the legal tradition that the two courts are based on, remains to be examined elsewhere. Yet it is interesting to observe that almost half of statements made on the ICJ – a court predominantly based on the civil law tradition[47] – are made by civil law states, while statements on the WTO AB – which is based on a mix of civil and common law rules[48] – are quite evenly distributed between common and civil law states. As for states adhering to other legal traditions, Islamic law states are quite vocal on the ICJ (17.72%), but only account for 1.35% of all statements

45 Joint ICJ statements encompass statements made jointly by Canada, New Zealand and Australia.

46 The numbers account for only one statement comprising 15 paragraphs/units made by Samoa in 1996.

47 Emilia Justyna Powell and Sara McLaughlin Mitchell, 'The International Court of Justice and the World's Three Legal Systems.' (2007) 62 *Journal of Politics* 387.

48 Donald McRae, 'What Is the Future of WTO Dispute Settlement?' (2004) 7 *Journal of International Economic Law* 19, 8.

prior to AB report adoption. Finally, states with mixed legal traditions engage more in debates on the AB (25.3%) than in UNGA debates on the ICJ (14% of all statements). The question is then, whether these differences in engagement on the two courts also translate into differences in their level of acceptance of the two courts' claims to authority. Figure 8.2 demonstrates that as for statements on the ICJ, there is generally little variation in the level of (dis)satisfaction with the Court. As for the AB there are similar proportions of (dis)satisfaction with the AB among its civil and common law members. Compared to the other groups, WTO members adhering to the Islamic law tradition are the most dissatisfied with the AB, but, again, as Figure 1 shows, they are accountable for less than 1% of all AB statements. Conversely, countries with mixed legal traditions overall express the most positive evaluations of the AB, in relative terms, with half of all statements being classified as 'Supportive'.

Turning to fluctuations in the legitimation of these two courts over time, the following section explores the practices within the two courts that have elicited the UN and WTO membership to express, in particular, negative evaluations of the two courts over the past 20 years.

Which issues have caused concern among UN and WTO members over the past 20 years?

Disaggregating statements into paragraphs, and classifying them into the three categories outlined above ('Supportive', 'Neutral' and 'Critical'), Figures 8.3 and 8.4

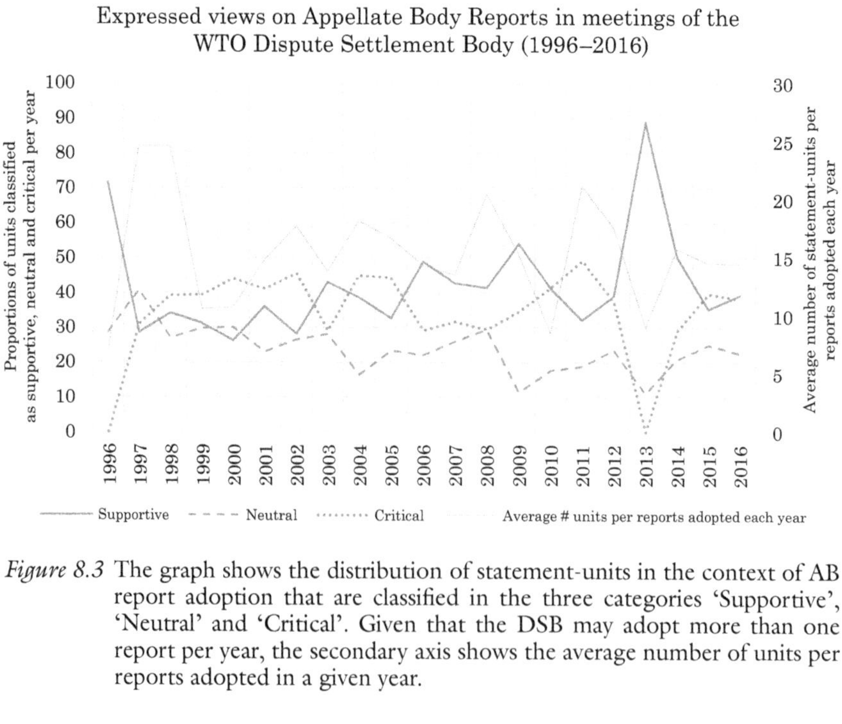

Figure 8.3 The graph shows the distribution of statement-units in the context of AB report adoption that are classified in the three categories 'Supportive', 'Neutral' and 'Critical'. Given that the DSB may adopt more than one report per year, the secondary axis shows the average number of units per reports adopted in a given year.

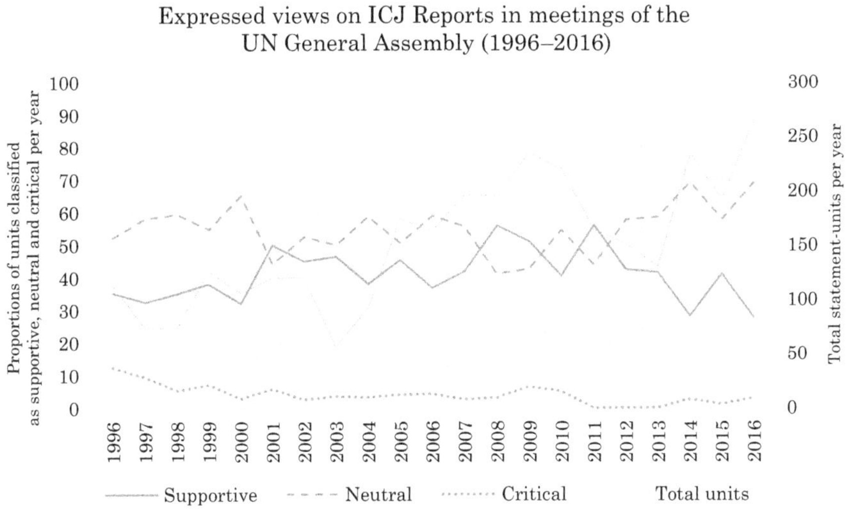

Figure 8.4 The graph shows the distribution of statement-units in the context of AB report adoption that are classified in the three categories 'Supportive', 'Neutral' and 'Critical'. The secondary axis provides the total number of units per report/year.

provide us with a picture of the fluctuations in the acceptance of the authority of these two courts among states over time. In the following, the analysis is focused on periods of delegitimation and those issues that have caused UN and WTO members to negatively evaluate the ICJ's and AB's exercise of authority. It focuses in particular on those issues that elicited concern among multiple members across the broader UN and WTO memberships.

As Figure 8.3 (AB) and Figure 8.4 (ICJ) show, UN members generally express far less criticism of the ICJ – in both relative and comparative terms. With two exceptions (1996 and 2013), the proportions of critical units on the AB vary between 30% and 45%, whereas the proportion of units classified as critical towards the ICJ rarely exceeds 10%. By extension, it is worth noting that WTO members generally express more *views* on the AB within their statements than UN members do on the ICJ, with generally far more units classified as 'Neutral' among UNGA statements. That said proportions of units within the three categories fluctuate from year to year on both courts, revealing certain trends in states' acceptance of these two courts' claims to authority over time.

The Appellate Body

Figure 8.3 provides an overview of the fluctuations in WTO members' support for the AB and shows that certain periods stand out as markedly critical with a set of findings and procedural decisions taken by the AB in the course of proceedings eliciting a wider set of the WTO membership to express criticism of the AB.[49]

After members' initial enthusiasm with the AB in 1996 settled, and similar proportions of expressed criticism and support in 1997, states consistently expressed higher proportions of criticism of the AB in the years 1998–2002. In three of those years – 1998, 2000 and 2002 – a wider set of members considered it necessary to voice concern over one recurring issue: *amicus curiae*.

Members first expressed criticism over the AB's assessment that panels had the right to consider amicus curiae briefs submitted by NGOs in *US – Shrimp*,[50] and then again when the AB found in *US – Lead and Bismuth II*[51] that it itself had the legal authority to accept and consider such submissions when it was 'pertinent and useful' to do so. Many members held that the AB had 'exceeded its authority' and that the 'evolutionary' interpretative approach [of the AB] was a recipe for adding to and diminishing the rights and obligations of Members'.[52] Later that same year, the issue again came up, when the AB adopted an additional procedure for filing of amicus curiae briefs by NGOs in the dispute *EC – Asbestos*.[53] The additional procedure elicited the convening of a special General Council meeting in which the membership discussed the practice and was able to send a clear signal to the AB that it believed it to be up to members to agree on the extent of panels' and the AB's right to accept and consider *amicus* briefs.[54] Despite this, the AB again caused controversy among its members when two years later (in *EC – Sardines*[55]) it decided to accept, albeit not take into account, unsolicited *amicus* briefs by one private individual and Morocco, that at the time was a WTO member but not a third party to the dispute. Many viewed this specific decision as giving Morocco – a non-party in the dispute – greater participation rights than passive third parties. On a more general level, many members expressed concern that the AB had ignored the 'overwhelming view' of WTO members expressed on preceding occasions.[56]

49 For an in-depth analysis of panel and AB reports that elicited engagement among third and non-parties, i.e. focal reports, readers are referred to Creamer and Godzimirska (n 2).

50 Appellate Body Report, *United States – Import Prohibition of Certain Shrimp and Shrimp Products*, WT/DS58/AB/R.

51 Appellate Body Report, *United States – Imposition of Countervailing Duties on Certain Hot-Rolled Lead and Bismuth Carbon Steel Products Originating in the United Kingdom*, WT/DS/138/AB/R.

52 Statement by Pakistan, DSB meeting on 6 November 1998, WT/DSB/M/50, 4–6 (para. 2). See also statements by Brazil, India, Malaysia and Thailand within the same meeting.

53 Communication from the Appellate Body to the Chairman of the Dispute Settlement Body on *European Communities – Measures affecting asbestos and asbestos-containing products*, WT/DS/135/9.

54 General Council meeting 22 November 2000, WT/GC/M/60.

55 Appellate Body Reports, *European Communities – Trade Description of Sardines* (WT/DS231/AB/R).

56 See statements by Chile, Egypt, India, Ecuador, Malaysia, Turkey and Hong Kong, DSB 23 October 2002, WT/DSB/M/134, 12–19.

In the remaining years, substantive issues, rather than procedural ones, elicited criticism from a wider set of members. In 1999 many expressed concern over two sets of issues arising from the conclusions and findings contained in the report in *India – Quantitative Restrictions*,[57] which represented the first time the WTO addressed the balance of payments issues in the context of a dispute. Many members expressed concern that the report, on the one hand, 'had not fully appreciated development concerns and imperatives of developing countries',[58] and on the other, that it upset the relationship between the judicial and political organs of the WTO.[59] In 2001, in turn, a wider set of the membership criticised the AB's ruling on causality in safeguard investigations in *US – Wheat Gluten*[60] for lack of clarity and inconsistency with precedents. Some members further argued that this was another issue that should be clarified by the political bodies of the WTO, and not by the judicial ones.[61]

In 2004 *EC – Tariff Preferences*[62] was put up for adoption. While almost a quarter of the units contained support for the AB's findings that developed countries, under certain conditions, could differentiate among nations exempted from the most favoured nation principle, there was overwhelming concern with the AB's interpretation of the term 'non-discriminatory'. Even governments that generally supported the report expressed discomfort over how developed countries would identify the criteria for 'similarly situated beneficiaries', and noted the AB's non-reliance on the Enabling Clause's negotiating history in interpreting the term 'non-discriminatory'. [63]

The high level of criticism in 2005 was largely driven by party statements, and no reports elicited critical comments from a wider set of the membership.[64] Over the next five years the AB continued to experience overall high levels of support, before two issues in 2011 prompted members to increase their level of criticism. The first set of critical comments related to a number of new, controversial interpretations in *US – Anti-Dumping and Countervailing Duties (China)*.[65] The

57 Appellate Body Report, *India – Quantitative Restrictions on Imports of Agricultural, Textile and Industrial Products*, WT/DS90/AB/R.

58 Statement by Jamaica, DSB meeting 24 September 1999, WT/DSB/M/68, 23 (para. 1).

59 See statements by Sri Lanka, Egypt, the Philippines, Cuba and Indonesia, DSB meeting 24 September 1999, WT/DSB/M/68, 23.

60 Appellate Body Report, *United States – Definitive Safeguard Measures on Imports of Wheat Gluten from the European Communities* and *United States – Definitive Safeguard Measures on Imports of Wheat Gluten from the European Communities*, WTO Doc. WT/DS166/R.

61 See e.g. statements by Chile, Uruguay, Hong Kong, DSB meeting 19 January 2001, WT/DSB/M/97, 2–8.

62 Appellate Body Report, *European Communities – Conditions for the Granting of Tariff Preferences to Developing Countries*, WTO Doc. WT/DS246/AB/R.

63 See e.g. statements by Brazil, Malaysia, Paraguay, DSB meeting 20 April 2004, WT/DSB/M/167, 17–22.

64 The increase in criticism is primarily driven by the disputing parties, as well as the EU and US in their capacity as third parties to *EC – Chicken Cuts* and *Mexico – Anti-Dumping Measures on Rice* respectively.

65 Appellate Body Report, *United States – Definitive Anti-Dumping and Countervailing Duties on Certain Products from China*, WTO Doc. WT/DS379/AB/R.

second related to the heavy workload of the AB and the consequences this had for the circulation of AB reports outside the strict time limits established by WTO members in the DSU. The lack of transparency with which the AB dealt with the issue reinforced the criticism voiced by many members.[66]

The International Court of Justice

Turning to UNGA statements, Figure 8.4 provides an overview of UN members' (de)legitimation of the ICJ over time. While those UN members that make statements generally express high levels of support for the Court, two periods – 1996–2000 and 2012–2016 – face somewhat lower levels of support, with slightly higher levels of criticism and increased levels of neutral units. Given that the proportions of critical statements are generally low as compared to the AB, and that the proportion of supportive statements often increases in tandem with increased criticism, it is, however, not as easy to pinpoint clear periods of delegitimation of the ICJ. A number of units classified as critical represent isolated views or positions of individual UN members. For example, certain individual members have expressed disappointment with the Court's interpretation in specific cases,[67] while again others have suggested improvements in the Court's dialogue with other international courts to avoid legal fragmentation.[68] A close reading of the critical units reveals, however, that four issues have raised concern among the broader UN membership.

The first issue to cause UN members – Asian and South American in particular – to express concern, have related to the composition of the bench, and the lack of representativeness of the 'the main forms of civilization'.[69] Some members, like Mexico, have argued that assuring that all the principal legal systems of the world be represented at the bench would strengthen the Court as 'a universal organ imparting justice and promoting respect for the rules of international law'.[70] Moreover, despite the absence of formal rules to ensure gender equality, the Philippines called for a greater gender balance at the Court's bench.[71]

The second issue to raise concerns regarded the Court's dissemination of information about its work, with many members expressing hope that it would 'be substantially improved in the near future'.[72] While most stressed the importance of an updated web page and dissemination of its publications to libraries around the world, some also encouraged an increase in the number and regional

66 See e.g. statements by Norway, Australia and Japan, DSB meeting 28 July 2011, WT/DSB/M/301, 5. Criticism with the delayed circulation of AB reports and the lack of transparency continued in 2012, and resurfaced in 2015.
67 See e.g. statement by South Africa, UNGA meeting 28 October 2010, A/65/PV.39, 3–5 (para. 8) expressing disappointment with the Court's Kosovo advisory opinion.
68 Statement by Ghana, UNGA meeting 29 October 2009, A/64/PV.30, 26–27 (para. 6).
69 Statement by Malaysia, UNGA meeting 15 October 1996, A/51/PV.34, 10–11 (para. 12).
70 Statement by Mexico, UNGA meeting 15 October 1996, A/51/PV.34, 13–14 (para. 9).
71 Statement by the Philippines, UNGA meeting 29 October 2009, A/64/PV.30, 7–9 (para. 12).
72 Statement by South Korea, UNGA meeting 26 October 1999, A/54/PV.39, 5–6 (para. 5).

distribution of speeches and presentations by the Court's judges.[73] By securing easy access to the Court's documents and increasing awareness about and understanding of the Court and jurisprudence,[74] members argued that states would be better equipped to both settle disputes, and possibly even prevent them.[75]

Third, and relatedly, at the turn of the century, another layer was added to the calls for improvement in the dissemination of the Court's work, when increasingly more members began to call upon the Court to update its websites and publish its various publications in the other UN languages. Some went as far as to suggest that the Court's *own* working languages should be updated to include the remaining four UN languages, given the Court's universal character and an increasing number of cases from all corners of the world.[76] Many more, however, just called upon the Court to translate its most important documents to the remaining UN languages in a timely manner. Given their involvement in multiple cases before the Court, Latin American members, in particular, called upon the Court (and still do), to make its judgments and opinions available in Spanish, arguing that this would allow their domestic constituents, and 'Spanish-speaking scholars and practitioners of international law'[77] to familiarise themselves with the Court's jurisprudence.[78]

Finally, the issue that has garnered the largest amount of critical comments over the years, and from the most diverse set of members, has been the issue of (in)efficiency. With the increase in the Court's docket after the end of the Cold War, the Court experienced challenges to keeping up with the pace of discharging its responsibilities. Despite part of the challenge stemming from the UNGA's hesitancy to increase the Court's budget, members began at the end of the century to raise concerns over 'the manner and quality of management by the Court of its caseload'.[79] Many indeed called for an increase in the Court's budget, but even more states called for an improvement in the working methods of the Court and its Registry, encouraging the Court to take greater advantage of technology and to streamline its proceedings,[80] warning at the same time that 'excessive delays, rather than facilitating the settlement of a dispute, may make it worse'.[81]

After the Court instituted concrete measures to improve its working methods in 1997, and an increase in its budget in 2001 that allowed it to address some of the challenges raised by members in previous years,[82] by 2007 concerns over the

73 Statement by Kenya, UNGA meeting 31 October 2003, A/58/PV.50, 7 (para. 6).
74 Statement by Nigeria, UNGA meeting 30 October 2001, A/56/PV.32, 16–17 (para. 6).
75 Statement by the Philippines, UNGA meeting 27 October 1997, A/52/PV.36, 8–9 (para 14).
76 Statement by Nigeria, UNGA meeting 26 October 2001, A/55/PV.41, 14–15 (para. 10).
77 Statement by Mexico, UNGA meeting 30 October 2009, A/64/PV.32, 4–5 (para. 7).
78 Interview 9.2, UN, New York, USA (27 October 2017).
79 Statement by Samoa, UNGA meeting 15 October 1996, A/51/PV.34, 15–16 (para. 8).
80 See statements by e.g. Brazil, Lesotho, Malaysia, Mexico, Samoa, Peru and the Philippines in UNGA meetings on the Report of the ICJ between 1996 and 2006.
81 Statement by Mexico, UNGA meeting 26 October 1999, A/54/PV.39, 6–8 (para. 5).
82 Alina Miron, 'Working Methods of the Court' (2016) 7 *Journal of International Dispute Settlement* 371.

Court's efficiency among the broader membership evaporated. There is reason to believe, though, that these concerns may resurface in the near future.

Conclusion and lessons for the future

The previous section analysed UN and WTO members' expressed views on the ICJ and the AB from the past 20 years. But what lessons can we draw from these statements? And what can we learn from the concerns expressed by the courts' primary constituents over the past 20 years when looking into the future?

First, both the ICJ and the WTO's Appellate Body enjoy substantial levels of support among their members; members seem generally satisfied with the way in which the courts exercise their authority. While government statements in UNGA and DSB meetings do not provide us with a complete picture of government satisfaction with these institutions, the analysis of statements and interviews conducted demonstrates that governments will and do raise their voice in these fora when they believe there to be room for improvement. Importantly, while many international courts do experience backlash or pushback these days as the other chapters show, the findings in this chapter do not show any dramatic decline in support among the *wider* UN or WTO memberships in recent years. This does not mean, though, that challenges do not loom on the horizon.

For the WTO AB the most pressing concern relates to the US' dissatisfaction with the court and the country's (thus far) successful, unilateral dismemberment of the Appellate Body. After voicing concern over the AB's rulings against its zeroing practices in anti-dumping investigations,[83] and demands to reform the dispute settlement system, the Trump administration adopted a new strategy in 2017 to get its way at the WTO by refusing to approve the initiation of the selection process for the appointment of new Appellate Body members. At the time of writing, the AB, which should consist of seven judges, only has four members on the bench, already creating serious challenges to the AB's settling of appeals within the time limits established in the DSU. The remaining WTO members might allow the AB some leeway in future months (and even years), but past DSB debates demonstrate that effective settlement and observance of the strict time limits lie at the core of the Dispute Settlement Mechanism's and hereunder Appellate Body's legitimacy. If the AB is unable to adhere to the strict time limits in the future, dissatisfaction among the broader membership may re-emerge, despite it being up to WTO Members to put an end to the current deadlock.

The ICJ's future does not seem as dire as that of the Appellate Body's, but it too may encounter renewed challenges in the years ahead that may spill over to UN members' usage of the Court. While the Court has proved able to adapt to changing circumstances, and increase its docket and efficiency over the past decades, one issue might again prompt governments to challenge the court's legitimacy in the coming years: the extensive practice of ICJ judges to serve as

83 Creamer and Godzimirska (n 2).

arbitrators in investment disputes.[84] A report by the International Institute for Sustainable Development in late 2017 revealed that 20 of the ICJ's past and current judges had worked as arbitrators while sitting on the ICJ bench in as many as 90 investor-state dispute settlement cases during their terms. The report spread like wildfire in academic circles and the debate that followed largely focused on the problem this double-hatting could have for perceptions of the independence and impartiality of ICJ judges. But the practice may also spur other assumptions and accusations. With evidence that many of the Court's judges take the role as arbitrators in time-consuming disputes, states might be less patient with the Court's administration of justice, and the long-lasting and widespread criticism witnessed in former UNGA debates of the Court's inefficiency might again resurface. If the Court manages to convince states that disputes are settled 'with the utmost integrity, impartiality and independence, and as expeditiously as possible'[85] there is reason to believe its docket will continue to rise. If it does not, states may turn to other, more appealing dispute settlement venues in the future, and put an aging Court as a sidelined spectator – instead of an active player – on the international dispute settlement arena.[86]

84 Nathalie Bernasconi-Osterwalder and Martin Dietrich Brauch, 'Is "Moonlighting" a Problem? The Role of ICJ Judges in ISDS' (International Institute for Sustainable Development 2017) <http://www.iisd.org/sites/default/files/publications/icj-judges-isds-commentary.pdf>.

85 Report of the International Court of Justice, 1 August 2016–31 July 2017, A/72/4, 8.

86 After this chapter was written and before it went to press, the President of the ICJ held his annual speech to the UN General Assembly during the presentation of the Annual Report of the ICJ. He noted that 'in light of the ever-increasing workload, the Court decided [...] to review this practice [...]' and [...]'will not normally accept [Members of the Court] to participate in international arbitration', by this pre-empting any criticism that might have been raised by states in the subsequent debate. Statement by President of the ICJ Judge Abdulqawi Ahmed Yusuf, UNGA meeting 25 October 2018, A/73/PV.24, 2–11

9 The future of investor-state dispute settlement

Armand de Mestral and Lukas Vanhonnaeker

Introduction

Quod vitae sectabor iter?

Crystal ball-gazing is always a hazardous exercise, especially when the object of speculation is both changing and controversial. Much has happened in recent years and no doubt much more will happen with respect to Investor-State Arbitration (ISA) in the coming years.[1] There is both a political debate and a debate over substantive rules all accompanied by new procedures and institutions. So the range of variables to be weighed is considerable. In the first place, there is the fact of the existence of more than 2,900 bilateral investment treaties (BITs). Added to this significant phenomenon in international law is the fact of the fast-growing number of regional trade agreements (RTAs) which include investment protection chapters. In recent years these phenomena have encountered a barrage of criticism coming from different sources and perspectives.[2] Some reflect the reaction against globalisation in general; others object to the principle of granting special treaty protection to foreign investors; others take exception to the particular standards of protection of foreign investors and, finally, some object specifically to the procedures traditionally involved in ISA. Criticism has been most strident in recent years in developed democracies where critics see ISA as constitutionally inappropriate and unnecessary, given the existence of domestic law and courts. Some developing countries have taken strong exception to ISA and are attempting to throw it off and many, perhaps in light of debates in developed countries, are seeking to make changes to their existing treaties. One is reminded of the Latin maxim *tot homines tot sententiae.*

1 The expression Investor-State Dispute Settlement (ISDS), which is generally used, is somewhat ambiguous as it covers both dispute settlement procedures between states and arbitration between private parties and states, i.e. investor-state arbitration (ISA). It is not always clear whether commentators and critics are referring to ISDS in general or only the ISA.

2 See Armand de Mestral, 'Investor-State Arbitration between Developed Democratic Countries' in Armand de Mestral (ed.), *Second Thoughts: Investor-State Arbitration between Developed Democracies* (CIGI 2017) 9–56.

As will be described below, major changes in the substance and procedure of ISA in some treaties have taken place and more are sure to follow. Does this mean that the system itself is at risk? In the view of the authors the evidence does not warrant any such conclusion. There is a lot of political noise and much serious principled objection from scholars, some of the best articulated in Canada.[3] Major international actors such as the EU are adopting very new positions and the United States has threatened to abandon Chapter 11 of the North American Free Trade Agreement (NAFTA) in the context of NAFTA renegotiation talks, and some developing countries are seeking to be released from their BIT treaty obligations. But they do so in the face of the existence of thousands of treaties in force, to which many are parties, and against the background of broad support in the global business community for ISA. The number of ISA arbitral claims has passed the 700 mark and continues to rise.[4] ISA presents one of the most interesting new developments in public international law, granting standing to private parties under investment treaties. It may change considerably in future years but it is unlikely to disappear.

What is happening?

Investor-State Dispute Settlement (ISDS) has evolved very considerably from its origins in the 1959 German-Pakistani BIT.[5] This agreement contained standards of protection and inter-state dispute settlement but no ISA provisions. ISA slowly emerged as an important element of most BITs and RTA investment chapters and was promoted by the World Bank in the so-called Washington Consensus period. It first appeared in an RTA in the 1994 NAFTA Chapter 11. It has continued to be a significant feature of investment and trade agreements concluded in the twenty-first century. At the present time the process of incremental change is the dominant trend and many countries are in the process of reviewing their model BITs and consequently their investment agreements.[6] Some countries have witnessed considerable controversy, particularly with respect to ISA and some have

3 See e.g. David Schneiderman, *Constitutionalizing Economic Globalization: Investment Rules and Democracy's Promise* (Cambridge University Press 2008); Howard Mann, 'Transparency and Consistency in International Investment Law: Can the Problems be Fixed by Tinkering?' in Kars Sauvant (ed.), *Appeals Mechanism in International Investment Disputes* (Oxford University Press 2008); Gus van Harten, 'Is it Time to Redesign or Terminate Investor-State Arbitration?', 11 April 2017, available at https://www.cigionline.org/articles/it-time-redesign-or-terminate-investor-state-arbitration, accessed 26 December 2017; Gus van Harten, *Investment Treaty Arbitration and Public Law* (Oxford University Press 2007). See generally Armand de Mestral (ed.), *Second Thoughts: Investor-State Arbitration between Developed Democracies* (CIGI 2017).

4 See UNCTAD, *World Investment Report 2017: Investment and New Industrial Policies* (UNCTAD 2018) at 91.

5 *Treaty between the Federal Republic of Germany and Pakistan for the Promotion and Protection of Investments*, signed 25 November 1959, entered into force 28 April 1962.

6 UNCTAD, *World Investment Report 2016: Investor Nationality – Policy Challenges* (UNCTAD 2016) at 109 *et seq.*

adopted more radical approaches to their prior foreign investment protection commitments.

The rapid development of BITs and RTAs with ISA has given rise to considerable comment and controversy. This has been particularly the case within developed democracies such as the NAFTA and EU countries as well as in Australia and Japan.[7] This criticism has taken the form of petitions from university-based groups[8] and political opposition from the Democratic Party and politicians in the United States,[9] in Canada the Green and New Democratic parties have expressed opposition,[10] in Australia the Labour government briefly abandoned recourse to ISA and several BITs and trade agreements were not concluded.[11] In Europe public opposition grew rapidly in the face of negotiations with the United States over the Transatlantic Trade and Investment Partnership (TTIP) after the transfer of competence over 'foreign direct investment' from member states to the EU itself with the Lisbon Treaty, which entered into force in 2009.

Governments in these countries have responded to criticism with some discomfort but have not given up recourse to ISA in investment agreements. Interestingly, it is particularly proceedings against Canada and the United States under NAFTA Chapter 11 or between members of the EU such as Germany and Sweden, under the 1994 Energy Charter Treaty, that have elicited the most public controversy. Yet in these same countries there has been virtual blindness and indifference to the many hundreds of agreements between developed countries and developing countries. The negotiating text of the EU-US TTIP,[12] which contains both investment protections and ISA, has provoked serious political opposition in the EU; perhaps because it was seen as a precursor to the TTIP, the Canada-EU Comprehensive Economic and Trade Agreement (CETA)[13] has

7 See generally de Mestral (ed.) (n 3).

8 In particular, letters expressing criticisms towards ISDS were circulated and signed by academics in 2015 and 2017. See <https://www.afj.org/wp-content/uploads/2015/03/ISDS-Letter-3.11.pdf>, accessed 26 December 2017 and <https://www.citizen.org/system/files/case_documents/isds-law-economics-professors-letter-oct-2017_2.pdf>, accessed 26 December 2017.

9 See David A. Gantz, 'Increasing Host State Regulatory Flexibility in Defending Investor-State Disputes: The Evolution of U.S. Approaches from NAFTA to the TPP' (2017) 50(2) *The International Lawyer* 232, at 249 *et seq.*

10 See Elizabeth May's Written submission in response to the Canada Gazette Notice RE: Consultations on the Renegotiation of the North American free trade agreement (NAFTA), <http://elizabethmaymp.ca/publications/2017/07/18/elizabeths-submission-to-the-consultations-on-the-renegotiation-of-the-north-american-free-trade-agreement-nafta/> accessed 28 December 2017.

11 See Gareth Hutchens, 'Labor pledges to review trade deals that let companies sue Australia', *The Guardian*, 7 June 2016.

12 *Transatlantic Trade and Investment Partnership (TTIP)*, under negotiation (draft text available at <http://trade.ec.europa.eu/doclib/press/index.cfm?id=1230>, accessed 19 December 2017).

13 *Comprehensive Economic and Partnership Agreement (CETA) between Canada, of the one part, and the European Union and its Member States, of the other part*, signed October 2016, provisionally applied 21 September 2017.

also been the object of controversy. This has led to the exclusion of the investment chapter from the provisional application of the CETA beginning in September 2017.[14] Most public concern in developed democracies has been aimed at ISA as a procedure and it is less clear that there is widespread public concern about the standards of protection of foreign investment themselves.

Objections to BITs and RTA investment chapters and ISA generally have not been limited to developed countries. The proceedings of the tobacco companies against Uruguayan and Australian plain packaging legislation provoked widespread condemnation. Previously, the many cases against Argentina arising out of the Argentine measures curtailing the rights of foreign investors after the 2002 financial crisis[15] provoked widespread comment and criticism, as did the content of some of the awards.[16] The governments of Venezuela and Bolivia have repudiated their BITs and together with Ecuador have taken particularly strong positions against ISA as a procedure by withdrawing from the Convention on the Settlement of Investment Disputes between States and Nationals of Other States (ICSID Convention).[17] The government of South Africa has sought to move from protection in BITs to protection of foreign investment in new domestic legislation. More generally, as is explained below, in some 50 other developing countries there is a move to review the form of the commitment to ISA and the standards of protection found in traditional BITs.

In the final analysis one may ask whether the objections that have been voiced against BITs and RTA investment chapters are not essentially political, reflecting the concerns of those who fear globalisation of the international economy, rather than focusing on the substantive standards of protection of foreign investors. At the present time the greatest concern appears to exist in developed democracies and is aimed at proceedings between these states, even though there continues to be general blindness concerning the 1500 agreements between developed and developing countries.

Changes currently taking place with respect to investment protection agreements in general and ISA in particular have taken many forms. The following is a summary of recent and current developments:

14 See *Canada-European Union Comprehensive Economic and Trade Agreement (CETA)*, available at <http://www.international.gc.ca/trade-commerce/trade-agreements-accords-commerciaux/agr-acc/ceta-aecg/index.aspx?lang=eng>, accessed 19 December 2017.

15 José E. Alvarez and Kathryn Khamsi, 'The Argentine Crisis and Foreign Investors: A Glimpse into the Heart of the Investment Regime' in Karl P. Sauvant (ed.), *Yearbook on International Investment Law & Policy 2008–2009* (Oxford University Press 2009) Chapter 10.

16 Ibid.

17 Pursuant to Article 71 of the ICSID Convention, the Plurinational State of Bolivia notified its intention to withdraw from the ICSID Convention on 2 May 2007, which took effect on 3 November 2007. Similarly, Ecuador submitted the written notice of its withdrawal on 6 July 2009, which became effective on 7 January 2010. Finally, the World Bank received the Bolivarian Republic of Venezuela's written notice of denunciation of the ICSID Convention on 24 January 2012, which took effect on 25 July 2012. Venezuela thus became the third state to withdraw from the ICSID Convention.

Incremental change

The most widespread response is found in incremental changes to the standards of protection and, to a lesser extent, the procedures of dispute settlement that states wish to see in the agreements they negotiate. These changes are evidenced first in model agreements published by governments in anticipation of future negotiations. In 2004 the United States adopted a Model BIT[18] which was subsequently altered in 2012.[19] The Model law was debated in Congress and, most recently, an acrimonious debate occurred in 2015 concerning the terms of the renewal of presidential authority to negotiate trade agreements.[20] The *Trade Priorities and Accountability Act 2015*[21] authorises investment protection, including ISA, in trade agreements and under President Obama the United States negotiated the Trans-Pacific Partnership (TPP) and TTIP texts which include ISA. However, both these agreements reflected the renewed standards of treatment proposed in the US Model BIT and the addition of significant procedural safeguards in the rules governing ISA. Thus, the text of the articles on fair and equitable treatment and expropriation contain language significantly limiting their application when compared to earlier texts such as the NAFTA Chapter 11. The United States also proceeds on the assumption that no investment protection commitment grants foreign investors greater rights than they would enjoy under US domestic law. Language was also included in both texts asserting that the right to regulate for purposes of protecting health, safety and environmental protection is not curtailed.[22] Similarly, changes are added to the articles on ISA to ensure the independence and impartiality of arbitrators, as well as the transparency of proceedings and the publication of documents. Provision is also made to allow states to exclude frivolous and unfounded claims at the inception of proceedings.[23] The TPP allows parties to exclude any recourse to ISA by tobacco companies.[24] Finally, there is also a reference to the possibility of adapting the TTIP to an international investment tribunal should such a tribunal ever emerge.[25]

These agreements and negotiations reveal the very strong influence of the Model BIT in the final TPP text and the negotiating proposals of the United States in the TTIP of the United States. At least until the arrival of President Trump the United States appeared committed to an approach to ISA based on

18 *Treaty between the Government of the United States of America and the Government of [Country] Concerning the Encouragement and Reciprocal Protection of Investment*, 2004.

19 *Treaty between the Government of the United States of America and the Government of [Country] Concerning the Encouragement and Reciprocal Protection of Investment*, 2012.

20 See Gantz (n 9) 244–248.

21 S.995, *Bipartisan Congressional Trade Priorities and Accountability Act of 2015*, 114th Congress (2015–2016).

22 *Trans-Pacific Partnership Agreement (TPP) (currently changed to the Comprehensive and Progressive Agreement for Trans-Pacific Partnership (CPTPP)*, under negotiation, Article 9.16 and TTIP (n 12) Article 2 (Chapter II).

23 TPP (n 22) Article 9.23(6) and TTIP (n 12) Articles 17 and 28(4) (Chapter II).

24 TPP (n 22) Article 29.5.

25 TTIP (n 12) Article 12 (Chapter II). No such provision occurs in the TPP.

making incremental substantive and procedural changes to the language of BITs and RTA investment chapters.

Canada has adopted a very similar course of incremental change to the negotiation of BITs and RTA investment chapters, the most significant examples being Canada's Model Foreign Investment Protection Act (FIPA)[26] and the text of the CETA[27] concluded on a provisional basis with the EU in September 2017. The Canadian formulation contains not only a strong assertion of the right to regulate but also significant rewriting of the protections of foreign investors of the two clauses when compared to traditional formulations. The Model FIPA clauses on exceptions, which are based on the General Agreement on Tariffs and Trade (GATT) Article XX, contain very significant recasting of the language designed to protect domestic measures adopted to protect public health, the environment and safety standards[28] and much of this was accepted by the EU in the CETA text.[29]

Similarly, perhaps because the EU Commission proved open to taking the Canadian approach of the Model FIPA, the CETA text is designed to guarantee the impartiality and transparency of the decision-making process. But the CETA text goes further than the Model FIPA. While the initial 2015 negotiated text of the draft CETA contained a very liberally worded version of ISA, in 2017 Canada agreed with the Commission to remove ISA and replace it by a standing Investment Tribunal which would hear all arbitral claims by foreign investors under CETA. Departing even further from traditional arbitration, the CETA text provides for the designation of Tribunal members for each case by the President of the Tribunal, rather than by the parties to the dispute. Canada thus agreed to join the efforts of the EU to move from the model of ISA based on classic commercial arbitration to a standing tribunal. Canada did this, while at the same time committing to more traditional ISA procedures in the 2017 TPP and the revised CPTPP of 11 states, subsequent to the withdrawal of the United States.

The European Union

Prior to acquiring competence over 'foreign direct investment' in 2009[30] the EU had no policy of its own. Member states had model BITs and had negotiated some 1000 BITs, as well as the Energy Charter. The standards of protection and procedures reflected a traditional 'gold standard' of protection of foreign

26 *Agreement between Canada and ____________ for the Promotion and Protection of Investments*, 2004 [hereinafter Canadian Model FIPA].

27 CETA (n 13).

28 Canadian Model FIPA (n 26) Arts. 10–11.

29 CETA (n 13) Chapter 28.

30 Following the entry into force of the Lisbon Treaty in 2009 (*Treaty of Lisbon amending the Treaty on European Union and the Treaty Establishing the European Community*, signed 13 December 2007, OJ C 306/01, 17 December 2007), the EU saw its competence extended in the field of external trade to encompass for the first time under the common commercial policy of the EU 'foreign direct investment' (*Consolidated Version of the Treaty on the Functioning of the European Union (TFEU)*, OJ C 326, 26 October 2012, Art. 207(1)).

investment and traditional arbitral procedures. As it sought to define its own approach, the EU Commission rapidly concluded that the traditional national gold standard was not politically acceptable and, while the Commission has not adopted its own model BIT it has clearly opted for the Canadian and American approach defining standards of protection in a manner designed to protect the right to regulate. The Commission has adopted an even more radical approach to ISA procedures by moving from classic investment arbitration. While the EU approach retains the process of arbitration, it places decision making in the hands of a standing Investment Tribunal whose president is empowered to name the members of the Tribunal charged with deciding the claim. This evolving EU approach is enshrined in the RTAs negotiated with Vietnam[31] and most recently the Canada-EU CETA.[32] Since these treaties involve a complex process of establishing tribunals for each one, the EU has embarked on a process of negotiating the establishment of a global Multinational Investment Tribunal designed to replace self-standing tribunals and in time to replace the ISA arbitration procedures found in treaties binding it and its member states. This is a long-term process which will involve not only negotiating new treaties and creating a new international court but it also requires the willing consent of the rest of the international community. So far only Canada appears to be actively assisting the EU.[33]

While the process of incremental change has been most publicly debated in Canada, the Unites States and the EU, other European states such as Norway[34] have recently adopted new model BITs. More generally, the United Nations Conference on Trade and Development (UNCTAD) reports that more than 50 developing countries around the world are in the process of reviewing and renewing their BITs or investment provisions in trade agreements. The process of incremental change is thus well under way in developing countries also. To give but a couple of examples, India has recently announced a new model BIT,[35] which maintains ISA but involves a return to domestic remedies and the strengthening of investors' obligations, while Indonesia[36] has announced a review of all of its trade and investment agreements.

Shift from BITs to investment chapters in RTAs

Part of the process of incremental change has been reflected in the emergence of many RTAs with investment protection chapters. The first major example of an RTA with chapters on services and investment was the Canada-US FTA of

31 *Free Trade Agreement between the European Union and the Socialist Republic of Viet Nam*, in negotiation, Chapter II, Section 3, Sub-section 3.

32 CETA (n 13) Chapter 8, Section F.

33 As illustrated by the conclusion of the CETA which provides for the creation of a standing investment Tribunal. See CETA (n 13) Chapter 8, Section F.

34 *Agreement between the Kingdom of Norway and __________ for the Promotion and Protection of Investments*, 2015.

35 *Model Text for the Indian Bilateral Investment Treaty – Bilateral Investment Treaty between the Government of the Republic of India and ________*, 2015.

36 UNCTAD (n 4) 112.

1988. This was renewed in 1994 with the adoption of the tripartite NAFTA, whose Chapter 11 included not only investment protection but also added Part B on ISA. The Energy Charter Treaty,[37] first concluded in 1994 between many European and Eurasian states also included investment protection clauses and ISA procedures. Many RTAs concluded in subsequent years have included investment chapters with ISA.[38] The logic of including enhanced investment protection results from the inherent link between services and investments, the limited coverage of the WTO Agreement on Trade-Related Investment Measures (TRIMS)[39] and hence the limited availability of dispute settlement. These investment chapters build on the BIT model but many contain more extensive language reflecting the emerging concern in developed states to ensure protection of their right to regulate.

The recourse to investment protection chapters in RTAs has had the effect of replacing some BITs and has probably had the effect of reducing the rate of increase of BITs, but it is far from replacing BITs altogether. Today, most states have a mix of BIT and RTA investment protection commitments, reflecting past history and the nature of their relations with other contracting states.

Plurilateral agreements

The years since 1994 have witnessed the emergence or strengthening of a number of plurilateral agreements with provisions on investment protection. To give but a few examples: the EU has only recently adopted an external policy on foreign investment but its internal rules, while phrased in terms of the rights of establishment, services and capital certainly touch on similar questions. NAFTA contains extensive chapters on investment and services. The Association of Southeast Asian Nations (ASEAN) signed an Investment Agreement in 2009.[40] The various African regional trade agreements[41] all include investment protections. MERCOSUR member states first adopted a Protocol on the Protection of Investments in 1994[42] and this was recently greatly expanded by a new Protocol.[43]

37 *Energy Charter Treaty*, concluded 17 December 1994, entered into force 16 April 1998, 1080 UNTS 95, 34 ILM 360 (1995) [hereinafter ECT].

38 See http://investmentpolicyhub.unctad.org/IIA/MostRecentTreaties#iiaInnerMenu, accessed 28 December 2017.

39 *Agreement on Trade-Related Investment Measures*, 15 April 1994, Marrakesh Agreement Establishing the World Trade Organization, Annex 1A, 1868 UNTS 186 [hereinafter TRIMS Agreement].

40 *ASEAN Comprehensive Investment Agreement*, signed 26 February 2009, entered into force 24 February 2012.

41 See e.g. *Treaty Establishing the African Economic Community/African Union*, signed 3 June 1991, entered into force 12 May 1994; *Treaty for the Establishment of the East African Community*, signed 30 November 1999, entered into force 7 July 2000, *esp.* Chapter 12; *Treaty establishing the Common Market for Eastern and Southern Africa*, signed 5 November 1993, entered into force 8 December 1994, *esp.* Chapter 26.

42 *Protocol of Colonia for the Promotion and Reciprocal Protection of Investments within MERCOSUR*, signed 17 January 1994.

43 *Intra-MERCOSUR Cooperation and Facilitation Investment Protocol*, signed 7 April 2017.

New paradigms: abandoning BITs

South Africa has been embarking these past years on a process of denouncing its existing BITs and replacing them with domestic legislation governing foreign investment.[44] The concerns expressed by the foreign business community led the government to propose additional legislation governing expropriation designed to allay these fears.[45] It is not clear that this new approach has been welcomed by the business community and there are rumours that foreign investors are requiring private investment contracts under new investment agreements.

New paradigms: rejection of ISA procedures

Venezuela, Bolivia and Ecuador have announced their withdrawal from the leading institution administering ISA procedures: the ICSID.[46] Notice of withdrawal from ICSID has been given but these countries continue to participate in ISA proceedings under other rules. Bolivia and Venezuela have served notice of abrogation of their BITs.

New paradigms: Brazil

The government of Brazil has always been sceptical of the advantages of ISA and has in the past negotiated 14 BITs but not ratified them. In recent years Brazil has however launched a new initiative, presented as an alternative model: the Agreements on Cooperation and Facilitation of Investments (ACFI). The seven agreements recently concluded with other states and the MERCOSUR[47] are designed to promote and facilitate foreign investment and avoid investment confrontations but do not contain ISA. Under the ACFI, there are institutions for problem solving and facilitation of investment, but formal disputes are to be settled only at the state-to-state level. So far, this approach is promoted only by Brazil but it has been accepted by a number of partners and may well spread more widely.

Pragmatism

Reflecting the popular unease with ISA, several developed democratic states appear to be adopting a very pragmatic approach to the inclusion or exclusion of ISA in investment protection agreements. Australia is the leader in this regard, having had a long public debate, marked by expressions of disapproval of ISA by

44 See http://investmentpolicyhub.unctad.org/IIA, accessed 24 December 2017.

45 Engela C. Schlemmer, 'An Overview of South Africa's Bilateral Investment Treaties and Investment Policy' (2016) 31(1) *ICSID Review* 167, at 180–181.

46 See above (n 17).

47 See generally <http://investmentpolicyhub.unctad.org/IIA/CountryGroupingTreaties/40#iiaInnerMenu> accessed 24 December 2017.

leading politicians and jurists on several occasions.[48] The Labour government, when it concluded a major RTA with the United States, did not include ISA in the agreement on the grounds that both countries had strong legal systems which were capable of protecting foreign investors. Subsequently, it decided that it would refrain from committing to ISA in any agreements. The current right wing government when it regained power in 2013 announced that it would adopt a more flexible policy with respect to ISA and has concluded a trade agreement with Japan[49] without ISA and one with South Korea[50] which does include it. Japan, which had a long history of support of ISA, has now also adopted a more pragmatic stance by agreeing to exclude ISA with Australia but include it in an RTA with Switzerland.[51]

It would appear that a sense of pragmatism has also infected the discussions around ISA in the Japan-EU FTA negotiations which were completed in December 2017.[52] Japan is apparently reluctant to accept the EU proposal for an Investment Tribunal replacing ISA. The compromise has been to separate ISA discussions from the agreed text and to continue separate negotiations on investment disputes.

Expressions of unease in developed democracies

One phenomenon that is highly relevant to this discussion is the increasing unease in a number of developed democracies at the use of ISA by foreign investors between themselves. As noted above the prime examples are claims made between Canada and the United States under NAFTA Chapter 11 or between European states under the Energy Charter Treaty. But as investment chapters are concluded between more developed democracies this sense of unease and attendant political objections are likely to increase, even within countries such as Germany and France. It is unlikely that politicians and the EU Commission can ignore this phenomenon. These countries are caught in the dilemma of not needing ISA between themselves, but not seeing how they can abandon ISA *inter se* without compromising the whole system in those countries where it is particularly needed.

48 See Kyla Tienhaara and Patricia Ranald, 'Australia's rejection of Investor-State Dispute Settlement: Four potential contributing factors', IISD, 12 July 2011, <http://www.iisd.org/itn/2011/07/12/australias-rejection-of-investor-state-dispute-settlement-four-potential-contributing-factors/> accessed 24 December 2017.

49 *Agreement between Australia and Japan for an Economic Partnership*, signed 8 July 2014, entered into force 15 January 2015, Chapter 14.

50 *Free Trade Agreement between Australia and the Republic of Korea*, signed 8 April 2014, entered into force 12 December 2014, Chapter 11, Section B.

51 *Agreement on Free Trade and Economic Partnership between Japan and the Swiss Confederation*, signed 19 February 2009, entered into force 1 September 2009, Article 94.

52 See EU Commission, 'EU and Japan finalise Economic Partnership Agreement', Press Release, 8 December 2017, <http://trade.ec.europa.eu/doclib/press/index.cfm?id=1767> accessed 24 December 2017.

Promotion of a global multinational investment court

The response of the EU Commission to the unease felt by many European critics of recourse to ISA in the intra-EU context has been first to promote the inclusion of an Investment Tribunal in its recent FTAs to replace arbitration and, secondly, to begin the process of negotiating the establishment of a global Multilateral Investment Court. Canada has agreed to support the Commission in its efforts. This may prove to be an arduous task and many states will have to be convinced that the devil they know is worse than the devil they do not know. The procedures and powers of such a court are all shrouded in mystery and the wisdom of having an appeals process included has been questioned. Some have already suggested that a powerful court, comparable to the WTO Appellate Body, with its power to bring order and uniformity to the law, might not be welcome.

What will be the future of ISA?

The authors have been asked to speculate – always a perilous course of action for an academic. The following is based on the authors' understanding of current trends, experience of involvement in the ISA process, research done for the Centre for International Governance Innovation (CIGI) on ISA between developed democracies,[53] and continuing involvement in a major CIGI research project to understand the reaction of developing countries to ISA as well as their own sense of what may happen in the future. Readers proceed at their peril.

In the view of the authors, the most likely future of ISA will probably take a variety of forms. 1) Abandonment of the international investment protection system by some states. 2) Emergence of other models of investment protection. 3) Survival through the weight of existing agreements. 4) Incremental change of form and procedure. 5) The emergence of investment tribunals. 6) Changes in major arbitral institutions. 7) The emergence of international commercial courts. 8) The expansion of the responsibility of the WTO for investment protection.

Abandonment of the international investment protection system

There can be little doubt that some states will be tempted to abandon the BIT system or the related procedural protections afforded by the ICSID. Three countries, Venezuela, Bolivia and Ecuador have done so and others may well be tempted to follow in time of crisis. It must be noted that due to the survival clauses in many BITs hasty departure is not easy. More likely than total abandonment may be the example of countries like Australia as well as the European Union where adverse political reactions have led governments to enter ISA commitments on a selective basis. There is no doubt that many governments of developed democratic countries are questioning the need for ISA – but not investment protection – with other democracies. There seems to be less political objection

53 Armand de Mestral (ed.) (n 3).

to BITs with developing countries. In any case, for strictly legal reasons, BITs between EU member states providing for ISA have been declared incompatible with EU law by the Court of Justice of the European Union (CJEU) on the ground that ISA offends against the monopoly of the CJEU on the settlement of disputes involving EU law.[54] It is much less likely that member states will be asked to abandon their BITs with the rest of the world or that the Commission will decide to abandon the effort to negotiate BITs or RTAs with investment chapters with developing countries. The only exception may be when and if BITs are negotiated for the EU which will automatically replace existing BITs.

The EU has experienced considerable political opposition to the inclusion of ISA provisions in its TTIP negotiations with the United States; this expanded to include opposition to the adoption of the CETA with Canada until the Commission proposed the replacement of ISA with a standing Investment Tribunal. Even after that, CETA was only approved on a provisional basis subject to the provisional exclusion of Chapter 8 provisions on the Investment Tribunal. One must therefore ask whether this signifies that the EU will have difficulty in concluding RTAs with foreign investment protections in future negotiations. If this were to materialise it would paralyse the efforts of a major negotiator of international investment protection. The decision in December 2017 to set aside the investment dispute provisions of the EU-Japan FTA for a future negotiation may well be indicative of a trend in this direction.

Emergence of new models of investment protection

Brazil has signed several but never ratified classic BITs and in recent years[55] has had some success in negotiating a new form of agreement based on principles of dispute avoidance rather than ISA. Brazil is currently negotiating with several other Latin American countries[56] and it may well succeed in convincing others to join in supporting its model *inter se*. It is unlikely that the Brazilian model will be more widely adopted outside the circle of its own treaty partners.

South Africa has moved to denounce its BITs and other regional ISA commitments and has replaced them with a new comprehensive foreign investment

54 CJEU, *Slovak Republic v. Achema B.V.*, Case C-284/16, Judgement of 6 March 2018.

55 States that have signed BITs with Brazil include Angola, the BLEU (Belgium-Luxembourg Economic Union), Chile, Colombia, Cuba, Denmark, Finland, France, Germany, Italy, the Republic of Korea, Malawi, Mexico, Mozambique, the Netherlands, Portugal, Switzerland, the United Kingdom and Venezuela. See http://investmentpolicyhub.unctad.org/IIA/CountryBits/27#iiaInnerMenu, accessed 25 December 2017.

56 In particular, since the unveiling of its Model Cooperation and Facilitation Investment Agreement (CFIA) in 2015, Brazil has signed CFIAs with Chile, Colombia, Mexico and Peru but also with African countries such as Angola, Malawi, Mozambique, Ethiopia and Suriname. The CFIA between Brazil and Angola was the first one to enter into force on 10 October 2017. See <http://investmentpolicyhub.unctad.org/IIA/CountryBits/27#iiaInnerMenu> accessed 25 December 2017.

protection law and a new expropriation law.[57] This is a major step by a BRIC country and its impact cannot be dismissed, but no other country as yet has followed this approach. Rumour has it that public ISA commitments under BITs have been replaced by private arbitral commitments in investment agreements required by foreign investors as a condition of new and continued investment, thus raising the spectre of arbitration going underground at a time when the public is calling for more publicity and transparency.

Survival through the weight of existing agreements

Many of the over 2900 BITs that exist as well as some of the investment chapters in RTAs contain 'survival clauses' that provide for the continuation of protection for a further 10 or 20 years after the denunciation of the treaty.[58] Thus, even if many states were to denounce their BITs unilaterally the system would survive for some time. Venezuela is currently subject to this rule under several of its BIT commitments.[59]

Incremental change of form and procedure

As suggested above, the most probable development of international investment protection, including ISA, is incremental change of both the substance and the procedure in future and existing treaties. This process has been going on constantly from the inception of the system. It continues unabated and at an increased pace today. Both substance and procedure are involved. UNCTAD reports that many countries are currently reviewing the substance of their BITs with a view to developing new models or renegotiating existing BITs.[60] A similar process can be seen in some major regional agreements such as the MERCOSUR,[61] the Southern African Development Community (SADC)[62] and the EU.[63] Canada[64] and the United States[65] have revised their highly influential model BITs and FIPA in recent years and have been followed by such influential players as the EU.[66] India

57 See Schlemmer (n 45).

58 UNCTAD (n 4) 132.

59 Sergey Ripinsky, 'Venezuela's Withdrawal from ICSID: What it Does and Does not Achieve', *Investment Treaty News*, 13 April 2012, <https://www.iisd.org/itn/2012/04/13/venezuelas-withdrawal-from-icsid-what-it-does-and-does-not-achieve/> accessed 25 December 2017.

60 UNCTAD (n 6) 109 *et seq.*

61 *Intra-MERCOSUR Cooperation and Facilitation Investment Protocol*, signed 7 April 2017.

62 See *SADC Model Bilateral Investment Treaty Template with Commentary*, July 2012, <http://www.iisd.org/itn/wp-content/uploads/2012/10/SADC-Model-BIT-Template-Final.pdf> accessed 28 December 2017.

63 The revised policy of the EU with respect to international investment law is illustrated by the content of the CETA's investment chapter. See CETA (n 13) Chapter 8.

64 See (n 26).

65 See (n 19).

66 See (n 63).

has recently adopted a model law which reverts to a system requiring exhaustion of local remedies and also seeks to place greater responsibility on investors.[67] It is questionable whether this is legally required, but *ex abundante cautela* many states are seeking to widen the exceptions designed to protect the general right to adopt regulatory measures for the protection of health, the environment and safety or otherwise reformulate the definition of 'fair and equitable treatment' or of 'indirect expropriation'. Evidence of the dynamism of the process of incremental change can be found in a significant number of recent RTAs and BITs.[68] This approach of incremental change is also being fostered by the work of UNCTAD[69] and recently by a new initiative of the United Nations Commission on International Trade Law (UNCITRAL).[70]

Incremental change takes the form of both substance and procedure. This process gained momentum from the NAFTA Chapter 11 parties when they began to require greater transparency of proceedings[71] as well as accepting amicus briefs after the *Methanex* case.[72] Proceedings have been made public and in principle all documents are also made public in Chapter 11 proceedings. This approach has been enshrined in the Canadian and United States Model FIPA and BITs and in agreements subsequently negotiated by them. For instance, the Transparency Rules[73] negotiated under the aegis of the UNCITRAL have been accepted by Canada[74] and appear to be gaining international support.

The EU has adopted the policy of attempting to negotiate the replacement ISA with an Investment Tribunal in its most recent RTAs.[75] This policy was adopted in response to considerable public concern over ISA in general and ISA in the draft TTIP with the United States in particular. Widespread concern had also been expressed in the European press and by some government

67 See (n 35).

68 Armand de Mestral and Lukas Vanhonnaeker, 'Exception Clauses in Mege-Regionals (International Investment Protection and Trade Agreements)' in T. Rensmann (ed.), *Mega-Regional Trade Agreements* (Springer 2017) 75–119.

69 See <http://unctad.org/en/Pages/themes.aspx> accessed 28 December 2017. See also <http://investmentpolicyhub.unctad.org/IIA> accessed 28 December 2017.

70 See UNCITRAL, *Report of Working Group III (Investor-State Dispute Settlement Reform) on the work of its thirty-fourth session (Vienna, 27 November–1 December 2017)*, Part I, 19 December 2017, A/CN.9/930, <http://www.uncitral.org/pdf/english/workinggroups/wg_3/WGIII-34th-session/930_for_the_website.pdf>, accessed 28 December 2017.

71 See NAFTA Free Trade Commission, Notes of Interpretation of 31 July 2001, <http://www.international.gc.ca/trade-agreements-accords-commerciaux/topics-domaines/disp-diff/NAFTA-Interpr.aspx?lang=eng> accessed 25 December 2017.

72 *Methanex Corporation v. United States of America*, UNCITRAL, Final Award of the Tribunal on Jurisdiction and Merits, 3 August 2005.

73 UNCITRAL Rules on Transparency in Treaty-based Investor-State Arbitration, effective date: 1 April 2014, <http://www.uncitral.org/pdf/english/texts/arbitration/rules-on-transparency/Rules-on-Transparency-E.pdf> accessed 25 December 2017.

74 See e.g. CETA (n 13) Art. 8.36.

75 See e.g. CETA (n 13) Chapter 8, Section F and EU-Viet Nam FTA (n 31) Chapter II, Section 3, Sub-section 3.

ministers[76] in the wake of the Vattenfall claim against Germany[77] and the examples of the Philip Morris claims against Uruguay and Australia.[78] In its explanatory memorandum[79] the EU Commission argued that an investment tribunal would provide much greater consistency in its decision making, would guarantee independence and impartiality and would abide by high standards of transparency in its proceedings, thus contributing to public confidence in the process. Critics have suggested that separate tribunals for each EU RTA would become unwieldy. For this reason, the Commission is now seeking to negotiate the establishment of a permanent Multilateral Investment Court.[80] This body would contain a first and an appellate level. It would be designed to accept cases under new treaties which are drafted to incorporate its services or under existing treaties which would be amended to allow recourse to it rather than to ISA. The ultimate success of this proposal remains in doubt. It has the obvious advantage of replacing *ad hoc* tribunals in individual treaties signed by the EU, but there remain many legal questions both as to how the permanent global tribunal would function and many political questions as to whether states are ready to subject themselves to the discipline of a single major new international court. One is reminded of the adage: 'Beware of obtaining what you seek.'

Another form of incremental procedural change would be the reform of the ICSID Convention review committee process. This has been mooted once in the past without success.[81] But there have been calls recently to turn the review committee process, which can lead to annulment of an ICSID award, into a genuine appeal process. This would have to be accomplished by amendment of the ICSID

76 See e.g. Sebastian Knauer, 'Vattenfall vs. Germany: Power Plant Battle Goes to International Arbitration', *Der Spiegel*, 15 July 2009, <http://www.spiegel.de/international/germany/vattenfall-vs-germany-power-plant-battle-goes-to-international-arbitration-a-636334.html> accessed 2 January 2018; 'Vattenfall vs. Germany: Nuclear Phase-Out Faces Billion-Euro Lawsuit', *Der Spiegel*, 2 November 2011, <http://www.spiegel.de/international/germany/vattenfall-vs-germany-nuclear-phase-out-faces-billion-euro-lawsuit-a-795466.html> accessed 2 January 2018; Claire Provost and Matt Kennard, 'The obscure legal system that lets corporations sue countries', *The Guardian*, 10 June 2015, <https://www.theguardian.com/business/2015/jun/10/obscure-legal-system-lets-corportations-sue-states-ttip-icsid> accessed 2 January 2018.

77 *Vattenfall AB and others v. Federal Republic of Germany*, ICSID Case No. ARB/12/12.

78 *Philip Morris Brands Sàrl, Philip Morris Products S.A. and Abal Hermanos S.A. v. Oriental Republic of Uruguay*, ICSID Case No. ARB/10/7, Award, Jul. 8, 2016 and *Philip Morris Asia Limited v. The Commonwealth of Australia*, UNCITRAL, PCA Case No. 2012–12, Award on Jurisdiction and Admissibility, 17 December 2015.

79 See European Commission, *Recommendation for a Council Decision authorising the opening of negotiations for a Convention establishing a multilateral court for the settlement of investment disputes*, 13 September 2017, COM(2017) 493 final.

80 See *infra* 'The emergence of new investment tribunals'.

81 See ICSID, 'Possible Improvements of the Framework for ICSID Arbitration', ICSID Secretariat, Discussion Paper, 22 October 2004. See also Christian J. Tams, 'An Appealing Option? The Debate about an ICSID Appellate Structure', Essays in Transnational Economic Law No. 57 / June 2006.

Convention and there is scant evidence of a general desire of ICSID parties to do this. Furthermore, among arbitration experts there is doubt as to the value of having a full-scale appellate process, which some see as unnecessarily prolonging an already lengthy process.[82] But were this to happen it would provide an important response to those who call for an appellate process to provide a check upon aberrant or outlying awards. This would not cover all ISA awards, but it would cover up to two-thirds of all ISA awards and would have a profound influence upon the development of the ISA system. Beside the question of the creation of an eventual appeal mechanism under the ICSID framework, ICSID announced on 3 August 2018 a proposal to update its investment dispute settlement rules. The proposed amendments to the ICSID rules include the introduction of a new set of mediation rules as well as enhanced transparency and disclosure with respect to decisions and order by ICSID tribunals, third-party funding as well as conflicts of interest by arbitrators, for example.[83]

For all these reasons, incremental change, while the most likely outcome in the future, may not provide a complete answer to those who fear globalisation of the international economy in general and policies of foreign investment protection through ISA in particular.

The emergence of new investment tribunals

As set out above, the EU has decided to replace ISA by an investment tribunal in all its future foreign direct investment agreements, first on an *ad hoc* basis in individual treaties and in the longer term in the form of a permanent Multilateral Investment Court potentially having wide jurisdiction over investment disputes. The EU has launched this proposal in response to much scepticism and political reaction to ISA in its member states. The EU has still to convince its population that it is a sufficient response and to convince the international community that such a new tribunal is necessary and feasible.

A permanent Multilateral Investment Court would for a long time be in competition with existing ISA procedures under several thousand BITs, as well as with other arbitral institutions and particularly with the ICSID which remains a popular and effective specialised arbitral institution. The political will to create a new permanent judicial institution is by no means obvious as indicated by the fact that the United States appeared to reject a tribunal in the (now dormant) TTIP negotiations and the difficulty of the EU to convince Japan to include a tribunal in the investment chapter of the FTA announced in December 2017.[84]

82 See Tams (n 81) 14–16.

83 See ICSID, 'ICSID Proposes Updated to Investment Dispute Settlement Rules', *ICSID News Release*, 3 August 2018, <https://icsid.worldbank.org/en/Pages/News.aspx?CID=286> accessed 5 September 2018 and ICSID, 'Proposals for Amendment of the ICSID Rules', 2 August 2018, <https://icsid.worldbank.org/en/Amendments>, accessed 5 September 2018.

84 See (n 52).

Many serious legal questions remain as to the efficacy of a new international tribunal. How could it be given jurisdiction over disputes arising under existing BITs and RTAs? How would it function? Who would be the adjudicators? Would it be an appellate body or have original jurisdiction coupled with an appeals level? Could it remand awards to the original arbitral panels? Do states really want a tribunal to unify the divergent tendencies in the existing arbitral awards? None of these questions has been answered as yet by the EU or other states like Canada which support the concept.

Changes in major arbitral institutions

It is possible that major arbitral institutions may respond to demands for change. Arbitral institutions such as the International Chamber of Commerce (ICC), the London Court of International Arbitration (LCIA) or the Stockholm Chamber of Commerce (SCC) cannot be expected to abandon arbitration. But they may well seek to offer various procedural changes and further guarantees as to the independence of arbitrators and even an appellate process. The Permanent Court of International Arbitration might make changes bringing it closer to the judicial than the arbitral model. The ICSID may well come forward with important changes to turn its review committee process into a genuine appellate procedure. All of these steps would be designed to give further guarantees as to the reliability and independence of the arbitral process. These changes would probably not satisfy many critics of ISA but they might well satisfy many governments.

The emergence of international commercial courts

The Commercial Court (England and Wales) is a specialised section of the Queen's Bench Division of the UK High Court which hears complex commercial cases including cases concerning arbitrations and is prepared to apply foreign law. It has functioned for many years on this basis and has been copied in various jurisdictions.[85] One of the most notable examples is the recently formed Singapore International Commercial Court which has jurisdiction exclusively over international commercial cases and which is seeking to decide cases that otherwise might be submitted to arbitration. Unlike the London court this court is designed to deal only with international cases. Like the London court it is open to pleas based in foreign law and even to pleas based on 'international commercial law'.

Were the Singapore court to succeed in attracting a great deal of business and were this model to be widely copied it is conceivable that lawyers might well prefer to refer their cases to a court composed of experienced commercial judges rather than to arbitration. The only major drawback of this court model is that its judgments are not arbitral awards enforceable under the New York Convention.[86]

85 See e.g. Dubai's Courts of the Dubai International Finance Centre and the Singapore International Commercial Court.

86 *Convention on the Recognition and Enforcement of Foreign Arbitral Awards*, concluded 10 June 1958, entered into force 7 June 1959.

The expansion of the responsibility of the WTO for investment protection

Currently only a narrow range of international investment disputes can be referred to the Dispute Settlement Body (DSB) of the World Trade Organization (WTO)[87] due to the limited application of the TRIMS Agreement,[88] and to the limited extent of binding commitments made by states under the General Agreement on Trade and Services (GATS)[89] with respect to services. The more extensive the commitments made on mode 3 services by WTO members, the broader the jurisdiction of the DSB will be over disputes arising under these commitments.

A further consideration is that there has always been some consideration given to expanding the coverage of the WTO over foreign investment protection. This might happen if WTO members decided that foreign investments had grown more important in promoting economic growth than trade. If this were to happen and the TRIMS Agreement were to be greatly expanded, the application of the DSU would follow. However, unless major procedural changes were made to the jurisdiction of the DSB this would still not cover the standard arbitral claims for damages by private parties under BITs and would remain an inter-state procedure. There is much to commend this development but there are obviously major procedural hurdles.[90]

If abandoned – what would replace ISA?

As suggested above, it is most unlikely that ISA will be abandoned as the default investment dispute-settlement procedure in the near future. The weight of over 3200 BITs and RTAs with investment chapters will be too great to allow this. Furthermore, there is the question of finding a suitable replacement. ISA was developed in the first place to remove the necessity for states to espouse the claims of their nationals. Despite the urgings of some enthusiasts[91] there does not seem to be any great willingness of governments to move investment protection law back to the inter-governmental level by shifting it to the WTO or by reverting to the political complexities of the traditional international claims procedures. There is also the fact that international business enterprises and their

87 DSU, *Dispute Settlement Rules: Understanding on Rules and Procedures Governing the Settlement of Disputes*, Marrakesh Agreement Establishing the World Trade Organization, Annex 2, 1869 UNTS 401, 33 ILM 1226 (1994).

88 TRIMS Agreement (n 39).

89 *General Agreement on Trade in Services*, 15 April 1994, Marrakesh Agreement Establishing the World Trade Organization, Annex 1B, 1869 UNTS 183, 33 ILM 1167 (1994).

90 *See generally* Armand de Mestral and Lukas Vanhonnaeker, 'How Best to Protect the Right to Regulate: The WTO or ISA?', CIGI papers No. 145 – September 2017.

91 Simon Lester, 'Game on: How to Devise International Investment Law", *National Interest*, 25 March 2015, <https://www.cato.org/publications/commentary/game-how-devise-international-investment-law> accessed 4 January 2018.

representatives have grown used to ISA and are generally in favour of maintaining the existing system.[92]

This being said, one cannot deny the political unease in many developed democracies at the availability of ISA remedies between the same developed democracies. To many this appears to diminish the role of domestic courts and creates an unwarranted privilege for foreign investors. There is also concern about the system in developing countries which is reflected in the proposals for change currently debated in at least 50 countries. Change is certainly the order of the day, but ISA is unlikely to disappear.

Many proposals, such as those made by Canada and the United States, for revision of the standards governing the treatment of foreign investors are being incorporated in new treaties around the world. There is increasingly powerful pressure to implement standards of transparency in the procedures governing most ISA claims. The EU is attempting something more radical: the shift from an arbitral to a judicial model of dispute settlement. The investment tribunal concept is designed to appeal to those who consider that an independent tribunal, functioning as a judicial institution, will provide better guarantees of independence, impartiality and predictability, thereby increasing public confidence in investor-state procedures. The EU proposal is focused on those hearing and deciding claims; it does not remove the legal protection of foreign investors. Those who are fearful of the impact of globalisation generally or those who object to any protection being given to foreign investors will not be convinced.

In the end the choice is political, and governments have to decide whether they will maintain their confidence in the substantive and procedural protections afforded to foreign investors at home and abroad. The system that exists is far from perfect and it will continue to be subject to calls for change or even abandonment – especially in the relations between developed democracies. But the system continues to serve a demonstrable purpose between capital exporting and capital importing states and it may be very difficult for developed democracies to subtract themselves from ISA without pulling down the pillars of the temple.

Should ISA be abandoned completely as an institution and even more seriously should BITs and investment chapters in RTAs be abandoned as a matter of general policy, it is by no means clear that investment disputes would disappear. The replacement solutions might be far worse than the current situation – despite its obvious failings. In the first place it is by no means clear that domestic courts would be able to resolve these problems. In some countries, domestic courts do not always have jurisdiction to award damages against the government for the acts of public authorities.[93] Even if they do in principle, the problems posed to

92 This is the position of the US Chamber of Commerce, for example. See <https://www.uschamber.com/issue-brief/13-myths-about-investment-agreements-and-investor-state-dispute-settlement-isds> accessed 4 January 2018.

93 See Armand de Mestral and Robin Morgan, 'Does Canadian Law Provide remedies Equivalent to NAFTA Chapter 11 Arbitration' in de Mestral (ed.) (n 2) Chapter 5. The authors are currently conducting research comparing recourses under BITs and before the domestic courts of a number of countries.

foreign investors of delays, unfamiliar legal systems, and possible corruption of the courts, all of which ISA is designed to avoid, will still remain. In this case, the obvious course of action for foreign investors and their legal counsel would be for ISA to be incorporated into private and probably confidential investment agreements, thus taking ISA underground. In other words, the critics of ISA may well regret getting what they have wished for.

10 Learning lessons through the prism of legitimacy

What future for international criminal courts and tribunals?

*Joanna Nicholson**

Ever since the first international criminal tribunal (ICT) opened its doors, they have attracted controversy and their legitimacy has been questioned. This is partly because ICTs are such unique forms of institutions, in that they are *courts*, *criminal* courts, and *international* criminal courts.[1] As courts, they are bound to uphold and apply the law in a way that is different to other types of institutions. Their decisions potentially have consequences reaching far beyond the immediate parties to a case, affecting the interpretation and development of the law.[2] As criminal courts, ICTs' primary concern is not with dispute settlement or compensation, but with determining individual guilt, dispensing punishment, and ensuring defendants receive a fair trial. That they are international criminal courts distinguishes them from domestic criminal courts, in that they are concerned with acts of extreme violence perpetrated on a massive scale, often involving a significant proportion of a society and often resulting in political change. Defendants appearing before ICTs tend to be high-ranking military or political leaders, including sitting heads of state. Trials can assume political overtones, causing tension between the requirements of politics and those of criminal justice. Due to the unique nature of ICTs and their relative newness on the international stage, they continually have to invest effort in enhancing their legitimacy and evidencing it to the world.[3]

* This work was partly supported by the Research Council of Norway through its Centres of Excellence funding scheme, project number 223274.

1 Silje Aambø Langvatn and Theresa Squatrito, 'Conceptualising and measuring the legitimacy of international criminal tribunals' in Nobuo Hayashi and Cecilia Bailliet (eds.), *The Legitimacy of International Criminal Tribunals* (Cambridge University Press 2017) 51–52.

2 Nienke Grossman, 'The normative legitimacy of international courts' University of Baltimore Legal Studies Research Paper No. 2014–03 and Langvatn and Squatrito ibid 47.

3 David Luban, 'After the honeymoon: Reflections on the current state of international criminal justice' 11 *Journal of International Criminal Justice* (2013) 505, 509 and Janine Natalya Clark, 'International criminal courts and normative legitimacy: An achievable goal?' 15 *International Criminal Law Review* (2015) 763, 764.

At present, the field of international criminal justice is experiencing a time of change. Several ICTs, including the International Criminal Tribunal for the former Yugoslavia (ICTY) and the International Criminal Tribunal for Rwanda (ICTR), have closed their doors; whereas others, for example the Extraordinary Chambers in the Courts of Cambodia (ECCC) and Special Tribunal for Lebanon (STL), have a limited lifespan. At the same time, a new generation of hybrid courts is emerging. The Kosovo Specialist Chambers (KSC) and the Special Criminal Court in the Central African Republic are taking shape; hybrid courts are proposed for South Sudan and Sri Lanka, as is a new regional court, the African Court of Justice, Human and Peoples' Rights (ACJHPR). This provides an important opportunity to reflect and learn lessons from the past. In doing so, this chapter argues that the concept of legitimacy can be used as a prism through which to evaluate and assess the past work of ICTs and shed light upon ways in which they can be proactive in enhancing their legitimacy in future.[4]

The chapter begins by considering the concept of legitimacy and advocates a three-pronged approach to the discussion of legitimacy in the context of ICTs. Part two focuses upon the first prong of this approach, namely how the creation of a court can contribute to its legitimacy. Part three discusses prong two: how the processes and procedures of an ICT help ensure its legitimacy; whereas part four turns to the third prong, the results and effects of ICTs. The final part of the chapter draws conclusions and asks what lies ahead for the international criminal justice project.

Legitimacy and international criminal tribunals

A substantial body of literature now exists examining the legitimacy of ICTs from numerous angles,[5] yet the term 'legitimacy' is frequently used with little or no explanation or reflection as to how it is being understood.[6] Legitimacy is an elusive and somewhat delicate thing. It is not fixed, but rather something that has to be continually worked at and enhanced. It is multilevelled: it is not down to one element, but rather involves an elusive mixture of many different things, all of which help contribute to the overall legitimacy of an institution. Furthermore, it is a nebulous concept that can mean different things to different people: lawyers, for example, tend to focus upon legal aspects of legitimacy; political scientists

4 Asad Kiyani, 'The antinomies of legitimacy: On the (im)possibility of a legitimate International Criminal Court', 8 *African Journal of Legal Studies* (2015) 1, 26 and 30–32.

5 For example see Vesselin Popovski, 'Legality and Legitimacy of International Criminal Tribunals' in Richard Falk, Mark Juergensmeyer and Vesselin Popovski, (eds.), *Legality and Legitimacy in Global Affairs* (Oxford University Press 2012); Gideon Boas *et al* (eds.), *International Criminal Justice: Legitimacy and coherence* (Edward Elgar 2012); Hayashi and Bailliet (n 2).

6 Daniel Bodansky, 'The Concept of Legitimacy in International Law' in R. Wolfrum and V. Röben (eds.), *Legitimacy in International Law* (Springer 2008), 309, 313.

upon issues of power and interest; while philosophers concentrate on normative or moral legitimacy.[7]

One commonly used distinction is between the normative and sociological aspects of legitimacy.[8] An institution is described as being legitimate in the normative sense if it has the 'right to rule'.[9] Sociological legitimacy, on the other hand, concerns whether an institution is widely believed to have a right to rule. Although these two meanings of legitimacy are distinct, they also overlap to a degree.[10]

In their comprehensive assessment of the concept of legitimacy in the context of ICTs, Langvatn and Squatrito advance a 'political and multidimensional' conception of legitimacy as being most suitable for evaluating the legitimacy of ICTs. They outline a three-dimensional framework requiring first, an assessment of the pedigree of the court, whether it was created by the sufficiently right agents; in a way that is sufficiently in accordance with established and recognised traditions and procedures; and in a way that is sufficiently procedurally just. Second, examinations of the processes whereby the court exercises its power and the procedures it follows in doing so, namely, that they are in accordance with the law and recognised traditions and are sufficiently fair or just. Third, an assessment of the results of the ICT, including its effectiveness and an assessment of its wider impact, for example, norm projection, effects on victim communities, and its deterrent effects.[11] This conception of legitimacy for ICTs requires evidence of 'sufficient adherence to established rules and procedures and a sufficient degree of both procedural and outcome justice'[12] with regard to all three dimensions, or with regard to the ICT's pedigree, procedures and results.

The remainder of this chapter will use this three-dimensional conceptualisation of legitimacy as a framework through which to analyse and discuss the legitimacy of ICTs and make suggestions as to future progression.

Legitimacy and the creation of international criminal tribunals

If one thing can be said of the field of international criminal justice, it is that it is nothing if not inventive. Since the early 1990s, an impressive number of ICTs

7 David Beetham, *The Legitimation of Power* (Macmillan 1991), 4.

8 Allen Buchanan and Robert O. Keohane, 'The Legitimacy of Global Governance Institutions', 20(4) *Ethics and International Affairs* 405.

9 Buchanan and Keohane define a right to rule as being 'where ruling includes promulgating rules and attempting to secure compliance with them by attaching costs to noncompliance and/or benefits to compliance' *see* ibid. 405. For a flavour of the complex discussion surrounding what the right to rule encompasses, *see* Allen Buchanan, 'The legitimacy of international law' and John Tasioulas, 'The legitimacy of international law', both in Samantha Besson and John Tasioulas (eds.), *The Philosophy of International Law'* (Oxford University Press 2012), 79–96 and 97–116, respectively.

10 Bodansky (n 6) 313.

11 Langvatn and Squatrito (n 1) 51–52. *Also see* Daniel Bodansky, 'The legitimacy of international governance: A coming challenge for international environmental law?' 93(3) *American Journal of International Law* (1999) 596, 612.

12 Langvatn and Squatrito (n 1) 52.

have been created to respond to a number of situations of mass atrocity, with each ICT operating according to its own unique institutional framework and legal basis.

Jurisdiction over the prosecution and punishment of individuals for crimes has traditionally been the preserve of states. That an affected state or states consent to the establishment of any court that will have jurisdiction over its territory or citizens will therefore add to the legitimacy of the institution.[13] The ultimate example of this is the International Criminal Court (ICC), which was created by a multilateral treaty, the ICC Statute.[14] The fact that states consent to become a state party to the Rome Statute gives the court significant legitimacy in terms of its creation.[15] Carter argues that the impressive number of member states is evidence of the acceptance and support for the Court and that 'The greater the number of states parties the more legitimacy the ICC will have.'[16] By the same token, that some states have refused to ratify the Statute, particularly powerful states such as the United States, China and India, potentially detracts from the Court's legitimacy.

The ICC's legitimacy can also be affected when states parties withdraw, or threaten to withdraw from the Statue, as occurred when a number of African states took steps to withdraw from the Statute.[17] Although the threatened collective withdrawal has not occurred, the possibility of it resulted in some bad publicity for the Court. The effect of state withdrawals upon the Court's legitimacy is not necessarily always negative, however. Kersten argues that comments made by Burundian President Pierre Nkurunziza concerning Burundi's proposed withdrawal from the ICC may have had the unintended consequence of bolstering the institution's legitimacy, in that Burundi is under investigation by the ICC's Office of the Prosecutor (OTP), and his remarks could be interpreted as the Burundian leadership running scared from a possible ICC case.[18] The same might

13 The UN secretary general noted of the ICTY and ICTR that a 'key lesson learned from those experiences was that the interested State should be associated in the establishment of the tribunal'. Report of the Secretary General pursuant to para. 6 of Resolution 1644 (2005), UN Doc. S/2006/176 (2006), para. 2.

14 Statute of the International Criminal Court, 1998.

15 The court can also be given jurisdiction over situations involving non state parties, *see* Rome Statute, Article 13(b) and for further information *see* Rogier Bartels, 'Legitimacy and ICC jurisdiction following Security Council referrals: Conduct on the territory of non-party states and the legality principle' in Hayashi and Bailliet (n 1) 141–178.

16 Linda E. Carter, 'The future of the International Criminal Court: Complementarity as a strength or weakness?' 12 *Washington University Global Studies Law Review* (2013), 495.

17 In 2016, South Africa, Burundi and the Gambia took steps to withdraw from the court, with Burundi's withdrawal taking effect on 27 October 2017. In 2017, African leaders adopted a strategy calling for a collective withdrawal from the court, *see* 'African leaders plan mass withdrawal from international criminal court', *The Guardian* (31 January 2017) <https://www.theguardian.com/law/2017/jan/31/african-leaders-plan-mass-withdrawal-from-international-criminal-court>

18 Mark Kersten, 'Burundi's awkward – and mostly pointless – farewell to the ICC' (*Justice in Conflict* 16 October 2016) <https://justiceinconflict.org/2016/10/16/burundis-awkward-and-mostly-pointless-farewell-to-the-icc/>

be said of the Philippines' President Rodrigo Duterte, who is withdrawing the state from the ICC Statute following the OTP opening an investigation into possible crimes within the jurisdiction of the Court having been committed within the state.[19]

The ICC stands alone in being the only permanent, multilateral ICT; all other such institutions were created in response to specific events. The picture surrounding state consent to the creation of these courts is variable. In some instances, states consented to the establishment of an ICT and remained cooperative throughout; in others, while a state may initially have consented to the establishment of an ICT, they have withdrawn support at a later stage; while on other occasions, state consent has been lacking throughout.

An example of the first category is the Special Court for Sierra Leone (SCSL). It is frequently pointed to as a success story in terms of its establishment, in that the court was created following a request by the president of Sierra Leone to the UN. Sierra Leonean authorities remained heavily involved throughout the negotiations,[20] which culminated in a treaty being signed between Sierra Leone and the UN to create the court. Consequently, while the court may have faced other challenges to its legitimacy, few have questioned the legitimacy of its creation.[21]

That a state supports the creation of an ICT is no guarantee that its establishment will be regarded as legitimate, however. For example, negotiations to form the ECCC began following a request from Cambodia. Over the following six years of discussions, the relationship between the UN and the Cambodian authorities became strained, causing the UN to withdraw from talks at one stage. UN negotiators were unwilling to agree to Cambodia's demand that it retain strong domestic control of the court, in that there was a fear that this could jeopardise international fair trial standards. Ultimately, the court was created as a domestic institution, established under Cambodian law.[22] Despite strong state participation in the creation process, the legitimacy of the court suffered because

19 Hannah Ellis-Petersen, 'Rodrigo Duterte to pull Philippines out of international criminal court' *The Guardian* (14 March 2016) <https://www.theguardian.com/world/2018/mar/14/rodrigo-duterte-to-pull-philippines-out-of-international-criminal-court-icc>

20 Agreement between the United Nations and the Government of Sierra Leone on the Establishment of a Special Court for Sierra Leone, 16 January 2002. The UN secretary general described the court as a 'treaty based *sui generis* court of mixed jurisdiction and composition'. UNSC, 'Report of the Secretary-General on the Establishment of a Special Court for Sierra Leone' (2000) UN Doc S/2000/915, 9.

21 The legal challenges brought by defendants at the SCSL are discussed below. For a discussion of the legitimacy challenges at the SCSL *see* Tim Kelsall, 'Insufficiently hybrid: Assessing the Special Court for Sierra Leone' 27 *Law Context: A Socio-Legal Journal* (2009) 132.

22 The Agreement between the United Nations and the Royal Government of Cambodia concerning the Prosecution under Cambodian Law of Crimes Committed during the Period of Democratic Kampuchea, 6 June 2003 <https://www.eccc.gov.kh/en/documents/legal/agreement-between-united-nations-and-royal-government-cambodia-concerning-prosecution>; and the Law on the Establishment of the Extraordinary Chambers in the Courts of Cambodia for the Prosecution of Crimes Committed During the Period of

of the circumstances surroundings its establishment and concerns that the court would be open to political manipulation.

Another scenario that can arise is where a state initially consents to the establishment of an ICT, but later withdraws its consent. This occurred with the STL, where the Lebanese authorities initiated discussions with the UN to establish a court and were actively involved in the process of designing it. However, due to a political deadlock within the Lebanese Parliament, the agreement between the UN and Lebanon, which would have created the court, was not ratified.[23] The UN Security Council (UNSC) subsequently stepped in to create the tribunal using its Chapter VII powers.[24] Some took the view that it was acceptable for the UNSC to override the Lebanese Parliament in this way, as Lebanon had been heavily involved in every aspect of the court's creation, and the passing of the UNSC Resolution to create the court was merely the final step.[25] For others, the fact that the court was ultimately created by the UNSC raised concerns that it had bypassed Lebanese sovereignty and Lebanese democracy by unilaterally establishing the tribunal,[26] rendering an early blow to the legitimacy of the institution.[27]

While state consent undoubtedly aids the establishment legitimacy of ICTs, it is not vital: both the ICTY and the ICTR began operation with little by way of state consent. Even in situations where state consent is absent, the creation of the court may still be legitimate providing that the threat to international peace and security is sufficiently high.[28] However, an ICT which begins its life with minimal or no state consent faces additional challenges. It must invest more in building its sociological legitimacy and convincing the affected population of its worth and validity. From a practical standpoint too, things are harder, in that it becomes more difficult to gain access to defendants, witnesses and other evidence without the consent and cooperation of the states concerned.

Which international organisation is involved in creating an ICT can also impact upon its legitimacy. The UN has been involved in establishing several ICTs and plays a role in the operation of the ICC. The power of the UNSC to establish ICTs as a measure to restore or maintain international peace and security under

---

Democratic Kampuchea passed by the Cambodian National Assembly in 2001, as amended 27 October 2004.

23 Agreement between the United Nations and the Lebanese Republic on the establishment of a Special Tribunal for Lebanon, Article 29.

24 Security Council Resolution 1757, 30 May 2007. *Also see* Sarah Williams, *Hybrid and Internationalised Criminal Tribunals: Selected jurisdictional issues* (Oxford and Portland 2012) 260–261.

25 Frédéric Mégret, 'A Special Tribunal for Lebanon: The UN Security Council and the Emancipation of International Criminal Justice' 21 *Leiden Journal of International Law* (2008) 485, 510–511.

26 Williams (n 24) 260–271 and Mégret ibid.

27 Dr. Bahige Tabbarah, 'The legal nature of the Special Tribunal for Lebanon' in Amal Alamuddin *et al* (eds.), *The Special Tribunal for Lebanon: Law and practice* (Oxford University Press 2014).

28 Mégret (n 25) 490.

Chapter VII of the UN Charter is well accepted.[29] Other UN bodies have also been involved in creating ICTs. The Special Panels for Serious Crimes (SPSC) in East Timor, for example, were created by the United Nations Transitional Administration, a mission created under Chapter VII authority[30] to assume governmental functions in the region.[31] This court is generally perceived as having been a failure.[32] That the court was created by what was essentially an administrative agency rather than by the power and authority of the UNSC did little to help the legitimacy of the institution.[33]

Organisations other than the UN have also been involved in creating ICTs. The KSC, an organ of the Kosovo court system situated in The Hague, was created with the support of the European Union.[34] This gives the court a strong international connection, which may help bolster perceptions that it is an independent and unbiased institution that complies with international fair trial standards. Another court, which at present exists only on paper, is the ACJHPR, created under the auspices of the African Union.[35] The fact that this is an 'African court created for African peoples' has the potential to give the court more sociological legitimacy in terms of its establishment, particularly in light of the soured relationship between several African states and the ICC.

Defendants have frequently challenged the legality of the establishment of ICTs. The first and most famous example is the *Tadić* case in the ICTY,[36] but

29 Williams (n 25), 258. Even when the UNSC first relied on this power to create the ICTY and the ICTR, there was near unanimous international acceptance of the legitimacy of the process. At the UNSC meeting to establish the ICTY, China argued that the ICTY should be established by treaty, but ultimately voted in favour of the resolution, *see* UNSC, Provisional Verbatim Record of the Three thousand two hundred and seventeenth meeting, S/PV.3217, 25 May 1993.

30 The mission had a wide mandate, which imparted it with 'all legislative and executive authority, including the administration of justice'. UNSC Resolution 1272 UN Doc. S/RES/1271 (1999) 2.

31 For a discussion of the work of the tribunal, *see* David Cohen, 'Accountability in the balance: Trials before the Special Panels for Serious Crimes in East Timor 1999–2005' 27 *Law Context: A Socio-legal Journal* (2009) 103.

32 Sylvia de Bertodano, 'East Timor: Trials and tribulations' in Cesare P.R. Romano *et al* (eds.), *Internationalized Criminal Courts and Tribunals* (Oxford University Press 2004).

33 Wayne Sandholtz, 'Creating authority by the Council: The international criminal tribunals' in Bruce Cronin and Ian Hurd (eds.), *The UN Security Council and the politics of international authority* (Routledge 2008) 138. For a discussion of the creation of the court, *see* Williams (n 24) 282–287.

34 Assembly of Republic of Kosovo, Law on Specialist Chambers and Specialist Prosecutor's Office, Law No. 05/L-053, 3 August 2015.

35 For a discussion of the court *see* Dorothy Makaza, 'African Supranational Criminal Jurisdiction: One-step towards ending impunity or two steps backwards for international criminal justice?' in Hayashi and Bailliet (n 1) 272–296.

36 *Prosecutor v Tadić*, case no. IT-94–1-T Decision on the Defence Motion on Jurisdiction (10 August1995) and *Prosecutor v Tadić*, case no. ICTY-94–1-AR72, Decision on the Defence Motion for Interlocutory Appeal on Jurisdiction (2 October 1995).

there have been other notable cases before other ICTs.[37] The main thrust of the legal argument has been that the creation of the respective institution violates the sovereignty of the concerned state and is not established by law as required by human rights law. Almost invariably, however, these legal challenges have failed.

The ICC aside, the legitimacy of the process of creating ICTs has sometimes been far from ideal. These courts are often established following or during times of extreme political and social unrest; where societies are divided and the rule of law has been absent for some time, it is almost inevitable that there will be challenges concerning their establishment that will impact upon their legitimacy. That most ICTs are created at all is a miracle in itself. If the legitimacy of these institutions depended solely upon the legitimacy of their creation, they would be poor institutions indeed. However, as Luban explains, 'The legitimacy of international tribunals comes not from the shaky political authority that creates them, but from the manifested fairness of their procedures and punishments.'[38] How well a court operates once it is up and running may ultimately be more decisive in building its legitimacy than the manner of its creation.

Legitimacy and the processes of international criminal tribunals

Many processes and procedures of a court can contribute to or detract from its legitimacy. Three key areas will be addressed here: the location and structure of the court; the exercise of prosecutorial discretion; and the accused's right to a fair trial.

First, the location and structure of a court can fundamentally impact its legitimacy, particularly from a sociological perspective. Both the ICTY and ICC, for example, have been criticised in the past for being too remote from affected populations.[39] Hybrid or mixed tribunals, combining national and international elements, were partly created to counter such critiques. Courts that are located locally and incorporate national law, judges, and staff, in theory allow for national 'ownership' of the court; allow for greater public connection and understanding

37 For example, for the ICTY *see Prosecutor v Milosević*, case no. IT-02–54, Decision on Preliminary Motions (8 November 2001). For the ICTR *see Prosecutor v Kanyabashi*, case no. ICTR-96–15-T, Decision on the Defence Motion on Jurisdiction (18 June 1997). For the SCSL, *see*: *Prosecutor v Moinina Fafana*, case no. SCSL-2004–14-PT, Decision on the Preliminary Motion on Lack of Jurisdiction Materiae: Illegal delegation of power by the UN (25 March 2004; (*Prosecutor v Charles Taylor*, case no. SCSL-2003–01–1, Decision of the Immunity from Jurisdiction (31 May 2004) [37].

38 David Luban, Fairness to rightness: Jurisdiction, legality and the legitimacy of International Criminal Law' in Besson and Tasioulas (n 9) 579. *Also see* Aaron Fichtelberg, 'Democracy legitimacy and the International Criminal Court: A liberal defence' 3 *Journal of International Criminal Justice* (2006) 765, 782.

39 Both courts have endeavoured to engage with affected communities through outreach programmes. For the ICC see <www.icc-cpi.int/about/interacting-with-communities> For the ICTY see <www.icty.org/en/outreach/outreach-programme>

of the court; and encourage domestic capacity and knowledge to be built. The extent to which localism aids legitimacy is highly dependent upon the particular circumstances within the concerned state, however.[40] If one considers the composition of the bench, for example, a preponderance of international judges might generate criticisms of imperialism;[41] while having a majority of national judges in societies whose legal institutions have been devastated can generate fears of judicial bias and judges who are open to political interference.[42] Achieving the right mix of national and international judges and staff can greatly contribute to the legitimacy of a court, but finding the right balance is rarely easy.[43]

Second, the selection of which situations to investigate and whom to prosecute can be critical to a court's sociological legitimacy. One of the most potent criticisms of the ICC has been that its OTP has placed undue focus upon investigating alleged crimes committed in African states. While some would contest the continuing merits of this argument,[44] it has had an important and enduring impact upon the legitimacy of the court that is proving hard to shift.

The use of prosecutorial discretion in selecting which individuals to prosecute has frequently been a matter of contention at ICTs.[45] Prosecutors have been criticised for pursuing potential perpetrators from one side of a conflict while largely ignoring perpetrators on the other side. The ICTR prosecutor, for example, was criticised for agreeing to temporarily put on hold investigations into crimes committed by Rwanda Patriotic Front soldiers following assurances being given by the Rwandan Prosecutor General that the cases were being investigated and would be prosecuted domestically.[46] The ICC OTP too has faced criticism for

40 Ellen Emilie Stensrud, 'New dilemmas in transitional justice: Lessons from the mixed courts in Sierra Leone and Cambodia' 46(1) *Journal of Peace Research* (2009) 5.

41 Kelsall (n 21).

42 Stensrud (n 40).

43 Hobbs argues in favour of a rebuttable presumption of there being a majority of international judges at hybrid courts *see* Harry Hobbs, 'Towards a principled justification for the mixed composition of hybrid international criminal tribunals', 30 *Leiden Journal of International Law* (2017) 177. *Also see* Erica Bussey 'Striking the right balance- Blending international and national components in hybrid courts' (*Justice in Conflict,* 14 March 2018) <www.justiceinconflict.org/2018/03/14/striking-the-right-balance-blending-international-and-national-components-in-hybrid-courts/>

44 The OTP is investigating situations in other parts of the world, including Georgia and is carrying out preliminary examinations in several non-African states. Also *see* Alette Smeulers *et al*, 'The selection of cases by the ICC: An empirically based evaluation of the OTP's performance' 15 *International Criminal Law Review* (2015) 1.

45 Allison Marston Danner, 'Enhancing the legitimacy and accountability of prosecutorial discretion at the International Criminal Court' 97(3) American Society of International Law (2003) 510.

46 See Statement by Justice Hassan B. Jallow, Prosecutor to the ICTR to the UN Security Council (4 June 2008) <www.ictr-archive09.library.cornell.edu/ENGLISH/speeches/jallow080604.html>. Also see Leslie Haskell and Lars Waldorf, 'The impunity gap of the International Criminal Tribunal for Rwanda: Causes and consequences' 34 *Hastings International and Comparative Law Review* (2011) 49 and Victor Peskin, 'Victor's Justice Revisited: Rwandan Patriotic Front crimes and the prosecutorial endgame at the ICTR' in Scott

prosecuting members of rebel groups while ignoring potential crimes committed by government perpetrators in Uganda and the Democratic Republic of Congo.[47] Prosecutors have also been criticised for indicting persons who are regarded as heroes by a certain section of a society. The legitimacy of the SCSL was damaged in the eyes of a significant number of Sierra Leoneans when members of the Civil Defence Forces were indicted, as they regarded them as war heroes who had been involved in defending the country.[48] The level of importance of indictees can also be critical. A successful capture and trial of a senior figure can help strengthen an ICT's legitimacy (the trials of Charles Taylor at the SCSL and Ratko Mladić at the ICTY are good examples of this); whereas the unsuccessful pursuit of senior figures comes at a cost: the ICC's reputation has suffered for failing to apprehend Sudanese President Omar al Bashir and the leader of the Lord's Resistance Army, Joseph Kony.[49]

Successfully juggling the political, legal and practical implications involved when selecting whom to indict is difficult, and it will rarely be possible to satisfy everyone. In order to boost the legitimacy of their decision making, prosecutors should be aware of the effects their selection of whom to prosecute can have upon the legitimacy of the court. They should endeavour to operate as transparently as possible in order to demonstrate that they are adhering to good process and that their decision making is principled, reasoned and impartial.[50]

A third key area of importance concerns the degree to which a court protects, and is seen to protect, the accused's right to a fair trial. Indeed, this is arguably one of the areas that is most vital to a court's legitimacy, in that while a fair trial may not be sufficient in itself to legitimise a court, an unfair trial will almost always delegitimise it.[51]

Straus and Lars Waldorf (eds.), *Remaking Rwanda: State Building and Human Rights after Mass Atrocities* (University of Wisconsin Press 2011) 173–183.

47 Phil Clark, 'Law, politics and pragmatism: The ICC and case selection in Uganda and the Democratic Republic of Congo' in Nicholas Waddell and Phil Clark (eds.), *Courting Conflict? Justice, Peace and the ICC in Africa* (Royal African Society 2008).

48 Thierry Cruvellier, 'From the Taylor trial to a lasting legacy: Putting the Special Court model to the test', International Center for Transitional Justice and the Sierra Leone Court Monitoring Programme (2009), 24–25

49 David Kaye, 'Who's afraid of the International Criminal Court: Finding the prosecutor who can set it straight', 90 Foreign Affairs (2011) 118 and Darryl Robinson, 'Inescapable dyads: Why the International Criminal Court cannot win', 28 *Leiden Journal of International Law* (2015) 323, 334–335.

50 See for example, ICC, Office of the Prosecutor, 'Policy paper on case selection and prioritisation' (15 September 2016) <www.icc-cpi.int/itemsDocuments/20160915_OTP-Policy_Case-Selection_Eng.pdf>

51 Kiyani (n 4) 27. In the *Šešelj* case, the ICTY noted that the right to a fair trial was not just a fundamental right of the accused but also 'a fundamental interest of the Tribunal related to its own legitimacy'. *Prosecutor v Šešelj,* case no. IT-03-67-PT, Decision on Prosecutor Motion for Order Appointing Counsel to Assist Vojislav Šešelj with his Defence (9 May 2003) [21].

ICTs have been keen to emphasise their adherence to international fair trial standards. The ICTR has described itself as providing a 'model of fairness'[52] for other legal systems to follow, and the ICTY has claimed to set the highest standards of justice[53] in this regard. McDermott agrees that ICTs have an obligation to set the highest standards of fairness, both for reasons of their own legitimacy and in order to spread respect for the rule of law.[54] However, she finds that in practice, the application of fair trial standards by ICTs has been inconsistent, both across the different ICTs and within different chambers of the same tribunals.[55]

An example of a fair trial right which can affect the legitimacy of ICTs is the principle of legality. Legality, or *nullum crimen sine lege, nulla poena sine lege,* requires that criminal liability and punishment be based upon prior legislative enactment of a prohibition that is expressed with adequate precision and clarity.[56] It has been described as a 'cornerstone' of ICL and found to be a *jus cogens* norm.[57] In practice, however, ICTs have adopted a soft approach to the principle. Judgments of ICTs have been criticised for imposing retroactive law;[58] for lacking foreseeability;[59] and for being insufficiently specific.[60]

This relaxed approach to legality has likely been tolerated in favour of the aim of progressing the field of international criminal law. Early ICTs, such as the ICTY and the ICTR, had little to guide them, barring their Statutes, which lacked detail, and a limited number of cases from the post-war period. If international criminal law was to become a viable and effective field of law, ICTs needed to add some flesh to the bones of the law they had been given. Thus, for example, in order for ICL to remain relevant in modern warfare, it was necessary for the ICTY to find in *Tadić* that breaches of international humanitarian law in

52 *Prosecutor v Ntagerura* et al, case no. ICTR 99–46-T, Trial Judgment and sentence (24 February 2004) Separate Opinion of Judge Pavel Dolenc [5].

53 *Prosecutor v Blaškić,* case no. IT-95–14-T, Decision on the objection of the Republic of Croatia to the Issuance of *Subpoena Duces Tecum* (18 July 1997) [61]. *Also see* Yvonne McDermott, *Fairness in International Criminal Trials* (Oxford University Press 2016), 131–133.

54 McDermott, ibid., 147 and *see* 125–147.

55 ibid.

56 Paul H. Robinson, 'Fair Notice and Fair Adjudication: Two Kinds of Legality', 154(2) *University of Pennsylvania Law Review* (2005) 335, 336.

57 STL, *Prosecutor v. Salim Jamil Ayyash* et al, case No. STL-11–01/I/AC/R176bis, Appeals Chamber, Interlocutory Decision on the Applicable Law: Terrorism, Conspiracy, Homicide, Perpetration, Cumulative Charging (16 February 2011) [76].

58 Susan Lamb, '*Nullum Crimen, Nulla Poena Sine Lege* in International Criminal Law' in Antonio Cassese *et al* (eds.), *The Rome Statute of the International Criminal Court: A Commentary, Volume 2* (Cambridge University Press 2002), 745 and Beth van Schaak, '*Crimen Sine Lege*: Judicial Law-making at the Intersection of Law and Morals', 97 *Georgetown Law Journal* (2008–2009) 119.

59 For an example where judicial law making was alleged, *see Prosecutor v. Tadić*, (n 37) [87–136] and for a critique *see* Christopher Greenwood, 'International Law and the *Tadić* Case', 7 European Journal of International Law (1998) 265; van Schaak, ibid., 150–152 and Joanna Nicholson, 'Strengthening the effectiveness of international criminal law through the principle of legality' 17(4) *International Criminal Law Review* (2017) 656.

60 Nicholson ibid. 113–117.

non-international armed conflicts constitute war crimes.[61] The field of substantive ICL is now well developed, and there are a significant number of cases interpreting international crimes. [62] It is unlikely that another *Tadić* is necessary, or would be tolerated, today. In order to strengthen the legitimacy of their decision making in future, ICTs should enforce a stronger version of the principle of legality, thereby placing the rights of the accused centre stage.

Legitimacy and the results of international criminal tribunals

The final dimension of the legitimacy framework involves a consideration of the wider impact of ICTs, including their results and their effectiveness. It is not sufficient to judge the effectiveness of ICTs merely upon the product of their trials. As Stahn explains, 'It does injustice to international courts to judge effectiveness merely by a number of visible and quantitative outcomes, such as the number of cases or decisions that they render . . . Some of the most important effects . . . are actually largely independent of the record of cases.'[63] However, the precise goals of ICTs are a matter of some debate.[64] They include those of national criminal law: retribution for wrongdoing, deterrence, incapacitation and rehabilitation, but also include a number of other aims, such as bringing to justice those responsible for serious violations of human rights and international humanitarian law; putting an end to such violations and preventing their recurrence; securing justice and dignity for the victims; establishing a record of what occurred; promoting national reconciliation, re-establishing the rule of law and contributing to the restoration of peace.[65] This is an impressive list, as Damaška notes: 'Even national systems of criminal justice, with their far greater enforcement powers and institutional support, would stagger under this load.'[66] Somewhat understandably, ICTs have struggled to meet many of these goals and to reconcile the tensions between them.

Turning for example, to deterrence, there is a growing body of empirical research investigating the extent to which ICTs can generally deter atrocity crimes. Most studies concentrate on the ICC, and the indications are that the court has a modest deterrent effect. Jo and Simmons, for example, have assessed the ICC's deterrent effect upon state and non-state actors concerning civilian killing, and have

61 *Tadić* (n 36) [128–134].

62 For a discussion of the legitimacy of ICTs relying on case law from other courts, *see* Joanna Nicholson, 'The role played by external case law in promoting the legitimacy of International Criminal Court decisions' 87(2) *Nordic Journal of International Law*, 189.

63 Carsten Stahn, 'Between "Faith" and "Facts": By what standards should we assess International Criminal Justice?' 25 *Leiden Journal of International Law* (2012) 251, 264.

64 Ibid. 254.

65 *See* Report of the Secretary General on the Rule of Law and Transitional Justice in Conflict and Post Conflict Societies, UN. Doc. S/2004.616 (23 August 2004) 38.

66 Mirjan Damaška, 'What is the point of international criminal justice?' 83 *Chicago-Kent Law Review* 329 (2008) 331.

found that states which have ratified the ICC Statute are more likely then states which have not ratified it to reduce, detect and prosecute such crimes domestically. Furthermore, non-state actors reduce intentional civilian killing when the ICC signals its intention to prosecute.[67] However, the deterrent effects of ICC interventions should not be overemphasised.[68] Dancy cautions that the court is but one factor among many that can influence the behaviour of state and non-state actors. He argues that the court has been 'more influential for what it *is* than what it *does*' and suggests that the court acts as a stigmatiser.[69] Jo and Simmons also evince caution, explaining that ICC interventions are powerful because '[T]hey are part of a package of efforts to rally support for ending impunity.'[70]

A second goal attributed to ICTs is that they have a positive impact upon the legal systems in the states in which they are involved, by encouraging domestic prosecutions; strengthening existing structures; and building capacity to try cases at a national level.[71] There have been some notable achievements in this regard: the ICTY helped contribute to the establishment of specialised war crimes chambers in the Balkans region, including the Section for War Crimes within the State Court of Bosnia and Herzegovina and the War Crimes Chamber of the Belgrade District Court. National prosecutions have also taken place in Rwanda, both within national courts and through the Gacaca lay court system.[72]

Research is only beginning to uncover what effects an ICC intervention can have upon the domestic legal system of the concerned state. Nouwen has found that ICC interventions in Uganda and South Sudan have had several catalysing effects,[73] and Dancy and Montal find systematic evidence that ICC involvement in a state can increase domestic prosecutions and convictions of human rights violators.[74] Notably, however, both studies conclude that the observed complemen-

67 Hyeran Jo and Beth A. Simmons, 'Can the International Criminal Court deter atrocity?', 70 *International Organization* (2016) 443, 469–470.

68 Geoff Dancy, 'Searching for deterrence at the International Criminal Court', 17(4) *International Criminal Law Review* (2017) 625.

69 Also see Jacqueline McAllister and James Meernik, 'Casting a Shadow over War Zones: The International Criminal Court's Impact on Rebel and Government Forces' Use of Violence against Civilians', 33, <web.isanet.org/Web/Conferences/CEEISA-ISA-LBJ2016/Archive/a7a5720e-fe27-48a6-8144-b816c183957d.pdf>; Courtney Hillebrecht, 'The deterrent effects of the International Criminal Court: Evidence from Libya', 42(4), International Interactions (2016) 616; and Benjamin J. Appel, 'In the shadow of the International Criminal Court: Does the ICC deter human rights violations?' *Journal of Conflict Resolution* (2016) 1.

70 Jo and Simmons (n 67) 470.

71 For example, the UNSC Resolution establishing the ICTR listed the goal of strengthening the Rwandan courts and judicial system, UNSC Res 955 (1994) UN Doc. S/RES/955.

72 Human Rights Watch, *Rwanda: Justice after genocide: 20 years on* (2014) <www.hrw.org/news/2014/03/28/rwanda-justice-after-genocide-20-years>

73 Sarah M. H. Nouwen, *Complementarity in the Line of Fire: The catalyzing effect of the International Criminal Court in Uganda and Sudan* (Cambridge University Press 2013).

74 Geoff Dancy and Florencia Montal, 'Unintended positive complementarity: Why International Criminal Court investigations increase domestic human rights prosecutions', Paper presented at the American Society of International Law Research Forum, Chicago

tarity effects were not caused directly by the intervention of the ICC within the states concerned, but rather for other reasons, including political pressure from the Security Council; economy of donor intervention;[75] or through reformer coalitions using the opportunities created by the ICC's involvement in the state to demand legal reforms, build local capacity and litigate human rights cases.[76] Expectations that ICTs could help strengthen and reform national justice systems have also not been as forthcoming as some had anticipated. [77] For example, hopes of building domestic legal capacity and a rule of law culture in Sierra Leone have not been met,[78] and a similar picture is emerging in Cambodia.[79] However, as Sperfeldt observes, 'Hybrid courts were never designed to transform entire judiciaries and succeed in building a rule-of-law culture within a few years.' Perhaps too much is being expected from these courts in this regard.

The potential of ICTs to establish some sort of record of what occurred is another oft-cited goal. Indeed, ICTs' truth-telling capacity has been found to be one of the most important to victims: in a recent survey in Cambodia, university students named the ability of the ECCC to educate their generation as to what happened as being the court's most important contribution.[80] However, the ability of these institutions to provide a historical record or to narrate the truth of what happened is limited by the restraints imposed by the requirements of the legal process. Holtermann, for example, argues that while it is a possible function of ICTs to tell the truth of what occurred, 'International criminal tribunals should not look for the full story (whatever that is) of past atrocities, but only to those facts relevant for the case in hand.' He cautions that truth is only one, possibly even subordinate, among other desiderata, including a fair trial, prevention, reconciliation and peace.[81]

Reconciliation is another stated goal of ICTs, but it is still open to question whether and to what extent they can contribute to this. Recent research concerning the ICTY has shown that despite the work of the ICTY 'Each ethnic group in the former Yugoslavia is still firmly attached to its own version of reality.'[82]

(November 2014), 40–41 <www2.tulane.edu/liberal-arts/political-science/upload/Dancy-Montal-IO-2014.pdf>

75 Nouwen (n 73) 406.

76 Dancy and Montal (n 74).

77 See for example, *Report of the Special Representative of the Secretary-General for Human Rights in Cambodia, Peter Leuprecht* (19 December 2003) UN Doc. E/CN.4/2004/105 [19].

78 Kelsall (n 21) 142–143.

79 Stensrud (n 40).

80 Caitlin McCaffrie *et al*, '"So we can know what happened" The Education potential of the Extraordinary Chambers in the Courts of Cambodia' (January 2018) <www.krttrialmonitor.files.wordpress.com/2018/01/so-we-can-know-what-happened-2018.pdf> and *see* Stensrud (n 40) 11.

81 Jakob v. H. Holtermann, '"One of the challenges that can plausibly be raised against them"? On the role of truth in debates about the legitimacy of international criminal tribunals' in Hayashi and Bailliet (n 1) 226.

82 Marko Milanović, 'The impact of the ICTY on the former Yugoslavia: an anticipatory post-mortem', 110(2) *American Journal of International Law* 233, 257.

One of the notable successes of ICTs has been their work in clarifying the law concerning international crimes and producing a strong body of jurisprudence that can serve as an important resource for international, regional and national jurisdictions in future. ICTs have also made substantial contributions to the development of international humanitarian law.[83] Indeed, it might be that this has been the most significant impact of ICTs. Luban states that the most important aim of ICTs is their potential to project norms through trials, punishments and jurisprudence. He argues that 'International criminal law uses trials, punishments and forms of law to project a radically different set of norms, one that reclassifies political violence from the domain of the sacred to the domain of ordinary thuggery.'[84] Rather than viewing political violence as being the prerogative of states, it is now regarded as a crime.[85] Today, when mass atrocities occur, as in Syria, Yemen, Myanmar or the Philippines, they are quickly labelled as such by international organisations, NGOs and others and demands for accountability are made. Although accountability may be slow in coming, the threat of it hangs there in a way which it did not before, and it might cause the senior leaders involved to sleep less easily in their beds.

Conclusion

Analysing ICTs through the prism of legitimacy shows that they are imperfect institutions. There are concerns surrounding the legitimacy of the creation of these courts; how they operate; and their wider effects. However, the exercise is also useful in indicating areas where ICTs can work to improve their legitimacy in future.

Ideally, when creating an ICT, the concerned state should consent to the establishment of the court and should remain actively engaged in the process. Realistically, however, this will not always be possible and it will often be the case that states will merely acquiesce to the court's creation or even evince active dissent. Clearly, the more that a state can be involved in the process the better, but even a complete lack of state consent or participation may not necessarily render a death-blow to an ICT's legitimacy, providing that the situation is grave enough and sufficiently threatens international peace and security. Perhaps we simply have to accept that, given the difficult political and social circumstances in which many ICTs are created, the manner of the establishment of ICTs will often be less than ideal and will impact upon the institution's legitimacy. Rather, the legitimacy of the court has to be built in other ways.

How a court operates once it is up and running is vital in this respect. The chapter has discussed only three aspects of this, namely, the structure of the court,

83 See for example the numerous references to the case law of ICTs in the International Committee for the Red Cross' customary international law study: ICRC, Customary IHL Database <www.ihl-databases.icrc.org/customary-ihl/eng/docs/home>

84 Luban (n 3) 510.

85 Ibid. 509.

the use of prosecutorial discretion and the protection of the rights of the accused. Other elements are also crucial: fact-finding procedures; the treatment of victims; the appeals process; sentencing processes; and restitution procedures. That these processes are normatively legitimate is important, but it is also important that the court takes active steps to build its sociological legitimacy while carrying out its work, by evidencing transparency and demonstrating to interested observers that its procedures are fair and just.

Finally, concerning the third aspect of the legitimacy framework, namely the results of ICTs, there is a need for a readjustment of expectations as to what ICTs can realistically achieve. At present, the lack of agreement surrounding what the goals of ICTs are damages the credibility of ICTs. Ultimately, ICTs are courts, and, as such, there are limits to what they can accomplish. There must be a greater degree of modesty as to what ICTs can do. There are signs that a reassessment is underway. The ICTY Dialogues Conference found, for example, that for future ICTs 'Expectations should be managed from the outset to avoid disappointing victims and affected communities, and the wider international community.'[86] Adjusting expectations as to the potential wider impact of ICTs; acknowledging their limitations and explaining this clearly to the public will greatly assist in enhancing the legitimacy of these institutions.

ICTs have legitimacy challenges, but this does not mean that they are illegitimate as such, or that they are not worth supporting. Rather, as we enter this new stage in international criminal justice and new ICTs open their doors, those involved should do so with their eyes open both to the possibilities of ICTs and to their limitations.

86 ICTY Legacy Dialogues, 'Outcome of the ICTY Legacy Dialogues Conference: Conclusions and recommendations' (22–24 June 2017) 3 <www.icty.org/sites/icty.org/files/articles/attachments/2017/170624-conclusions-and-recommendations-sarajevo-legacy-conference.pdf>

Part III

Procedural challenges

11 How the application of teachings can affect the legitimacy of the International Court of Justice

Sondre Torp Helmersen

Introduction

This chapter discusses how the application of 'teachings' can affect the legitimacy of the International Court of Justice. 'Teachings' are mentioned in the International Court of Justice (ICJ) Statute Article 38(1)(d), according to which the Court 'shall apply [. . .] the teachings of the most highly qualified publicists of the various nations [. . .] as subsidiary means for the determination of rules of law'. The term 'teachings' is similar to 'academic literature', 'scholarship', and 'doctrine', and will for the purposes of this chapter be taken to cover academic books and articles that comment on legal questions. Legitimacy is important to the international judiciary not least because it probably affects compliance with judicial decisions.[1] This is particularly important in international law, compared to many national legal systems, due to the lack of enforcement powers.[2] Legitimacy may also affect the weight accorded to judicial decisions.[3] The term 'legitimacy' can be used in at least two senses: the normative and the sociological. The normative sense can be defined as having 'the right to rule according to pre-defined standards', while the sociological sense can be defined as '*perceptions or beliefs* that an institution has such a right to rule'.[4] This chapter focuses on legitimacy in the sociological sense.

The 'perceptions or beliefs' about an international court or tribunal depend on who the perceiver is.[5] Following Prott, the audiences of the ICJ include 'at the very least the litigants, the professional legal elite, national governments (who are of course also potential litigants), and peoples of the world or at any rate,

1 See for example Alan Boyle and Christine Chinkin, *The Making of International Law* (Oxford University Press 2007) 301.

2 See for example C G Weeramantry, *Universalising International Law* (Martinus Nijhoff 2004) 3.

3 See for example Boyle and Chinkin (n 1) 301.

4 See for example Harlan Grant Cohen and others, 'Introduction: Legitimacy and International Courts' in Harlan Grant Cohen and others (eds.), *Legitimacy and International Courts* (Cambridge University Press, forthcoming) 3.

5 See for example Harlan Grant Cohen and others (n 4) 3.

the educated and interested parts of their populations'.[6] The discussions in this chapter are not limited to any specific audience. The discussions are linked to broader ongoing normative debates in international law. These debates are found in teachings, but are often driven by other constituencies, including states. For example, the geographical concentration of power in international law, which is a debate that underlies the arguments about the diversity of the writers cited by the ICJ, is not just of concern to scholars. It also matters in practice, for example when states leave or threaten to leave international institutions such as the International Criminal Court (ICC) or International Centre for Settlement of Investment Disputes (ICSID) (as noted below). The existence of the broader debates means that at least some audiences share the concerns that are debated, even though other audiences may disagree. While it is not possible to know exactly what the members of each audience thinks, the mere existence of the broader debates that are invoked below should mean that the relevant concerns are shared by at least some audience members. An accurate way of discovering the views of the Court's different audiences would be to poll or interview relevant individuals, but that is beyond the scope of this chapter.

Rules about recusal for judges in international and national courts focus on perceptions rather than substance. The essential aim of such rules is not only to ensure that 'justice [is] done', but also that it is '*seen to be done*'.[7] Thus it is not relevant whether a recused judge was not actually influenced or biased by the facts that led to the recusal. This has a parallel to the arguments in this section, which focus on how legitimacy of the ICJ can be improved rather than on trying to show that the judges are biased or that their behaviour is wrong.

Diversity as a legitimacy issue

Introduction

This section discusses diversity as a legitimacy issue. It is based on an observation about the (lack of) diversity among the writers who have been cited in ICJ opinions. This in turn is connected to broader debates on the geographic concentration of power in international law, and with the words 'of the various nations' in the ICJ Statute Article 38(1)(d). Counterarguments against increased diversity are also considered, in that the current citations may be a result of availability, relevance or familiarity, or of quality.

The most-cited writers are homogeneous

This section will show that the most-cited writers in individual ICJ opinions comprise a homogeneous group. Table 11.1 below shows the 20 most-cited writers

6 Lyndel V Prott, *The Latent Power of Culture and the International Judge* (Professional Books 1979) 152.

7 E.g. English High Court of Justice, *R v. Sussex Justices, Ex parte McCarthy* [1923] 1 KB 256, 259 (emphasis added).

Table 11.1 National affiliations of the top 20 most-cited writers

Writer	*Citations*	*Nationality*	*Education*	*Employment*
Rosenne, Shabtai	233	UK/Israel	UK/Israel	UK/Israel
Lauterpacht, Hersch	119	Austro-Hungary/UK	Austro-Hungary/Austria/UK	UK
Fitzmaurice, Gerald	67	UK	UK	UK
Hudson, Manley O.	55	US	US	US
Oppenheim, Lassa	53	Germany/UK	Germany	Germany/Switzerland/UK
Jennings, Robert	52	UK	UK/US	UK
de Visscher, Charles	51	Belgium	Belgium	Belgium
Brownlie, Ian	42	UK	UK	UK
Watts, Arthur	32	UK	UK	UK
Stone, Julius	32	UK?	UK/US	UK/NZ/Australia
Schwarzenberger, Georg	31	Germany/UK	Germany/UK	UK
Higgins, Rosalyn	30	UK	UK	UK
Schachter, Oscar	30	US	US	US
Guyomar, Geneviève	28	France?	France?	France?
Aréchaga, Eduardo Jiménez de	28	Uruguay	Uruguay	Uruguay
Jenks, C. Wilfred	24	UK	UK/Switzerland	Switzerland
McNair, Arnold	24	UK	UK	UK
Hambro, Edvard	24	Norway	Norway/Switzerland	Norway
Brierly, James Leslie	23	UK	UK	UK
Guillaume, Gilbert	22	France	France	France/Belgium

(not counting self-citations) in individual ICJ opinions, and lists their nationality as well as the countries where they were educated and employed. Thirteen of the writers had British citizenship. Two were from the US, two from France, and one each from Italy and Belgium. Only one was a citizen of a non-Western country, Eduardo Jiménez de Aréchaga of Uruguay, and he has been described as 'very close to the US and European traditions'.[8] The numbers for the top 20 writers' countries of education and employment are similar, with the United Kingdom being dominant and Jiménez de Aréchaga being the only non-Western writer. Thus, while the court itself is relatively heterogeneous in terms of geography and culture,[9] the teachings cited by the Court are less so. The heterogeneity of the Court's membership is mandated by the ICJ Statute Article 9. There is no similar regulation regarding teachings.

8 Antonio Cassese, *Five Masters of International Law* (Hart 2011) ix (and similarly 49–50).

9 Shabtai Rosenne with the Assistance of Yaël Ronen, *The Law and Practice of the International Court 1920–2005*, Vol 1 (4th edn, Martinus Nijhoff 2006) 388.

Figure 11.1 illustrates the results from the table. It lists states along the horizontal x-axis, and the number of top 20 writers who have a nationality, education, or employment affiliation with that state along the vertical y-axis.

The same patterns show up in other contexts

The under-representation of non-Westerners is not unique to teachings cited by the ICJ; the same patterns show up in many different contexts in international law. A study of lawyers who appeared before the ICJ between 1999 and 2012 found that they were mostly a small group of Western men.[10] The same is true for international investment arbitrators,[11] and investment arbitration counsel.[12] Roberts finds that textbooks from various parts of the world 'tended to focus primarily on material from Western states in general, and core English-speaking Western states in particular' when 'looking at the practice of foreign states or the writings of foreign scholars'.[13] She finds a comparable pattern among the staff in two international institutions with public data about employee nationalities (the ICC and the World Trade Organization (WTO)).[14] A possible contrast is provided by Pauwelyn, who finds that '52% of WTO panelist positions are nationals from countries considered in the WTO as "developing",' although 'when using not the broad WTO definition of "developing countries" but World Bank country classifications', the share is only 36%.[15] Roberts finds that the notable representation of developing country nationals 'is mainly explained by the rule that WTO panelists may not be nationals of disputing parties and third parties to disputes, unless the disputing parties agree'.[16] Roberts concludes that 'Actors, materials, and approaches from some states and regions have come to dominate certain transnational flows and forums in ways that make them disproportionately influential in constructing the "international" – a point that holds true for

10 Shashank P Kumar and Cecily Rose, 'A Study of Lawyers Appearing before the International Court of Justice, 1999–2012' (2014) 25 *European Journal of International Law* 893, 901–904; similarly Kurt Taylor Gaubatz and Matthew MacArthur, 'How International Is "International" Law?' (2001) 22 *Michigan Journal of International Law* 239, 250–260.

11 See for example Susan D Franck, 'Empirically Evaluating Claims about Investment Treaty Arbitration' (2007) 86 *North Carolina Law Review* 1, 78; Sergio Puig, 'Social Capital in the Arbitration Market' (2014) 25 *European Journal of International Law* 387, 405; ICSID, 'The ICSID Caseload – Statistics (Issue 2017–2)' (2017) <https://icsid.worldbank.org/en/Documents/resources/ICSID%20Web%20Stats%202017-2%20(English)%20Final.pdf> accessed 6 December 2017, 19.

12 Malcolm Langford, Daniel Behn, and Runar Hilleren Lie, 'The Revolving Door in International Investment Arbitration' (2017) 20 *Journal of International Economic Law* 301, 316.

13 Anthea Roberts, *Is International Law International?* (Oxford University Press 2017) 165.

14 Ibid. 258.

15 Joost Pauwelyn, 'The Rule of Law without Lawyers? Why Investment Arbitrators are from Mars, Trade Adjudicators from Venus' (2015) 109 *American Journal of International Law* 761, 771 (footnotes omitted).

16 Roberts (n 13) 259, citing the DSU Article 8.3.

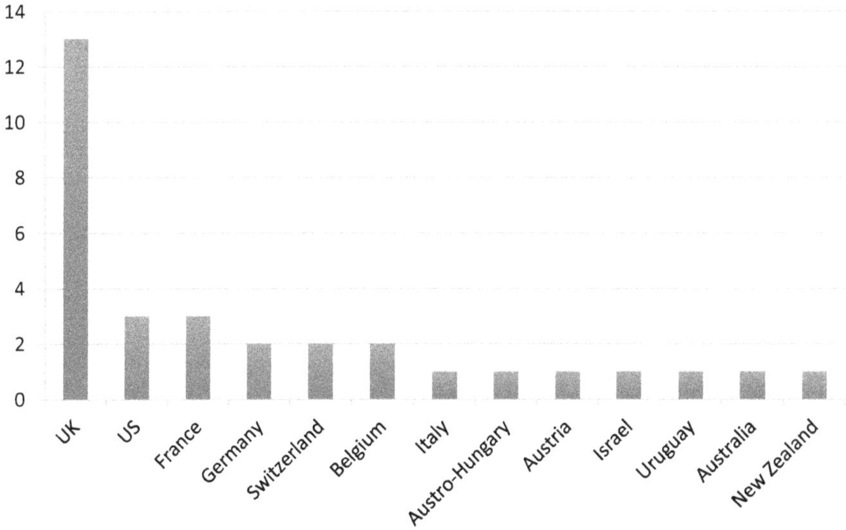

Figure 11.1 National affiliations of the top 20 most-cited writers.

Western actors, materials, and approaches in general, and Anglo-American ones in particular.'[17] This is interesting, since it means that the diversity issue that is identified in this chapter is part of a broader trend. It also means that the counter-arguments discussed below, as well as the proposed regulation in the conclusion, could be of interest in other global institutions and areas of international law.

Diversity as part of the 'international' in international law

The lack of diversity among scholars cited by the ICJ can be linked to broader debates about the 'international' nature of international law. International law seeks to be global, insofar as it applies to every state in the world. States are nonetheless different in many ways, also in how they approach international law. As Kennedy argues, 'International law is different in different places.'[18] Because of these differences, international legal methodology 'must presumably aim to be universal in character, encompassing all cultural traditions'.[19] This should include

17 Roberts (n 13) 5.
18 David Kennedy, 'The Disciplines of International Law and Policy' (2008) 12 *Leiden Journal of International Law* 9, 17.
19 Philip Allott, 'Interpretation – An Exact Art' in Andrea Bianchi, Daniel Peat, and Matthew Windsor (eds.), *Interpretation in International Law* (Oxford University Press 2015) 373, 384 (talking about 'interpretation').

the application of teachings. Thus Bohlander asks: 'Is it simply true that courts that purport to be "international" *should* or must take care to draw on a truly international set of sources?'[20] According to Roberts, '[T]he ideal of international suggests that it draws equally on people, materials, and ideas from all national and regional traditions.'[21] Many writers make the analogous argument that 'representative deficiency' (i.e. diversity among the judges) may be a 'legitimacy' issue for the ICJ.[22] This chapter extends this argument to cover the writers that the judges cite.

Despite their differences, states are supposed to be 'equal' under international law (see e.g. the reference to 'sovereign equality' in the UN Charter Article 2(1)). Even so, international law is sometimes accused of being dominated by a limited number of Western European states.[23] For example, there may be a bias against Third World states in investment arbitration awards.[24] In that context it may be particularly problematic when most ICSID arbitrators are Western,[25] '. . . and the most-cited writers in investment ICSID awards are also Western.'[26] Western lawyers could be seen as being helped by Western governments in arguing before Western arbitrators, who cite Western teachings, in cases aimed at curbing the regulatory space and political freedom of less developed countries. The perceived bias of the investment arbitration system has had practical repercussions, with several developing states criticising or leaving it.[27] Similarly, the ICC has been accused of 'bias against Africa',[28] possibly because 'The African countries are not represented adequately among the decision-makers of the court.'[29] Several Afri-

20 Michael Bohlander and Mark Findlay, 'The Use of Domestic Sources as a Basis for International Criminal Law Principles' (2002) 2 *Global Community Yearbook of International Law and Jurisprudence* 3, 22.
21 Roberts (n 13) 255.
22 See for example Boyle and Chinkin (n 1) 306–307.
23 See for example Allen Buchanan, 'The Legitimacy of International Law' in Samantha Besson and John Tasioulas (eds.), *The Philosophy of International Law* (Oxford University Press 2010) 79, 88.
24 See for example Gus Van Harten, 'Arbitrator Behaviour in Asymmetrical Adjudication: An Empirical Study of Investment Treaty Arbitration' (2012) 50 *Osgoode Hall Law Journal* 211, 252, although Susan Franck, 'Conflating Politics and Development: Examining Investment Treaty Outcomes' (2014) 55 *Virginia Journal of International Law* 1, 70 disagrees.
25 The same patterns show up in other contexts.
26 Tony Cole, 'Non-Binding Documents and Literature', in Tarcisio Gazzini and Eric De Brabandere (eds.), *International Investment Law: The Sources of Rights and Obligations* (Martinus Nijhoff 2012) 289, 305–306 lists the writers.
27 See for example Emmanuel Gaillard, 'The Denunciation of the ICSID Convention', Transnational Dispute Management (2007) <www.transnational-dispute-management.com/article.asp?key=1074> accessed 12 October 2017.
28 The Economist, 'Nice idea, now make it work' (4 December 2014) <www.economist.com/news/international/21635470-international-criminal-court-struggling-justify-itself-amid-accusations-bias> accessed 13 October 2017.
29 Vera Shikhelman, 'Diversity and Decision-Making in International Judicial Institutions' (2017, forthcoming) 36 *Berkeley Journal of International Law*, 4.

can states have threatened to leave the ICC,[30] and Burundi has done so.[31] The ICC too cites many Western teachings. They include German criminal law teachings, which may not be suitable to a 'specific African context'.[32]

It is not certain whether more consultation and citations of non-Western writers in ICJ opinions would result in different substantive outcomes in specific cases. Non-Western authors may have (systematically and in aggregate) different attitudes, assumptions, preferences and prejudices than their non-Western counterparts, which may shape how they approach specific questions of international law. Frank reports that 'The outcome of investment treaty arbitration was not reliably associated with [. . .] the development status of the presiding arbitrator.'[33] In a study of the UN Human Rights Committee, Shikhelman finds 'certain voting patterns that are associated with geographical origin, domestic legal systems, professional background, and possibly gender', although 'on many issues' she 'did not find that [. . .] background [. . .] had a significant influence on [. . .] voting patterns'.[34] Thus the substantive outcomes of specific cases are not necessarily connected with nationality.[35] The argument made here does not rely on substantive outcomes. It is rather an argument about representation. The argument is equally valid even if it turns out that increasing the diversity of cited writers has no effect on the outcome of any future case.

Diversity and the ICJ Statute Article 38(1)

According to the ICJ Stature Article 38(1)(d), the ICJ 'shall apply [. . .] the teachings of the most highly qualified publicists *of the various nations*' (emphasis added). This should be read as urging the judges to consult texts from different parts of the world. It is not certain whether this would lead to a more diverse selection of authors being *cited*, just as it is not clear whether judges already consult texts from different parts of the world. In any case, consulting a diverse range of authors is more in line with the wording of the ICJ Statute Article 38(1)(d)

30 See for example Associated Press in Addis Ababa, 'African leaders plan mass withdrawal from international criminal court', *The Guardian* (31 January 2017) <www.theguardian.com/law/2017/jan/31/african-leaders-plan-mass-withdrawal-from-international-criminal-court> accessed 12 October 2017.

31 Agence France-Presse, 'Burundi becomes first nation to leave international criminal court', *The Guardian* (28 October 2017) <www.theguardian.com/law/2017/oct/28/burundi-becomes-first-nation-to-leave-international-criminal-court> accessed 21 November 2017.

32 Elies van Sliedregt, 'International Criminal Law: Over-studied and Underachieving?' (2016) 29 *Leiden Journal of International Law* 1, 7.

33 Susan D Franck, 'Development and Outcomes in Investment Treaty Arbitration' (2009) 50 *Harvard International Law Journal* 438, 487.

34 Shikhelman (n 32) 6.

35 Eg Susan D Franck, 'The Diversity Challenge: Exploring the "Invisible College" of International Arbitration' (2015) 53 *Columbia Journal of Transnational Law* 429, 498.

than not doing so,[36] as the International Law Commission (ILC) recognised in the *Customary International Law Conclusions.*[37]

One reason judges cite mainly Western writers may be that the writers the judges consider to be 'the most highly qualified' happen to be from Western countries (which is discussed as a possibility in the next-but-one section below). If so, the wording of the ICJ Statute Article 38(1)(d) can explain, and in one sense justify, at least some of the dominance of Western nationals among the writers cited by the ICJ. However, the phrase 'the most highly qualified' is subjective. It is largely up to the individual judges to decide whom they consider 'qualified'.

Counterargument: availability, relevance and familiarity

The ICJ is in some writers' opinion afflicted with 'structural bias'.[38] This bias may extend to the Court's choice of teachings. However, the skewed representations of different groups of writers in the teachings cited by the ICJ does not have to be the result of bias, conscious or unconscious, among judges.[39] Judges searching for teachings may not even be aware of the nationality of the different authors, even if they cared about it at all. Bias is a possibility, but the numbers cited here do not prove it.

The different rates of citation of Western and non-Western writers may instead reflect patterns in the teachings that are published. Different levels of university funding in different countries probably play a role, since 'The size of the community of international legal scholars [. . .] depends on the funding made available by public authorities.'[40] Another important factor is how 'developed' a country's 'legal education [system]' is.[41] When discussing appointments to investment arbitration panels, Franck believes '[T]here may be structural, educational, social, and financial barriers that prevent arbitrators from gaining [. . .] expertise,'[42] and the same points apply to the production of teachings.

Western teachings may also be more available to the judges, for example if they are preferred by the Court's librarians or clerks, or if they are easier to acquire or consult in The Hague or other cities where the judges spend time. As Kammerhofer puts it, the choice to cite a certain work 'may be as banal as the judge who drafts a judgment just happening to have standard work A, but not B or C on his

36 Michel Virally, 'The Sources of International Law', in Max Sørensen (ed.), *Manual of Public International Law* (St. Martin's Press 1968) 116, 153.
37 International Law Commission, *Report of the International Law Commission Sixty-eighth session (2 May–10 June and 4 July–12 August 2016) (A/71/10)* (United Nations 2016) 112.
38 Eg Martti Koskenniemi, *From Apology to Utopia: The Structure of International Legal Argument* (2nd edn, Cambridge University Press 2006) 607.
39 Similarly Miguel de Figueiredo and Eric A Posner, 'Is the International Court of Justice Biased?' (2005) 34 *Journal of Legal Studies* 599, 624.
40 Jean d'Aspremont, 'Wording in International Law' (2012) 25 *Leiden Journal of International* Law 575, 587.
41 Franck (n 38) 465.
42 Franck (n 12) 80.

or her desk at the time'.[43] Additionally, judges may be more familiar with certain teachings. This may depend, for example, on the teachings they were instructed to read as students.[44] In that context, it is worth noting that most judges, including the non-Western ones, have studied at Western universities.[45]

Of the 20 most-cited writers, ten are originally from the UK, two from the US, and two from France. Thus 12 out of 20 writers, or 60%, can be presumed to be native English speakers. A further two, 10%, are native French speakers.[46] Since English is the dominant international law language,[47] and French and English are the official languages of the Court,[48] it is fair to assume that more judges can read them than can read most other languages. This is probably one reason why the Court cites many English-speaking and some French-speaking writers.[49] This can in turn explain some of the dominance of Western writers in ICJ opinions, since English and French are Western languages. Thus, generally, the role of language in international law and in the ICJ does to some extent explain why the ICJ's citations of teachings are skewed in favour of Western writers. This does not fully explain the preponderance of British writers over other English speaking and French speaking writers, though. The over-representation of British writers may also, for example, be a result of a British tradition of writing general textbooks, which are popular with courts, and from many non-British judges having studied in Britain or lived under British rule.

That being said, non-native English writers can, and do, write in English. Among the top 20 most-cited writers, Hersch Lauterpacht grew up in a Polish-speaking city (Lviv), studied in a German-speaking city (Vienna), and subsequently moved to the UK and wrote in English. Lassa Oppenheim was born and studied in Germany, but wrote in English after moving to the UK. The same story is true for Georg Schwarzenberger. Eduardo Jiménez de Aréchaga was a native Spanish speaker, but mostly wrote in English. Edvard Hambro was Norwegian, but wrote

43 Jörg Kammerhofer, 'Lawmaking by scholars' in Catherine Brölmann and Yannick Radi (eds.), *Research Handbook on the Theory and Practice of International Lawmaking* (Edward Elgar 2016) 305, 323.

44 Neil Duxbury, *Judges and Jurists: An Essay on Influence* (Hart Publishing 2001) 20–21, citing Louis J Sirico Jr and Jeffrey B Margulies, 'The Citing of Law Reviews by the Supreme Court: An Empirical Study (1986) 34 *UCLA Law Review* 131, 133–134.

45 Eg Prott (n 6) 203; Gaubatz and MacArthur (n 11) 262; Gleider I Hernández, *The International Court of Justice and the Judicial Function* (Oxford University Press 2014) 133–134.

46 This is similar to the ICTY, where Bohlander notes the dominance of English and French teachings: Michael Bohlander, 'The Influence of Academic Research on the Jurisprudence of the International Criminal Tribunal for the Former Yugoslavia – A First Overview' (2003) 3 *Global Community Yearbook of International Law & Jurisprudence* 195, 197.

47 Clive Parry, *The Sources and Evidence of International Law* (Manchester University Press 1965) 108; Roberts (n 15) 47 and 260–267.

48 ICJ Statute Article 39(1).

49 Similarly, according Bohlander and Findlay (n 23) 6, '[A]t the ICTY the language of justice is mainly English, and to a somewhat lesser extent French. Anything not written down in these idioms does not seem to be accorded great relevance for purposes of legal research into authorities.'

his most significant international law works in English. This shows that non-native English speakers can write in English, even though they may do so less often or less successfully than native speakers. It is more difficult to write well in a non-native language, especially if that language is radically different from one's native language. Because non-native speakers can, in principle, write in English (or French), the Court's preference for English (and French) teachings may not be all that problematic. As long as all judges can read English or French, and English is the dominant international law language, non-Western writers who wish to influence the ICJ should be encouraged to write in those languages.[50]

The conclusion is that the citation of teachings in ICJ judges' opinions is probably to a large extent determined by familiarity, availability and relevance. Changing this will require broader changes in the languages used by international lawyers and the Court, as well as in the geographic distribution of international law research and publications. However, it is still possible to make the argument that more diverse citation patterns would improve the Court's legitimacy. Regardless of *why* ICJ judges cite mostly Western writers, the Court is a global institution applying international law that is supposed to be universal. Judges can therefore still be encouraged to consult non-Western teachings, as proposed in the conclusion.

Counterargument: the quality of teachings

Different teachings probably have different weight. If Western teachings have more weight, judges may prefer to cite them in order to maximise the authority of their own judicial opinions. For example, quality is a factor that should affect the weight of teachings, and objectivity, as noted above, is one aspect of quality. Scholars from some regions may be systematically more objective than others. In this connection it may be noted that scholars from certain states tend to unanimously support their own state's positions on controversial issues, while scholars from other states dare to criticise their own government's record of compliance with international law. For example, Julian Ku compares the unanimous support of Chinese scholars of the Chinese non-cooperation and non-compliance with the 2016 *South China Sea Arbitration*[51] with the divided reaction of US scholars to the country's non-cooperation and non-compliance with the ICJ's *Nicaragua*[52] decision.[53] Anton Moiseienko notes that 'Any criticism of Russia's

50 Although there are problems involved in encouraging everyone to write in English. While it does ease cross-border communication, it poses risks to the intellectual richness and global legitimacy of international law, as discussed by Roberts (n 15) 264–269.

51 Permanent Court of Arbitration, *The South China Sea Arbitration (The Republic of Philippines v. The People's Republic of China)*, Case 2013–19, Award, 12 July 2016.

52 *Military and Paramilitary Activities in and against Nicaragua (Nicaragua v. United States of America), Merits, Judgment. I.C.J. Reports 1986*, p. 14.

53 Julian G Ku, 'China's Legal Scholars Are Less Credible After South China Sea Ruling', Foreign Policy (14 July 2016) <http://foreignpolicy.com/2016/07/14/south-china-sea-lawyers-unclos-beijing-legal-tribunal> accessed 14 October 2017. Similarly Roberts (n 15) 240.

annexation of Crimea largely remains a marginal idea in Russian legal media.'[54] This can, for example, be contrasted with the responses of British (and UK based) international lawyers that are posted on the website of the Chilcot Inquiry, where they critically discussed the legality of the UK's participation in the 2003 Iraq Invasion.[55] A lack of scholarly objectivity may be prompted by governmental interference.[56] Roberts suggests 'explicit and implicit Chinese censorship' as an explanation for the unanimity among Chinese scholars.[57] Malksoo reports that an 'MGIMO history professor [. . .] was fired in March 2014 because of his criticism of Putin's annexation of Crimea'.[58] If scholars are unable to be critical of their own government due to outside pressures, this can mar the objectivity and thus the quality of their writings. It is natural that their writings are given less weight, at least on issues that are politically important to their own state.

The writer's expertise is another factor that should affect the weight of teachings. Western countries may have more experts on international law.[59] This chapter does not investigate this possibility further.

In short, judges may prefer certain teachings because they increase the weight of their opinions. Similarly, in studies of ICJ counsel and investment arbitrators, authors suggest that 'governments [. . .] insist[ing] upon being represented by the "best" counsel' and 'different actors behaving rationally and independently' are explanations for low diversity.[60] The lack of diversity that is discussed here could be seen as a collective action problem. Citation of more diverse teachings could improve the ICJ's legitimacy, but if the practice is a result of the varying quality of teachings, it could also reduce the authority of the individual judge's opinion. Regulation, as proposed in the conclusion, could be one way to alleviate this collective problem, by coordinating the incentives of the individual judges. This collective action problem is also one reason why no particular measures have been taken to improve the diversity of the teachings that are cited in this chapter, despite the chapter itself highlighting such diversity as an issue. The choice of teachings has also been restricted by language proficiency and by what has been available in relevant libraries.

Thus, there seems to be some basis for saying that some of the lack of diversity among the writers cited by the ICJ is because there is a perception that Western writers have more expertise and official authority, and produce works of higher

54 Anton Moiseienko, 'Guest Post: What do Russian Lawyers Say about Crimea?', Opinio Juris (24 September 2014) <http://opiniojuris.org/2014/09/24/guest-post-russian-lawyers-say-crimea/> accessed 14 October 2017. Similarly e.g. Oleksandr Zadorozhnii, 'To Justify against All Odds: The Annexation of Crimea in 2014 and the Russian Legal Scholarship' (2015) 35 *Polish Yearbook of International Law* 139, 168–169.

55 The Iraq Inquiry, 'International Law Submissions' (undated) <www.iraqinquiry.org.uk/other-material/submissions-international-law/> accessed 14 October 2017.

56 Roberts (n 15) 231.

57 Roberts (n 15) 231 and 241.

58 Lauri Mälksoo, *Russian Approaches to International Law* (Oxford University Press 2015) 31.

59 E.g. Antonio Cassese (n 8) 254.

60 Kumar and Rose (n 10) 912. Similarly Puig (n 12) 423.

quality. Because of this, increasing the diversity of teachings may negate one of their advantages. Teachings can save judges time, not least because judges can trust the legal analyses in authoritative works. If judges were to consult and cite less authoritative works, this benefit may disappear.[61]

Conclusion

In light of the counterarguments discussed above, some of the uniformity in the citation of a narrow range of writers in ICJ opinions may be due to factors judges cannot, should not or may not wish to attempt to counter. This does not affect the potential for improving the ICJ's legitimacy through a more diverse citation practice. It does, however, mean that increased diversity has to be balanced against the counterarguments.[62] It seems that this balance can be struck in a way that results in somewhat more diversity than is found in current citation practices. Whether it will actually do so in the future is a more open question. That the same patterns are found in a wide variety of areas and institutions suggests that they are deeply entrenched in international law generally. Some form of official regulation, as proposed in the conclusion, could be a beginning.

Transparency as a legitimacy issue

Introduction

Citations of teachings are almost completely absent from the ICJ's majority opinions.[63] The ICJ probably uses teachings far more often than they are cited in the Court's decisions and opinions. For example, Kammerhofer reports 'anecdotal evidence about the Court's internal procedures' which 'supports the intuition that the judges and the Registry utilise scholarship to a significant degree'.[64] This section argues that if judges' citation of teachings were more in line with how often teachings are actually used, the application of teachings would be more transparent, and this may improve the ICJ's legitimacy.

The term 'transparency' is used through this section. The ICJ's citation of teachings is only one particular aspect of a broad and complex concept. For example, Philippe Sands has previously 'raised the issue of lack of transparency as a problem in the Court', but only 'discussed the appointment of experts', 'the

61 Avidan Kent and Jamie Trinidad, 'International Law Scholars as Amici Curiae: An Emerging Dialogue (of the Deaf)?' (2016) 29 *Leiden Journal of International Law* 1081, 1088 make a similar argument about amicus curiae briefs and 'the writings of any researcher who has enough ambition and an Internet connection'.

62 Shikhelman (n 32) 47.

63 Robert Jennings and Arthur Watts (eds.), *Oppenheim's International Law*, vol 1 (9th edn, Longman 1992) 42–43; Michael Peil, 'Scholarly Writings as a Source of Law: A Survey of the Use of Doctrine by the International Court of Justice' (2012) 1 *Cambridge Journal of International and Comparative Law* 136, 151.

64 Kammerhofer (n 46) 307.

assessment of evidence', 'when judges are acting as arbitrators', and 'the bar at the Court'.[65]

The transparency issue that is discussed in this section is not limited to teachings. The ICJ also refrains from citing judicial decisions from other courts and tribunals,[66] and has been criticised for citing too little state practice.[67] The issue is also not limited to the ICJ, although many other international courts and tribunals as well as national courts cite teachings in their decisions more often than the ICJ does. This includes the International Criminal Tribunal for the former Yugoslavia (ICTY),[68] the WTO Appellate Body (AB),[69] and ICSID tribunals,[70] as well as arbitral tribunals[71] and national courts.[72]

Transparency as part of the rule of law

Transparency is often touted as an essential component of the rule of law.[73] For example, it may be argued that there is 'no duty to obey secret laws',[74] and that democratic states have 'a significant presumption in favor of judicial honesty'.[75] Legal philosopher Lon Fuller has argued that non-transparent rules should be excluded from the concept of 'law' altogether.[76] This line of argument can be extended to sources and instruments applied by judges when deciding cases,

65 Philippe Sands quoted in Amelia Keene (ed.), 'Outcome Paper for the Seminar on the International Court of Justice at 70' (2016) 7 *Journal of International Dispute Settlement* 238, 249.
66 Boyle and Chinkin (n 1) 297; D J Harris, *Cases and Materials on International Law* (8th edn, Sweet & Maxwell 2015) 41–42.
67 Eg Fernando Lusa Bordin, 'Reflections of Customary International Law: The Authority of Codification Conventions and ILC Draft Articles In International Law (2014) 63 *International and Comparative Law Quarterly* 535, 548.
68 Bohlander (n 49) 198–202.
69 Sondre Torp Helmersen, 'The Use of Scholarship by the WTO Appellate Body' (2016) 7 *Goettingen Journal of International Law* 309, 317.
70 Ole Kristian Fauchald, 'The Legal Reasoning of ICSID Tribunals – An Empirical Analysis' (2008) 19 *European Journal of International Law* 301, 351. Similarly S A Riga Sureda, *Investment Treaty Arbitration: Judging under Uncertainty* (Cambridge University Press 2012) 132.
71 Alina Kaczorowska, *Public International Law* (4th edn, Routledge 2010) 59; James Crawford, *Brownlie's Principles of Public International Law* (8th edn, Oxford University Press 2012) 43.
72 E.g. Malcolm N Shaw, *International Law* (7th edn, Cambridge University Press 2014) 80; Sandesh Sivakumaran, 'The Influence of Teachings of Publicists on the Development of International Law' (2017) 66 *International and Comparative Law Quarterly* 1, 27.
73 E.g. Boyle and Chinkin (n 1) 302; Samantha Besson, 'Theorizing the Sources of International Law' in Samantha Besson and John Tasioulas (eds), *The Philosophy of International Law* (OUP 2010) 163, 172.
74 David Lefkowitz, 'The Sources of International Law: Some Philosophical Reflections' in Samantha Besson and John Tasioulas (eds), *The Philosophy of International Law* (Oxford University Press 2010) 187, 195.
75 Fábio P Shecaira, *Legal Scholarship as a Source of Law* (Springer 2013) 80.
76 Lon Fuller, *The Morality of Law, New Haven* (Yale University Press 1965) 49–51, in light of 38–41. Similarly Bordin (n 70) 562.

including teachings. Dealing with such sources and instruments in a transparent manner 'generally enhances the legitimacy of the adjudicative process'.[77] It allows the actors in the legal system to know more accurately how decisions are made, and makes it easier to predict one's legal position. Transparency is not just about citing teachings. Judges can also show and explain how teachings affected their decision, by 'engaging' with teachings, which the ICJ and its judges rarely do. For example, judges could consistently refer to and rebut perspectives that go against the legal solution favoured in a decision,[78] and evaluate the argument found in teachings on their merits.[79]

Transparency and the ICJ Statute Article 38(1)

The ICJ Statute Article 38(1)(d) says that the ICJ 'shall apply' teachings when deciding cases based on international law. The use of the words 'shall' and 'apply' suggest an obligation to at least consider teachings, but probably not an obligation to cite them. Thus, while a more transparent application of teachings by international judges could improve the Court's legitimacy, such action is not mandated by the ICJ Statute.

Plagiarism

Judges can, of course, consult and be influenced by works they do not cite. In so doing, they may even adopt the text of those works more or less verbatim.[80] Unlike writers, judges who take ideas or even repeat text verbatim from teachings without acknowledgment are not guilty of plagiarism in a strict legal sense.[81] The ethics are nonetheless somewhat similar.[82] Many academic institutions and subject areas have guidelines mandating a transparent citation practice, but courts do not.

Counterargument: length and complexity

Citing teachings in a judicial decision makes the decision longer,[83] which means that it takes longer to read and longer to write. It can also make the decision

77 J Romesh Weeramantry, *Treaty Interpretation in Investment Arbitration* (Oxford University Press 2012) 137.
78 Similarly Cole (n 29) 289, 310 and 316; Fábio P Shecaira (n 78) 80.
79 Cole (n 29) 316.
80 Jack Beatson, 'Legal Academics: Forgotten Players or Interlopers?' in Andrew Burrows, David Johnston, and Reinhard Zimmermann (eds.), *Judge and Jurist: Essays in Memory of Lord Rodger* (Oxford University Press 2013) 523, 524 gives specific examples (from national law).
81 E.g. Richard A Posner, *The Little Book of Plagiarism* (Pantheon 2007) 21.
82 E.g. Robert Y Jennings, 'Reflections on the Subsidiary Means for the Determination of Rules of Law', in *Studi di diritto internazionale in onore di Gaetano Arangio-Ruiz*, vol 1 (Editoriale Scientifica 2004) 319, 329.
83 E.g. Russell Smyth, 'Citing Outside the Law Reports: Citations of Secondary Authorities on the Australian State Supreme Courts Over the Twentieth Century' (2009) 18 *Griffith Law Review* 692, 701.

more complex, by obscuring the judge's reasoning.[84] This makes the decision less accessible to readers.[85] Prott criticises 'exaggerated reliance on citations' as 'clumsy' and 'diminish[ing] the persuasive force of the opinion', and highlights a specific example, the opinion of 'Van Wyk in the *South West Africa Case 1962*'.[86] The added length and complexity are thus counterarguments against citing teachings frequently in judicial decisions.

Counterargument: lack of official authority

Authors of teachings have no official authority, in that their writings have not been endorsed, directly or indirectly, by states.[87] By contrast, treaties and customary international law are created by states, and judicial decisions are created by courts and tribunals that have been set up by states. Thus Wolfke, for example, notes that 'Formally speaking there are no grounds for awarding an independent role to the opinions of private persons.'[88] This lack of official authority is an argument against the citing of teachings in judicial decisions. Rodger argues (in the context of English law) that 'The parties [. . .] want to see something that appears to embody the judge's own views as a result of listening to the arguments, rather than views which he or she has taken [. . .] from some academic author.'[89] The ICJ may be pre-empting this expectation by not citing teachings. This approach is arguably encapsulated in the wording of ICJ Statute Article 38, which says that the Court's 'function is *to decide* [. . .] such disputes as are submitted to it' (emphasis added).

Counterargument: exposing lack of diversity

The ICJ may refrain from citing teachings because writers tend to stem from 'a handful of countries', as noted earlier. Increased reference to teachings would expose this lack of diversity. This lack of diversity can be used as a counterargument against transparency. Having said that, the lack of diversity seems to be the main issue, not the risk that the issue gets exposure.

Conclusion

This section has identified arguments for and against increased transparency in ICJ judges' application of teachings. It is up to each judge to strike a balance

84 Lord Rodger of Earlsferry, 'Judges and Academics in the United Kingdom' (2010) 29 *University of Queensland Law Journal* 29, 32.
85 E.g. Deborah J Merritt and Melanie Putnam, 'Judges and Scholars: Do Courts and Scholarly Journals Cite the Same Law Review Articles' (1996) 71 *Chicago-Kent Law Review* 871, 876–877.
86 Prott (n 6) 127.
87 G J H Van Hoof, *Rethinking the Sources of International Law* (Kluwer 1993) 177.
88 Karol Wolfke, *Custom in Present International Law* (2nd edn, Martinus Nijhoff 1993) 156.
89 Lord Rodger of Earlsferry (n 87), 32.

between these competing arguments. However, it seems likely that the ICJ's legitimacy would be improved by a somewhat higher degree of transparency in the application of teachings than what is currently practised.[90] However, Judge Tomka seems adamant about not citing teachings in majority opinions, having stated that 'The Court would never refer to the writings of qualified publicists.'[91] Future judges may nonetheless take a different approach.

The need for regulation

Regulation as a legitimacy issue in itself

Various writers argue, in different ways, that anything that affects the outcomes of specific legal decisions and contributes to the development of the law should ideally be subject to some form of regulation. For example. it may be argued that any 'governance activity' that reduces the 'freedom' or 'unilaterally' shapes the 'legal or factual situation' of 'individuals, private associations, enterprises, states, or other public institutions' (whether or not it is 'legally binding') should be subject to 'legal standards'.[92] Such regulation may affect 'legitimacy', 'according to a deeply held popular belief that [. . .] a system of rules' should 'be firmly rooted in a framework of formal requirements about how rules are made, interpreted and applied'.[93] This line of argument can be extended to the ICJ's application of teachings.

Regulation may alleviate other legitimacy issues

Appropriate regulation could also be a way to alleviate the legitimacy issues of transparency and diversity mentioned above. It would increase judges' incentive to be transparent in their application of teachings, and increase awareness of the effect that this may have on the Court's legitimacy. For the 'collective action problem' of diversity, regulation may encourage judges to consider a more diverse selection of teachings. In her study of gender representation on international courts, Grossman finds that in 'courts where states were required by statute to take sex into account when nominating or voting for judges, a higher percentage of women sat on the bench'.[94] The statutes in question do not require a specific number or proportion of female judges. They may nonetheless have had

90 Cole (n 29) 316 similarly argues for greater transparency by investment tribunals about their application of teachings.
91 Judge Tomka quoted in Keene (n 68) 260.
92 Armin von Bogdandy, Philipp Dann, and Matthias Goldmann, 'Developing the Publicness of Public International Law: Towards a Legal Framework for Global Governance Activities' (2008) 9 *German Law Journal* 1375, 1376–1382.
93 Thomas M Franck, *Fairness in International Law and Institutions* (Oxford University Press 1998) 7–8.
94 Nienke Grossman, 'Achieving Sex-Representative International Court Benches' (2016) 110 *American Journal of International Law* 82, 82.

some effect, which suggests that even an informal or open-ended regulation of the application of teachings by the ICJ could make a difference.[95]

The appropriate form of regulation

The application of teachings cannot be regulated in the form of rules. There is no sense in, for example, proposing strict instructions about when and what teachings should be cited. While many international courts have specific regulations to ensure a regionally diverse membership, this would not be realistic in practice for the production or citation of teachings. There cannot be quotas on how many authors from each region are to be cited in each opinion, for example. A better approach would be to encourage (rather than oblige) judges to consult a diverse range of teachings, through guiding principles rather than strict rules.

A further question is what kind of instrument is most appropriate for regulating the application of teachings. One possibility is a binding treaty. For the ICJ, this would mean amending the ICJ Statute. However, this would not only be unrealistic, it would also be impractical and inflexible. An alternative would be to add certain principles to the ICJ Rules of Court. This would be more flexible and practical, and more realistic to accomplish. The application of teachings by judges could also be a subject of discussion in bodies such as the ILC, the IDI, the ILA, and the like.

Conclusion

The ICJ and most of the judges cite teachings less often than they consult teachings, and the teachings that they do cite are largely written by male writers from Western countries. The Court's and the judges' application of teachings is largely unregulated, beyond the skeletal instructions in the ICJ Statute Article 38(1)(d). It is difficult to know precisely how relevant audiences perceive the Court's legitimacy, but it seems plausible that a more transparent and diverse application of teachings, based on a firmer regulatory framework, would have a positive effect on the Court's legitimacy.

More frequent citation of teachings would make the Court's and the judges' opinions more closely aligned with how cases are actually decided in practice, which would make it easier for states and others to predict their legal positions. Ideally, judges should cite different perspectives that appear in the teachings that they consult, and rebut those that go against the legal solution favoured in their opinion. This could improve the quality of judicial decisions, by encouraging judges to sharpen and justify their views in light of the teachings they cite. It would also say something about the role that teachings play in the judges' reasoning process, especially compared with the common practice of simply citing

95 Nienke Grossman, 'Shattering the Glass Ceiling in International Adjudication' (2016) 56 *Virginia Journal of International Law* 339, 388.

teachings in a footnote without further comment. Judges could also be more open about their reasons for preferring specific teachings, such as the quality of the work, or the author's expertise or official positions, or that multiple authors agree. This too would contribute to parties' ability to predict their legal position. If they can know why certain authors or works are preferred and how their relative weight is assessed, they have a better chance of predicting how judges would decide a potential case. Additionally, judges should be open about how their application of teachings conforms to the ICJ Statute Article 38(1), for example by occasionally saying whether they believe that Article 38 permits or obliges them to consult or cite teachings, or by specifying whether their criteria for preferring some teachings over others are derived from the text of Article 38. The Court and the judges are bound by Article 38, and they must stay within this legal framework when deciding cases.

As for diversity, judges should make some effort to consult teachings by writers who are citizens of or have studied or worked in non-Western countries. Even where such works are found and consulted in a specific case, this may not change the outcome of the case, or even bring any new perspectives to the table (although the odds of that will probably increase). These are not the main purposes of the proposal, however. The main purpose is rather to show that this part of international law, too, aspires to be global and universal, even if this ideal is often achieved only imperfectly in practice.

These changes would also have costs, however. The lack of diversity among writers seems to be a broader issue in international law more generally. It should be possible for judges to at least try to seek out alternative teachings beyond what is available in pleadings and libraries, but this could be costly in terms of time and other resources. The alternative works could also be of lower quality, and when consulting them judges may have to spend more time assessing the quality of each individual work rather than trusting the views of writers they are already familiar with. A more transparent application of teachings would have a negative effect on the length and readability of opinions, and it would further expose the lack of diversity among writers. Citing teachings in majority opinions could also have a negative effect on the Court's prestige and authority, since teachings have less prestige and authority than the Court does.

In the end it is the Court's judges who must balance these competing interests when drafting opinions, either individually or as part of the Court's drafting committee. The argument made in this section is that there is a potential for increased transparency, diversity and regulation, and that utilising some (but not too much) of this potential would have a net positive effect on the Court's legitimacy.

12 Towards separate opinions at the Court of Justice of the European Union

Lessons in deliberative democracy from the International Court of Justice and elsewhere

*David Yuratich**

Introduction

The Eurozone crisis precipitated a shift towards intergovernmental forms of EU governance involving executive dominance and a reduced role for the European Parliament, and consequently it spotlighted the EU's democratic legitimacy.[1] It provoked prescriptions for a more deliberative EU whose citizens have more opportunities to effectively contest its direction. This chapter argues that the Court of Justice of the European Union (CJEU) could assist this if its judges were able to issue separate opinions. It draws on the International Court of Justice (ICJ), other international and domestic courts, and deliberative theory to demonstrate the democratic potential of such a reform. In sum, moving away from its current univocal format would encourage clearer and more discursive judgments which articulate different legal solutions and catalyse what Hübner Mendes calls 'post-decisional'[2] deliberation.

It proceeds as follows. It first examines the EU's democratic imperatives. Next it introduces Hübner Mendes' framework for assessing a court's deliberative quality. The link between his framework and a court's judgment style is then considered, noting in particular the CJEU's shortcomings. The previous approaches of EU scholars are then considered, before the final sections detail the deliberative benefits of separate opinions.

The EU and deliberative democracy

Several recent contributions to the EU democracy literature argue that the intergovernmental shift has reduced possibilities for EU citizens to exercise

* I would like to thank the three editors of this volume, the various contributors to the 'Future of International Courts' symposium at the University of East Anglia in June 2017, and Dr Eleni Frantziou for their helpful comments on earlier drafts. All errors remain my own.

1 See e.g. Kaarlo Tuori and Klaus Tuori, *The Eurozone Crisis: A Constitutional Analysis* (CUP 2014).

2 Conrado Hübner Mendes, *Constitutional Courts and Deliberative Democracy* (OUP 2015) 110.

self-determination, and that the CJEU is complicit since it is generally an object and agent of EU integration, a tool for establishing an autonomous supranational legal order.[3] Whereas EU law is typically used to foster integration by depoliticising policy issues, these analyses propose that law should create more opportunities for popular contestation of the EU's direction.[4] Dawson and De Witte's suggestion is typical: to reduce the EU's legal path-dependency, policy objectives should be removed from the Treaty on European Union to prevent the CJEU interpreting law in accordance with an autonomous doctrine of integration.[5] Instead the CJEU should guard the political processes enclosing EU competences. For example, the current approach to subsidiarity – does the court deem the EU best-placed to achieve *x* – could become a different question inviting political contestation: has there been an effective and inclusive dialogue about whether *x* should be pursued?[6] The court thereby becomes a vessel for constructive political conflict, protecting those procedures 'necessary to guarantee the political process between free and equal citizens'.[7] Similarly, Azoulai argues that law must do more than hold the EU together; it should create 'preconditions necessary to foster genuine collective action',[8] and Grimm seeks to move away from the judicial constitutionalisation that transformed vast political questions around topics such as citizenship into narrower legal ones.[9] Each prescribes a deliberatively democratic system which 'tries to make good political decisions by systematically connecting them to the reasons that equal citizens give each other for and against those decisions'.[10]

These concepts loosely relate to formal and informal dialogues between the CJEU and the political and legal elites in member states which ultimately contextualise its decisions within competition between the domestic and the supranational. For example, recent CJEU decisions restricted when EU citizens can claim social benefits in their host state, partially tracking domestic political concerns about welfare tourism.[11] Similarly its fundamental rights jurisprudence has long juggled the constitutional preferences and duties of national courts with the primacy of the EU legal order.[12] The deliberation outlined in the previous para-

3 Mark Dawson and Floris de Witte, 'From Balance to Conflict: A New Constitution for the EU' (2016) 22 ELJ 204, 222. See generally Gerard Conway, *The Limits of Legal Reasoning and the European Court of Justice* (CUP 2012) ch 1.
4 Ibid. 221.
5 Ibid.
6 Ibid.
7 Ibid. 223.
8 Loïc Azoulai, '"Integration Through Law" and Us' (2016) 14 ICON 449, 463.
9 Dieter Grimm, 'The Democratic Costs of Constitutionalisation: The European Case' (2015) 21 ELJ 460, 471.
10 Michael Neblo, *Deliberative Democracy Between Theory and Practice* (CUP 2015) 2.
11 Panos Koutrakos, 'A Realist Court?' (2018) 42 EL Rev 311, 312.
12 Luis Arroyo Jiménez, 'Constitutional Empathy and Judicial Dialogue in the European Union' (2018) 24 EPL 57.

graph, and focussed on by this chapter, is different. It seeks to move the CJEU beyond dialogue with national elites and tie its decisions into a wider process of deliberation about the EU that better incorporates EU citizens.

Using courts to protect deliberation recurs in deliberative theory, generally in a Habermasian sense, where they ensure that those laws germinating deliberation – such as voting and expression rights – are respected.[13] Hence, one way to approach the law of deliberative democracy in the EU is to examine whether the law seeds effective democratic conditions.[14] Another way the CJEU may enhance the EU's deliberative qualities is by encouraging its judgments to become sites for popular deliberation. The following argues that its decisions currently discourage contestation and that permitting separate opinions may help the CJEU plumb greater popular deliberation into the EU. As explained below, this is because they encourage all submitted arguments to be addressed, promote clearer decisions, and enable dissentients to publicly discuss alternative jurisprudences. The next section frames this argument by introducing Hübner Mendes' model for a deliberative court, the yardstick for this chapter's assessment of how separate opinions would boost the CJEU's deliberative legitimacy.

The deliberative court

Hübner Mendes identifies three ways courts can protect and promote deliberation. First is the Habermasian view sketched above.[15] Second, courts may be Rawlsian public reasoners which require laws and administrative actions to be justified or else invalidated.[16] Gerstenberg has identified this within the EU: if asked, the CJEU requires EU institutions to give defensible reasons for the legal basis and substance of legislation and executive action.[17] This ties the EU into a justificatory dialogue between citizens, institutions, and member states.[18] Third, courts may be assessed internally. If judicial percolations meet deliberative expectations, the decision is more likely to be soundly reasoned; be clearer and thus a better public reasoner; display different opinions to the public; and encourage greater confidence.[19] A constitutional court operating effectively within the custodial, interlocutory and internal vectors will tend towards being a 'special deliberator'.[20] They are both micro-sites for deliberation on specific legal problems and

13 Jürgen Habermas, *Between Facts and Norms* (Polity 1995) 458. See generally Ron Levy and Graham Orr, *The Law of Deliberative Democracy* (Routledge 2016).

14 See e.g. David Yuratich, 'Article 13(2) TEU: Institutional Balance, Sincere Co-Operation, and Non-Domination During Lawmaking?' (2017) 18 GLJ 99.

15 Hübner Mendes (n 2) 85.

16 Ibid. 86–91.

17 Oliver Gerstenberg, 'Law's Polyarchy: A Comment on Cohen and Sabel' (1997) 3 ELJ 343, 357.

18 Joshua Cohen and Charles Sabel, 'Directly-Deliberative Polyarchy' (1997) 3 ELJ 313, 335.

19 Hübner Mendes (n 2) 91.

20 Ibid. 4.

macro-sites for broader deliberation, catalysing and provoking it through their judgments. Three interrelated phases of a judicial decision provide a seedbed:

1. *Pre-decisional*: The period between a court receiving and disposing of a case. This phase is distinctively concerned with deliberation exhibited during litigation, inside and outside the courtroom, by lawyers, judges and the wider non-legal community.[21]
2. *Decisional*: The judiciary must interact collegially during decision making, promoting a well-reasoned judgment reflecting the totality of the deliberations.[22]
3. *Post-decisional*: A deliberative judgment enables the community to 'keep talking about that specific controversy so long as disagreement persists'.[23] It is crucial that it is open to contestation: it must carry an air of contingency so that it may spark engagement with its impact and its future. It must also be understandable to educated members of the public or campaigners as well as legal actors.[24] This encourages and enables popular debate and cements its position in future pre-decisional phases.[25]

Hübner Mendes is ultimately ambivalent about separate opinions. Whilst he notes that they may have significant deliberative benefits, he focuses on the decisions' rhetorical qualities, and it is possible to have a clear and fallible single judgment.[26] The CJEU does not generally create such judgments and thus lacks deliberative quality by post-decisional standards. Its reasoning is, as discussed below, too often oracular and constrained. Separate opinions would help the CJEU overcome this problem and catalyse a more deliberative European order in the post-decisional phase; they may also have applications in the decisional and pre-decisional phases, but space precludes such analysis. The first step is a general examination of how judgment style relates to deliberative democracy.

Judgment style and deliberative democracy

The structure of court rulings varies between and within jurisdictions depending on the prevailing conditions under which legal power is and should be determined.[27] This is evident from Lasser's comparison between France's *Cour de cassation*, the Supreme Court of the United States (SCOTUS) and the CJEU. The *Cour* is built on a fiction that law is solely promulgated by the legislature and

21 Ibid. 107–108.
22 Ibid. 108.
23 Ibid. 110.
24 Ibid.
25 Ibid. 116–117. See further Lani Guinier, 'Courting the People: Demosprudence and the Law/Politics Divide' (2009) 89 BULR 539.
26 Ibid. 138–139; 170–171.
27 M Todd Henderson, 'From Seriatim to Consensus and Back Again: A Theory of Dissent' (2008) 7 *Sup Ct Rev* 283, 291.

technocratic judges merely apply it.[28] To maintain this posture, its judgments insist that the judge is not unduly developing the law.[29] Its rulings are short and formal, 'plugging applicable legislative provisions and the bare minimum of relevant facts into the formal mold, mechanically . . . producing the judgment'.[30] This purposefully makes its decisions unhelpful guides to the law's development, disguising backroom judicial discussions to maintain the legislature's pre-eminence.[31] In contrast, the SCOTUS, which embraces concurrence and dissent, 'generates its legitimacy primarily by publicly argumentative means'.[32] Each judge must align themselves with a colleague or publish and justify their own decisions, creating space for ongoing public education and argument about their reasoning and the meaning and future of federal law.[33]

These approaches – welcoming or forbidding separate opinions – are not an either/or choice. Even in jurisdictions allowing polyphony, judges will frequently agree, or not wish to write separately.[34] A single judgment may be preferable if it creates clarity and certainty; hence even if judges do disagree, courts which allow separate opinions often issue a single, possibly compromise, majority judgment because it may be crucial to have a clear *ratio*.[35] Apex courts in India, Canada, the USA, Australia, and New Zealand produce a single 'Opinion of the Court' alongside individual concurrences and dissents, as does the European Court of Human Rights (ECtHR) and the ICJ.[36] The UK's House of Lords (UKHL) strove to produce a single majority judgment if clarity was especially important, and the UK Supreme Court (UKSC) has continued this approach.[37] In 20 EU member states (19 after Brexit), courts which engage in constitutional review allow dissent even if this is prohibited in non-constitutional courts.[38] This reflects democratic cultures which prize a discursive approach in some or all circumstances, and for reasons explored below, feeds a deliberative post-decisional phase.

The CJEU's current approach to polity-building presents itself in its single composite judgment. It is an authoritative voice that closes off contestation and

28 Mitchel Lasser, *Judicial Deliberations: A Comparative Analysis of Transparency and Legitimacy* (OUP 2009) 37–38, 169–174.
29 Pierre Legrand, *Fragments on Law-As-Culture* (WEJ Tjeenk Willink 1999) 69.
30 Lasser (n 28) 34.
31 Ibid. 329.
32 Ibid. 338.
33 Ibid. 339–340.
34 Alan Paterson, *The Law Lords* (MacMillan 1982) 102.
35 See e.g. *Doherty v Birmingham City Council* [2006] EWCA Civ 1739, [62] (Carnwath LJ).
36 Mads Andenas and Duncan Fairgreave, 'Simply A Matter of Style? Comparing Judicial Decisions' (2014) 25 *EBL Rev* 361, 369.
37 Ibid. 366–369, 371–375.
38 Rosa Rafaelli, 'Dissenting Opinions in the Courts of Member States' (European Parliament 2012), available online at: <http://www.europarl.europa.eu/document/activities/cont/201304/20130423ATT64963/20130423ATT64963EN.pdf> accessed 13 April 2018, 25–29.

pursues integration as inevitable legal *telos* rather than political choice.[39] Its continued appropriateness depends on certain assumptions: foundationally, that the EU still benefits from this specific style; and practically, that it is indeed clear. Both are flawed. First, in the EU's current crisis of self-determination, integration must be contestable; mandatory univocality sits uncomfortably with this imperative, in contrast with its suitability for the EU's integration through law phase. As Dawson notes, up to 27 judges can hear the most contentious and important cases. Enforced unanimity is ill-suited to such conditions: 'Loose agreement on outcomes but not on detailed reasons . . . could leave us with the unsatisfactory and ironic outcome that precisely the most important judgments may often be the ones with the least rigorous reasoning.'[40] The CJEU could be shifted towards an argumentative model if enforced unanimity was bypassed by allowing separate opinions, whilst maintaining the advantages of a single opinion by publishing a single 'Opinion of the Court'. At present, the CJEU's judgments are often, as Lasser describes, terse compromises:

> . . . unsigned, univocal, magisterial ('authoritarian'), and largely deductive documents that reveal decidedly less than they might . . . the Court's shorthand reference to, and axiomatic application of, such systemic policies as 'the effectiveness' of Community law, 'legal certainty and uniformity', and/or the 'legal protection' of Community rights tend to leave much – and at times, virtually everything – unsaid. One need only look, for example, at the ECJ's repeated, contradictory, largely unexplained, and yet utterly determinative references to 'the system of the Treaty' and to 'institutional balance' . . . In the face of the EU's daunting transnational political pressures, ECJ decisions therefore remain quite uninformative and thus remarkably discursively unaccountable.[41]

Similarly, Lord Neuberger complained that some CJEU judgments: '. . . (i) are incomprehensible, (ii) have internally inconsistent reasoning, (iii) do not answer the issue that has been referred, or (iv) manage to enjoy all these three regrettable characteristics.'[42] An infamous example is the *Ruiz Zambrano* case,[43] which revolutionised EU citizenship law by holding that in certain circumstances, cross-border activity was no longer required for an EU citizen to activate their EU rights. Its reasoning was curt, flowing from the laconicism that EU citizens must not be deprived of the 'genuine enjoyment of the substance of the rights

39 Vlad Perju, 'Reason and Authority in the European Court of Justice' (2009) 49 Va J Intl L 308, 331.

40 Mark Dawson, 'How Does the European Court of Justice Reason? A Review Essay on the Legal Reasoning of the European Court of Justice' (2014) 20 ELJ 423, 433.

41 Lasser (n 28) 351–352 (footnotes omitted).

42 Lord Neuberger, 'No Judgment – No Justice' (First Annual BAILII Lecture, London, 20 November 2012) <https://www.supremecourt.uk/docs/speech-121120.pdf> accessed 23 April 2018, para. 11.

43 Case C-34/09 *Ruiz Zambrano v Office national de l'emploi* [2011] ECR I-1177.

conferred by virtue of their status as citizens of the Union'.[44] For Kochenov, this and consequent cases displayed 'worrisome vagueness';[45] the CJEU abdicated its duty to develop clear guidance on autonomous EU concepts, leaving national courts to produce their own, possibly fragmented, interpretations. Nic Shuibhne was equally exasperated: 'Having conflated all of the issues and questions into one constitutional maelstrom, the Court would rewrite the fundamentals of EU law in just seven slender paragraphs of "reasoning" . . . How can the Court possibly think that such a brief and opaque articulation of its reasoning is remotely adequate or acceptable?'[46] A defence was mounted by the CJEU's president, Koen Lenaerts. He argued that case law must be read as a step-by-step development of the law restraining itself to specific questions raised in individual cases. Weiler responded that nonetheless, 'All too often the reasoning in the *questions it does answer* is cryptic.'[47] This was symptomatic of the CJEU's 'institutional constraint . . . which prevents it from issuing fully reasoned, less apodictic, more discursive decisions',[48] suggesting in passing that the CJEU prevents forced compromise and permits dissent.[49]

The Advocate General (AG) is often identified as a remedy. The AG hears each case alongside the CJEU and prior to the court's deliberations issues an advisory Opinion. This is usually detailed and enlightening; Lasser compares it to how *doctrine* unpacks French judicial decisions.[50] It has been asked whether AGs are substitutes for separate opinions. It is important to stress a fundamental difference: the AG is not a judge and does not observe or participate in the Court's deliberations. Solanke's interviews found that AGs saw themselves as giving preparatory advice and starting a conversation or framing the case, but not as giving judgments.[51] This is not to diminish the AG, but to stress their different function; they are better viewed as very high-calibre scholarship in their ability to encourage better deliberation about EU law within the legal field, without rendering the CJEU's decisions more open or discursive.[52]

The AG's limits are evident in two ways. First, the CJEU need neither refer to, nor follow, their Opinion. The AG normally addresses every argument before the court, but the CJEU will usually only engage with those sufficient to settle the

44 Ibid. para. 42.
45 Dimitry Kochenov, 'The Right to Have *What* Rights? EU Citizenship in Need of Clarification' (2013) 19 *ELJ* 502, 504.
46 Niamh Nic Shuibhne, 'Seven Questions for Seven Paragraphs' (2011) 36 *EL Rev* 161, 161–162.
47 Joseph HH Weiler, 'Epilogue: Judging the Judges – Apology and Critique' in Maurice Adams, Henri De Waele, Johan Meeusen and Gert Straetmans (eds.) *Judging Europe's Judges: The Legitimacy of the Case Law of the European Court of Justice* (Hart 2013) 250 (my emphasis).
48 Ibid.
49 Ibid. 252.
50 Lasser (n 28) 39–51.
51 Iyiola Solanke, 'The Advocate General: Assisting the CJEU of Article 13 TEU to Secure Trust and Democracy' (2011–2012) 14 CYELS 697, 709.
52 Tamara Ćapeta, 'The Advocate General: Bringing Clarity to CJEU Decisions? A Case-Study of *Mangold* and *Kücükdeveci*' (2011–2012) 14 CYELS 563, 586.

case, making it difficult to trace the extent to which the CJEU agrees with the AG on certain points of law and thus reducing the AG's role as a 'marketplace of ideas'.[53] Second, the Opinion does not necessarily help its readers interpret the judgment, either because the judgment does not directly refer to the Opinion or because the CJEU's curtness cannot sufficiently articulate agreement and disagreement. For example, in *Ynos*, the operative part of the CJEU's judgment was a single paragraph with an unclear relationship to AG Tizzano's Opinion; in *Zambrano*, the CJEU ignored AG Sharpston's human rights arguments, and the judgment was so cryptic that her Opinion was of little interpretative use.[54] Similarly, in *Mangold* and *Kücükdeveci* the CJEU's published judgment was 'entirely non-responsive'[55] to their Opinions. Such observations abound.[56] Hence, the AG's influence often falls to be derived from statistical, not qualitative, analysis.[57] This frustrates the argumentative form of legitimation evident in jurisdictions where judges writing separately after their deliberations engage in post-decisional dialogue.[58] If the CJEU is to serve as a site of deliberation, it cannot persevere with composite judgments buttressed by AG Opinions. The *court* is only going to catalyse effective debate on EU law if its judgments are more capable of deliberative engagement. From a post-decisional perspective, the AG's Opinion is insufficiently related to the judgment; by design it does not react to the specific holding that comes to shape EU law. The purpose of the post-decisional phase is to open a specific *judicial decision* up to more effective contestation. The spotlight should move to the question of separate opinions.

Towards separate opinions?

Rules on separate opinions reflect the democratic ecosystem in which the judgment is issued.[59] That ecosystem and associated judicial practices can evolve. Chief Justice Marshall's reign at the SCOTUS discouraged separate opinions; like the CJEU, he saw a single voice as enhancing the new court's authority.[60] This norm

53 Ibid. 585.

54 Adam Łazowski, 'Advocates General and Grand Chamber Cases: Assistance with the Touch of Substitution' (2011–2012) 14 CYELS 635, 660; Julia Laffranque, 'Dissenting Opinion in the European Court of Justice – Estonia's Possible Contribution to the Democratisation of the European Union Judicial System' (2004) IX *Juridica International* 14, 18–19.

55 Ćapeta (n 52) 585.

56 Weiler (n 47) 244–245; Sophie Turenne, 'Advocate Generals' Opinions or Separate Opinions? Judicial Engagement in the CJEU' (2011–2012) 14 CYELS 723, 735.

57 Carlos Arrebola, Ana Júlia Maurício and Héctor Jiménez Portilla, 'An Econometric Analysis of the Influence of the Advocate General of the Court of Justice of the European Union' (2016) 5 CJICL 82.

58 Conway (n 3) 162.

59 Henderson (n 27) 285.

60 'Note: From Consensus to Collegiality: The Origins of the "Respectful Dissent"' (2011) 124 *Harvard L Rev* 1305, 1307–1308.

dissipated around Chief Justice Stone's appointment in 1941. For Henderson, an increase in civil liberties cases tended towards unresolvable disagreement, requiring Stone to empower 'the Court to act even *without unanimity*'.[61] In contrast, Sunstein hypothesises that Stone encouraged dissent to better probe legal principles, and was supported by associate justices Frankfurter and Douglas – former academics willing to run judicial conferences like seminars.[62] Both accounts suggest that separate opinions can improve judicial authority, whether by enabling sensitive decisions or improving their reasoning. Similarly, in Ireland, a 2013 constitutional amendment permitted separate opinions during constitutional review of post-1937 statutes. There had been decades of opposition to the old unanimity rule due to arguments explored shortly: separate opinions repel inadequate compromise, improve judicial clarity, promote discursiveness, and map alternative approaches.[63] Courts can and should alter practices on separate opinions to reflect new norms, whether based on workplace conditions or jurisprudential, political or social needs.[64]

Separate opinions have not gone unnoticed by EU scholars.[65] Relevant contributions generally aim at broader questions concerning the CJEU's authority. They do not assess a relationship between separate opinions and deliberative democracy, much less the post-decisional phase. Turenne worries that at present, the CJEU can merely declare rather than justify its claim that EU fundamental rights follow from the common constitutional traditions of member states; separate opinions could create 'space for pluralism of interpretations of rights . . . facilitating the search for a credible overlap between legal systems'.[66] Perju comes closest to relating separate opinions to post-decisional deliberation. He argues that a court's power derives from good reasoning. If the CJEU allowed separate opinions, its reasoning would become livelier and more transparent, including 'in the public reason giving process the substantive legal debate about doctrinal choices and jurisprudential visions that inform [its decisions]'.[67] He then shifts to defeating objections to introducing separate opinions rather than dwelling on why they would achieve a deliberative turn.[68] Similarly, Laffranque argues that the CJEU requires greater democratic authority.[69] She touches on the link between separate opinions and deliberation – especially its capacity to foster public debate

61 Ibid. 330 (emphasis in original).
62 Cass Sunstein, 'Unanimity and Disagreement on the Supreme Court' (2015) 100 Cornell L Rev 769, 790–791.
63 Nora Ni Loinsigh, 'Judicial Dissent in Ireland: Theory, Practice and the Constraints of the Single Opinion Rule' (2014) 51 *IJ* 123, 138.
64 Robert Post, 'The Supreme Court Opinion as Institutional Practice: Dissent, Legal Scholarship, and Decisionmaking in the Taft Court' (2000–2001) 85 *Minn L Rev* 1267, 1289.
65 Turenne (n 56) 737; Laffranque (n 54) 21–22; Perju (n 39) 338–345.
66 Ibid. 744.
67 Perju (n 39) 328.
68 Ibid. 345–374.
69 Laffranque (n 54) 21.

and understanding – but is primarily concerned with the notion of authority, not deliberation.[70]

A deliberative court may well be more authoritative, but the concepts are distinct. Alter, Helfer and Madsen's concept of an international court's *de facto* authority – its clout that predicts compliance – does not require deliberative norms.[71] They suggest three other factors. First, generous access rules combined with few alternative dispute resolution methods will encourage litigants, so the court naturally gains authority.[72] Second, authority relies on how far the court's interlocutors accept its decisions.[73] Third, geopolitics: is the court supported by the politics of its affiliated organisation?[74] Neither requires deliberatively strong prevailing conditions; as Kelemen demonstrates, deliberation was not why the CJEU's *de facto* authority was accepted by national governments and courts.[75] That said, as he notes, the criteria satisfying each factor may evolve, especially as the CJEU continues to adjudicate on sensitive policy areas and member states become increasingly sovereignty-focused.[76] Indeed, the calls for greater space for contestation within EU law arose for that reason: the EU regulates increasingly salient matters, so member states and citizens demand greater justification for the CJEU's actions. This forces a reassessment of the CJEU's judgment style focused on providing deliberative advantages rather than general authority. The following section examines, primarily through comparison with the ICJ, why separate opinions would facilitate this shift.

Separate opinions and deliberation

Separate opinions are 'speech acts'[77] signalling the contestability of judgments and malleability of law. This is especially helpful for the post-decisional phase, which requires the court to speak in a contingent voice. *Brown*,[78] for example, saw disagreement about whether one could legally consent to serious bodily harm. For Alder this discord was rooted in divergent views on utilitarianism and individualism and reflected a broader, arguably incommensurable, debate about substantive values ill-suited to an artificially binary decision.[79] Similarly, he found frequent disagreement when decisions pivoted on individual views of the judicial role,

70 Ibid. 21–22.
71 Karen Alter, Laurence Helfer, and Mikael Rask Madsen, 'How Context Shapes the Authority of International Courts' (2016) 79 LCP 1, 9–10.
72 Ibid. 20–21.
73 Ibid. 22.
74 Ibid. 26.
75 R Daniel Kelemen, 'The Court of Justice of the European Union in the Twenty-First Century' (2016) 79 *LCP* 117.
76 Ibid. 140.
77 Note (n 60) 1305.
78 [1994] 1 AC 212.
79 John Alder, 'Dissents in Courts of Last Resort: Tragic Choices?' (2000) 20 *OJLS* 221, 227–228.

for example the use of literal or purposive interpretation.[80] Similar conclusions are found in analyses of the USA, New Zealand and Ireland.[81] Separate opinions demonstrate and precipitate disagreement about the content and scope of fundamental legal concepts. Judicial decisions, as Cover argues, are 'jurispathic'.[82] They close off alternative meanings and narratives, denying diversity of opinion and shutting down debate. Separate opinions highlight this, partly explaining why the CJEU pushed integration law through unanimity. Yet is it not necessary to *hide* the problem by forcing a single voice upon the law. It can be *embraced*.

Separate opinions demonstrate alternative perspectives, suggesting that the decision is contingent and may be open to revision; it is contestable in the post-decisional sense. *Ostendorf v Germany*[83] is a good example. This ECtHR case concerned whether Article 5 of the European Convention on Human Rights (ECHR) permitted preventative detention. The Court was split as to whether Article 5(1)(b) or 5(1)(c) allowed it. For the minority, 5(1)(b) could not apply. First, its application could permit detention in troublingly wide circumstances, including a very general obligation to obey the law.[84] Second, they sought to correct decades of case law which had moved away from the ECtHR's first interpretation of Article 5 by confining Article 5(1)(c)'s scope to criminal proceedings.[85] The concurrence was subsequently adopted by the UKSC, deemed a better way of preventing arbitrary detention whilst permitting short-term, necessary, preventative detention.[86] The concurrence provided benefits congruent with post-decisional deliberation. The judgment thus became deeper; the majority could state their view clearly and the concurrences provided a forum in which to posit and analyse an alternative approach and question an entire body of law. This helped later judges make sense of transnational law and align it with national requirements. These benefits, now unpacked in turn, suggest that separate opinions can help reposition the CJEU as a deliberative institution.

Meticulousness

Separate opinions indicate meticulousness, that the majority has covered multiple angles and defeated criticisms. This helps justify judicial power, since judicial

80 Ibid. 228.
81 Sunstein (n 62); Robin White and Iris Boussiakou, 'Separate Opinions in the European Court of Human Rights' (2009) 9 *HRLR* 37; Ni Loinsigh (n 60) 140–146; Victoria Heine, 'Institutional Unity v Freedom of Expression: A Dissent Analysis of the Richardson Courts' (2002) 33 Victoria U Wellington L Rev 581, 587; Andrew Lynch, '"The Intelligence of a Future Day": The Vindication of Constitutional Dissent in the High Court of Australia – 1982–2003' (2007) 29 *Syd LR* 195, 202.
82 Robert Cover, 'Foreword: *Nomos* and Narrative' (1983) 97 *Harvard LR* 4, 40.
83 App no. 15598/08 (7 March 2013).
84 Ibid., joint Concurring Opinion of Judges Lemmens and Jäderblom, para 3.
85 Ibid. para 4.
86 *R (Hicks) v Commissioner of Police for the Metropolis* [2017] UKSC 9, [38] (Lord Toulson).

legitimacy rests on popular acceptance of their deliberative and intellectual authority.[87] For Stack:

> . . . only delivering a single opinion would not demonstrate that the Court's judgment is the product of a reasoned dialogue among the Justices. The publicity of dissenting opinions and the indication of Justices' individual endorsements of particular opinions reveal that the Justices do confront each other with their disagreements about matters of principle through the exchange of opinions and the conversation that surrounds them . . . without this practice, those of us outside the Court would have no way to see the Court as embodying a deliberative process of judgment.[88]

The ICJ is a useful example. It is conceptually similar to the CJEU; it develops a legal order in the face of differing national legal traditions and, especially in its advisory opinions, sensitive sovereign matters. This is evident from its statute: Article 9 requires that its judges represent the world's 'main forms of civilization and . . . principal legal systems'. The court necessarily engages with heterogeneous legal traditions and political powers, and Article 9 is partly intended to ensure it maintains its legitimacy as an arbiter. It means international law is developed by a judiciary whose intellectual background broadly reflects the international community, one that can navigate national difference and present an acceptable face for an *international* legal order. Hence it issues a collective judgment which is assumed to reflect its diversity of background and thought.[89] Should this not assist, the simultaneous publication of individual opinions shows that competing approaches have been thoroughly digested. The ICJ thereby presents as a deliberative body. This model would benefit the CJEU because it combines a magisterial face that settles the immediate dispute with individual opinions which enable judges to illuminate the Court's decision, to catalyse the production of better judgments; and, the present focus, to show the parties it duly considered the range of options litigated upon.[90] The need to consider all arguments is encapsulated by Lauterpacht's differentiation between domestic and international law:

> [Domestic law may] disregard the susceptibilities of either of the parties by ignoring such of its arguments as are not indispensable to the decision. This cannot properly be done in international relations, where the parties are

87 Paul Horwitz, 'Law's Expression: The Promise and Perils of Judicial Opinion Writing in Canadian Constitutional Law' (2000) 38 *Osgoode Hall LJ* 101, 116.

88 Kevin Stack, 'The Practice of Dissent in the Supreme Court' (1996) 105 *Yale LJ* 2235, 2257. See further Andrew Lynch, 'Dissent: The Rewards and Risks of Judicial Disagreement in the High Court of Australia' (2003) 27 *MULR* 724, 729–736.

89 Bardo Fassbender, 'Article 9', in Andreas Zimmermann, Christian Tomuschat, Karin Oellers-Frahm, and Christian J Tams (eds.) *The Statute of the International Court of Justice: A Commentary* (2nd edn, OUP 2012) 314–317; Gleider Ignacio Hernández, *The International Court of Justice and the Judicial Function* (OUP 2014) 96.

90 Hernández (n 89) 96–97.

> sovereign States, upon whose will the jurisdiction of the Court depends in the long run, and where it is of importance that justice should not only be done but that it should also appear to have been done.[91]

Separate opinions mean the Court does not shut down the losing party. They allow their arguments to be endorsed or given more detailed attention, which may suggest a future way forward or explain why their arguments did or did not work. *Barcelona Traction*[92] provides a good example.[93] Four opinions stressed the need to analyse litigated matters absent from the judgment, to provide rigorous legal guidance to the parties and promote informed debate judicially and extra-judicially. This bleeds into an advantage considered in more depth below – providing alternative jurisprudences – but the current focus is how they enhance the possibilities of post-decisional deliberation by indicating the comprehensiveness of the judgment. In *Barcelona Traction*, Judges Jessup and Fitzmaurice explicitly endorsed Lauterpacht's view.[94] Indeed, Jessup cited five cases where the Lauterpachtian approach led to jurisprudential benefit – particularly regarding knotty jurisdictional issues – using this to justify his own discussion of when shareholders may be afforded diplomatic protection.[95] Similarly, Fitzmaurice addressed 'part of the long series of questions debated by the Parties'[96] concerning equity in international law, the relevance of shareholder nationality to diplomatic protection, bankruptcy, and local remedies. Judge Ammoun stressed that separate opinions allow exhaustive discussion of the legal issues presented and ensure a judgment that contributes to the development and legitimacy of international law.[97] He discussed diplomatic protection from the perspective of international responsibility, since:

> a rigid conservative kind of law, cannot adapt the emerging reality to sacrosanct rules rooted in the remote past. It must, on the contrary, adapt itself to the imperious needs of an international society which is moving towards universalism; it must adapt itself thereto in order to avoid confrontation between peoples, and lest it lose its footing in the upward march of progress towards better justice and the common aspiration towards the ideals of prosperity and peace.[98]

91 Hersch Lauterpacht, *The Development of International Law by the International Court* (reprinted edn, CUP 2010) 39.
92 *Barcelona Traction, Light, and Power Company, Limited (Belgium v Spain)* [1970] ICJ Rep 1.
93 Hugh Thirlway, 'Judical Activism and the International Court of Justice' in Nisuke Ando, Edward McWhinney, Rüdiger Wolfrum (eds.), *Liber Amicorum Judge Shigeru Oda* (Kluwer 2002) ch 7.
94 *Barcelona Traction* (n 92), Separate Opinion of Judge Jessup, para. 2; Separate Opinion of Judge Fitzmaurice, para 2.
95 Ibid., Separate Opinion of Judge Jessup, paras. 4–9.
96 Ibid., Separate Opinion of Judge Fitzmaurice, paras. 3.
97 Ibid., Separate Opinion of Judge Ammoun, para. 1.
98 Ibid., para. 3.

Judge Tanaka posited that judges must be allowed to pursue their own logic. Helpfully this was a rebuttal to Sir Percy Spender's Declaration on separate opinions in *South West Africa*; the contrast illuminates the conversational potential of separate opinions.[99] Spender sought to regulate when ICJ judges should write separately, asserting that they should not address matters absent in or irrelevant to the majority decision, even if they were raised by the parties, since this could undermine or confuse the judgment.[100] This preference for magisterial judicial discourse generally parallels the CJEU's current model. It is not inherently problematic but reflects a paradigm where deliberation about and contestation of the law are less important than a specific conception of legal certainty. The separate opinions in *Barcelona Traction*, each adding something valuable to deliberation on international law, illustrate one of the flaws in Spender's argument. As Judge Higgins wrote in the *Wall* case, advisory opinions in particular should 'elaborate and develop international law'.[101] She expressed dismay that the judgment did not analyse which aspects of international humanitarian law Israel had violated, then took her opportunity to provide commentary. Given the frequent recourse to separate opinions that deliberately go beyond the judgment, these sentiments have generally triumphed; the consequence is that the ICJ is able to maintain a post-decisional dialogue that allows continued deliberation over the law and a sense of contestation.[102]

Confusion is not a necessary consequence of multiple judgments, and as is apparent from the CJEU, clarity does not necessarily follow from single opinions. Separate opinions may sometimes muddy the waters, but if a deliberative approach is sought – as it is for the CJEU – benefits outweigh the negatives since this can lead to fuller, enduring analysis.[103] The ICJ's use of separate opinions to provide deliberative satisfaction to competing legal traditions in sensitive proceedings indicates that moving the CJEU towards multi-vocality could open channels for post-decisional deliberation.

Clarity

The possibility and existence of separate opinions improves judicial expression. This feeds into the post-decisional phase; a court obstructs post-decisional conversation if its decision is hard to understand. For example, the UKHL permitted separate opinions, but when its judges sat as the Judicial Committee of the Privy Council (JCPC) – which was the final appellate court for many British colonies

99 Separate Opinion of Judge Tanaka, p. 114.

100 *South West Africa (Ethiopia v South Africa; Liberia v South Africa)* [1966] ICJ Rep 6, Declaration of President Spender, para. 20.

101 *Legal Consequences of the Construction of a Wall in the Occupied Palestinian Territory (Advisory Opinion)* -2004] ICJ Rep 136, Separate Opinion of Judge Higgins, para. 23.

102 Thirlway (n 93) 95.

103 Peter Hogg and Ravi Amarnath, 'Why Judges Should Dissent' (2017) 76 *UTLJ* 126, 141.

and remains so for many Commonwealth nations – they were discouraged.[104] Until 1966 the JCPC had to issue a single composite judgment; concurrences remain rare, albeit dissents less so.[105] Several judges felt that the single opinion often paid mere lip service to its doubters, or simply reflected a single author's views rather than the totality of judicial deliberation.[106] This re-emerged following Lord Diplock's preference for a single UKHL judgment.[107] Some colleagues foresaw two risks now associated with the CJEU: lowest-common-denominator compromise and reification. The former created a weak or unclear judgment; as to the latter, if a judgment did not express the nuances of differing judges, it risked being treated almost as a statute instead of a contingent, albeit authoritative, interpretation of the law.[108] Neither comply with the post-decisional phase. In contrast, as discussed below, separate opinions do. They grant individuals a voice and reduce the possibility of a constrained judgment that cannot advance the law or its public understanding. Hernández points to the ICJ's separate opinions as countering a tendency towards reductionist reasoning; its separate opinions prevent terseness and retain, as seen above, analytical 'vitality'.[109]

Judges stress that individual opinions force reflection and improve persuasion. Justice L'Heureux-Dubé notes:

> [D]issenting judges will often make a conscientious effort to demonstrate the weak links in the majority's reasoning. In some cases, this may lead the majority to make changes . . . It may even lead to a change in who ultimately writes for the majority, if the dissenting judge is able to persuade several colleagues of the soundness of his or her criticism. Thus, dissenting judges will strive to provide a rigorous analysis of the questions at issue in order to persuade both their colleagues and the public.[110]

The first part of this statement – a threatened dissent might change the panel's minds – is widely chronicled.[111] Its second part shows that that even without a winning-over, the possibility of separate judgments aids clarification. First, they provoke interaction between judges during opinion-writing. A more rigorous judgment prevails, one with a more defensible or nuanced position that may answer the concerns of a critic or putative dissentient; their separate opinion

104 Lynch, 'Dissent' (n 88) 738.
105 Lord Neuberger, 'The Judicial Committee of the Privy Council in the 21st Century' (2014) 3 CJICL 30, 41.
106 Paterson (n 34) 99.
107 Alan Paterson, *Final Judgment: The Last Law Lords and the Supreme Court* (Hart 2013) 101.
108 Ibid. 100–102.
109 Hernández (n 89) 113.
110 Claire L'Heureux-Dubé, 'The Dissenting Opinion: Voice of the Future?' (2000) 38 *Osgoode Hall LJ* 495, 515.
111 Paterson, *Judgment* (n 107) 186; Lynch, 'Dissent' (n 88) 741; Sunstein (n 59) 804; Hernández (n 89) 113–114; Marie-Clair Belleau and Rebecca Johnson, 'Ten Theses on Dissent' (2017) 67 *UTLJ* 156, 166–170.

may be withdrawn, or a colleague's comments may simply lead to a tightened opinion. Second, published separate opinions will often implicitly or explicitly interact, as seen with *Ostendorf v Germany*. Partly this continues the previous point, in that the majority's rebuttal of a dissent may strengthen its argument. Another consequence is that when the holding is unclear, identifying differences can establish common ground.[112] Again the ICJ is instructive. It stresses the indissoluble relationship between separate opinions and the judgment: 'The decision itself, reviewed as it finally is with knowledge of the [separate] opinions, cannot be fully appreciated in isolation from them.'[113] Separate opinions will reflect key lines of internal judicial discussion and, because they are not compromises, they can provide clearer statements of relevant principles and may corroborate, correct or clarify aspects of the judgment; hence the ICJ deems writing separately 'wise practice'.[114] *Barcelona Traction* is again a useful example. In its judgment on the preliminary objections, the ICJ used the opinions in *Aerial Incident of 27 July 1955 (Israel v Bulgaria)* to help clarify whether that case helped determine whether the Permanent Court of International Justice (PCIJ)'s jurisdiction carried over into the present dispute.[115]

If the CJEU were to introduce separate opinions it is likely that a similar clarification would develop alongside a less terse judicial style. Even if the main judgment remains unclear, separate opinions could clarify it, and unlike the AG's Opinion, the opinions would come from a judge with detailed insight into the court's deliberations.[116]

Alternative jurisprudences

Separate opinions feed the post-decisional phase by encouraging effective deliberation about the law's future within and outside the legal profession. Alternative jurisprudences help courts articulate and weigh up forking approaches before settling on which befits the situation and can also prompt a sense of, as well as actual, public involvement in the development of the law by encouraging the 'ongoing community discussion'[117] central to post-decisional deliberation. For example, the USA's constitutional canon contains dissents by Holmes and Harlan.[118] Their importance lies not just in their arguments against a specific holding. They offered constitutional imaginings and ideological disagreements that fed political and cultural discourse.[119] More recent dissents have become a

112 Hernández (n 89) 112–113; Paterson, *Judgment* (n 107) 111.
113 Rainer Hoffman and Tilmann Laubner, 'Article 57', in Zimmermann, Tomuschat, Oellers-Frahm, and Tams (n 89) 1396.
114 Hernández (n 89) 113.
115 *Barcelona Traction (Preliminary Objections)* [1964] ICJ Rep 29–30.
116 Ibid. 122.
117 Lynch, 'Dissent' (n 88) 733.
118 Richard Primus, 'Canon, Anti-Canon, and Judicial Dissent' (1998) 48 *Duke LJ* 243, 243–245.
119 Ibid. 252.

rallying point for controversies such as capital punishment.[120] Similarly, Canadian dissents concerning constructive trusts and intoxication as a criminal defence reflected social positions around women's equality and the meaning of a fair trial that were adopted in later cases.[121] When the UK's Parliament debated the maintenance of its ban on prisoners voting following the adverse decision in *Hirst v UK (No. 2)*,[122] its dissents were relied upon by several MPs seeking to maintain the ban since it supported their views on the margin of appreciation.[123] This political use was counterbalanced by its legal assistance; the UKSC used the dissents and others on the same subject to indicate that there was no choice but to follow the relevant case law.[124] Separate opinions enabled post-decisional dialogue about the application and evolution of the law, rather than leaving it as a *fait accompli*.

A court's ability to discern alternative jurisprudences and position them within legal and social debate is particularly beneficial for courts like the CJEU which must develop transnational legal orders and reconcile competing national positions. Such courts hold particularly jurispathic powers, and the ability of separate opinions to open up post-decisional dialogue by developing a catalogue of alternatives aids their legitimacy. Hence, Fitzmaurice called the ICJ's separate opinions a 'rich mine in which to quarry for general pronouncements of law and principle'.[125] This was even recognised by Spender; despite his criticisms in *South West Africa*, he endorsed those offering 'side by side'[126] disagreement and alternative approaches. Hofmann and Laubner note several examples of such separate opinions have helped develop international law. At least twice – the *Case of the SS Lotus* and *Reservations to the Convention on the Prevention and Punishment of the Crime of Genocide* – dissents were later codified, respectively in various instruments on the law of the sea and Article 20 Vienna Convention on the Law of Treaties.[127] Various other individual opinions have influenced the ICJ's future jurisprudence on a range of matters: the international personality of the UN, the undesirability of automatic reservations, the correctness of dynamic treaty interpretation, and the binding character of provisional measures.[128] These examples show how an international court, tasked with adjudicating and evolving a complex and evolving legal order, has greatly benefitted from the use of separate opinions to catalogue alternative approaches, which have helped it shape international law transparently and deliberatively. Judge *ad hoc* Franck, writing in

120 Alison Orr Larsen, 'Perpetual Dissents' (2008) 15 *Geo Mason L Rev* 447.
121 L'Heureux-Dubé (n 110) 505–506.
122 (2005) 42 EHRR 849.
123 HC Deb 10 February 2011, vol 523, cols 498, 473, 519, 557, 573.
124 *R (Chester) v Secretary of State for Justice* [2013] UKSC 63, [21]-[34] (Lord Mance).
125 Gerald Fitzmaurice, 'Hersch Lauterpacht – The Scholar as Judge. Part One' (1961) 37 BYBIL 1, 15.
126 Spender (n 100), para. 12.
127 Hoffman and Laubner (n 113) 1398.
128 Ibid. 1399.

Sovereignty over Pulau Ligitan and Pulau Sipadan (Indonesia v Malaysia), made the point most clearly:

> The function of the dissent, therefore, is multiple. It assures the losing party that its arguments, far from being overlooked, were considered extensively by the entire Court. It facilitates the reasoned and balanced exchange of research and written views among the judges during the deliberative process. And, perhaps, it presents to the law's universal market place of ideas certain principles of law and nuances of analysis which, even if not adopted in the instant case, may be of use in another, as yet unforeseen, context.[129]

Franck unifies the three strands of the relationship between separate opinions and post-decisional deliberation. The key to the post-decisional phase is that the court's decision is transparent and ultimately contingent: these two factors combine to create a contestable decision whose specific reasoning, as well as the wider legal issues it encapsulates, are open to discussion and debate in search of a better understanding of the law's present and its future. Franck rightly shows that separate opinions achieve this by creating three interlinked effects, each discussed above: satisfaction to the losing party, better and multifaceted reasoning, and the marketplace of ideas. If the CJEU is to become a more deliberative court, the introduction of separate opinions would assist.

Conclusion

This chapter has sought to demonstrate how the deliberative imperatives faced by the EU – in particular the lack of effective contestation over its future – may be ameliorated if the CJEU is re-conceptualised as a site of deliberation in itself and that this is actualised by introducing the possibility of separate opinions. At present, the CJEU's reasoning is generally laconic. It does not promote post-decisional deliberation, a democracy-enhancing process whereby judicial decisions encourage rather than deny popular and professional contestation. The use of separate opinions in other jurisdictions, particularly the ICJ, effectively encourages this phenomenon, and this strongly suggests that the CJEU and consequently the EU would benefit from permitting separate opinions.

129 [2001] ICJ Rep 575, Separate Opinion of Judge *ad hoc* Franck, para. 11

13 From warfare to 'lawfare': increased litigation and rise of parallel proceedings in international courts

A case study of Ukraine's and Georgia's action against the Russian Federation

Iryna Marchuk

Introduction

Despite the ongoing discussion of the waning legitimacy of international courts, there is a growing tendency of increased litigation and a rise of parallel proceedings in international courts. Over the last ten years, we have witnessed that states are keen on 'forum shopping' and tend to pursue complex litigation strategies by initiating parallel proceedings before various international courts, in order to maximise their chances to obtain effective remedies for the violations of their rights. Nowadays, it is not uncommon that essentially the same dispute is being adjudicated by different international courts, each from its own jurisdictional angle. By taking the example of Georgia and Ukraine, which decided to pursue parallel proceedings in different international courts (the International Court of Justice (ICJ), the International Criminal Court (ICC) and the European Court of Human Rights (ECtHR)) as their litigation strategy to respond to Russia's military involvement in both countries, the chapter examines the benefits and pitfalls of pursuing such complex litigation tactics, as well as the matters of international law underlying such disputes.

The chapter focuses on the states' litigation strategy and discusses what the wronged states attempt to achieve by pursuing parallel proceedings. Does the pressure exerted on states by parallel proceedings before various international courts lead to greater compliance? Do states maximise their chances to obtain the relief sought by pursuing parallel proceedings? Is this the only possible 'winning' litigation strategy if the wronged state is at loggerheads with another state that has a more powerful geopolitical presence? Drawing on the case studies of Ukraine and Georgia, the chapter also explores whether parallel proceedings could lead to a richer judicial dialogue on the matters of international law among various international courts.

Background

Georgia

ECtHR

Georgia decided to pursue parallel proceedings in different international courts as its litigation strategy in response to Russia's military involvement in South Ossetia and Abkhazia during the 2008 Russia-Georgia war. The first inter-state application lodged by Georgia dealt with Russia's pre-conflict implementation of unlawful administrative practices against a large number of Georgians on the territory of the Russian Federation.[1] As a result, the ECtHR established the violations of Articles 3, 5 and 13 of the Convention as well as Article 4 of Protocol 4.[2] However, the judgment fell on Russia's deaf ears, as its implementation is still open.

The subsequent inter-state application, Georgia v Russia (II) (no. 38263/08), directly concerns the armed conflict, which Georgia argues gave rise to a number of serious violations under the Convention, in particular Articles 2 and 3, all of which were alleged to be attributable to Russian forces and/or separatist forces under their control.[3] Russia denied all the allegations, arguing that the Russian armed forces acted in defence of the civilian population of South Ossetia.[4] It also raised a preliminary objection based on jurisdiction, arguing that the application was incompatible *ratione materiae* with the Convention, as it concerned an international armed conflict governed by the rules of international humanitarian law.[5] Interestingly, Russia also contended that the application lodged by Georgia to the ICJ on the basis of the alleged violations of the International Convention on the Elimination of All Forms of Racial Discrimination (CERD) precluded the ECtHR from dealing with similar issues pending determination by the ICJ.[6] However, this argument was dismissed by the ECtHR in light of the ICJ judgment of 1 April 2011, which declined jurisdiction of the ICJ in the absence of Georgia's fulfilment of procedural preconditions under CERD. At the same time, the ECtHR held that the rule precluding parallel consideration of similar issues by various courts did not apply to inter-state applications.[7] The judgment on the merits is however still pending, notwithstanding that the application has been considered by the ECtHR for a decade.

1 *Georgia v Russia* (I), Application no. 13255/07, 26 March 2007.
2 *Georgia v Russia* (I) [GC], no. 13255/07, Judgment of 3 July 2014, *dispositif.*
3 *Georgia v Russia* (II), Application no. 38263/08, 12 August 2008.
4 *Georgia v Russia* (II), no. 38263/08, ECtHR (Fifth Section), Decision of 13 December 2011, paras 39–46.
5 Ibid para. 69.
6 Ibid para. 77.
7 Ibid para. 79–80.

ICJ

In parallel to the ECtHR inter-state applications, Georgia launched a lawsuit against Russia before the ICJ on the basis of the alleged violations of CERD.[8] Georgia invoked Article 22 of CERD as a jurisdictional basis, which stipulates a number of procedural prerequisites to be fulfilled prior to bringing the case before the ICJ. Russia submitted a number of procedural objections to the ICJ jurisdiction, arguing that Georgia had not honoured the procedural requirements laid down in Article 22.[9] The Court upheld Russia's preliminary objection and dismissed the case on procedural grounds, concluding that Georgia neither attempted to negotiate CERD-related matters with the Russian Federation nor invoked any other procedures expressly provided for in CERD to settle the dispute.[10] Needless to say, the outcome of the ICJ case was hugely disappointing for Georgia, yet hailed as a big victory by Russians.[11] However, there is a good chance that at least *some* discriminatory aspects of the alleged human rights violations, which were not considered on their merits by the ICJ, will be addressed by the ECtHR in *Georgia v Russia* (II).

ICC

The Russia-Georgia conflict also prompted the ICC Prosecutor to look into the alleged crimes against humanity and war crimes committed by all three parties involved in the conflict, i.e. the Georgian armed forces, the South Ossetian forces, and the Russian armed forces. The ICC Prosecutor initiated the preliminary examination into the situation on 14 August 2008 and took seven long years to seek the Pre-Trial Chamber's authorisation to open an investigation, which was finally granted on 27 January 2016.[12] The ICC Prosecutor's statement explains the slow pace of progress at the preliminary examination stage with reference to ongoing national proceedings, both in Georgia and in

8 International Court of Justice, *Case Concerning Application of the International Convention on the Elimination of All Forms of Racial Discrimination* (*Georgia v Russian Federation*), Application Instituting Proceedings (12 August 2008) (hereinafter – ICJ *Georgia v Russia* Application).

9 Ibid. paras 18–19.

10 International Court of Justice, *Case Concerning Application of the International Convention on the Elimination of All Forms of Racial Discrimination* (*Georgia v Russian Federation*), Preliminary Objections, Judgment of 1 April 2011, paras 182–184. However, the ICJ refrained from ruling on whether the two modes of dispute settlement provided for in Article 22 of CERD are cumulative or alternative.

11 Михаил Денисов, 'Международный суд ООН отклонил иск Грузии к России' (Mikhail Denisov, 'The ICJ declined Georgia's lawsuit against Russia') BBC (1 April 2011) <https://www.bbc.com/russian/russia/2011/04/110401_icj_geo_russia> accessed 1 July 2018.

12 ICC, Situation of Georgia, Pre-Trial Chamber I, Decision on the Prosecutor's request for authorisation of an investigation, ICC-01/15-12, 27 January 2016.

Russia,[13] as she only decided to move ahead with an investigation when national proceedings were indefinitely suspended in Georgia. The prospects of the ICC Prosecutor focusing on the Russian side are bleak, as the same statement mentions that the Office of the Prosecutor (OTP) continues to monitor relevant ongoing proceedings in Russia.[14] However, it is unclear how the ICC Prosecutor is able to monitor such national proceedings, especially after Russia ceased any cooperation with the Court following the symbolic withdrawal of its signature from the Rome Statute.[15]

Ukraine

The strategy of pursuing parallel proceedings was largely replicated by Ukraine, which lodged multiple lawsuits against Russia in the wake of the annexation of Crimea and the waging of Russia's proxy war in eastern Ukraine. In fact, Ukraine takes a lead with respect to the number of disputes brought against its adversary by lodging (1) six inter-state applications in the ECtHR;[16] (2) two declarations accepting the ad hoc jurisdiction of the ICC;[17] and (3) bringing action against Russia before the ICJ on the basis of CERD and the International Convention for the Suppression of the Financing of Terrorism (ICSFT).[18] At first sight, the

13 International Criminal Court, Press Release, 'The Prosecutor of the International Criminal Court, Fatou Bensouda, requests judges for authorisation to open an investigation into the Situation of Georgia' (ICC-OTP-20151013-PR1159, 13 October 2015) <https://www.icc-cpi.int/Pages/item.aspx?name=pr1159> accessed 1 July 2018.

14 Ibid.

15 Russia's Ministry of Foreign Affairs, Press Release (in connection with Russia's withdrawal of its signature from the Rome Statute) (16 November 2016) <http://www.mid.ru/ru/foreign_policy/news/-/asset_publisher/cKNonkJE02Bw/content/id/2523566?p_p_id=101_INSTANCE_cKNonkJE02Bw&_101_INSTANCE_cKNonkJE02Bw_languageId=ru_RU> accessed 1 July 2018. See also: 'Phakiso Mochochoko: No Cooperation from Moscow, Tskhinvali in ICC Investigation' Civil Georgia (9 October 2017) <https://old.civil.ge/eng/article.php?id=30502> accessed 1 July 2018.

16 *Ukraine v Russian Federation*, Application No 20958/14, 13 March 2014; Ukraine v Russian Federation (II), Application No 43800/14, 13 June 2014; *Ukraine v Russian Federation* (III), Application No 49537/14, 9 July 2014 (struck off the list on 1 September 2015); *Ukraine v Russian Federation* (IV), Application No 42410/15, 26 August 2015; *Ukraine v Russian Federation* (V), Application No 8019/16, 13 March 2014; *Ukraine v Russian Federation* (VI), Application No 70856/16, 27 August 2015.

17 Declaration of the Verkhovna Rada of Ukraine to the ICC on the recognition of the jurisdiction of the ICC by Ukraine over crimes against humanity, committed (. . .) during peaceful protests within the period 21 November 2013–22 February 2014, 25 February 2014, case no. 790-VII ('Declaration I'); Declaration of the Verkhovna Rada of Ukraine to the ICC on the recognition of the jurisdiction of the ICC by Ukraine over crimes against humanity and war crimes committed by senior officials of the Russian Federation and leaders of the Russian Federation and leaders of terrorist organizations "DNR" and "LNR" (. . .), 4 February 2015, case no. 145-VIII ('Declaration II')

18 International Court of Justice, *Case Concerning Application of the International Convention for the Suppression of the Financing of Terrorism and of the International Convention on the*

disputes are very diverse in nature, touching upon various regimes of international law. However, the common thread is that *all* these disputes stem from the existence of an armed conflict (or illegal occupation in the case of Crimea) that has had a profound impact on other regimes of international law.

ECtHR

On 13 March 2014, following the assumption of control by Russia over the Crimean Peninsula and secessionist movements in eastern Ukraine, Ukraine lodged its first inter-state application against Russia (application no. 20958/14). In its application, the Ukrainian government maintained that, as of 27 February 2014, by virtue of exercising effective control over Crimea and the separatist armed groups in eastern Ukraine, Russia exercised jurisdiction over the situation marred by serious violations of the ECtHR.[19] The catalogue of the alleged violations of the Convention, which Ukraine attributes to Russia, is vast, including the violations of Articles 2, 3, 5, 6, 8, 9, 10, 11, 13 and 14; Article 1 of Protocol No. 1 and Article 2 of Protocol No. 4 to the Convention.[20] Ukraine drew particular attention to the hardship encountered by Crimean Tatars who have been subjected to numerous human rights violations on account of their ethnic origin.[21]

Shortly afterwards, on 13 June 2014, Ukraine lodged its second inter-state application against Russia (*Ukraine v Russia* (II), no. 43800/14), which concerned the alleged abduction of orphan children and the accompanying adults in eastern Ukraine and their temporary transfer to Russia. However, the situation was resolved by diplomatic efforts between the Ukrainian and Russian authorities, as the children and adults were returned to the territory of Ukraine.[22] Ukraine's third inter-state application (*Ukraine v Russia* (III), no. 49537/14) concerned the deprivation of liberty and ill-treatment of a Ukrainian national on the account of his Crimean Tatar ethnicity in the context of criminal proceedings conducted by the Russian authorities. The case was later struck out of the Court's record, since an individual application (*Dzhemilov v Ukraine*, no. 49522/14) was lodged on the same subject matter.

Ukraine's fourth inter-state application (*Ukraine v Russia* (IV), no. 42410/15) is a logical extension of its first application and covers the time framework beyond that of September 2014. Similarly, it revolves around Russia's exercise of effective control over Crimea and de facto control over the separatist armed groups in eastern Ukraine. The Ukrainian government attributes numerous human rights violations to Russia analogous to those specified in *Ukraine v Russia* (I), as well

---

Elimination of All Forms of Racial Discrimination (Ukraine v Russian Federation), Application Instituting Proceedings (16 January 2017) (hereinafter – ICJ Application (*Ukraine v Russia*)).

19 ECtHR, Press Release, 'European Court of Human Rights deals with cases concerning Crimea and Eastern Ukraine', ECHR 345 (2014), 26 November 2014.

20 Ibid.

21 Ibid.

22 Ibid.

as violations of Article 18 of the Convention, and Article 2 of Protocol No. 1 and Article 3 of Protocol No. 1 to the Convention.[23]

In order to expedite the processing of Ukraine's first inter-state application, the Court decided to group it according to a geographical criterion. All allegations related to the events in Crimea up to 2014 are registered as *Ukraine v Russia* (no 20958/14), whereas allegations concerning the events in eastern Ukraine up to 2014 are registered as *Ukraine v Russia* (V), case no. 8019/16. With respect to continuing alleged violations of the Convention from September 2014 onwards, detailed in *Ukraine v Russia* (IV) (no. 42410/15), they were similarly divided upon geographical criteria. Those concerning Crimea are registered as case no. 42410/15 *Ukraine v Russia* (IV); and those concerning eastern Ukraine are currently registered under the case no. 70856/16 *Ukraine v Russia* (VI). Inter-state applications lodged by Ukraine include a wide range of the alleged violations of the Conventions covering all aspects of Russia's involvement in the conflict in eastern Ukraine and its annexation of Crimea. Given that the ECtHR is notoriously slow in handling inter-state applications, it will take years for Ukraine's applications to be adjudged by the Court.

ICJ

On 17 January 2017, Ukraine submitted its lawsuit against Russia at the International Court of Justice (ICJ) alleging numerous violations of the ICSFT and the CERD.[24] This is the second contentious case that involves Russia as a party to the dispute before the ICJ, and the first one in which state-sponsored terrorism was alleged as the violation of ICSFT.

Although the major issue at stake is the unlawful use of force by Russia by annexing Crimea and conducting the war by proxy in eastern Ukraine, Ukraine chose to invoke the breach of the two UN conventions that, although relevant to the issues at stake, do not directly address the core of the dispute with Russia.[25] Given that Russia does not recognise the compulsory jurisdiction of the Court, the strategy of Ukraine is understandable, as it had no other choice but to limit its claims to the breach of its rights under the Conventions that have been both ratified by Ukraine and Russia. While preparing its application to the ICJ, Ukraine attempted to avoid Georgia's ill-fated litigation strategy, which eventually led to the dismissal of its case on jurisdictional grounds. Unlike Georgia, the Ukrainian government did not rush with its lawsuit to the ICJ but took time to document the futility of negotiations with Russians over the alleged

23 ECtHR, Press Release, 'European Court of Human Rights communicates to Russia new inter-State case concerning events in Crimea and Eastern Ukraine', ECHR 296 (2015), 1 November 2015.

24 ICJ Application (*Ukraine v Russia*).

25 Iryna Marchuk, "Ukraine Takes Russia to the International Court of Justice: Will It Work?" *EJIL: Talk!* (26 January 2017) <https://www.ejiltalk.org/ukraine-takes-russia-to-the-international-court-of-justice-will-it-work/> accessed 1 July 2018.

breaches of CERD, as well as attempted to fulfil the procedural prerequisites under ICSFT.[26]

Although the case is still pending, the ICJ recent order on indication of provisional measures alludes to the possible outcome of the case. The majority found that all the prerequisites for the indication of provisional measures had been satisfied with respect to *some* claims under CERD;[27] however, it dismissed the plausibility of the existence of the asserted rights by Ukraine under ICSFT and therefore denied provisional measures in relation to this claim.[28] Notwithstanding Ukraine's failure to meet the required plausibility standard under ICSFT, this does not preclude Ukraine from advancing its submissions on the breaches of ICSFT at a later stage of proceedings, given that 'Some of the allegations made by Ukraine appear to be capable of falling within the scope of the ICSFT *ratione materiae*.'[29] The preliminary outcome for Ukraine is rather disappointing, since the ICJ declined to indicate provisional measures under ICSFT, with very bleak prospects of those claims to be addressed later on merits, and only indicated provisional measures with respect to some breaches under ICERD. As argued elsewhere, Ukraine's best-case scenario would be to have at least some of its CERD claims to be heard on merits.[30]

ICC

Being a non-state party to the Rome Statute, Ukraine triggered the exercise of the ICC jurisdiction by accepting the ad hoc jurisdiction of the Court pursuant to Article 12(3) of the Rome Statute. Initially, the Ukrainian government lodged its declaration accepting the ad hoc jurisdiction of the Court with respect to the Maydan crimes orchestrated by Ukraine's former political regime against its own population.[31] Following the annexation of Crimea and escalation of violence in eastern Ukraine, the Ukrainian government submitted another declaration with respect to the alleged crimes committed during the post-annexation climate in Crimea and during the fighting in eastern Ukraine from 2014 onwards.[32] The first declaration submitted by Ukraine was shelved by the ICC Prosecutor, as

26 Iryna Marchuk, "Ukraine v Russia at the ICJ Hearings on Indication of Provisional Measures: Who Leads?" *EJIL: Talk!* (16 March 2017) <https://www.ejiltalk.org/ukraine-v-russia-at-the-icj-hearings-on-indication-of-provisional-measures-who-leads/> accessed 1 July 2018.

27 International Court of Justice, *Application of the International Convention for the Suppression of the Financing of Terrorism and of the International Convention on the Elimination of All Forms of Racial Discrimination (Ukraine v Russian Federation) (Order)*, General List No 166, 19 April 2017, para. 99 ('*Ukraine v Russia Order*').

28 Ibid. paras 75–76.

29 Ibid. para. 30.

30 Iryna Marchuk, "Ukraine's Dashed High Hopes: Predictable and Sober Decision of the ICJ on Indication of Provisional Measures in Ukraine v Russia" *EJIL: Talk!* (24 April 2017) <https://www.ejiltalk.org/ukraines-dashed-high-hopes-predictable-and-sober-decision-of-the-icj-on-indication-of-provisional-measures-in-ukraine-v-russia/> accessed 1 July 2018.

31 Declaration I, *supra note* 17.

32 Declaration II, *supra note* 17.

she did not find that the Maydan crimes satisfied the threshold of crimes against humanity.[33] As for the second declaration, dealing with a broad catalogue of the alleged crimes in Crimea and eastern Ukraine, the ICC Prosecutor continues to examine numerous allegations of war crimes and crimes against humanity.

Similar to the ECtHR, the ICC examines the situation of Ukraine by applying a geographical criterion, looking into the allegations in Crimea and in eastern Ukraine separately. As for Crimea, the ICC Prosecutor rather swiftly found that the situation in Crimea amounts to an international armed conflict between Ukraine and Russia,[34] having taken as a starting point 26 February 2014, when Russia deployed its armed forces on the territory of Crimea without the consent of the Ukrainian government. It was further explained that the rules of International Humanitarian Law (IHL) continue to apply after the annexation 'to the extent that the situation within the territory of Crimea and Sevastopol factually amounts to an ongoing state of occupation'.[35] It will be interesting to observe whether the ECtHR and the ICJ will adopt the findings of the ICC Prosecutor. Although neither of the two courts is expected to pronounce on the legal qualification of the situation in Crimea, they do not operate in a vacuum and will have to contextualise the alleged human rights violations under ECHR and the alleged breaches of rights under CERD.

The thorniest issue on the ICC Prosecutor's desk is the assessment of the degree of Russia's involvement in the conflict in eastern Ukraine and ensuing classification of the conflict. The ICC Prosecutor established that by 30 April 2014, the level of intensity of hostilities between Ukrainian government forces and pro-Russian separatist armed groups, as well as the level of organisation of the parties, qualified the situation as a non-international armed conflict.[36] In parallel to that, the Prosecutor found that evidence of direct military engagement between Russian and Ukrainian armed forces suggested the existence of an international armed conflict in eastern Ukraine from 14 July 2014 onwards.[37] The ICC Prosecutor continues examining allegations whether Russia has exercised overall control over the separatist armed groups in eastern Ukraine, which could establish the existence of a *single* international armed conflict in eastern Ukraine.[38]

33 International Criminal Court, Office of the Prosecutor, Report on Preliminary Examination Activities (12 November 2015) <http://.legal-tools.org//ed2/> accessed 1 July 2018, para. 101 ('2015 OTP Report'). See also: Iryna Marchuk, 'No Crimes Against Humanity During the Maydan Protests in Ukraine? Or the ICC Prosecutor's Flawed Interpretation of Crimes Against Humanity?' (2017) *Boston University International Law Journal* 35(1), 39.

34 International Criminal Court, Office of the Prosecutor, Report on Preliminary Examination Activities (14 November 2016) <http://.legal-tools.org//a53/)> accessed 1 July 2018, para. 155 ('2016 OTP Report').

35 Ibid.

36 Ibid. para. 168.

37 Ibid. para. 169.

38 Ibid. para. 170. See also: International Criminal Court, Office of the Prosecutor, Report on Preliminary Examination Activities (4 December 2017), para. 95 ('2017 OTP Report').

Phenomenon of parallel proceedings

Litigation strategy and tactics pursued by states

One of the main questions to be reflected upon in this chapter is what the wronged states attempt to achieve by pursuing parallel proceedings. Ukraine openly pursues the strategy of 'lawfare' against Russia – a term frequently referred to by the Ukrainian politicians.[39] The term 'lawfare' is not novel, as it has been widely used to describe 'a strategy of using – or misusing – law as a substitute for traditional military means (. . .)'.[40] The term was further picked up by foreign policy experts, lawyers and academics attributing various connotations to the term, both positive (as a strategy to achieve policy objectives through enforcing legal obligations under international law) and negative ones (the use of international law against a powerful law-abiding adversary).[41] In this context, litigation before international courts bears a positive connotation as it enables a party with a weaker geopolitical presence to take on a powerful adversary.

By pursuing proceedings in various international courts, Ukraine intends to maximise its chances to obtain the relief sought. Apart from seeking that Russia cease the breaches of its treaty obligations both in the ECtHR and the ICJ, Ukraine also seeks monetary compensation as a result of the alleged breaches of the conventions in question. Whereas Ukraine's pecuniary interest in litigation is clear, given the losses sustained over the annexation of Crimea and tremendous costs associated with the conflict in eastern Ukraine, this does not suggest the Ukrainian government is oblivious to a high risk of Russia's possible non-compliance with the decisions of international courts if ruled in favour of Ukraine.[42]

Accounting for possible non-compliance

Russia's strained relationship with the ECtHR strongly suggests that neither Georgia nor Ukraine would succeed in obtaining just satisfaction in the form of monetary compensation in the inter-state applications pending determination by the Court. The ECtHR decision in a highly politicised *Yukos* case, which ordered Russia to pay compensation in the amount of 1.9 billion euros in pecuniary

39 'Україна подала до ЄСПЛ ще один позов проти Росії' ('Ukraine yet submitted another lawsuit against Russia') Depo.ua (26 October 2017) <https://www.depo.ua/ukr/politics/ukrayina-podala-do-yespl-sche-odin-pozov-proti-rosiyi-20171026664373> accessed 1 July 2018.

40 Dunlap Jr, Charles J. 'Lawfare Today: A Perspective' (2008) *Yale J. Int'L Aff.* 3, 146.

41 Orde F. Kittrie, *Lawfare: Law as a Weapon of War* (OUP 2016). See: Michael A Becker '*Lawfare: Law as a Weapon of War*. By Orde F. Kittrie' (2017) *British Yearbook of International Law* 86(1), 199.

42 'Зеркаль: "Україна може подати ще один позов проти Росії до Міжнародного суду ООН"' ('Zerkal: "Ukraine can lodge another lawsuit against Russia at the ICJ"') Vysokyy Zamok (12 March 2017) <https://wz.lviv.ua/article/194468-ukraina-v-haazi-zbroiu-boiovykam-postachaie-rosiia> accessed 1 July 2018.

damages, prompted a powerful backlash against the authority of the ECtHR in Russia.[43] As a result, the Russian Constitutional Court in its controversial ruling of 14 July 2015 introduced a legal mechanism that could be invoked to stall the enforcement of the ECtHR judgments that are deemed contrary to the Constitution of the Russian Federation.[44]

High risks associated with possible non-compliance with decisions of international courts in the future is also evident from Russia's justificatory rhetoric over its intervention in the breakaway regions of South Ossetia and Abkhazia and the incorporation of Crimea into the territory of the Russian Federation.[45] In the first instance, Russia portrayed itself as a peacekeeper that intervened in Georgia's breakaway republics to protect the rights of the ethnic Russian population, having acted upon the R2P doctrine.[46] As for Crimea, Russia has consistently denied any wrongdoing justifying 'reunification' of the peninsula with its 'historical homeland' following the exercise by the Crimean 'people' of its right to self-determination.[47] Any decisions of international courts that would go against this mainstream rhetoric in Russia will feed into the public perception of the Western bias and hostility against Russia.

Seeking interim measures

As part of their litigation strategy, both Georgia and Ukraine sought indication of provisional measures (interim measures) in the ICJ and the ECtHR, which to a certain extent perform an early alert function of the conflict related issues, broadcasting them to the international community. Whereas interim measures rendered by international courts do not have the power to stop the war, they nevertheless perform an important symbolic function by signalling the concern

43 Marina Aksenova and Iryna Marchuk, 'The Tale of *Yukos* and of the Russian Constitutional Court's Rebellion against the European Court of Human Rights' *Osservatorio Constituzionale* (6 April 2017) <http://www.osservatorioaic.it/the-tale-of-yukos-and-of-the-russian-constitutional-court-s-rebellion-against-the-european-court-of-human-rights.html> accessed 1 July 2018.

44 Decision of the Constitutional Court of the Russian Federation on The Review of Constitutionality of Article 1 of Federal Law "On Ratification of the Convention for The Protection of Human Rights and Fundamental Freedoms and Additional Protocols Thereto" (. . .), No. 21-П, 14 July 2015, para. 2.2.

45 For more, on Russia's interpretation of international law, see: Marina Aksenova and Iryna Marchuk, 'Reinventing or Rediscovering International Law? The Russian Constitutional Court's Uneasy Dialogue with the European Court of Human Rights' (2018) *International Journal of Constitutional Law*.

46 Gareth Evans, 'Russia and the 'Responsibility to Protect'' *International Crisis Group* (originally published in *Los Angeles Times*) (31 August 2008) <https://www.crisisgroup.org/europe-central-asia/caucasus/russianorth-caucasus/russia-and-responsibility-protect> accessed 1 July 2018.

47 Крым. Путь на Родину. Документальный фильм Андрея Кондрашова (Crimea: Way Back Home. Documentary by Andrei Kondrashov), *Russia-24* (per Vladimir Putin).

of the international community over the conflict and exerting pressure over the parties to refrain from further escalation of fighting.

In the midst of the ongoing conflict with Russia in August 2008, Georgia requested the Court to indicate interim measures under Rule 39 seeking that the Russian government 'refrain from taking any measures which may threaten the life or state of health of the civilian population and to allow the Georgian emergency forces to carry out all the necessary measures in order to provide assistance to the remaining injured civilian population and soldiers via humanitarian corridor'.[48] The Court partly satisfied Georgia's request by granting more general measures primarily aimed at ensuring compliance with Articles 2 and 3 of the Convention, although it refrained from indicating more specific measures sought by Georgia with respect to securing humanitarian assistance in the conflict zone.[49] Similarly, in the early days of the conflict, Ukraine followed in Georgia's footsteps and sought interim measures before the ECtHR, which were granted immediately calling upon both parties to refrain from taking any military action which might bring about violations of the Convention rights of the civilian population.[50] However, despite this swift action by the Court, they have never been followed, as the conflict continued to deteriorate.

A similar strategy of seeking indication of provisional measures was replicated by both Georgia and Ukraine in the ICJ. By the narrowest majority vote (8–7) in *Georgia v Russia*, the Court generously granted provisional measures sought by Georgia and ordered both parties to refrain from: (1) any act of racial discrimination under CERD against any affected persons, groups of persons or institutions; (2) placing any impediments to humanitarian assistance in support of the rights under ICERD; and (3) any action that might aggravate or extend the dispute before the Court.[51] Ukraine was less fortunate in obtaining provisional measures which it sought to protect its rights under ICERD and ICSFT. The Court only chose to indicate provisional measures with respect to Ukraine's claims under CERD requesting Russia 'to refrain from maintaining or imposing limitations on the ability of the Crimean Tatar community to conserve its representative institutions, including the Mejlis' (by thirteen to three) and 'ensure the availability of education in the Ukrainian language' by a unanimous vote.[52] Further to this, the Court indicated an additional measure of general nature, with the view of further non-aggravation of the dispute between the parties.[53]

48 ECtHR, Press Release, 'European Court of Human Rights grants request for interim measures', ECHR 581 (2008), 12 August 2008.

49 Ibid.

50 ECtHR, Press Release, 'Interim measure granted in inter-State case brought by Ukraine against Russia', ECHR 073 (2014), 13 March 2014.

51 International Court of Justice, *Application of the International Convention on the Elimination of All Forms of Racial Discrimination (Georgia v Russian Federation) (Order)* [2008] ICJ Rep 2008, para. 149 *(Georgia v Russia Order)*.

52 *Ukraine v Russia Order*, *supra note* 27, para. 106.

53 Ibid., paras 103, 106.

As for ICSFT, the Court was not convinced about the plausibility of rights asserted by Ukraine under the Convention and therefore did not indicate provisional measures with respect to Ukraine's claims in that regard. Although no provisional measures were granted under ICSFT, the Court nevertheless highlighted the seriousness of the ongoing fighting in eastern Ukraine and spoke of its expectation for the parties, 'through individual and joint efforts, to work for the full implementation of [the Minsk Agreements] in order to achieve a peaceful settlement of the conflict in the eastern regions of Ukraine'.[54]

The oral proceedings on provisional measures which precede the Court's order provide an excellent overview of the parties' litigation strategy and major arguments that they intend to develop throughout the court proceedings. In *Georgia v Russia*, the parties clashed over the extraterritorial scope of the obligations of a state party under CERD, with Russia claiming that the CERD provisions could not be applied extraterritorially and govern a state's conduct outside its territory.[55] This argument was nevertheless dismissed by the ICJ that affirmed the extraterritorial scope of CERD.[56] In *Ukraine v Russia*, the parties fiercely clashed over the parallel application of the rules of IHL and the suppression of terrorism framework.[57] The Court did not elaborate on this important matter at this stage, which is bound to re-emerge at a later stage of proceedings. These are just a few examples of the issues that form the backbone of each party's litigation strategy that have already become evident at the provisional measures stage.

Parallel proceedings as the only possible 'winning' strategy against a more powerful state?

The action taken by Georgia and Ukraine against Russia in different international courts also brings up a question as to whether such course of action may be the only possible 'winning' litigation strategy if the wronged state is at loggerheads with a state that has a more powerful geopolitical presence. Neither Georgia nor Ukraine could withstand Russia militarily, which explains why the *battlefield* has moved to the courtroom of international courts. Although the risk of non-compliance on the part of Russia is high, one should not underestimate reputational pressure that could be exerted by the authority of international courts.[58] In fact, there appears to be a gradual shift at the international arena when states with a less prominent geopolitical presence are no longer afraid of

54 Ibid., para. 104.

55 *Georgia v Russia Order*, para. 108.

56 Ibid., para. 109.

57 For more, see: Iryna Marchuk, 'Application of the International Convention for the Suppression of the Financing of Terrorism and of The International Convention on The Elimination of All Forms of Racial Discrimination (Ukraine v Russia)' (2018) *Melbourne Journal of International Law* 18(2), 426, 450–453.

58 Roger P. Alford, 'The Proliferation of International Courts and Tribunals: International Adjudication in Ascendance' (2000) *Proceedings of the ASIL Annual Meeting* 94, Cambridge University Press, 160, 163.

taking action against more powerful states. The representatives of the Ukrainian government also noted the utility of pursing action against Russia in different international courts as a way to achieve other diplomatic goals, i.e. maintaining sanctions against Russian officials, Russia's exclusion of full participation in the Parliamentary Assembly of the Council of Europe (PACE), etc.[59]

Parallel proceedings as an opportunity for a richer dialogue among international courts?

In his public appearances and academic work, the former ICJ Judge Bruno Simma reflected on the impact of parallel proceedings on both the convergence and divergence of international law, noting that convergence remains the most likely outcome rather than the widely feared divergence.[60] Instead of viewing parallel proceedings as contributing to the fragmentation of international law and bearing a negative connotation, Judge Simma rightly notes that 'Contradictory jurisprudence of international courts (. . .) remains the exception' and 'Courts have gone to great length to avoid contradicting each other.'[61] Another former International Criminal Tribunal for the former Yugoslavia (ICTY) judge emphasised upon a 'legal duty' of international courts 'to take account of the need for coherence in the whole field' [of international law] in rendering their decisions.[62] In support of the very same 'coherence argument', Martinez puts forward a sensible suggestion that the court should engage with precedents of other international courts, 'not depart from them unless necessary for the decision in the case at hand', and when departure from the precedent is inevitable, the court in question should articulate the reasons for taking this path.[63] In order to preserve coherence of international law as a system in response to 'proliferation' of courts and ensuing 'fragmentation' of international law, there have been calls for a meaningful judicial dialogue. This responsibility rests with judges of international courts who are expected to keep themselves abreast of the case law developments in other courts and foster an inter-judicial dialogue on the important matters of international law.[64]

59 E.g. Council of Europe Parliamentary Assembly ('PACE'), Reconsideration on substantive grounds of the previously ratified credentials of the Russian delegation, 10 April 2014, Resolution 1990 (2014).

60 Bruno Simma, 'Universality of International Law from the Perspective of a Practitioner' (2009) *European Journal of International Law* 20(2), 265, 279–284.

61 Ibid., 278.

62 ICTY, *The Prosecutor v Laurent Semanza*, Case No ICTR-97-20-A, Appeals Chamber, Separate Opinion of Judge Shahabuddeen, 31 May 2000, paras 28–29.

63 Jenny S Martinez, 'Towards an International Judicial System' (2003) *Stanford Law Review* 56, 429, 487.

64 Gilbert Guillaume, 'The Proliferation of International Judicial Bodies: The Outlook for the International Legal Order', Speech by his Excellency Judge Gilbert Guillaume, President of the International Court of Justice, to the 6th Committee of the General Assembly of the United Nations) (27 October 2000).

However, the most recent jurisprudence of international courts demonstrates that the problems arising from parallel proceedings do not only concern the matters of law but also the matters of fact-finding. To illustrate this point, one may turn to the example of proceedings pursued by Bosnia before the ICJ alleging state responsibility of Serbia with respect to the violations of its obligations under the Genocide Convention, which were taking place at the background of parallel proceedings at the ICTY dealing with the matters of individual criminal responsibility for international crimes, including the crime of genocide. Many commentators criticised the ICJ for blindly accepting the findings of the ICTY, without doing any serious fact-finding on its own.[65]

ECtHR-ICC possible judicial dialogue

The international courts tasked with adjudicating the conflict in Ukraine are facing difficult dilemmas with respect to fact-finding. In each case, the judges of international courts will have to ascertain the role that Russia played both in the occupation of Crimea and in fuelling the conflict in eastern Ukraine. As for Ukraine's inter-state applications pending determination by the ECtHR, many commentators referred to the earlier case law of the Court, most notably *Ilascu v Moldova and Russia*, which raises similar issues regarding the attribution of responsibility when a state is prevented from exercising effective control over the whole or part of its territory.[66]

In *Ilascu*, the judges pondered over a degree of responsibility for the violations of the Convention to be assigned to Moldova and Russia that had taken place on the territory of Transnistria – the self-proclaimed republic that formally belongs to Moldova but is under effective control of Russia. They found that a 'State's responsibility may be engaged where, as a consequence of military action – whether lawful or unlawful – it exercises in practice effective control of an area situated outside its national territory'.[67] In such a situation, the state exercising effective control is bestowed with obligations to guarantee the rights and freedoms in the Convention by virtue of the exercise of such control 'whether it be exercised directly, through its armed forces, or through a subordinate local administration'.[68] This, however, does not relieve a state which is prevented from exercising control over its territory from its positive obligations towards persons within its territory under Article 1 of the Convention. As clarified by the ECtHR, 'The State in question must endeavour, with all the legal and diplomatic means available to it *vis-à-vis* foreign States and international organisations, to

65 Richard J. Goldstone and Rebecca J. Hamilton, '*Bosnia v Serbia*: Lessons from the Encounter of the International Court of Justice with the International Criminal Tribunal for the Former Yugoslavia' (2008) *Leiden Journal of International Law*, 21, 95, 97.

66 ECtHR, *Ilascu and Others v Moldova and Russia* (Application No 48787/99), Judgment, 8 July 2004.

67 Ibid. para. 314.

68 Ibid.

continue to guarantee the enjoyment of the rights and freedoms defined in the Convention.'[69] With this line of reasoning in mind, it is logical that the violations of the Convention complained of in Crimea could be attributed to Russia by virtue of its effective control over the peninsula, as well as equally to Ukraine that retains responsibility in light of its positive obligations under the Convention. However, it is important to bear in mind that the ECtHR is limited in its scope of the judicial inquiry, as it cannot make a legal assessment of the lawfulness or unlawfulness of occupation, but instead would focus on the fact of occupation itself and its significance for assigning shared responsibility to Russia and Ukraine (in light of its positive obligations).

The legal assessment of the situation in eastern Ukraine is more complicated, as the degree of Russia's control over the part of the territory is yet subject to discussion. In the first individual application adjudged by the ECtHR, concerning the situation arising out of the armed conflict in eastern Ukraine (*Khlebik v Ukraine*), the Court found no violation of Article 6 on the part of Ukraine, as the area in which the applicant found himself serving his prison sentence was no longer under the Ukrainian government's control and therefore his appeal against the conviction could not have been examined by domestic courts.[70] At the same time, the Court noted that the Ukrainian authorities 'had done all in their power under the circumstances to address the situation'.[71] This, however, does not mean that the Court relieves Ukraine from its positive obligations to protect the rights of its citizens in the territories which are not under the control of the Ukrainian government. At some point, the ECtHR will have to assess the degree of Russia's control when considering both inter-state applications and individual applications arising out of the conflict in eastern Ukraine lodged against Russia (or against both Russia and Ukraine).

As mentioned above, the extent of Russia's control in eastern Ukraine is also examined by the ICC Prosecutor through the lens of the 'overall control test' for the purposes of determining the nature of the conflict.[72] Whereas establishing the degree of control serves different purposes in the ECtHR and the ICC ('effective control' for attributing state responsibility v. 'overall control' for qualifying the nature of the conflict), both courts embark on a similar fact-finding mission, thus opening up the possibility of a judicial dialogue in future.

An important precedent for the inter-state proceedings in *Ukraine v Russia* will be set once the ECtHR delivers its judgment in *Georgia v Russia* (II) arising out of a similar situation of an armed conflict. Given that the ECtHR held its final hearing in May 2018, the outcome in *Georgia v Russia* is imminent, with the judgment anticipated to be delivered in the very near future. In this highly

69 Ibid. para. 333.
70 ECtHR, Press Release 'Ukrainian authorities not responsible for appeal remaining unexamined due to inability to retrieve criminal case file from area beyond their control', ECHR 256 (2017), 25 July 2017.
71 Ibid.
72 OTP 2017 Report, para. 95.

sensitive case, the Court will have to examine the role Russia played in the 2008 military stand-off with Georgia in the breakaway regions of South Ossetia and Abkhazia, and what degree of responsibility for the alleged violations of the Convention it would entail. The ICC Pre-Trial Chamber had earlier established the existence of an armed conflict between Georgia and Russia in the period between 1 July 2008 and 10 October 2008, covering the period before direct intervention based on Russia's exercise of overall control over the South Ossetian forces, direct armed hostilities between Georgia and Russia, and subsequent Russian occupation of parts of Georgian territory.[73] Therefore, of particular interest is whether the ECtHR will choose to account for the ICC fact-finding in its judgment.

ECtHR-ICJ possible judicial dialogue

In the context of the legal wrangling between Georgia and Russia, the opportunity for a judicial dialogue between the ICJ and the ECtHR was missed, as Georgia failed to convince the ICJ on satisfying the jurisdictional prerequisites under CERD and therefore the proceedings did not progress to the point where the alleged breaches under CERD had been addressed by the Court. Similar to Georgia's litigation strategy, Ukraine's ICJ case revolves around the alleged breaches of treaty obligations provided for in CERD. In its application, Ukraine alleges that Russia pursues a 'policy of cultural erasure through a pattern of discriminatory actions' targeting the non-ethnic Russian population of Crimea, and, as a result, breaches Articles 2, 3, 4 and 5 of CERD. [74] As mentioned above, the issues of racial discrimination lie largely on the periphery of both conflicts, with the illegal use of force evidently being at the heart of the dispute in both cases. Both disputes raised important background questions on the legal contours of the right to self-determination in the context of secession. The breakaway republics of South Ossetia and Abkhazia have been stirring troubles within Georgia, as they were largely detached from the parent state and unsuccessfully sought to have their formal independence recognised.[75]

As for Ukraine, a big elephant in the room is the legality of Russia's annexation of Crimea in light of the contested exercise by the Crimean population of its right to self-determination. More broadly, the situation in Crimea revives the discussion on the interpretation of the concept of self-determination under international law, the validity of unilateral secessionist declarations and whether remedial self-determination – as invoked in the Kosovo case – could serve as a justificatory ground for secession of Crimea.[76] Another important question is the legality of

73 ICC, Situation of Georgia, Pre-Trial Chamber I, Decision on the Prosecutor's request for authorisation of an investigation, ICC-01/15–12, 27 January 2016, para. 29.

74 ICJ *Ukraine v Russia* Application, para. 131.

75 Phoebe Okowa. 'The International Court of Justice and the Georgia/Russia Dispute' (2011) *Human Rights Law Review* 11(4), 739, 743–744.

76 ICJ, *Accordance with International Law of the Unilateral Declaration of Independence in Respect of Kosovo (Advisory Opinion)* 2010 I.C.J. 141.

an aided secession in international law given the continuous presence of Russian troops at the time of the contested referendum. If the ICJ were to proceed with the examination of Ukraine's claims under CERD, it would only focus narrowly on the alleged breaches of CERD, without addressing big questions underlying the human rights situation in Crimea. However, the ICJ would not be able to avoid a bigger picture altogether and would have to deal with the question of secession and annexation of Crimea as a background for the violations of CERD. The dialogue between the ICJ and the ECtHR on the issues underlying the alleged breaches of state obligations under the human rights instruments will be particularly welcome.

Concluding words

The examples of excessive litigation pursued by Georgia and Ukraine against Russia demonstrate how the matters of IHL have an impact on the broader spectrum of issues under international law. However, these developments also signify creative litigation strategies pursued by states that find themselves unable to raise the real questions at stake, i.e. the use of force and the violation of the principle of sovereignty and territorial integrity. Hence, by initiating proceedings at various international courts the wronged state(s) maximise their chances to obtain the relief sought and exert reputational damage on the state that breached international law. This does not make easier the job of international judges who – while not being able to adjudge the real matters at stake – address peripheral issues brought by the wronged state(s) as a tactic to satisfy the jurisdictional prerequisites.[77]

Georgia's action against Russia in the ICJ on the basis of CERD clearly raised a few eyebrows given the instrument's remoteness to the real substantive issues at stake. While Georgia's case fell apart due to its failure to meet the necessary jurisdictional prerequisites, Ukraine pursues a similar litigation strategy at the ICJ, having invoked two instruments that are relevant, albeit not directly related, to the core of the dispute. Therefore, while not being able to address a big picture, international courts can only examine various matters of international law in a piecemeal fashion. Each international court seized of the matter(s) related to the conflict in Georgia and Ukraine will embark on their independent fact-finding missions, which could open up a possibility of judicial dialogue. As discussed above, such dialogue will be particularly welcome between the ECtHR and the ICC, and between the ICJ and the ECtHR (with respect to Ukraine only). The

77 E.g. see Judge Crawford's comment in the *Marshall Islands* case on the interpretation of the existence of a dispute in *Georgia v Russian Federation*. Although he did not question the existence of a dispute, he doubted whether the dispute concerned racial discrimination under *CERD* or whether it was being used as a 'device to bring a wider set of issues before the Court'. ICJ, *Obligations Concerning Negotiations Relating to Cessation of the Nuclear Arms Race and to Nuclear Disarmament (Marshall Islands v United Kingdom) (Preliminary Objections)* ICJ Rep, 6 [19] (per Judge Crawford).

concerted effort of international courts in clarifying the interaction between various regimes of international law (i.e. international human rights law and IHL, terrorism suppression regime and IHL) should strengthen the landscape of international law and advance the peaceful settlement of international disputes.

As for the ability of international courts to increase compliance, there is hardly any solid empirical evidence on that. However, the international legal process in itself may yield positive effects going beyond the authoritative value of the final ruling by potentially producing out-of- court dispute resolution alternatives. As described above, in the present context, there is a heightened risk of Russia's non-compliance if any decisions of international courts were to be ruled in favour of Georgia and/or Ukraine. However, one should not underestimate reputational pressure exerted by the authority of international courts' judgments that – even when not complied with – may be invoked by the winning party to apply continuous political pressure at the international level to achieve foreign policy objectives. The intervention of international courts is particularly valuable (even at the interim measures stage) when litigation takes place in the midst of the ongoing armed conflict, as it may facilitate peace processes and contain the ongoing violence. Turning to international courts may prove to be the only available option for states that are at loggerheads with more powerful states, that they cannot fight by military means, and thus turn to 'lawfare' as the means of last resort. Ultimately, moving the battlefield to the courtrooms of international courts is not a bad development in itself, as this avenue is not only useful for advancing the field of international law, but may also serve for the good of international diplomacy and international conflict resolution.

14 Amicus curiae participation in international proceedings

Forever friends?

Avidan Kent and Jamie Trinidad

Introduction

Few procedural phenomena excite more scholarly interest than the rules governing third-party amicus participation in International Courts (ICs).[1] The role of the amicus in international adjudication is often – although not without controversy – associated with 'progressive' values such as transparency, public participation and democracy. From the 1990s onwards, civil society organisations have increasingly sought to participate as third-party amici in international proceedings. Legal academics, in addition to observing and critiquing the amicus phenomenon from a multitude of angles, are themselves participating as amici curiae in ever greater numbers.[2] Such developments have been facilitated by rules of procedure that are permissive of third-party participation, notwithstanding the transaction costs associated with this form of participation, for the tribunals and for the parties. The general direction of travel is one of 'creeping acceptance'.[3]

It should nevertheless be emphasised that the evolving practice of amicus intervention across international courts and tribunals, which this chapter sets out to survey and critique, cannot be reduced to a simple progress narrative. Certain tribunals, most famously the International Court of Justice (ICJ), maintain their traditional resistance to amicus briefs (especially unsolicited amicus briefs). As will be seen, amici curiae have found themselves the focus of North-South tensions, amid accusations that they serve as voice boxes for narrow, Western vested interests. A related criticism is that amici with an international profile and the financial and human resources necessary to intervene effectively, may not always be well placed to give voice to the public interests that are engaged by the proceedings in question.

Our chapter will begin with a historical review of the practice of amicus intervention, discussing some of the drivers that led to the expansion of this trend.

1 We are not concerned in this chapter with other types of participation that draw the label 'amicus', notably court-appointed representatives of unrepresented defendants.

2 Avidan Kent and Jamie Trinidad, 'International law scholars as amici curiae: An emerging dialogue (of the deaf)?' (2016) 29(4) *Leiden Journal of International Law* 1081.

3 Avidan Kent, 'The principle of public participation in NAFTA Chapter 11 disputes', in Hoi Kong and Kinvin Wroth (eds.) *NAFTA & Sustainable Development* (CUP 2015) 283.

It will then discuss some of the controversy generated by this burgeoning form of participation. It will finally identify areas where further research is required in order to evaluate the usefulness of various forms of amicus participation and the impact of regulatory choices on the efficiency and legitimacy of international proceedings.

The origins and evolution of amicus participation: a brief history

References to amicus curiae interventions in court proceedings appear in the English legal system as early as 1353.[4] The term 'amicus curiae' was traditionally understood to encompass two elements – neutrality and expertise. The amicus was defined as an objective, independent expert, whose role was to assist the court in its work.[5] This view of the amicus has evolved over the years in certain domestic legal systems. Krislov describes the evolution of the amicus role within the US legal system as a shift from 'neutral friendship to positive advocacy and partisanship'.[6] The focus used to be on the representation of the interests of unrepresented individuals, but today it is on the protection of broader public interests.[7]

This development can be attributed in part to idiosyncratic aspects of the US system, such as the federal-constitutional system and the potential impact of private disputes on constitutional questions.[8] The 'advocate amicus' has thrived in this context. No longer viewed as a non-partisan expert 'bystander', the amicus in the US has come to be seen primarily as a representative of explicit agendas and goals.

The rise of the 'advocate amicus' began in the early years of the twentieth century in the US, as amicus interventions in favour of public interests began to mushroom.[9] Today the role of the 'advocate amicus' as the protector (or the representative) of public interests is widely accepted in the US. In 2013, an average of 14 amicus briefs were submitted to the US Supreme Court per case,[10] the vast majority of which touched on issues of public importance. For example, during the 2012—2013 term, 156 amicus briefs were submitted in same-sex marriage

4 See review in S. Chandra Mohan, 'The amicus curiae: Friends no more?' (2010) 2 *Singapore Journal of Legal Studies* 4–5.

5 This is reflected in a variety of definitions provided by legal dictionaries. See Avidan Kent and Jamie Trinidad, 'International law scholars as amici curiae: An emerging dialogue (of the deaf)?' (2016) 29(4) *Leiden Journal of International Law* 1081.

6 Samuel Krislov, 'The amicus curiae brief: From friendship to advocacy' (1962) 72 *Yale Law Journal* 694.

7 Ibid.

8 Ibid. 697.

9 Ibid. 706–707.

10 Anthony Franze and Reeves Anderson, 'The Supreme Court's reliance on Amicus Curiae in the 2012–13 term' (2013) *National Law Journal*, available online: <http://www.arnoldporter.com/resources/documents/NLJ_The%20Supreme%20Court's%20Reliance%20on%20Amicus%20Curiae%20in%20the%202012-13%20Term_Franze%20and%20Anderson.pdf.>

cases, and during the 2011–2012 term 136 briefs were submitted in health care cases.[11]

The 'advocate amicus' model that is today so prevalent in the US is also the dominant model in ICs. Most amici in international proceedings are agenda-driven, and openly so. Having said that, the 'bystander' amicus – the old-fashioned expert – also features in international proceedings, albeit less frequently. As we have shown elsewhere,[12] the 'expert amicus' is making a resurgence, partly in the form of academics who consider the submission of amicus briefs an effective way to achieve academic impact, or through the migration of yet another US-led phenomenon into the world of international litigation: the submission of 'group' amicus briefs, often signed by scores of academics or law school 'clinics'.

A creeping acceptance by international courts

Despite some resistance by certain international courts (most famously the ICJ), the amicus trend in international proceedings is on the rise. The 'creeping' acceptance of amicus submissions is due to a combination of persistence on behalf of amici and to progressive forces within the ICs, which have resulted in changes to procedural rules and the formalisation or legalisation of the processes whereby amici are permitted to intervene.[13]

The first successful attempts to submit amicus briefs on the international level were made during the early 1980s. When it came to human rights tribunals (notably the European Court of Human Rights (ECtHR)[14] and the Inter-American Court of Human Rights (IACtHR)[15]) amici found they were knocking on an open door. That may appear unsurprising given the significance such ICs attach to values like public participation and inclusivity, but by the 1990s the amicus phenomenon was flourishing in other types of ICs too.

The rise of global civil society and the public 'backlash' against global economic institutions (and globalisation more generally) coincided with a more permissive approach towards amici curiae in economic tribunals.[16] The World Trade

11 Ibid.

12 Kent and Trinidad (n 5).

13 A few examples of tribunals that led the way in different areas of law are *Suez v. Argentina* (ICSID), *Methanex v. USA* (NAFTA/UNCITRAL), *US-Shrimp* (WTO), *Responsibilities and Obligations of States Sponsoring Persons and Entities with Respect to Activities in the Area* (ITLOS), '*Other Treaties*' Advisory Opinion (IACtHR), *Winterwerp v. The Netherlands* (ECtHR).

14 See review in Anna Dolidze, 'Bridging comparative and international law: Amicus curiae participation as a vertical legal transplant' (2015) 26(4) *European Journal of International Law* 851.

15 See review in Charles Moyer, 'The Role of Amicus Curiae in the Inter-American Court of Human Rights', in *La Corte-Interamericana de Derechos Humanos, Estudios y documentos*, (Instituto Interamericano de Derechos Humanos, 1986) 103.

16 On the role of NGOs in pressuring the WTO AB, see the *US-Shrimp* case (in which the Appellate Body 'changed the rules' on amici interventions) in Jagdish Bhagwati, 'After Seattle: Free trade and the WTO' in R. Porter, P. Sauve, A. Subramanian, and A. Zampetti (eds.),

Organization's Appellate Body (WTO AB) and a variety of investment tribunals declared that they would accept amicus briefs, usually on the basis that nothing in the tribunals' procedural rules explicitly prohibited the acceptance of amicus briefs.

The backlash against investment law's dispute settlement mechanism (the 'notorious' Investor-State Dispute Settlement mechanism (ISDS), often described as secretive, non-democratic and corporate-biased) has led several investment institutions effectively to codify the procedural decisions of earlier tribunals regarding amicus participation into their procedural rules. Notable examples are Rule 37 of the Convention on the Settlement of Investment Disputes between States and Nationals of Other States (ICSID), the North American Free Trade Agreement International Trade Commission's (NAFTA ITC) Statement and the more recent United Nations Commission on International Trade Law (UNCITRAL) Rules on Transparency, some of which will be discussed further below.

Ideological developments in transitional justice and the associated re-emergence of international criminal courts further contributed to the rise of amicus participation in the 1990s. Unlike the other ICs, the international criminal courts were explicitly empowered from birth to accept amicus interventions,[17] and they have made use of this power to a significant extent. This hardly seems surprising when one considers the importance of non-state actors (for example, victims) in such proceedings and the prominent role that civil society played in pressuring governments to establish these tribunals in the first place.

The expansion of the amicus phenomenon has continued apace into the twenty-first century. In 2006 amicus submissions were accepted in the first ever case of the East African Court of Justice (EACJ).[18] In 2011 the International Tribunal for the Law of the Sea (ITLOS) implicitly allowed amici to intervene for the first time.[19] Despite past resistance,[20] the Economic Community of West African States (ECOWAS) Court has recently begun accepting amicus interventions.[21]

A complete historical review would be impossible within the confines of this short chapter. The examples referred to above, however, indicate that there has

---

Equity, Efficiency and Legitimacy: The Multilateral System at the Millennium (Washington, DC: Brookings Institution Press, 2001) 225. On the various dimensions of 'backlash', see generally David Caron and Esmé Shirlow, 'Dissecting Backslash: The Unarticulated Causes of Backlash and Its Unintended Consequences' King's College London Legal Studies Research Paper, No 2016–37 (2016).

17 Avidan Kent and Jamie Trinidad, 'The management of third-party amicus participation before international criminal tribunals: Juggling efficiency and legitimacy' (2017) 17 *International Criminal Law Review* 728.

18 See review in Frans Viljoen and Adem Kassie Abebe, '*Amicus Curiae* participation before regional human rights bodies in Africa' (2014) 58(1) *Journal of African Law* 22, 38–39.

19 *Responsibilities and Obligations of States Sponsoring Persons and Entities with Respect to Activities in the Area*, Case No. 17 (1 February 2011).

20 See discussion in Viljoen and Abebe (n 18) 39.

21 The ECOWAS Court for example accepted amici briefs from several NGOs in *Federation of African Journalists et al. v. The Republic of Gambia* (Judgment, 13 March 2018) Suit No: ECW/CCJ/APP/36/15, at para 2(b).

been a gradual (albeit uneven) expansion of amicus participation in ICs in recent decades. While this expansion shows no signs of abating, there are significant pockets of resistance.

The resistance

Not all ICs are open to amicus participation. Most famously, the ICJ has long maintained that it will only accept amicus briefs from 'public international organizations'.[22] NGOs and academics have sought to intervene in proceedings, but they have not received a welcoming response.[23] Judge Guillaume once referred to the 'thousands of letters' received by the Court during the *Nuclear Weapons* advisory proceedings, continuing with the reassurance: 'I am sure that the pressure brought to bear in this way did not influence the Court's deliberations.'[24]

ITLOS seemed to signal the adoption of a more liberal approach in its 2010–11 advisory opinion, only to take a step back two years later and reject a different application (made by the same amicus) in the *Arctic Sunrise* case. The Tribunal gave no reasons explaining its U-turn, but the geopolitical context of the dispute, and Russia's explicit objection to the submission of amicus briefs in this case, may have influenced the Tribunal's decision. Other commentators regard decisions made by ITLOS in the *Arctic Sunrise* case, as well as in later Annex VII arbitration decisions (which also rejected amicus applications), as a careful step forward. In the context of Annex VII tribunals, Yeng-Chiang Chang argues persuasively that the fact that amicus submissions are no longer flatly rejected, but are instead sent to the parties for comments, is suggestive that tribunals now consider themselves as having the discretion to accept these submissions.[25]

Another interesting (and slightly more nuanced) example of a pocket of resistance is the WTO's dispute settlement mechanism. The WTO is often heralded as an example of an institution in which the rules on amicus interventions have been relaxed, as a result of decisions of the WTO AB.[26] A closer examination reveals a more complicated picture.

22 Art 66(2), ICJ Statute.

23 See Letter from Professor WM Reisman to the Registrar, 10 September 1970, ICJ Pleadings 1971, Vol. II, 636; Letter from the Registrar to Professor Reisman, 6 November 1970, ICJ Pleadings 1971, Vol. II, 638.

24 Legality of the Threat or Use of Nuclear Weapons, Advisory Opinion, Separate Opinion of Judge Guillaume ICJ Rep [1996] 287.

25 Yeng-Chiang Chang, 'How does amicus curiae submission affect a tribunal decision?' (2017) 30(3) *Leiden Journal of International Law* 647, 657–658.

26 Notably *United States – Import prohibition of certain shrimp and shrimp products*, WT/DS58/AB/R (1998) para 104–110. This decision was later reaffirmed in several other cases, see for example *United States – Imposition of countervailing duties on certain hot-rolled lead and Bismuth carbon steel products originating in the United Kingdom,* Report of the Panel, WT/DS138/R, 1999, at para 6.8. The Panel in this case rejected the amicus submission as it was submitted too late; *United States – Imposition of countervailing duties on certain hot-rolled lead and Bismuth carbon steel products originating in the United Kingdom,* WT/DS138/AB/R, (2000) at para 39; *Australia – Measures affecting importation of*

While WTO tribunals have been open to the submission of amicus briefs, they rarely acknowledge any interaction with such briefs. In fact, in the overwhelming majority of the cases in which amicus briefs were accepted, the Panel/AB dismissed these briefs with the cursory explanation that it 'did not find it necessary to rely' on them. In several cases, Panels have allowed the submission of amicus briefs only where these are annexed to the submissions of the parties.[27] This later practice can be viewed as a *de facto* elimination of the right to submit *independent* amicus briefs. The practice of WTO tribunals owes much, arguably, to the political context: by accepting amicus briefs but avoiding any meaningful engagement with them, tribunals can appease civil society organisations and at the same time avoid antagonising those member states that object to the involvement of third-party interveners.

The regulation of amicus interventions in ICs

The regulation of amicus participation in ICs is variable, but it is possible to discern a general trend towards more permissive procedural frameworks that are open in principle not only to third-party interventions that offer 'bystander' expertise, but also to those that engage in advocacy.

Investment tribunals provide a useful example of this phenomenon. Investment arbitrations are regulated by numerous investment treaties and different procedural rules. The rules most often relied upon are the ICSID Arbitration Rules and the UNCITRAL Arbitration Rules. Rule 37(2)(a) of the ICSID Arbitration Rules dictates:

> The non-disputing party submission would assist the Tribunal in the determination of a factual or legal issue related to the proceeding by bringing a perspective, particular knowledge or insight that is different from that of the disputing parties[.]

A similar instruction can be found in other investment arbitration rules.[28] Beyond mere expertise (or 'particular knowledge'), Rule 37(2)(a) also welcomes 'perspectives' and 'insights' that are 'different from that of the disputing parties' – a clear nod to third-party advocacy.

According to Rule 37(2)(c) the amicus must have a 'significant interest in the proceeding'. Whether this requirement makes it more difficult for traditional

---

salmon – recourse to Article 21.5 by Canada, WT/DS18/RW, 2000, at paras 7.8–7.9; *European Communities – Trade Description of Sardines* (2002) WT/DS231/AB/R, at para 157.

27 See for example Canada Certain Measures Affecting the Renewable Energy Generation Sector (2012) WT/DS412/R at 1.12.-13; United States – Certain Country of Origin Labelling (COOL) Requirements (2011) WT/DS384/R at para 2.9–10; European Communities – Anti-Dumping Measure on Farmed Salmon from Norway (2007) WT/DS337/R, at paras 1.12–13; United States – Final Countervailing Duty Determination With Respect To Certain Softwood Lumber From Canada (2003) WT/DS257/R at para 7.1; United States – Investigation of the International Trade Commission in Softwood Lumber From Canada (2004) WT/DS277/R at para 7.10.

28 See for example para 6 of the NAFTA's 'Statement of the Free Trade Commission on non-disputing party participation', and Art 4(3) of the UNCITRAL Rules on Transparency in Treaty-based Investor-State Arbitration.

'bystander' amici to intervene is debatable. On the one hand, several investment tribunals have stated that mere legal expertise in investment law will not, of itself, be sufficient for satisfying the 'significant interest' test.[29] On the other hand, investment tribunals have accepted expert submissions on matters that went beyond the tribunals' core expertise.[30]

The rules adopted by international criminal tribunals are fairly general and inclusive. Consider for example Art 74 of both the International Criminal Tribunal for the former Yugoslavia (ICTY) and the International Criminal Tribunal for Rwanda (ICTR) rules ('A Chamber may, if it considers it desirable for the proper determination of the case, invite or grant leave to any State, organization or person to appear before it and make submissions on any issue specified by the Chamber'), and the rules of 'hybrid' criminal tribunals (for example Sierra Leone (SCSL), Cambodia (ECCC) and Lebanon (STL)). Rule 103 of the International Criminal Court (ICC) is a slightly more elaborate version of this rule, in that it gives the prosecutor and the defence the right to respond to amicus interventions.

The ICTY has done more than any of the other criminal tribunals to establish a detailed framework for the management of amicus briefs. In 1997 it published a document entitled 'information concerning the submission of amicus curiae briefs'.[31] This note includes technical submission rules and a requirement to disclose the relationship (if any) between the amicus and the parties. Interestingly, the note also states that the tribunal *may* invite amici to participate in 'oral argument'.

A similar approach is enshrined in the Rules of the African Court on Human and Peoples' Rights (African HR Court), which states that the Court may hear 'representatives of parties, witnesses, experts, or such persons as the Court may decide to hear.'[32] Art 70 adds (with respect to Advisory Opinions): 'Any other States [sic] Parties may submit written submissions on any of the issues raised in the request. Any other interested entity may be authorized by the Court to do the same.' As described by Viljoen and Abebe, the practice of the African HR Court is to ask amici to describe the nature and the type of contribution that they intend to make.[33] They observe that '[T]his criterion is the only guide in the court's exercise of its discretion to allow or refuse requests.'[34]

The fact that the ICJ and ITLOS have not been able to open up to amicus participation to the same extent as other ICs is arguably a function of their respective statutes. Article 34 of the ICJ Statute permits the Court to accept submissions only from inter-governmental organisations. Rules 133 (advisory proceedings) and 84 (contentious proceedings) provide for similar restrictions in the ITLOS.

29 See for example *Resolute Forest Products Inc v. Canada* (Procedural Order No 6. 29 June 2017), PCA Case No 2016–13, para 4.4; *Apotex v. USA* (Procedural Order, 4 March 2013) ICSID Case No ARB(AF)/12/1, para 40.

30 For example *Eli Lilly v. Canada* (Procedural Order No 4, 23 February 2016) Case No. UNCT/14/2.

31 ICTY, *Information concerning the submission of amicus curiae briefs* (16 February 2015) IT/122/Rev.1 <http://www.icty.org/x/file/Legal%20Library/Miscellaneous/it122_amicuscuriae_briefs_en.pdf>.

32 Rule 27(3), Rules of the African Court on Human and Peoples' Rights.

33 Viljoen and Abebe (n 18) 36.

34 Ibid.

The ICJ's practice is to place any amicus briefs that are received in the Court's library, but there is no data available on whether they are consulted, or by whom. The ITLOS, as previously mentioned, has authorised the transfer of an amicus brief to the parties. This was done 'at the request of the President'[35] and the Tribunal stated that the brief would be posted on the ITLOS' website. It was not, however, a sign of a general 'opening up' to amicus submissions, as evidenced by the Tribunal's rejection, without explanation, of the subsequent amicus brief in the *Arctic Sunrise* case.

The WTO approach is even more ambivalent. As has already been noted, the WTO has no fixed procedural rules with respect to amicus submissions, and the practice of WTO tribunals is to accept briefs – occasionally with the requirement that they be attached to the submissions of a party to the proceedings – and then ignore them.

The impact of amicus participation on the adjudicative process of ICs

There are obvious transaction costs associated with amicus participation. Third-party briefs place an administrative burden on registries, judges and parties to proceedings. Depending on the level of participation, there is a risk that the efficient conduct of proceedings could be compromised. In the *Nuclear Tests* cases, for instance, 'thousands' of unsolicited letters were received, according to Judge Guillaume. Had the ICJ engaged with all of them, even to the extent of filtering the submissions and singling out those that were most useful, the impact on the Court's efficiency would have been considerable.

Some courts deal with a much higher number of amicus submissions than others. According to Pasqualucci, the Inter-American Court of Human Rights has received more than 500 briefs since its establishment in 1979.[36] The ECtHR has also received a large number of submissions; recent data was unavailable to the authors at the time of writing, but according to Dolidze, up to 2015, amici intervened in 34.5% of all the ECtHR's Grand Chamber's cases (133 out of 386 cases).[37] There are concrete examples of cases in which a relatively large number of amici attempted to intervene. Notable examples are the ECtHR's *Lautsi vs Italy* in which six NGOs, a group of MEPs, and ten different states asked to intervene. In the ICTY's *Blaskic* case, 20 amicus submissions were made. In the NAFTA Chapter 11 *Eli Lilly* case, nine amicus submissions were made. Other well-known examples include the IACtHR'S *Artavia Murillo vs Costa Rica* case (46 submissions), and the *Atala Riffo vs Chile* case (32 submissions). Reviewing and commenting on such a large number of submissions comes at a considerable cost in terms of time and resources.

35 Ibid.
36 Jo Pasqualucci, *The Practice and Procedure of the Inter-American Court of Human Rights* (Cambridge University Press 2013) 72.
37 Dolidze (n 14) 864.

In our view, the 'floodgates' argument is important, but it should not be overstated. There are occasional examples of cases in which a 'flood' materialised. However, most cases before ICs do not attract any third-party interventions. In the ECtHR, which receives a relatively high number of amicus interventions, research has shown that in most cases where interventions were made, only one or two amici attempted to intervene, and only rarely did this number exceed three.[38]

During the first two decades of the twenty-first century, the writing and submission of amicus briefs have been open to anyone with an internet connection and sufficient motivation. The flow of submissions may increase in the future, but the fact that it has rarely up to this point resulted in a flood suggests that it is unlikely ever to do so.[39]

At the same time, it is important not to dismiss the time and cost implications that the involvement of even a small number of amici can entail. Parties are often asked to comment on these submissions and tribunals are often required to make procedural rulings on the admissibility and applicability of these submissions. These costs may not be debilitating for most tribunals, but they are significant.

The transaction costs of amicus participation must be weighed against the ostensible benefits. For a start, amici bring special knowledge and perspectives that may not be available to the tribunal, and it could be argued that this has the potential to improve the quality of decisions. This is particularly true when *specialised* courts are asked to deal with complex legal matters in which different areas of law could be relevant, or where complicated factual questions are disputed.

When ICs have limited resources and expertise, amicus participation may even increase the efficiency of the judicial process. As Viljoen and Abebe argue (regarding the African HR Court):

> Given the limitation of time emanating from its ad hoc nature and the human resource constraints the court faces, allowing individuals and NGOs to participate in its proceedings can overcome some of the difficulties of undertaking expensive and time-consuming research, thereby enhancing the quality of the court's decisions [FN omitted]. Amicus briefs also enable the court to access legal opinion and practical information that a resource and time-constrained court would not otherwise obtain. Without the support of experts and NGOs, the role of the court will be marginal at best [FN omitted].[40]

Others contend that amicus participation enhances the legitimacy and accountability of courts. For example, Eckersley argued in 2007 that 'Amicus curiae

38 Laura Van den Eynde, 'An empirical look at the amicus curiae practice of human rights NGOs before the European Court of Human Rights' (2013) 31(3) *Netherlands Quarterly of Human Rights* 271.

39 Consider, in a similar vein, that NGOs were at the vanguard of a hard-fought battle to make WTO proceedings public, and when they eventually got their way (for example *EC-Seals*), hearing rooms remained almost as empty as before.

40 Viljoen and Abebe (n 18) 37.

briefs are likely to remain the most promising mechanism of external accountability in the WTO, in this case, of the judicial arm of the WTO to broader publics, via specialized, cosmopolitan public spheres.'[41]

Such claims are however contestable and, to the best of our knowledge, are not supported by empirical studies. Recently, critical approaches have begun to cast doubt on the desirability of an enhanced role for amici curiae in international proceedings. We outline some of the main critiques below.

Are they actually helpful?

As stated at the beginning of this chapter, the purpose of amicus curiae interventions is to assist the court, to contribute a unique perspective or specialised knowledge that will enrich and improve the court's decision. Most of the relevant procedural rules require that amicus intervention will *assist* the tribunal in its work.[42] Empirically, however, it is difficult to determine how useful amicus curiae briefs are in reality.

Judges may consider and even rely on amicus submissions, but they may not necessarily acknowledge that they have done so.[43] On the other hand, judges may acknowledge amicus briefs in order to create the appearance of an open and inclusive procedure, but in reality attach little importance to them. The drive for openness and transparency could therefore be shaping the way that ICs *say* they are engaging with amicus submissions. In the context of investment arbitration, for instance, it was noted by one tribunal that the 'Chapter 11 arbitral process could benefit from being perceived as more open or transparent; or conversely be harmed if seen as unduly secretive.'[44] Statements by arbitral tribunals concerning amicus participation and the benefits thereof cannot therefore be taken at face value.

As previously discussed, WTO Tribunals overwhelmingly disregard amicus interventions, flatly explaining that they 'did not find it necessary to rely' on these. Investment tribunals have also rejected several briefs on the basis that they were simply unhelpful. Even within the amicus-friendly ECtHR there are some who will admit that many submissions do not in fact assist the Court; in a blog post from 2015, Paul Harvey, a UK lawyer and former employee in the Registry of the ECtHR, disclosed that in cases that are based on Art 8 and 9 ECHR[45] 'too many'

41 Robyn Eckersley, 'A green public sphere in the WTO?: The *amicus curiae* interventions in the transatlantic biotech dispute' 13(3) *European Journal of International Relations* (2007) 329, 351.

42 See for example NAFTA 'Statement of the Free Trade Commission on non-disputing party participation', para 6(a); rule 74 of the ICTY Rules; rule 74 of the ICTR Rules, Art 36 ECHR, and more.

43 See for example Yen-Chiang Chang's claim that the PCA's arbitral tribunal indeed discreetly considered the CSIL's amicus submission during the South-China Sea Arbitration. Chang (n 25).

44 *Methanex v. USA* (Decision of the tribunal on petitions from third persons to intervene as "amici curiae", 15 January 2001) UNCITRAL, para 49, cited later by *Biwater Gauff vs Tanzania* (Procedural Order No 5, 2 February 2007) ICSID Case No ARB/05/22.

45 Art 8 ECHR concerns 'right to respect for private and family life' and Art 9 ECHR concerns 'freedom of thought, conscience and religion'.

amici 'rely almost exclusively on philosophical or religious arguments. Without in any way criticising the sincerity of the beliefs or philosophies upon which these submissions are based, the reality is that they provide little assistance.'[46]

It is impossible to know how widespread such attitudes are, but it is perhaps significant that among the many amicus submissions identified by the present authors, examples of ICs engaging with amicus submissions in an open and meaningful way are the exception rather than the norm.

Against this, it should be noted that there are several examples of cases from international criminal and economic tribunals in which the courts did rely on amicus interventions and even rely on these in their reasoning.[47] Dolidze argues with respect to the ECtHR that amici are engaged with extensively by the Court.[48] Moreover, it is quite possible for an amicus brief to inform a judge's thinking and yet not be acknowledged in the judgment. In short, there is some evidence to suggest that amicus submissions are considered useful by some ICs, but the evidence varies from tribunal to tribunal and general narratives of 'usefulness' require careful critical scrutiny.

'Unfriendly' behaviour and 'animus curiae'

Amici whose main motivation is advocacy cannot always be relied on to be true 'friends' of the court. Some have been accused by tribunals of acting in bad faith and with conflicting interests.[49] In other cases amici were accused of publishing confidential information on their website. A WTO Panel commented on this specific incident:

> It should be noted, in addition, that the Institute for Agriculture and Trade Policy and Friends of the Earth submitted *amicus curiae* (friend-of-the-court) briefs, requesting the Panel to accept and consider their briefs [FN omitted]. The Panel acknowledged receipt of these briefs, shared them with the Parties and Third Parties, and accepted them as such [FN omitted]. In the light of this, it is surprising and disturbing that the same NGOs which claimed to act as *amici*, or friends, of the Panel when seeking to convince the Panel to accept their unsolicited briefs subsequently found it appropriate to

46 Paul Harvey, 'Third party interventions before the ECtHR: A rough guide', Strasbourg Observers (24 February 2015) <https://strasbourgobservers.com/2015/02/24/third-party-interventions-before-the-ecthr-a-rough-guide/>.

47 Kent and Trinidad (n 3); Kent and Trinidad (n 17) 728.

48 Dolidze (n 14).

49 See for example the ICTY's *Prosecutor* v. *Ante Gotovina and Mladen Markac*, (Decision on the application and proposed amicus curiae brief) (2012) Case No. IT-06–90-A, para 12; NAFTA Chapter 11's *Apotex Holdings Inc and Apotex Inc* v. *The United States of America*, ICSID Case No. ARB(AF)/12/1 (Procedural Order on the Participation of the Applicant, Mr. Barry Appleton, as a Non-Disputing Party), in which the Tribunal stated: 'It seems that the Applicant's "significant interest" in this arbitration lies only in having this Tribunal adopt legal interpretations of NAFTA that he favours that could be advantageous to his clients in his pending and possible future NAFTA cases.'

> disclose, on their own websites, interim findings and conclusions of the Panel which were clearly designated as confidential.[50]

The criticism goes beyond a mere accusation of misbehaviour – it suggests that some are using the amicus process not for the purpose of assisting the court, but for the purpose of self-promotion. Academics attempting to achieve 'impact', or law school clinics attempting to achieve educational (and promotional) goals might also be accused of falling within this rubric. Even in the amicus-friendly ECtHR, some doubts exist as to what the real motivation of amici may be. Paul Harvey observes in this respect:

> Too often third party interventions have passed from being welcome and valued *amicus curiae* to being *animus curiae*. However sincere and well intentioned such interventions are, they often leave the impression that the intervention has been made, not out of a desire to assist the Court, but so that the intervener can be seen to have intervened.[51]

Legitimacy?

As stated above, the assumption that amicus intervention enhances the legitimacy of ICs is a major justification for the wide acceptance of this phenomenon. That assumption is open to question, however. Birnie, Boyle and Redgwell comment as follows on NGOs' interventions in international environmental disputes:

> NGOs are not in reality representative of the international community, but at best only of their own members. Their policies and priorities may be driven by factors other than a rational appreciation of true global needs. Many of the wealthiest and most influential NGOs are American or European, and do not necessarily reflect Third World concerns or perspective.[52]

Claims that amicus participation promotes legitimacy can also be called into question in the context of international criminal courts.[53] The present authors have shown elsewhere that while the subject matter of international criminal proceedings is often 'local' in nature (in the sense that atrocities took place within specific communities) the intervening amici are, more often than not, foreign actors – a fact that arguably diminishes the representativeness of the dispute settlement process and potentially also its legitimacy in the eyes of affected communities.

50 *EC-Measures affecting the approval and marketing of biotech products* (Panel Report, 29 September 2006) WT/DS291/R, para 196.
51 Harvey (n 47).
52 Patricia Birnie, Alan Boyle and Catherine Redgwell, *International Law & the Environment* (OUP 2009) 254.
53 See generally Kent and Trinidad (n 17).

Within economic institutions, some states have openly questioned the fairness and the legitimacy of a process that arguably privileges interventions by Western NGOs, whose human and financial resources far exceed those of grassroots organisations. As one state commented:

> . . . constraints of financial resources would prevent non-governmental entities in developing countries from effectively participating in the dispute settlement process even if amicus curiae briefs were permitted.[54]

Looking to the future

What kind of a role should amici curiae play in the future? And what kind of regulatory reform is required, if any? In order to answer these questions, further research – both empirical and analytical – is required.

First of all, we need a better understanding of the way amicus briefs are used by ICs, and how helpful they are in practice. We have argued in this chapter that the assumption that amicus submissions are generally helpful cannot be accepted uncritically. Judges in ICs are mostly seasoned legal experts in their fields. It is therefore somewhat presumptuous of amici such as law schools' clinics or NGOs to assume that they can 'educate' these judges and add something useful to the legal process. Nevertheless, international judges do occasionally acknowledge, explicitly or implicitly, that they have relied on amicus submissions and even that they have found them helpful.

Such instances tend to fall into two broad categories: (a) when ICs invite specific amici to intervene, or indicate they would welcome submissions from expert amici addressing a particular issue in a given case,[55] and (b) when unsolicited amicus briefs focus on areas that are beyond the IC's core expertise (for example, EU Commission briefs on EU Competition Law submitted to investment tribunals, or 'fact-finding' briefs submitted by NGOs[56]).

While we have the benefit of snippets of information from individuals who have worked at ICs (like Paul Harvey at the ECtHR), which suggest a sceptical

54 Minutes of meeting held in the Centre William Rappard (23 October 2002), WTO Doc. wt/dsb/m/134, para 63.

55 For an example of an IC positively engaging with invited expert submissions, see the effusive comments of the Special Court for Sierra Leone on the interventions of Professors Sands and Orentlicher: *Prosecutor v. Taylor (Charles Ghankay)*, Decision on Immunity from Jurisdiction, Case No SCSL2003–01-I, SCSL-03–01-I-059, ICL 25 (SCSL 2004), 31 May 2004, Appeals Chamber (SCSL). For an example of an IC engaging with amicus briefs following an 'open ended' call for expert submissions, see the approach taken in *Prosecutor v. Tihomir Blaskic* (Judgment on the request of the Republic of Croatia for review of the decision of trial chamber II of 18 July 1997) (1997) Case No. IT-95–14.

56 E.g. Human Rights Watch amicus brief, submitted in *Prosecutor v. Fulgence Kayishema*, 16 December 2008, ictr, Case No. ictr-01–67-R11, Decision on the prosecutor's request for referral of case to the Republic of Rwanda.

approach towards amicus participation, the views of current and former IC officials on this issue have never been systematically canvassed.

It is hoped that further research along these lines will shed light on the impact of amici within ICs. That work will lay the foundations for a critical evaluation of the impact of amicus participation on the legitimacy of the adjudicative process in ICs. Much has been written about the concept of legitimacy in ICs, which encompasses notions of transparency, inclusivity and representativeness.[57] It is at least arguable that amicus participation undermines such values in certain instances. The aim of broadening public participation may be laudable, but the specialised NGOs and US law school clinics which often intervene in proceedings may not always be well placed to give voice to public concerns. In the worst cases, amicus submissions can be vehicles for vested interests cloaked as expertise, and can undermine the integrity of proceedings.

The issue therefore goes deeper than a mere balancing of the transaction costs of amicus participation against the benefits of broadening participation. More work is necessary to develop an analytical framework for understanding the impact of various forms of amicus participation – from invited expert opinions to unsolicited NGO submissions – on the legitimacy of ICs and international adjudicative processes. For the time being, an amorphous (and questionable) desire to enhance 'legitimacy' by broadening participation will most likely continue to fuel an upward trend in amicus participation.

Admittedly, the questions that we have posed in this chapter are not at the forefront of the agenda in ICs. Civil society organisations – so often the drivers of change – are unlikely to challenge the presumption that increased participation necessarily leads to increased legitimacy and better judicial decisions. It would therefore be surprising if we witnessed dramatic changes in the way that amici participate in international proceedings, at least in the short to medium term.

It nevertheless seems to us that one procedural approach, adopted most famously by the ICTY in the *Blaskic* case, has obvious merits. The Tribunal in *Blaskic* issued an open call for amicus submissions dealing with the question of whether it could issue a *subpoena duces tenum* to a sovereign state or government officials. It received 20 submissions in response, and the decision of the ICTY shows that it engaged with, and relied upon, these submissions to a significant extent, citing them a total of 11 times.[58]

When an IC is in the habit of indicating in which cases it is receptive to amicus submissions, prospective amici are more likely to focus their efforts on such cases, and are less likely to flood the IC with submissions in other cases. Amicus submissions are likely to be more valuable to an IC as a result, as suggested by the extent of the *Blaskic* Tribunal's reliance on the amicus briefs that were received. The *Blaskic* model also promotes pluralism. Whereas some ICs seeking the benefit of

57 We survey some of the literature in the context of international criminal courts in Kent and Trinidad (n 17) 227–228.

58 *Blaskic* (n 55) fns 20–22, 38, 49, 61, 64, 71, 74, 75, 79, 101.

expertise will invite specific experts to intervene,[59] the *Blaskic* Tribunal cast the net wider by inviting submissions from *any* interested amicus, and it benefited from doing so.

If the *Blaskic* approach is rolled out more widely, it could prove unpopular with civil society organisations, in that – in practice at least – it could effectively narrow the range of cases in which they are able to intervene. On the other hand, the approach has the potential to focus the efforts of would-be interveners more effectively, reduce the overall transaction costs associated with amicus interventions and improve the decision-making processes of ICs.

The 'fine-tuning' of the procedural rules and practices on amicus interventions is not, it must be admitted, a matter of fundamental importance for the future of ICs. It is however one of a multitude of areas in which the efficiency and legitimacy of ICs is at stake, and as such it should not be neglected.

59 *Taylor (Charles Ghankay)* (n 55).

15 Not just a wit, but a cause of wit in others

The influence of human rights in international litigation

Jason Rudall

Introduction

Such has been the influence of human rights in the last century that it has been suggested they now provide a dual foundation for international law today.[1] A human rights culture is driving more comprehensive and deeper human rights protection through the architecture of international law. To illustrate this phenomenon, it is interesting to observe how the International Bill of Rights – the Universal Declaration of Human Rights, the Covenant on Civil and Political Rights and the Covenant on Economic, Social and Cultural Rights – have been complemented by more specific human rights initiatives over time. This has included both the negotiation of further treaties as well as monitoring and enforcement mechanisms.[2] National and international NGOs, advocacy groups and civil society have all contributed to the human rights culture behind this progressive human rights agenda.[3] In this context, international courts and tribunals have been affected by and played a part in the development of this culture.

As early as 1907, with the establishment of the Central American Court of Justice, there have been permanent international courts with an individual complaints mechanism for violations of human rights.[4] This development has had a transformative impact on certain aspects of the form and substance of international law. Antônio Augusto Cançado Trindade has commented in this respect that:

> The very advent of permanent international jurisdiction at the beginning of the twentieth century, before the creation of the PCIJ, was thus *not* marked by a purely inter-State outlook of the international *contentieux*.[5]

1 Itamar Mann, *Humanity at Sea: Maritime Migration and the Foundations of International Law* (CUP 2016) 216.

2 See David Held, 'Law of States, Law of Peoples: Three Models of Sovereignty' (2002) 8 *Legal Theory* 1, 9.

3 Ibid. See also, David Held, Anthony McGrew, David Goldblatt and Jonathan Perraton, *Global Transformations: Politics, Economic and Culture* (Polity Press 1999) Chapter 1.

4 Antônio Augusto Cançado Trindade, 'A Century of International Justice and Prospects for the Future' in Mads Andenas and Eirik Bjorge (eds.), *A Farewell to Fragmentation: Reassertion and Convergence in International Law* (CUP 2015) 57.

5 Ibid.

The role of human rights courts and tribunals in the humanisation of international law has been said to represent the most significant development in international legal thinking since the Second World War.[6] Indeed, individual recourse to international justice had been an idea explored in various initiatives in the early twentieth century. This included, for example, the systems of minority protection, and mandates and petitions of islands at the time of the League of Nations. Moreover, stretching back even further is the practice of mixed arbitral tribunals and compensation commissions.[7] But, international courts and tribunals, of other specialisations and none, have more recently begun to engage with human rights issues. In 2005, for example, 'human rights' were apparent for the first time in the *dispositif* of an International Court of Justice (ICJ) decision.[8] Similarly, various international courts and tribunals have had opportunities to develop norms through what has been termed 'norm-brokering'.[9] This is concerned with the way in which courts take heed of other interpretations of human rights, including those interpretations of non-judicial bodies, and is normally aimed at extending the reach of human rights norms.[10]

This chapter unravels some of the elements behind this developing human rights approach in different international courts and tribunals.[11] It identifies several ways in which a human rights culture is being propagated through international dispute settlement, it asks why this may be happening, and offers some insights on where this may lead in the future. The chapter proceeds in four main parts. First, it explores certain influences of specialised human rights courts and expert bodies on other international courts and tribunals. Second, the chapter looks at how particular legal vehicles have been utilised for extending human rights protection. Third, the chapter considers the professional profiles of judges, and particularly how judges with human rights expertise or inclinations sitting on courts with general jurisdiction has strengthened the human rights culture at these courts. Finally, it appraises how this human rights culture may present both opportunities

6 Ibid. 65.
7 Ibid. 57–58, footnote 9.
8 Armed Activities on the Territory of the Congo (*Democratic Republic of the Congo v. Uganda*), Judgment, ICJ Reports 2005, 168; Bruno Simma, 'Human Rights before the International Court of Justice: Community Interest Coming to Life', in Christian J. Tams and James Sloan (eds.), *The Development of International Law by the International Court of Justice* (OUP 2013) 586.
9 Michael Hamilton and Antoine Buyse, 'Human Rights Courts as Norm-Brokers', 2018 18(2) *Human Rights Law Review* 205.
10 Ibid; Mark Beeson, 'Living with Giants: ASEAN and the Evolution of Asian Regionalism', (2013) 1(2) *TRaNS: Trans-Regional and National Studies of Southeast Asia* 303.
11 Similar trends are evident with general courts engaging in other specialised areas of law. See in the context of international environmental law, for example, Jason Rudall, 'Certain Activities Carried Out by Nicaragua in the Border Area (*Costa Rica v. Nicaragua*). Compensation Owed by the Republic of Nicaragua to the Republic of Costa Rica' (2018) 112(2) *American Journal of International Law* 288; Jorge E. Viñuales, 'The Contribution of the International Court of Justice to the Development of International Environmental Law' (2008) 32 *Fordham International Law Journal* 232.

and challenges for international dispute settlement at large in the future. While an exhaustive exploration of the ways in which a human rights culture is being propagated through dispute settlement would be beyond the scope of this chapter, it nevertheless seeks to shine a light on some of the emerging pathways.

The influence of specialised tribunals and bodies

One major source of the human rights culture in general courts and tribunals is through the influence of specialised human rights tribunals and bodies. It is evident that there is increasing interaction between international courts and tribunals and specialised human rights institutions.[12] These bodies refer to each other in their development of the law, and courts are relying on the jurisprudence of specialist tribunals and bodies for interpretative guidance in an increasing number of cases. This is one aspect of law as an 'intersubjective enterprise' and highlights that law often relies on a discursive process for its development. There is a dialogue that occurs between courts and tribunals through what might be termed 'cross-judging'.[13] The result of this process can be 'substantive complementarity', which is where legal norms in one legal space may be affected by the legal norms of another legal space.[14] New norms can be introduced, particular norms may be given a higher status, their application may be extended to other subjects or categories of behaviour, and new positive obligations may be created as a result of judicial norm development.[15] As Teitel and Howse describe:

> Interpretation responds to and normalizes the proliferation and fragmentation of legal orders; since there is no original context-less 'intended' meaning to the law. . . . Judicial interpretation is well-suited to making sense of diverse normative sources under conditions of political conflict and moral disagreement. . . . [C]ourts, whether domestic or international, are inherently in dialogue with other institutions and actors that also play interpretive roles.[16]

12 See, for example, Vaughan Lowe and Antonios Tzanakopoulos, 'The Development of the Law of the Sea by the International Court of Justice' in Tams and Sloan (eds.), op. cit., 181; James Sloan and Gleider Hernández, 'The Role of the International Court of Justice in the Development of the Institutional Law of the United Nations', in Tams and Sloan (eds.), op. cit.; James Crawford, 'The International Court of Justice and the Law of State Responsibility' in Tams and Sloan (eds.), op. cit., 77.

13 Ruti Teitel and Robert Howse, 'Cross-judging: Tribunalization in a Fragmented but Interconnected Global Order' (2008–2009) 41 *New York University Journal of International Law and Politics* 959; Ruti Teitel and Robert Howse, 'Cross-judging Revisited' (2013–2014) 46 *New York University Journal of International Law and Politics* 867.

14 Dana Burchardt, 'Intertwinement of Legal Spaces in the Transnational Sphere' (2017) 30(2) *Leiden Journal of International Law* 305, 324.

15 Wayne Sandholtz, 'Expanding Rights: Norm Innovation in the European and Inter-American Courts of Human Rights' in Alison Brysk and Michael Stohl (eds.), *Expanding Human Rights: 21st Century Norms and Governance* (Edward Elgar 2017) 158.

16 Teitel and Howse, 'Cross-judging: Tribunalization in a Fragmented but Interconnected Global Order', op. cit., 967.

There are several concrete examples that help to elaborate this point. The first concerns the case law of the ICJ in which the Court confirmed that the International Covenant on Civil and Political Rights could apply extraterritorially.[17] This was the position previously laid down by the Human Rights Committee,[18] which the Court in the *Wall Opinion* relied upon, and *DRC v. Uganda* followed.[19] The Court also confirmed the extraterritorial application of the Convention on the Rights of the Child in these cases, and by doing so followed the approach of the Committee on the Rights of the Child (although the Court did not expressly refer to the Committee's position).[20] Interestingly, in the *Wall Opinion*, the Court similarly confirmed the extraterritorial application of the International Covenant on Economic, Social and Cultural Rights, albeit in a different and more creative way.[21] As such, the Court confirmed that the latter Covenant applied extraterritorially by reading into it a particular concept of jurisdiction. As a result, the Court adopted an approach – not strictly relevant to the case at hand – that had been developed by another human rights institution; it generalised that approach and applied it to a differently drafted treaty.[22] Moreover, the development of the presumptive extraterritorial applicability of human rights treaties in the jurisprudence of human rights suggests that state action beyond its borders will be regulated by human rights law. This approach follows that of the Inter-American Commission on Human Rights and the Human Rights Committee.[23]

In another context, the ICJ in the *Diallo* case said of the Human Rights Committee's jurisprudence:

> Although the Court is in no way obliged, in the exercise of its judicial functions, to model its own interpretation of the Covenant on that of the

17 Armed Activities on the Territory of the Congo (*Democratic Republic of the Congo v. Uganda*), Judgment, ICJ Reports 2005, 168.

18 See Human Rights Committee, General Comment No. 31 on The Nature of the General Legal Obligation Imposed on State Parties to the Covenant, 29 March 2004, UN Doc. CCPR/C/21/Rev.1/Add., para 10 (noting that '. . . a State party must respect and ensure the rights laid down in the Covenant to anyone within the power or effective control of that State Party, even if not situated within the territory of the State Party').

19 See Legal Consequences of the Construction of a Wall in the Occupied Palestinian Territory, Advisory Opinion, ICJ Reports 2004, 136, paras 109–110 and Armed Activities on the Territory of the Congo (*Democratic Republic of the Congo v. Uganda*), Judgment, ICJ Reports 2005, 168, para 216.

20 Legal Consequences of the Construction of a Wall in the Occupied Palestinian Territory, Advisory Opinion, ICJ Reports 2004, 136, para 113 and Armed Activities on the Territory of the Congo (*Democratic Republic of the Congo v. Uganda*), Judgment, ICJ Reports 2005, 168, paras 216–217.

21 Legal Consequences of the Construction of a Wall in the Occupied Palestinian Territory, Advisory Opinion, ICJ Reports 2004, 136, para 112.

22 Ralph Wilde, 'Human Rights Beyond Borders at the World Court: The Significance of the International Court of Justice's Jurisprudence on the Extraterritorial Application of International Human Rights Law Treaties' (2013) 12(4) *Chinese Journal of International Law* 639, 667.

23 Ibid. 670.

> Committee, it believes that it should ascribe great weight to the interpretation adopted by this independent body that was established specifically to supervise the application of that treaty. The point here is to achieve the necessary clarity and the essential consistency of international law, as well as legal security, to which both the individuals with guaranteed rights and the States obliged to comply with treaty obligations are entitled.[24]

As such, the *Diallo* case evidences the importance accorded to the views and opinions expressed by the Human Rights Committee. In doing so, it recognises that in extending human rights protection, it should be consistent with the more specialised jurisprudence on the matter. At the same time, the Court was cautious in acknowledging the influence of this body on its decision making.

Turning to a different example again, the ICJ has followed the lead of the International Law Commission (ILC) as regards the development of the law of state responsibility. This was evident in the *Barcelona Traction* case,[25] in which the approach to state responsibility reflected the views of former Special Rapporteur on State Responsibility, Roberto Ago. In particular, the approach is a comprehensive one that encompasses breaches of public interest obligations in the areas of human rights, as well as environmental law and decolonisation. The classical conception of state responsibility had simply encompassed violations of bilateral obligations, such as those existing in the context of diplomatic relations.[26] In the *Wall Opinion* the ICJ also followed the approach of the ILC when the Court used the same language as Article 41 of the Draft Articles on State Responsibility, even though it did not formally cite the Articles.[27] This signified a departure from the traditional concept of state crimes.

The influence of human rights mechanisms on the case law of courts and tribunals can have the effect of elevating human rights norms to a new level of bindingness. Unlike the human rights treaty bodies, for example, the judgments of the ICJ are binding. This is significant for the propagation and enforcement of human rights more generally.

To illustrate the substantive impact of specialised tribunals on international law, two notable contributions of human rights courts are the circumscription of state voluntarism[28] and the greater emphasis placed on the *ordre public* in their jurisprudence. The human rights cases of *Belilos*,[29] *Loizidou*,[30] and *Ilaşcu and others v. Moldova and Russia*[31] are examples of this phenomenon in the European context,

24 Ahmadou Sadio Diallo (*Republic of Guinea v. Democratic Republic of the Congo*), Merits, Judgment, ICJ Reports 2010, 639, 663.
25 Barcelona Traction, Light & Power Co. (*Belgium v. Spain*), Judgment, ICJ Reports 1970, 3.
26 Crawford, 'The International Court of Justice and the Law of State Responsibility, op. cit., 77.
27 Ibid. 82.
28 Ibid. 65.
29 *Belilos v. Switzerland* (1988) 10 EHRR 466.
30 *Loizidou v. Turkey* (1995) 20 EHRR 99.
31 *Ilaşcu and others v. Moldova and Russia* (2005) 40 EHRR 46.

whereas the cases *Constitutional Tribunal*,[32] *Ivtcher Bronstein* (Jurisdiction),[33] and *Hilaire, Constantine and Benjamin et al* (Preliminary Objections)[34] show a similar tendency in the practice of the Inter-American Court. These are important precedents of the way in which specialised tribunals are contributing to the dismantling of classical precepts of international law and how they are constructing new norms. Both of these processes and their impact on the development of international law are not limited to the work of specialised human rights tribunals. Rather, their influence can be detected in the jurisprudence of other international courts and tribunals.

In an analogous way, 'tribunalisation' has led to other specialised regimes breaking their banks, so to speak. Criminal justice, for example, has been populated with tribunals from Nuremburg to the International Criminal Tribunal for the Former Yugoslavia (ICTY) and the International Criminal Tribunal for Rwanda (ICTR) to the International Criminal Court. This has led to a mainstreaming of international criminal justice in understandings of conflict from a political perspective.[35] These specialised tribunals have had normative consequences on the development of international law, such as through the extension of international jurisdiction, for example.[36] Tribunalisation has also assisted in breaking down disciplinary boundaries between self-contained regimes. This can be seen particularly with certain concepts that have spread across the laws of war, human rights law and humanitarian law.[37] And this is perhaps not surprising with specialised or *ad hoc* tribunals. Without a comprehensive code, long precedent or detailed mandate, tribunals are forced to look beyond their disciplines for guidance in interpretation and developing the law. This too can prompt dialogue between international courts and tribunals.

International economic law has also been affected, albeit to a lesser degree, by the propagation of human rights. Investment tribunals allow for the submission of amicus curiae briefs as a way of giving consideration to human interests beyond the economic issues at stake in the case.[38] As for the effect of tribunalisation on investment law, it is not yet fully apparent how it will play out. That said, investment tribunals have often looked to other judicial bodies for the development of norms and interpretative guidance, as has been the case with the way in which

32 *Case of the Constitutional Tribunal (Camba Campos et al) v. Ecuador*, Inter-Am. Ct. H.R. (ser. C) No. 268.

33 *Ivtcher Bronstein v. Peru*, Competence, Inter-Am. Ct. H. R. (ser. C) No. 54.

34 *Hilaire, Constantine and Benjamin et al v. Trinidad and Tobago*, Preliminary Objections, Judgment, Inter-Am. Ct. H. R. (ser. C) No. 80.

35 Teitel and Howse, 'Cross-judging: Tribunalization in a Fragmented but Interconnected Global Order', op. cit., 969.

36 Ibid. 970, noting that international jurisdiction in the international criminal justice sphere has been extended to matters occurring in peacetime and internal conflict.

37 Ibid. 975–976.

38 See, for example, *Methanex v. United States*, Decision of the Tribunal on Petitions from Third Persons to Intervene as Amici Curiae (NAFTA, 15 January 2001).

the standard of 'fair and equitable treatment' has been crafted for example.[39] Teitel and Howse have predicted that '. . . one result might be, in the spirit of anti-fragmentation, a global movement for a new international investment law that embodies what is perceived as a just, humanity-oriented balance of rights and obligations.'[40] As will be further explored in the next section, there is some evidence for this in recent jurisprudence from investment tribunals.

The World Trade Organization's (WTO) system of dispute settlement evolved in a different way. Previously the General Agreement on Tariffs and Trade (GATT) and panels had been composed primarily of technocrats, and their approach was characterised by self-referentiality. They were fairly insulated from external factors, and particularly other courts and tribunals. Their driving normative force was that of free trade and they had little need or desire to look beyond their own discipline for guidance in judicial interpretation or practice.[41] However, with the WTO and the influence of the Appellate Body, a 'community of jurists' rather than 'WTO technocrat insiders'[42] began to make a mark on dispute settlement in this area. Rather, they were outward looking. They have had to consider how international trade law addresses human rights, the environment, development, and other matters beyond their classic discipline. Moreover, it has also begun to allow diverse human interests to be heard in the system of dispute settlement through tools like *amicus curiae* submissions, for example.

The ways in which international courts and tribunals are using legal tools to further human rights is the subject of the next section.

Legal vehicles for propagating human rights

International courts and tribunals have used various tools to extend human rights protection. This section seeks to reveal some of these vehicles and how they assist in the cross-pollination of human rights norms. It is important to point out, however, that the exploration of vehicles set out below is not exhaustive and there are other ways in which a human rights culture has been propagated. These, nevertheless, are illustrative and give an insight into the mechanics of judicial norm development and dialogue in international law.

One of the vehicles judges have utilised is the recourse to general principles of law. Sir Hersch Lauterpacht argued that, historically, it is courts that have been charged with integrating morals into the law, and principles are an important tool for this task. While international courts had to exercise caution, the

39 Teitel and Howse, 'Cross-judging: Tribunalization in a Fragmented but Interconnected Global Order', op. cit., 989.

40 Ibid. 981.

41 Joseph Weiler, 'The Rule of Lawyers and the Ethos of Diplomats: Reflections on WTO Dispute Settlement' in Roger Porter et al (eds.), *Efficiency, Equity and Legitimacy: The Multilateral Trading System at the Millennium* (Brookings Institution Press 2001) 336–337.

42 Teitel and Howse, 'Cross-judging: Tribunalization in a Fragmented but Interconnected Global Order', op. cit., 983.

development of international law in this way was not an insignificant part of the judicial function.[43] Similarly, according to Judge Antônio Augusto Cançado Trindade, principles

> . . . inform and conform the norms and rules of international law, being a manifestation of the universal juridical conscience; in the *jus gentium* in evolution, basic considerations of humanity play a role of the utmost importance.[44]

Indeed, general principles of law have long played an important role in international dispute settlement.[45] Emphasising the discretion inherent in the judicial function and the role that principles can play in this respect, Judge *Ad Hoc* Dugard has said:

> Where authorities are divided, or different general principles compete for priority, or different rules of interpretation lead to different conclusions, or State practices conflict, the judge is required to make a choice. In exercising this choice, the judge will be guided by principles (propositions that describe rights) and policies (propositions that describe goals) in order to arrive at a coherent conclusion that most effectively furthers the integrity of the international legal order.[46]

Recourse to principles has been particularly significant in the area of peremptory human rights. Here, it is interesting to observe that principles have been resorted to for the development of the law by judicial actors, rather than attempting to identify custom.[47] In this context, general principles have been arrived at through a process that is similar to the creation of customary international law. That said, these principles have had less stringent requirements than custom, partly because they do not have to derive from classically understood notions of state practice. Instead they can be determined by 'moral and humanitarian considerations'.[48]

43 Hersch Lauterpacht, *The Development of International Law by the International Court* (CUP 1982) 172.
44 Trindade, 'A Century of International Justice and Prospects for the Future, op. cit., 73.
45 Ibid. 73; see also, Katarzyna Grabarczyk, *Les principes généraux dans la jurisprudence de la Cour Européenne des Droits de l'Homme* (Presses Universitaires d'Aix Marseille 2008), 375–473; Mohamed Shahabuddeen, *International Criminal Justice at the Yugoslav Tribunal – A Judge's Recollection* (OUP 2012), 55, 57, 86, 88–89, 185 and 203.
46 Case Concerning Armed Activities on the Territory of the Congo (*Democratic Republic of the Congo v. Rwanda*) (New application: 2002), Separate Opinion of Judge *Ad Hoc* Dugard.
47 Bruno Simma and Philip Alston, 'The Sources of Human Rights Law: Custom, Jus Cogens and General Principles' (1989) 12 *Australian Yearbook of International Law* 82, 82; see also, Andrea Bianchi, 'Human Rights and the Magic of Jus Cogens' (2008) 19(3) *European Journal of International Law* 491, 493.
48 Bianchi, 'Human Rights and the Magic of Jus Cogens', op. cit., 493; Simma and Alston, 'The Sources of Human Rights Law: Custom, Jus Cogens and General Principles, op. cit., 105.

The recourse to principles suggests that certain norms may find legal expression in the corpus of international law without stringent reliance on the will of states.[49] Moreover, the drafters of the ICJ Statute envisaged that general principles of law would not simply be drawn from those existing *in foro domestico*, but that they could also be created at the international level. While principles do ultimately require general acceptance and recognition by states, to find application they do not require conclusive evidence of widespread state practice and *opinio juris*.[50] In this way, human rights law principles can and have come before practice.[51] Indeed, the normative role that general principles have played at the ICJ where it has had to extend or deepen human rights protection is evident in many cases.[52]

Principles thus play an important role in propagating human rights protection, especially where this cannot be achieved through treaties. Given that in the area of human rights law states participate in treaties at their discretion and, as a result, the substance of such treaties can be less than adequate on important matters of human rights, it has been argued that these judicial vehicles are essential alternative sources of human rights.[53] Newly created principles by international

49 For a detailed consideration of the ways in which international law is created other than by states, see in particular Christian Tomuschat, 'Obligations Arising for States Without or Against their Will' (1994) 241 *Collected Courses of the Hague Academy of International Law* 195; see also, Oscar Schachter, 'International Law in Theory and Practice: General Course in Public International Law' (1982) 178 *Collected Courses of the Hague Academy of International Law* 21, 333–342 and 334 (noting that human rights come into existence in a multitude of ways, including beyond the '. . . usual processes of customary law formation').

50 Simma and Alston, 'The Sources of Human Rights Law: Custom, Jus Cogens and General Principles', op. cit., 105. Similarly, Judge Tanaka in the *South West Africa case* argued that general principles under Article 38(1)(c) of the ICJ Statute encompassed '. . . the concept of human rights and of their protection . . .' and that Article 38(1)(c) '. . . does not require the consent of States as a condition of the recognition of the general principles'. As such, 'From this kind of source international law could have the foundation of its validity extended beyond the will of States, that is to say, into the sphere of natural law and assume an aspect of its supra-national and supra-positive character.' South West Africa Cases (*Ethiopia v. South Africa; Liberia v. South Africa*), Second Phase, ICJ Reports 1966, 6, 298

51 Simma and Alston, 'The Sources of Human Rights Law: Custom, Jus Cogens and General Principles', op. cit., 107.

52 See, for example, Corfu Channel Case, Judgment, ICJ Reports 1949, 4, 22 ('obligations . . . based . . . on certain general and well-recognised principles' as including 'elementary considerations of humanity'); Reservations to the Convention on the Prevention and Punishment of the Crime of Genocide, Advisory Opinion, ICJ Reports 1951, 15, 23 ('. . . the principles underlying the Convention are principles which are recognised by civilised nations as binding on States, even without any convention obligation'); Barcelona Traction, Light & Power Co. (*Belgium v. Spain*), Second Phase, ICJ Reports 1970, 3, at 32 (*erga omnes* obligations derive '. . . from the principles and rules concerning the basic rights of the human person'); United States Diplomatic and Consular Staff in Tehran, Judgment, ICJ Reports 1980, 3, 42 (to '[w]rongfully deprive human beings of their freedom and to subject them to physical constraint in conditions of hardship is in itself manifestly incompatible with the principles of the Charter of the United Nations, as well as with the fundamental principles enunciated in the Universal Declaration of Human Rights').

53 See Simma and Alston, 'The Sources of Human Rights Law: Custom, Jus Cogens and General Principles', op. cit., 107.

tribunals can assist in the development of human rights instruments. To take one significant example, the legal principles developed in the Nuremburg trials and the United Nations War Crimes Commission established in the aftermath of the Holocaust fed into the Human Rights Division of the United Nations and the Universal Declaration of Human Rights.[54]

Other vehicles similarly serve to further the cause of human rights through international courts and tribunals. The advisory jurisdiction of these bodies has provided a means through which judges can develop international law. Those advisory opinions of the ICJ in *Reparation for Injuries* (1949),[55] *Namibia* (1971),[56] *Immunity from Legal Process of a Special Rapporteur of the UN Commission on Human Rights* (1999),[57] the *Wall Opinion* (2005),[58] and many others have clarified and developed legal rules, particularly in the field of human rights. Moreover, certain advisory opinions of the Court have helped to strengthen the human rights machinery of the UN by, for instance, confirming that UN special rapporteurs on human rights have immunity.[59] In this context, it has been asserted that international courts and tribunals have a 'self-perceived role as guardians of the international legal system rather than as resolvers of specific, bilateral interstate disputes',[60] and have, in certain cases, used the latitude afforded by their advisory jurisdiction to further a human rights agenda. It is interesting to note that, when the major human rights treaties and the ICJ were being conceived, some states had seen a role for the ICJ in reviewing human rights through its advisory function by virtue of a request from the General Assembly. But this was later dismissed.[61]

While the Permanent Court of International Justice (PCIJ) and the ICJ were not endowed with a mechanism for hearing individual complaints, the judges of these courts have nevertheless pronounced upon the place or plight of individuals

54 Johannes Morsink, *The Universal Declaration of Human Rights: Origins, Drafting and Intent* (University of Pennsylvania Press 1999), Chapter 2 and 345.

55 Reparation for Injuries Suffered in the Service of the United Nations, Advisory Opinion, ICJ Reports 1949, 174.

56 Legal Consequences for States of the Continued Presence of South Africa in Namibia (South West Africa) notwithstanding Security Council Resolution 276 (1970), Advisory Opinion, ICJ Reports 1971, 16.

57 Immunity from Legal Process of a Special Rapporteur of the UN Commission on Human Rights, Advisory Opinion, ICJ Reports 1999, 62.

58 Legal Consequences of the Construction of a Wall in the Occupied Palestinian Territory, Advisory Opinion, ICJ Reports 2004, 136.

59 See Applicability of Article VI, Section 22, of the Convention on the Privileges and Immunities of the United Nations, Advisory Opinion, ICJ Reports 1989, 177; Difference Relating to Immunity from Legal Process of a Special Rapporteur of the Commission on Human Rights, Advisory Opinion, ICJ Reports 1999, 62.

60 Eyal Benvenisti, 'Sovereigns as Trustees of Humanity: On the Accountability of States to Foreign Stakeholders' (2013) 107(2) *American Journal of International Law* 295, 331.

61 See Simma, 'Human Rights Before the International Court of Justice: Community Interest Coming to Life?', op. cit., 580, citing a Report of the Australian delegation to the Second Session of the UN Commission on Human Rights in December 1947.

or groups. This is particularly evident, for example, in advisory opinions of the PCIJ in *German Settlers in Poland* (1923),[62] *Jurisdiction of the Courts of Danzig* (1928),[63] *Greco-Bulgarian 'Communities'* (1930),[64] *Access to German Minority Schools in Upper Silesia* (1931),[65] *Treatment of Polish Nationals in Danzig* (1932),[66] or *Minority Schools in Albania* (1935).[67] As such, even these courts, officially endowed with jurisdiction only over inter-state disputes, nevertheless engaged in developing international law beyond the dimension of purely inter-state relations and state interests.[68]

It is particularly notable that the ICJ is engaging more profoundly with human rights in light of the systemic obstacles that could prevent it from doing so. First, the Court's jurisdiction is based on state consent and is not compulsory. Only five of the major human rights treaties contain a compromissory clause providing for ICJ jurisdiction,[69] and it is only the Genocide Convention that provides access to the Court directly and immediately. Second, the ICJ can solely deal with inter-state matters and will have to frame issues concerning human rights violations as matters of state responsibility.[70] A state must also decide to bring the case of an individual or individuals whose human rights have been violated to the Court

62 Advisory Opinion given by the Court on 10 September 1923 on Certain Questions Relating to Settlers of German Origin in the Territory ceded by Germany to Poland, PCIJ Reports 1923, Series B, No. 6.

63 Jurisdiction of the Courts of Danzig, PCIJ Reports 1928, Series B, No. 15.

64 Greco-Bulgarian 'Communities', PCIJ Reports 1930, Series B, No. 17.

65 Access to German Minority Schools in Upper Silesia, PCIJ Reports 1931, Series A/B, No. 40.

66 Treatment of Polish Nationals and Other Persons of Polish Origin or Speech in the Danzig Territory, PCIJ Reports 1932, Series A/B, No. 44.

67 Minority Schools in Albania, PCIJ Reports 1935, Series A/B, No. 64.

68 See Trindade, 'A Century of International Justice and Prospects for the Future', op. cit., 59; Catherine Brölmann, 'The PCIJ and International Rights of Groups and Individuals', in Christian Tams and Malgosia Fitzmaurice (eds.), *Legacies of the Permanent Court of International Justice* (Nijhoff 2013), 123–143.

69 These include the Convention on the Prevention and Punishment of the Crime of Genocide 1948, 78 UNTS 277; Convention on the Political Rights of Women 1952, 193 UNTS 135; International Convention on the Elimination of All Forms of Racial Discrimination 1965, 660 UNTS 195; Convention on the Elimination of All Forms of Discrimination Against Women 1979, 1249 UNTS 13; and Convention Against Torture and Other Cruel, Inhuman or Degrading Treatment or Punishment 1984, 1465 UNTS 85. See Simma, 'Human Rights before the International Court of Justice: Community Interest Coming to Life', op. cit., 586.

70 See Simma, 'Human Rights before the International Court of Justice: Community Interest Coming to Life', op. cit., 587; Robert McCorquodale, 'Impact on State Responsibility', in Menno T. Kamminga and Martin Scheinin (eds.), *The Impact of Human Rights on General International Law* (OUP 2009), 236.

in the first place, as per *Mavrommatis*.[71] However, despite these hurdles, Bruno Simma has observed of the ICJ, in an extra-judicial capacity, that:

> . . . the Court has now begun to tackle human rights issues in more straightforward ways and has turned to deciding cases focusing squarely on allegations of human rights violations.[72]

As for international tribunals in other fields, some examples show a human rights approach being adopted by the amendment of traditionally established concepts. In the investment law field, for instance, the *Urbaser v. Argentina*[73] case is the first investment tribunal to accept jurisdiction over a counterclaim on human rights. In that case, the tribunal allowed what it determined to be a sufficient factual connection between the initial claim and the counterclaim. In particular, the tribunal noted that the claims were 'based on the same investment, or alleged lack of sufficient investment, in relation to the same Concession'.[74] This is a much more liberal approach than has been taken in previous awards, which have required a legal connection between the claim and counterclaim.[75] Moreover, the tribunal in *Urbaser* rejected the argument that it could not accept jurisdiction for a human rights claim.[76] Further still, the tribunal lowered the procedural burden by only requiring the host state to establish a *prima facie* case for jurisdiction.[77] During the merits, the tribunal was of the view that the bilateral investment treaty at issue did not constitute a 'closed system'.[78] As a result, the state was entitled to invoke legal obligations beyond the treaty. The tribunal also rejected the argument that the claimant, being a non-state entity, could not be bound by human rights obligations.

This way in which courts and tribunals develop the law was welcomed by Sir Hersch Lauterpacht, and indeed he noted in *The Function of Law in the*

71 Mavrommatis Palestine Concessions, PCIJ Reports 1924, Series A, No. 2, 12: 'By taking up the case of one of its subjects and by resorting to diplomatic action or international judicial proceedings on his behalf, a state is in reality asserting its own rights – its right to ensure, in the person of its subjects, respect for the rules of international law. Once a State has taken up a case on behalf of one of its subjects before an international tribunal, in the eyes of the latter the State is the sole claimant'.

72 Simma, 'Human Rights before the International Court of Justice: Community Interest Coming to Life', op. cit., 590. It should be said that there are some exceptions to the general trend that can be detected in the ICJ's recent case law. Jurisdictional Immunities of the State (*Germany v. Italy: Greece Intervening*), Judgment, ICJ Reports 2012, is a case in point.

73 *Urbaser SA and Consorcio de Aguas Bilbao Bizkaia, Bilbao Biskaia Ur Partzuergoa v. The Argentine Republic*, ICSID Case No. ARB/07/26, 8 December 2016.

74 Ibid. para 1151.

75 See, for example, *Saluka Investments BV v. The Czech Republic*, Decision on Jurisdiction over the Czech Republic's Counterclaim, UNCITRAL, 7 May 2004.

76 *Urbaser SA and Consorcio de Aguas Bilbao Bizkaia, Bilbao Biskaia Ur Partzuergoa v. The Argentine Republic*, ICSID Case No. ARB/07/26, 8 December 2016, para 1154.

77 Ibid. para 1153.

78 Ibid. para 1191.

International Community that 'judicial activity is nothing else than legislation *in concreto*'.[79] This is perhaps to be expected, and indeed all institutions have a tendency to move beyond the intentions of those who conferred a mandate upon them.[80] In the case of international courts and tribunals it is evident that they are developing the law with and without state consent. Indeed, many judicial actors have taken a wider view of their function such that their judgments involve functional normativity, that is to say they further certain values or goals.[81] This self-perceived role is, I submit, part of the product of a human rights culture and has led to the vehicles described above being constructed by the international judiciary to further a human rights agenda. We might ask why this is so. The next section begins to answer that question.

The human rights culture among international judges

A human rights culture among international judges is cultivated and catalysed by the context in which these judges operate, their backgrounds and ancillary professional activities. It has been said that international judges are important in part because 'Men and women around the world have embraced the idea of international human rights, and the laws protecting those rights are enforced in international courts and tribunals.' In this context 'The work of international judges represents an avenue of hope for millions of individuals whose own governments may fail or abuse them.'[82] We might venture to suggest that certain international judges have served as missionaries for the cause of human rights. Judges are part of an 'interpretative community'[83] in which there are certain accepted practices and customs. This informs the available interpretations open to the judge. For a substantial part of the post-Cold War period, there were calls for the extension and universalisation of human rights. Ruti Teitel argues that the contemporary international legal order has been increasingly shaped by 'humanity law',[84] and that people – rather than sovereignty – more frequently provide the basis for that legal order. Indeed, a human rights culture is increasingly part of the normative environment in which international judges form their decisions.

79 Hersch Lauterpacht, *The Function of Law in the International Community* (first published 1933, OUP 2011), 320.

80 Franklin Berman, 'The International Court of Justice as an Agent of Development?' in Tams and Sloan (eds.), op. cit., 20

81 Armin von Bogdandy and Ingo Venzke, 'The Spell of Precedents: Lawmaking by International Courts and Tribunals' in Cesare P. R. Romano, Karen J. Alter, and Chrisanthi Avgerou (eds.), *The Oxford Handbook of International Adjudication* (OUP 2014) 519.

82 Daniel Terris, Cesare P. R. Romano and Leigh Swigart, *The International Judge: An Introduction to the Men and Women Who Decide the World's Cases*, International Courts and Tribunals Series (OUP 2007) xii.

83 Ian Johnstone, 'The Power of Interpretative Communities' in Michael Barnett and Raymond Duvall (eds.), *Power in Global Governance* (CUP 2005).

84 Ruti Teitel, *Humanity's Law* (OUP 2013).

International law has often been the product of 'people with projects', and individuals have regularly had a very significant impact on developments in the law.[85] The work of members of the *Institut de Droit International* helps to illustrate this point.[86] More recently, Philippe Sands has traced the influence of Sir Hersch Lauterpacht and Raphael Lemkin on the legal definition of crimes against humanity and genocide.[87] Their projects led to the materialisation of fundamental legal standards. In fact, Raphael Lemkin coined the term 'genocide' in 1944. By 1946, the UN General Assembly adopted Resolution 96 (I) and the Convention on the Prevention and Punishment of the Crime of Genocide was approved and proposed for signature and ratification or accession by General Assembly Resolution 260 A (III) in 1948. The latter Convention entered into force on 12 January 1951. As for the role that international lawyers have played in the evolution of sovereignty, Philip Alston has observed that:

> International lawyers have, in many respects, served as the handmaidens of the changes wrought by globalization. Indeed, the characteristics of sovereignty have changed so much partly because of the role they have played in facilitating many of those changes and in seeking to reflect the new realities, both in their normative and institutional dimensions.[88]

Today, the agents of international law continue to be engaged in a purposive enterprise and are directed by their own conception of international law and what international law should seek to achieve.[89] The agents of international law include, of course, the international judiciary.

Analysing the career profiles of international judges is particularly revealing.[90] It is pertinent to point out that judges of international courts have regularly been engaged with issues of human rights outside the courtroom.[91] As for the ICJ, to take a few examples, Judge Rosalyn Higgins was previously a member of the UN Human Rights Committee, Judge Pieter Kooijmans was formerly the UN Special Rapporteur on Torture as well as President of the UN Commission on Human

85 See Andrea Bianchi, *International Law Theories: An Inquiry into Different Ways of Thinking* (OUP 2016) 168–169.
86 Ibid. 169–170.
87 Philippe Sands, *East West Street: On the Origins of Genocide and Crimes Against Humanity* (Weidenfeld and Nicolson 2016).
88 Philip Alston, 'The Myopia of the Handmaidens: International Lawyers and Globalization', (1997) 3 *European Journal of International Law* 435.
89 Patrick Capps, *Human Dignity and the Foundations of International Law* (Hart 2009) 24.
90 See Terris, Romano and Swigart, *The International Judge: An Introduction to the Men and Women Who Decide the World's Cases*, op. cit., 20; Ruth Mackenzie, Kate Malleson, Penny Martin, and Philippe Sands, *Selecting International Judges: Principle, Process and Politics* (OUP 2010).
91 See Wilde, 'Human Rights Beyond Borders at the World Court: The Significance of the International Court of Justice's Jurisprudence on the Extraterritorial Application of International Human Rights Law Treaties', op. cit., 647.

Rights, Judge Thomas Buergenthal had been President of the Inter-American Court of Human Rights and a member of the UN Human Rights Committee prior to his appointment at the ICJ, while Judge Bruno Simma previously served as a member of the UN Committee on Economic, Social and Cultural Rights. Several other judges engaged with human rights in other ways: Judge Leonid Slotnikov and Peter Tomka were diplomats, Judges Ronny Abraham and Kenneth Keith were human rights lawyers and national judges, and Judge Bernado Sepulveda-Amor was a human rights scholar. In this context, Rosalyn Higgins observed in a personal capacity that:

> The presence of these judges on the bench, providing a 'critical mass' of persons particularly versed in human rights law, has contributed, I believe, to human rights being viewed as in the centre of what the Court does, not at the margin.[92]

This resonates with studies conducted around judicial decision making, in particular at the ICJ, which reveal that judges can be driven more by experience and values than state interests. Indeed, commenting on their study about biases in international dispute settlement, Eric Posner and Miguel de Figueiredo noted that:

> We . . . have not shown that judges – consciously or unconsciously – vote in a manner that promotes the strategic interests of their home states, [but] it is possible that the judges vote in a manner that reflects their own psychological or philosophical biases.[93]

Moreover, in the context of the European Court of Human Rights, Erik Voeten has noted that '. . . judges may have personal policy preferences that influence how they evaluate cases, in a way similar to that in which political scientists generally presume that US Supreme Court justices are motivated by policy.'[94] Similarly, it has been asserted that judges are often policy-seekers.[95] This fits with the attitudinal model of judicial decision making, i.e. that a judge decides cases by squaring their ideological values with the legal facts arising in the given case. Extending this argument further, judges have been shown to move policy in the direction of their own preferences.[96] This is amplified somewhat in the international context given that the law is less settled and there is more room for manoeuvre than in domestic decision making.[97]

92 Rosalyn Higgins, 'Human Rights in the International Court of Justice' (2007) 20(4) *Leiden Journal of International Law* 745, 746.
93 Eric Posner and Miguel de Figueiredo, 'Is the International Court of Justice Biased?' (2005) 34 *Journal of Legal Studies* 599, 625.
94 Erik Voeten, 'The Impartiality of International Judges: Evidence from the European Court of Human Rights' (2008) 102(4) *American Political Science Review* 417, 418.
95 Lawrence Baum, 'What Judges Want: Judges' Goals and Judicial Behaviour' (1994) 47 *Political Research Quarterly* 749.
96 Lee Epstein and Jack Knight, *The Choices Judges Make* (CQ Press 1997).
97 Voeten, 'The Impartiality of International Judges: Evidence from the European Court of Human Rights', op. cit., 422.

Certain sections of the international judiciary are becoming part of an increasingly homogenous epistemic community. They remain different in many ways but can share common ideas and ideals.[98] They constitute a 'network of knowledge-based experts' who have a 'shared belief or faith in the verity of and the applicability of particular forms of knowledge or specific truths'.[99] As many international judges share similar professional backgrounds, education and commitments to the rule of law and certain universal rights, their decisions will continue to converge, regardless of the forum in which they practise. Indeed, a comprehensive study conducted by Daniel Terris, Cesare Romano and Leigh Swigart has revealed that:

> Asked what their institutions are ultimately *for*, judges give a variety of answers. Despite the many differences among the types of courts they sit on and cases they hear, their responses fall into three areas: the establishment of a community of law, the preservation of the dignity of the individual, and the prevention of violence and war.[100]

This helps to illustrate that, among many international judges, there is some consensus on the purpose of their judging. Overall, the experience, values and environment of international judges contribute to the cultural context of the interpretive community in which they make their decisions and, consciously or unconsciously, develop legal norms.[101]

Looking to the future of international courts and tribunals: challenges and opportunities in a human rights culture

International judges play a part in the development of international law and, in concert with other specialised human rights institutions, help to propagate human rights protection.[102] Generally speaking,

> The steady insistence on the need to respect human rights, by international law-making and monitoring bodies, and the impact these bodies have gradually had on States' behaviour, has produced a significant ripple effect.[103]

98 Peter Haas, 'Introduction: Epistemic Communities and International Policy Coordination' (1992) 46(1) International Organization 1; Terris, Romano and Swigart, *The International Judge: An Introduction to the Men and Women Who Decide the World's Cases*, op. cit., 63. That said, there are of course other sections who remain outside this characterisation.

99 Haas, 'Introduction: Epistemic Communities and International Policy Coordination', op. cit., 2–3.

100 Terris, Romano and Swigart, *The International Judge: An Introduction to the Men and Women Who Decide the World's Cases*, op. cit., 229.

101 Stanley Fish, *Is There a Text in This Class* (Harvard University Press 1980) 147–174.

102 See Simma and Alston, 'The Sources of Human Rights Law: Custom, Jus Cogens, and General Principles', op. cit., 82 (noting that '. . . treaty law on its own provides a rather unsatisfactory basis on which to ground the efforts of international institutions whose reach is truly universal, such as the General Assembly and the Commission on Human Rights').

103 Antonio Cassese, *International Law* (OUP 2005) 396.

The human rights rhetoric of international courts and tribunals reinforces what might be termed 'perspective-taking'[104] and this in turn helps to reinforce a culture of human rights beyond the courtroom. To demonstrate, we may refer to the symbolism and rhetoric of war crimes tribunals like Nuremburg and Tokyo.[105] Similarly, the establishment of the ICTY and the International Criminal Court (ICC) were catalysed by the 'coincidence of imagery' between mass atrocities and the Holocaust.[106] Indeed, the narratives of international courts and tribunals help in expanding the circle of empathy for the plight of others by universalising victimhood after mass atrocities. A good example is provided by the emergence of crimes against humanity during the Nuremburg trials. In the case of the Holocaust, the crimes against the Jewish people were presented as being crimes against humanity at large.[107] The creation of a new legal category was justified through the universalisation of victimhood and associating it with the established crime against the peace. The Jewish people represented humanity at large, and their suffering was also the suffering of human society at large.

I submit that a human rights culture has developed in international courts and tribunals through a process of institutionalisation, and will continue to become part of institutional responses. The institutionalisation of beliefs, values or emotions can occur when those with authority within an established institution draw upon beliefs or emotions '. . . to acquire and organise knowledge and to formulate a response to conditions or complete a task'.[108] Over time, this process develops into a routine and the institutionalised emotions and beliefs come to change and characterise the behaviour of the institution itself. In other words, exceptional behaviour or responses become normalised and established practice.[109] In a similar way, Antonio Cassese has said of the influence of international institutions and human rights rhetoric that:

> The whole international ethos has gradually, if almost imperceptibly, changed, so much so that some international supervisory bodies now consider it warranted to depart from notions they themselves traditionally upheld.[110]

104 On the importance of perspective-taking for the development of human rights protection and institutions, see Daniel Levy and Natan Sznaider, 'The Institutionalisation of Cosmopolitan Morality: The Holocaust and Human Rights' (2004) 3(2) *Journal of Human Rights* 143.

105 Ibid., 145. On how international criminal trials can shape historical narratives, see Barrie Sander, Doing Justice to History: The Construction of Historical Narratives within International Criminal Courts (PhD thesis, Graduate Institute of International and Development Studies 2017).

106 Samantha Power, *A Problem from Hell: America and the Age of Genocide* (Basic Books 2002).

107 Levy and Sznaider, 'The Institutionalisation of Cosmopolitan Morality: The Holocaust and Human Rights', op. cit., 149.

108 Marlier and Crawford, 'Incomplete and Imperfect Institutionalisation of Empathy and Altruism in the "Responsibility to Protect" Doctrine' (2013) 5(4) *Global Responsibility to Protect* 397, 402.

109 Ibid.

110 Cassese, *International Law*, op. cit., 396.

In a context where the international human rights machinery is populous and increasingly fragmented, certain courts and tribunals will likely struggle to find common ground. Similarly, a real challenge will be developing consistent jurisprudence on human rights as more and more international courts and tribunals engage with human rights problems. Each international court or tribunal can approach human rights issues through different lenses depending on their particular mandate and, as a result, may establish different interpretations of similar rights and obligations. That said, to date there have not been significantly problematic contradictions in human rights jurisprudence.[111]

Looking ahead, a human rights culture will probably continue to develop alongside traditional inter-state litigation.[112] It is my prediction that these strands will coexist in better ways. International courts will be more willing and adept at dealing with the human rights dimensions of international cases. Moreover, there is evidence to suggest that courts of general jurisdiction will deal with more 'pure' human rights cases, as state parties bring them directly, as opposed to those courts simply dealing with human rights issues as matters tangential to the *dispositif* issues in a given case. Those same courts of general jurisdiction will, if present practice continues, most likely rely on specialised tribunals and other human rights mechanisms to guide them through what are still relatively uncharted waters for them.

That said, it will be important to maintain a balance with more traditional approaches in inter-state dispute settlement. Courts of specialised jurisdiction, such as regional human rights courts and other human rights mechanisms, will have their own methods of interpretation that may not always be appropriate for courts of general jurisdiction or of another specialisation. Vice versa, there is a danger that those latter courts' progressive human rights jurisprudence may be watered down by courts of general jurisdiction, such as the ICJ.[113] Unhelpful cross-pollination of this nature should be avoided. A similar but distinct critique has been aimed at human rights courts. Indeed, those specialised courts have been the subject of criticism for simply indiscriminately aggregating various external norms, adopting them without giving consideration to whether they may be appropriate in the new context.[114] Courts must carefully appraise the way in which the norms they import were created and previously applied.

Further still, adopting an approach that is profoundly unpopular with its constituency, i.e. states which expect consensual mechanisms of inter-state dispute settlement, may also be counterproductive for the cause of progressive human

111 Erika De Wet and Jure Vidmar, *Hierarchy in International Law: The Place of Human Rights* (OUP 2012); Laurence Boisson de Chazournes, 'The EJIL Foreword: Plurality in the Fabric of International Courts and Tribunals: The Threads of A Managerial Approach' (2017) 28(1) *European Journal of International Law* 13.

112 For a similar prediction, see Simma, 'Human Rights before the International Court of Justice: Community Interest Coming to Life', op. cit., 598.

113 Ibid. 599–600.

114 See Hamilton and Buyse, 'Human Rights Courts as Norm-Brokers', op. cit., 19.

rights.[115] A middle ground for courts and tribunals engaging with human rights (other than specialised human rights tribunals) might be what has been termed the 'judicial mainstreaming of human rights', which consists of 'integrating this branch of the law into the fabric of both general international law and its various other branches'.[116]

Concluding remarks

This chapter has revealed that a human rights culture has been propagated among international courts and tribunals beyond those fora with a specialised human rights mandate. This is evident in a number of ways. First, the interaction between specialised human rights bodies and tribunals and other international courts has materially affected the judgments of those latter courts. Second, certain legal tools have been utilised by judges in international courts to extend human rights protection, especially in areas where human rights have to date been absent. Third, a human rights profile is evident in some sections of the international judiciary, and this likely has an impact on the orientation of their decisions.

A few caveats are, however, necessary. First, it is important to point out that the means referred to are not exhaustive. There are other ways in which such a culture is being propagated, but those mentioned in this chapter provide illustrative examples of a broader trend. Second, this culture is not being propagated to the same extent among all types of tribunals. As indicated above, it is much more prevalent in courts of general jurisdiction like the ICJ than it is in economic tribunals for example. This could be linked to the nature of the tribunals constituted in a specific regime. In the investment law regime, for example, dispute settlement is constituted by *ad hoc* arbitration panels rather than courts. As such, there may be less of an impulse to deliver justice or ensure systemic coherence, in contrast to other areas of law which have established courts.[117] Nonetheless, as the *Urbaser* case exemplifies, human rights considerations are becoming present in international economic law tribunals.[118] Third, it should be noted that there exists some resistance to human rights at the national level. This is the case, for example, in the UK towards the European Court of Human Rights, where certain segments of society are calling for the UK

115 See ibid. 600.

116 See ibid. 601 and Viñuales, 'The Contribution of the International Court of Justice to the Development of International Environmental Law', op. cit.

117 See Teitel and Howse, 'Cross-judging: Tribunalization in a Fragmented but Interconnected Global Order', op. cit., 960, noting the shift from 'dispute settlement' by arbitration as an idiom of diplomacy, a mere instrument of cooperation or coexistence among sovereigns, to a system of adjudication that supposes international 'dispute settlement bodies' increasingly have the character of courts and less so that of *ad hoc* arbitration panels. In other words, the judges understand themselves less as playing the role of fostering compromise-building and conflict avoidance or de-escalation in international politics, and more as rendering justice between the parties and building genuine jurisprudence.

118 For some evidence on an analogous trend in the investment sphere, see Ibrahim Shihata, 'Towards A Greater Depoliticization of Investment Disputes: The Roles of ICSID and MIGA' (1986) 1(1) *ICSID Rev. - Foreign Inv. L.J.* 1.

to leave the European Convention on Human Rights. It remains to be seen what effect this might have on international courts and tribunals.

In their interpretative endeavours, international courts and tribunals do not seem to be constrained by formal methodology – such as through Article 31.3(c) of the Vienna Convention on the Law of Treaties – but are influenced by, and import norms from, other areas of law.[119] Part of this interpretative exercise has derived from what has been referred to as cross-judging. The evolution in cross-judging and the influence of tribunalisation has meant norms are being imported across disciplinary boundaries and between tribunals more frequently. This is particularly evident in the ICJ's recourse to decisions of the ICTY and ICTR when it has had to address questions already dealt with by those tribunals, while the WTO's Appellate Body has also sought guidance from external sources when it has encountered new issues, particularly the exceptions under the GATT. It is similarly the case for investment tribunals, which have referred to the PCIJ for guidance for example.[120] Looking ahead, Teitel and Howse predict that:

> Sophisticated legal interpretation, the province of tribunals (ideally), allows for and indeed arguably requires greater openness to various kinds of outside and diverse influences or factors than diplomatic and technocratic cultures of international regimes.[121]

There are both challenges and opportunities with a human rights culture developing among the international judiciary. Courts and tribunals have a wealth of norms to choose from given the proliferation of 'norm-generating bodies'[122] and extending human rights is, in principle, a good thing, not least because this brings greater protection and better standards of living to more people. But there are also risks, such as the watering down of specialised human rights jurisprudence as well as the need to ensure that those tribunals without the requisite expertise to decide human rights cases do not do more harm than good. More broadly, courts and tribunals are amassing a greater portfolio of functions, beyond simply the settlement of disputes.[123] In the future they will continue to be empowered with other roles, including norm-development. But with great power must come great responsibility.

119 Teitel and Howse, 'Cross-judging: Tribunalization in a Fragmented but Interconnected Global Order', op. cit., 988–989.

120 Ibid. 989.

121 Ibid. 988.

122 Hamilton and Buyse, 'Human Rights Courts as Norm-Brokers', op. cit., 20, who emphasise the need for courts and tribunals to take so-called 'norm-brokering' seriously. On the proliferation of courts and tribunals, and potential problems thereto, see Benedict Kingsbury, 'Foreword: Is the Proliferation of International Courts and Tribunals a Systemic Problem?", (1999) 31 *N.Y.U. J. Int'l. L. & Pol.* 679.

123 See for example Laurence Boisson de Chazournes, 'Review Essay: The International Judicial Function in Its (In)finite Variety' 109(2) (2015) *American Journal of International Law* 433; Armin von Bogdandy and Ingo Venzke, 'On Functions of International Courts: An Appraisal in Light of their Burgeoning Public Authority' (2013) 26 *Leiden Journal of International Law* 49.

16 The future of international courts

What next?

Most of the authors in this volume take the view, at least implicitly, that the ground beneath ICs is not as stable as it once was. Whether we are witnessing a momentary tremble or a genuine seismic event remains to be seen. It would seem, however, that some of the more alarmist predictions of the impending demise of ICs may be overblown. For instance, the potential 'mass withdrawal from the ICC' that was reported by media outlets[1] has yet to materialise. Similarly, the denunciation by several Andean states of the ICSID Convention has not led to large-scale abandonment of this system, as some predicted it would. The same applies to the ECtHR. For all of Russia's protestations, there is no sign that it will abandon the Strasbourg Court. Meanwhile, the UK government – despite Brexit – seems to have shelved its plans for a withdrawal from the Council of Europe system of protection of human rights. Tribunals such as the ICJ and the WTO's AB still enjoy high levels of support.

On the other hand, Alter's description of the current moment as a 'critical juncture' is apt. The pages of this volume are infused with the view that there is a sense of disenchantment with the work of ICs, among the public as well as among states. The celebratory tone of some of the 1990s scholarship on ICs is noticeably absent from the contributions to this book; authors have instead drawn attention to the 'backlash' against ICs, whose legitimacy is now routinely called into question.

The fear that powerful states will politicise ICs through passive-aggressive threats or weaken them by ignoring their decisions is well-founded. It has been fuelled by episodes such as the United States' attempt to *de facto* shut down the WTO's Appellate Body, and China's approach to the South-China Sea Arbitration.

The current 'critical juncture' did not materialise overnight. It reflects broader trends in international law and global governance. For instance, the age of treaty proliferation is now behind us, and achievements on the scale of the establishment of the WTO or the conclusion of the Rome Statute now seem unimaginable. The

1 See headlines from the BBC <https://www.bbc.co.uk/news/world-africa-38826073> and *The Guardian* <https://www.theguardian.com/law/2017/jan/31/african-leaders-plan-mass-withdrawal-from-international-criminal-court>.

global/multilateral institutions that were expected to lead the process of international governance have delivered little progress in the last ten to 20 years. Even an underwhelming achievement such as the conclusion of the Paris Agreement on climate change was treated as a cause for celebration by incredulous treaty negotiators and media outlets.

One feature of the current landscape is that the expectations placed on ICs are unrealistic, even contradictory. In troubling times, ICs are sometimes seen as a panacea. ICs are often expected to do more than resolve disputes; they are expected to *govern*, and to develop the law that lawmakers are unable to deliver. The progressive jurisprudence of tribunals such as the WTO's AB and the CJEU shows that some ICs are prepared to take up this challenge. A 'governance' role for ICs, however, inevitably leads to questions of accountability and democracy. 'In whose name?' is the title of an oft-cited paper by Armin von Bogdandy and Ingo Venzke.[2] The answer, according to these authors, is:

> In the Kantian tradition, and this is the best one we have, there is philosophically only one answer to the question: the starting point of democratic justifications are the individuals whose freedom shapes the judgments, however indirect and mediated this may be. In this vein, international adjudication in the post-national constellation should be guided by the idea of transnational and possibly cosmopolitan citizenship.[3]

At the time of writing, in the midst of rising nationalism and populist regimes, the idea of acting in the name of 'transnational and possibly cosmopolitan citizenship' seems hard to sell. Events such as the Brexit campaign demonstrate the change in the environment in which ICs must now operate; the CJEU was portrayed by the Leave campaign as a remote institution, imposing foreign rules and values on the British public. As the Vote Leave campaign's website put it: 'In a world with so many new threats, it's safer to control our own borders and decide for ourselves who can come into this country, not be overruled by EU judges.'

In short, the current environment requires institutions, including ICs, to tread carefully and to adjust their practices in response to external challenges. The evidence suggests that they are indeed doing so. Examples include attempts to reform the ISDS *inter alia* by creating an investment court; the rise of regionalism in areas such as international trade; and the preference for hybrid courts in international criminal law. Authors in this book suggest further fine-tuning that could assist ICs in confronting present challenges, for instance in relation to the management of amicus submissions, reliance on scholarship, delivery of separate opinions, and more.

2 Armin von Bogdandy and Ingo Venzke, 'In whose name? An investigation of international courts' public authority and its democratic justification' (2012) 23(1) *European Journal of International Law* 7.

3 Ibid.

Some of the challenges of our politically polarised world may demand deeper structural change. For example, if the ICC has lost traction with African states, perhaps an African Criminal Court is the solution. If the WTO is no longer trusted by some, perhaps regional integration is the answer. If the ISDS has lost its credibility, perhaps an investment court will be more publicly acceptable. Having said that, regional integration is also far from uncontested and clearly has its limits as Brexit and the debate over the ECtHR show.

As academics, our role is to observe the evolution of ICs and their practices closely. It is our responsibility to comment on developments, to explain trends, to identify problems and to offer solutions. This is what the authors in this book have set out to do, from a variety of angles. They have also offered future-facing insights, anchored in an analysis of historical and current developments.

The consensus is that ICs are not about to disappear, but that they will have to adapt if they are to survive today's challenges. The impulse to globalise and multilateralise courts (for example the WTO and ICC) will have to be moderated. The expectation in some quarters that ICs will develop the law progressively and effectively *govern* will also have to be kept in check. But in the absence of any viable alternative, ICs are here to stay as one of the main expressions of a rule-based international order.

Index

For Product Safety Concerns and Information please contact our EU representative GPSR@taylorandfrancis.com
Taylor & Francis Verlag GmbH, Kaufingerstraße 24, 80331 München, Germany

www.ingramcontent.com/pod-product-compliance
Ingram Content Group UK Ltd.
Pitfield, Milton Keynes, MK11 3LW, UK
UKHW020015200926
475702UK00014B/1896
9781032241388